ENVISIONING TAIWAN

Asia-Pacific: Culture, Politics, and Society

Series editors: Rey Chow, H. D. Harootunian,

and Masao Miyoshi

ENVISIONING TAIWAN

Fiction, Cinema, and the Nation

in the Cultural Imaginary

June Yip

DUKE UNIVERSITY PRESS *Durham and London 2004*

Duke University Press gratefully acknowledges
the support of two organizations that provided
funds toward the production of this book:
Chiang Ching-kuo Foundation
Taiwanese American Foundation of San Diego

For
David, Justin, Dylan, and Griffin,
who make everything
worthwhile

CONTENTS

ACKNOWLEDGMENTS

I am grateful to Reynolds Smith and the staff at Duke University Press for helping me to finally bring this book to print. I also want to thank the Taiwanese American Foundation of San Diego for the generous grant supporting its publication. It has truly been a long, long road.

This project has been through numerous incarnations and is the result of many, many years of on-again, off-again writing. It would be impossible, therefore, for me to thank by name all of those who have touched it along the way. Instead, I would like to offer my heartfelt gratitude to the countless individuals—professors, colleagues, and students—at Harvard, Princeton, New York University, and UCLA—who have helped this project to fruition. Your teachings have inspired me, your enthusiasm has sustained me, and your insights and critiques have been invaluable to my work. My deepest dept of appreciation, though, is reserved for those who have been most intimately affected by my commitment to this project: my family. To my parents, Wai-lim and Tzu-mei, thank you for your patience, for your guidance, and for never allowing me to quit. To my husband, David, thank you for your unconditional love and nurturing throughout these many years. Finally, I especially want to thank my children, Justin, Dylan, and Griffin, who have sacrificed more than they know. Thank-you for bringing me such joy and for reminding me daily of my priorities in life. Thank-you for your patience and respect—for understanding that my closed office door means "Not now, Mom has to work." I'm so happy I can finally say, without hesitation: "Boys, let's play!"

Introduction:
Envisioning Taiwan in a
Changing World

Nationalism is not the awakening of nations to self-consciousness;
it *invents* nations where they do not exist. —Ernest Gellner

China, Taiwan, and the Rhetoric of "Nation"

During an interview with a German radio station in July of 1999, Lee
Teng-hui (李登輝), Taiwan's first native born, democratically elected
president, touched off a political firestorm with his seemingly offhand
remark that Taiwan and the People's Republic of China (PRC) enjoy a
"special state-to-state relationship"—a surprising departure from the intentionally ambiguous terminology in which Taiwan's status has traditionally been shrouded and a statement that many in the international
community thought came perilously close to describing Taiwan as an independent nation. Both Beijing and Washington interpreted Lee's words
as a rejection of the "one China" formula that has maintained peace in
the region for half a century, and they reacted with alarm. The former
responded by conducting military exercises in and around the Taiwan
Strait, and the latter hurriedly dispatched envoys to both Beijing and
Taiwan to try to calm the waters. Eleven days later, Taiwanese officials
sought to "clarify" President Lee's description of the relationship between
Taiwan and China by expressing their belief that "there is one nation and
two countries." As journalists quickly pointed out, these remarks were
made in English rather than Chinese.[1] When invited to repeat the statement in Chinese, the government spokesman politely declined, saying,
again in English, that "we are still looking for the right words." In Chinese, of course, there is only one term—*guo jia* (國家)—that might be

used to describe Taiwan's undefined status. English, on the other hand, has several different words—*nation, state, country,*—whose slight gradations of meaning appeal to Taiwanese officials, who have long relied on slippery semantics to describe the island's separate but not quite independent status since the end of the Chinese civil war in 1949.

Local, National, Global: Reframing the Terms of Cultural Analysis

Taiwan's quandary over how to define itself and the alarming fallout over President Lee's remarks present a fascinating illustration of just how volatile the idea of "nation" continues to be—even in a world that has increasingly been described as "global" or "postnational." Much of recent cultural criticism—in disciplines ranging from history, sociology, and political science to literary and cinema studies—has focused on the interrogation and demythologizing of a number of fundamental terms of cultural analysis. Foremost among the cultural configurations that are being challenged and reevaluated is the category of nation—long the primary organizing principle for people's economic and political activities as well as the main vessel for their social and cultural identities.[2] Those who prophesy the "withering away of the nation" attribute its decline to several dimensions of geopolitical change that have, in the last several decades, radically reshaped the modern world. These include the collapse of the three-world cosmology and rigid polarities of the Cold War era, the spread of multinational capitalism, a dramatic increase in mass migrations, and the development and proliferation of new electronic media, such as the Internet, which circulate postmodern culture around the globe at ever-increasing speeds. All of these factors—but particularly the new diasporic flows of capital, people, images, and ideas—have, it is argued, undermined traditional boundaries and condemned the idea of nation to irrelevance. One of the surprising hit books of 2001, for example, was *Empire*,[3] a dense and lengthy analysis whose central argument is that political authority and the power to regulate economic and cultural exchange no longer reside in the sovereign nation-states of the imperialist era but are now completely deterritorialized and distributed into hybrid, unpredictable, and ever-changing global networks.[4] The authors envision their new global narrative of empire as a revolutionary and all-encompassing paradigm that supplants all others, "suspends history," and "operates on all registers of the social order." In the book's preface, for instance, the authors state that "The passage to Empire emerges from the twilight of modern sovereignty. In contrast to imperialism, Empire establishes no territorial center of power and does not rely on fixed boundaries or barriers. It is a de-centered and deterritorializing apparatus of rule that progressively incorporates the entire global realm within its open, expanding frontiers. Empire manages hybrid identities, flexible hierarchies, and plural exchanges through modulating networks of command. The distinct national colors of the imperialist map of the world have merged and blended in the imperialist global rainbow."[5] Yet, despite the almost euphoric and emancipatory tone that the authors of *Empire* take in declaring the nation-state dead and gone, the daily realities of global events remind us that even as the world globalizes the concept of nation continues to exert a profound influence on the perceptual frameworks of contemporary peoples. As the mounting tensions precipitated by identity politics and ethnic and religious fundamentalism in all its varieties make clear, the territorial impulse toward drawing borders and defining an "us" against a "them" remains vigorous. What the proliferation of studies on nation and nationalism over the last four decades has pointed out, however, is that it is a cultural category very much in a state of crisis.[6]

We find ourselves, then, at a fascinating and paradoxical juncture in which two concurrent and conflicting—though not always contradictory—modes of understanding are shaping not only the production but also the study of culture worldwide. On the one hand, there are theories of cultural multiplicity and hybridity, which emphasize the transnational nature of the newly emerging cultural spaces; on the other, there are studies that insist—perhaps in response to the perceived homogenizing power of globalization—on the continued importance of local differences and indigenous popular cultures and seek to reinscribe, if you will, the nation into the critical discourse of globalization.[7] While the critical terrain they inhabit may be tense and contested, these two modes of understanding are not strictly oppositional. Both are posited, as with most recent critical discourse, on a conception of nation not as something that is simply and empirically identifiable—a legally defined political entity; a geographical unity; or a linguistic, ethnic, or religious community—but as something much more nebulous: what Ernest Renan in 1882 called "a spiritual principle" that binds people together with common memories and a shared will, and what Benedict Anderson, in his influential 1983 work, reconceptualized as an "imagined community."[8] The work of Anderson and others marked a significant shift in thinking about the nation because, while acknowledging that its appeal is essentially emotional—a sense of identity that often arises from common experiences in a struggle against invaders or overlords from someplace else, for example—it unveils these communal sentiments as culturally constructed. Hence, the idea of nations as "natural" communities linked by the "facts" of common blood, language, race, or soil is replaced by the recognition that they are products of the *imagination*—the totality of discursive and representational practices that defines and legitimizes a specific unified community (a republic) and constructs individuals as members of that collective (citizens).[9] As such, nation is seen as thoroughly ideological—not the "natural destiny" of a people but a projection of their collective fears and desires. In response to globalization and as part of a larger trend in postcolonial and postmodernist theory, the most recent critical discourse on nationhood has also moved away from a classical reliance on the traditional dyadic oppositions generated by imperialism—East/West, native/foreign, traditional/modern, past/present—toward a view of nations less categorical than relational, as interconnected structures created and re-created through repeated enunciations of cultural differences between multiple complex and historically specific influences. In the postcolonial/postmodernist understanding of the term, *nation* becomes ever more fluid, an always contingent and unstable discursive surface, and a continuous process of articulating difference. Unlike the retrospective gaze of the "myth of nation," it focuses not only on memories of the past but also on the needs of the present and the desires of the future, more fully recognizing the role of the rhetoric of nation and cultural identity in the ongoing struggles for sociopolitical power.

If the contest for sociopolitical power is intimately tied up with the cultural production and manipulation of nationhood, then there are a number of reasons why modern Taiwan, with its persistent uncertainty over the issue of national identity, presents a particularly provocative site for examining the complex problematics of the local, the national, and the global. It is, after all, an island struggling to define itself and its place in the new world order at a time when categories such as nation and cultural identity are steadily being undermined. As the ongoing tensions with the People's Republic of China have underlined, the very existence of Taiwan poses a fundamental challenge to the idea of a unified Chinese nation—an imagined coherence that has, in any case, never adequately accounted for the internal tensions and myriad linguistic, ideological, and experiential differences that have shaped modern Chinese societies.[10] In addition, the island's political democratization over the last two decades and its focused efforts to integrate itself into new networks of global exchange have led to a sociocultural diversity that conventional conceptions of "Chineseness" can no longer encompass.[11] The capital city of Taipei, for example, has increasingly taken on the contours of a peculiar type of global city. The city itself is a curiously hybrid space, with unpredictable juxtapositions of tradition and modernity and a remarkably diverse mix of Asian and Western cultural influences. As in Hong Kong, an influential sector of its population is affluent, educated, and well traveled. The complex cultural heterogeneity of major Asian cities such as Taipei and the breadth and scope of the Chinese diaspora are important to current discussions of culture and globalization because they highlight the changes in global dynamics that have undermined the efficacy of existing categories of cultural analysis, particularly by exposing the limitations of conventional models of the nation.

Postcolonial Global Awareness and the Indigenization (本土化) of Post–Martial Law Taiwan

Taiwan in the twenty-first century is, even to the casual observer, a remarkably different place than it was fifteen or twenty years ago. Today the people of Taiwan enjoy a healthy economy, one of the highest standards of living in Asia, and a diverse array of consumer goods, services, and entertainment whose variety and availability rivals that of any Western industrial nation. The population is relatively well educated and well traveled, contributing to the enrichment of a culture that has become increasingly tolerant of diversity. The island's freewheeling print and electronic media have proliferated in recent years and, like the raucous street demonstrations and boisterous legislative sessions that are now so commonplace, have become public forums for lively and enthusiastic debate about all manner of topics—personal, social, or political. In short, Taiwan is well on its way toward becoming a truly democratic society. What is most astonishing about Taiwan's democratization is how, after so many decades of autocratic and repressive rule in which Taiwanese natives had no political voice, the mainlander minority has, gradually and with relatively little turmoil, transferred control of the island's government and cultural institutions to the Taiwanese majority. Indeed, the process of liberalization that has allowed Taiwan to evolve, in a mere two decades, from severe and authoritarian one-party dictatorship with zero tolerance for political dissent or unorthodox ideas to a vigorous young democracy in which almost anything goes was initiated from within the long-ruling Kuomintang (國民黨), or KMT, regime itself. It was Generalissimo Chiang Kai-shek's (蔣介石) son and successor, Chiang Ching-kuo (蔣經國), who first set the wheels of reform in motion. Before his death in 1988, Chiang Ching-kuo took several steps toward shifting the balance of power in Taiwan back to the native population. These included selecting Taiwan-born men to serve as his vice president in 1978 and 1984, allowing previously illegal opposition groups to merge and form the Democratic Progressive Party in 1986, and lifting martial law in 1987. Whatever Chiang's objectives were in initiating these liberalizations, though, it is unlikely that he could have imagined the breadth and depth of change that characterizes today's Taiwan. In all dimensions of life—cultural and social, as well as political—the island is rapidly being "indigenized," looking less and less like the Republic of China and more and more like Taiwan.

Chiang was succeeded, for instance, by a president, Lee Teng-hui, and a premier, Lien Chan (連戰), who are both Taiwanese. Thanks to the institution of direct elections in the early 1990s, the majority of members in the National Assembly and Legislative Yuan—once monopolized by elderly mainlanders—are also native-born islanders. In the years since the lifting of martial law, many former political prisoners jailed by the KMT have been released, and dissidents who went into forced or self-imposed exile have returned to participate in the young democracy. The Nationalists's sacred vision of a unified Republic of China suffered severe blows in 1993, when the objective of "recovering the mainland" was formally abandoned, and again in 1997, when Taiwan's provincial government was dissolved. All of these factors have contributed to the increasingly strong demands for a reassessment of the island's "national" identity, including the possibility of an independent Taiwan. As president, Lee Teng-hui was notably tolerant of pro-independence agitators. While he continued to at least pay lip service to the idea of a reunified China, he never tried to hide his own lack of historical or sentimental attachment to the mainland. Born in 1923 to a Taiwanese rice farmer, Lee is a devout Christian who received an elite education under the Japanese, first at one of the island's best colonial schools and later at Kyoto Imperial University.[12] He also spent several years doing graduate work in agronomy in the United States, receiving a master's degree from Iowa State University, and a doctorate from Cornell. In private and in public, he is fond of emphasizing his cultural hybridity and frequently points out that he did not learn Mandarin until the age of twenty-one and still speaks it with a heavy Taiwanese accent. He also acknowledges that he has always considered the KMT government, which arrived in Taiwan in 1945, to be a foreign regime. As for his official position on Taiwan's status, Lee prefers maintenance of the status quo—"no reunification and no independence"—a deliberately vague strategy that he himself calls "creative ambiguity."[13] He articulated his views most clearly in his 1999 book *The Road to Democracy: Taiwan's Pursuit of Identity*, which demonstrated his determination to carve out and define a space for the island in the new world order.[14] Lee's vision of Taiwan revolves around two central ideas—existence and experience—

which in many ways reflect the current tensions and interplay between globalization and the persistent appeal of the national. Unable to declare Taiwan's independence as a nation-state yet determined to continually articulate and assert its undeniable existence and central importance in the new global community, Lee made it a priority to integrate the island into emergent networks of transnational exchange—whether strengthening economic ties worldwide, entering into joint ventures in manufacturing, or encouraging cultural interaction via student exchange programs, the Internet, and other forms of global communication. While Lee envisions recognition in the United Nations as Taiwan's ultimate goal in its quest for legitimization, he feels that active participation in other international organizations—the World Trade Organization, the International Monetary Fund, the World Bank—are equally vital. As president, he found creative ways to rally support for Taiwan through the use of unorthodox tactics that one analyst has dubbed "dollar diplomacy, vacation diplomacy, and golf diplomacy."[15]

While he was reaching out across borders to ensure Taiwan's participation in global networks, however, Lee was also encouraging the exploration and closer examination of the historical, sociological, and cultural specifics of the Taiwanese experience. Hence, it is not only that the island's affluence and increasing integration into global networks have made Taiwan a more culturally diverse, less sinocentric society, but also that in recent years the island has been redefining itself by deliberately rejecting the mainland Chinese heritage imposed by the KMT in favor of a more local identity.[16] The enthusiastic rediscovery of Taiwan's historical past and indigenous culture—discouraged if not altogether forbidden in the days before reform—can be seen in any bookstore, where shelves are suddenly overflowing with books about all things Taiwanese: history, literature, visual arts, crafts, music, folklore, and politics. Trendy restaurants, teahouses, and pubs not only feature Taiwanese cuisine, but also strive, in their decor, to re-create the ambiance of the island's pre-KMT past. Emblematic of this assertion of Taiwanese identity is the revival of the local dialect. Where it was once considered vulgar to speak Taiwanese, it is now not only acceptable in any social context but even fashionable.[17] Anyone campaigning for public office, for example, must at least try to speak the local dialect.[18]

Lee Teng-hui was succeeded as president in 2000 by Chen Shui-bian (陳水扁), another native Taiwanese who is a member of the pro-independence Democratic Progressive Party. Despite his party's official stance, Chen has not taken the step of declaring Taiwan an independent nation but instead has continued on the course of "creative ambiguity" pursued by his predecessor,[19] taking incremental but steady steps toward asserting Taiwan's existence and global significance—all with an eye toward ending its diplomatic isolation.[20] Like Lee, he has also sought to nurture a sense of separate Taiwanese identity both within the island and without. Chen's government, for instance, continues to encourage the reexamination of Taiwanese history and has opened up the processes of democratization to include members of the island's population who have long been suppressed and neglected.[21] The government has also taken small but significant steps that signal its determination to assert Taiwan's separateness from China and the KMT legacy. In January of 2002, for instance, it decided to stamp its passports with the phrase "Issued in Taiwan" rather than "Issued in the Republic of China." It is also considering a plan to rename its overseas liaison bureaus—defacto embassies that are called Taipei Economic and Cultural Affairs Offices in deference to Beijing's sensitivities—Taiwan Representative Offices.[22]

Taiwan: The Nation in the Cultural Imaginary

> National liberation is essentially an act of culture.
> —Frantz Fanon and Amilcar Cabral

Democratization, indigenization, the emergence of a vigorous native Taiwanese consciousness—all these recent changes have emboldened, even compelled, the island's residents to challenge long-held assumptions about their status as a people, about their relationship with China, about their role in determining the island's future, in short, to ask questions about Taiwan's identity as a nation. While political democratization since the martial law era has been dramatic and the "indigenization" of Taiwan has contributed to the surfacing of a newly vital and refreshingly uncensored native consciousness, it is important to understand that these changes are not so much manifestations of a cataclysmic shift in Taiwanese life as the culmination of a decades-long process of social and cultural decolonization—a process in which the island's popular cultural forms have been deeply implicated, particularly in the construction and articulation of a Taiwanese nation. Indeed, many of the issues surrounding Taiwanese identity that are only now being debated in the island's political circles have long found articulation in Taiwanese literature and cinema. This study, therefore, puts aside the question of whether Taiwan is a nation in any legal or political sense in order to focus on the island's cultural polemics, attempting to trace the growth and evolution of a Taiwanese sense of itself as a separate and distinct entity through an examination of the diverse and multiple ways in which the rhetoric of nation has been produced, manipulated, and transformed in the Taiwanese cultural imagination.[23] At the heart of this investigation are two cultural phenomena — one literary and one cinematic — whose textual and visual representations of the "Taiwan experience" during the past several decades have been critical for the emergence of a uniquely Taiwanese consciousness and whose histories have intersected and engaged the rhetoric of nation in volatile and mutually illuminating ways.[24] The study begins with the literary movement known as *hsiang-t'u* (鄉土), regionalist or nativist literature that first emerged in Taiwan during the late 1960s and flourished in the 1970s. One of the earliest attempts to articulate a distinctly Taiwanese cultural identity, this influential literary movement included native Taiwanese authors such as Wang Chen-ho (王禎和) and Ch'en Ying-chen (陳映真), but its undisputed master, Hwang Chun-ming (黃春明), is the primary focus of analysis.[25] Hwang's *hsiang-t'u* stories are notable not only for the richness and complexity of their depictions of contemporary Taiwanese life but also for their inherently cinematic qualities.[26] It is these qualities that not only put his writing at the center of inspired debates about aesthetic and cultural nationalism among his contemporaries but also gave his works lasting resonance and influence among those who followed, including the filmmakers who were part of the cinematic movement known as Taiwanese New Cinema (臺灣新電影). Emerging in the 1980s, Taiwanese New Cinema put Taiwanese filmmaking on the international map and is thought by many to be the heir to the nativist cultural traditions of hsiang-t'u literature. Many of its participants do indeed have direct links to the literary movement that preceded it, and one of the key works that marked its birth was in fact an anthology film based on three of Hwang Chun-ming's short stories.[27] Hwang's counterpart in Taiwanese New Cinema is the director Hou Hsiao-hsien (侯孝賢), a filmmaker who shares Hwang's commitment to capturing the everyday realities of the Taiwanese sociohistorical experience. He has come to represent, both in Taiwan and to the international community, this new direction in Taiwanese filmmaking.[28] It is on Hou's body of work, therefore, that this study focuses.

What unites the literature of Hwang Chun-ming and the films of Hou Hsiao-hsien and makes their works central to any investigation of Taiwanese nationhood is their common fascination with the sociohistorical specificities of the modern Taiwanese experience and their attempts to formulate a sense of Taiwanese cultural identity. Hwang and Hou represent the generations whose formative years coincided with the decades of enormous economic and sociocultural change that Taiwan experienced following World War II, during which time the island was transformed from a primarily rural agrarian society to a modern urban industrial economy. They and their contemporaries have personally experienced the rewards of this explosive growth: an increase in material wealth, improved standards of living, and Taiwan's entry into the global order as a rising economic power. They have also, however, witnessed the costs: overcrowding, pollution, an increasingly pronounced gap between metropolitan cities and rural villages, a breakdown of traditional social relationships, and manic consumerism precipitated by a deluge of American, European, and Japanese products into the Taiwanese market. Moreover, they have been shaped by the tensions and conflicts that arose between the island's mainlander ruling elite and its native population, imported ideologies and indigenous traditions, and global imperatives and local needs. It is on these experiences of economic, cultural, and political colonialism, therefore, that they draw in their quest for an understanding of the modern Taiwanese experience. Deeply concerned about the future trajectory of the island's development, they turn a critical eye on the past and the present in search of answers to essential questions of culture and identity: What is Taiwan, how did it get here, and where is it likely to go? What are the most urgent problems and challenges it faces today? What does it mean to be Taiwanese now and what might it mean in the future?

The opening chapters of this study aim both to establish a theoretical framework drawn from a broad diversity of critical discourses—including historiography, literary and film criticism, and postcolonial cultural studies—and to articulate points of intersection between current cultural debates and the unique characteristics of Taiwan's sociohistorical development over the last several decades. Beginning with an examination of the specific historical and cultural contexts underlying the emergence of hsiang-t'u literature in the 1960s and 1970s and the phenomenon of Taiwanese New Cinema in the 1980s, I explore the ideological significance of the themes and aesthetic strategies that set these cultural practices apart from earlier modes of writing and filmmaking in Taiwan. I offer an initial overview of the way these themes and strategies are manifested in Hwang Chun-ming's fiction and Hou Hsiao-hsien's films and examine the varying ways in which the rhetoric of nation is deployed by the critical discourse surrounding the texts. By emphasizing the critical positioning of these texts within the broader context of Taiwanese cultural discourse, I hope to suggest some ways in which the concepts and issues raised by contemporary cultural theory might illuminate the emergence of hsiang-t'u literature and Taiwanese New Cinema at their particular junctures in Taiwan's history. While tracing the ways in which cultural elaborations of nation shift in the transition from hsiang-t'u literature (textual) to Taiwanese New Cinema (visual), I also attempt to be particularly sensitive to the very different circumstances of production, strategies of representation, and ideological and economic imperatives associated with each medium—differences that in turn determine their sometimes similar, often disparate, but always mutually illuminating relationships with the problematics of nation.

Subsequent chapters focus on more detailed analyses of the literary and cinematic texts themselves and are organized around dominant tropes and specific issues often associated with the discourse of nationhood—the treatment of history, the role of language, the question of modernization, and alternative conceptions of identity. By exploring the changing cultural constructions of a Taiwanese nation in hsiang-t'u literature and Taiwanese New Cinema, I hope to highlight a perceptible shift from conceptions of nation and cultural identity based on unitary coherence and authenticity toward alternative models that emphasize multiplicity and fluidity—models that perhaps better reflect the multicultural, transnational consciousness of today's Taiwan, which, with its history of multiple colonizations and its globally mobile population, is very much at the forefront of cultural hybridity. My purpose throughout is not to shoehorn Taiwan into any particular metanarrative of global cultural understanding, which is in any case still in a state of instability and change, but instead to offer it as a site where broader cultural themes—the relation between popular culture and collective identity and tensions between local/global, national/international, identity/difference, and purity/hybridity—are played out in distinct and provocative ways. The problem of how to define and analyze the newly emerging globalized cultural spaces is an ongoing project, and my hope is that the following pages, by revealing how the complexities of Taiwanese literature and film have themselves necessitated a reassessment of conventional assumptions about the local, the national, and the global, will be a relevant contribution.

1

Confronting the Other, Defining a Self:
Hsiang-t'u Literature and the Emergence of
a Taiwanese Nationalism

Encountering the Other: Taiwan's Colonial History

Since the concept of nation is intimately tied to the processes of imperialism and colonialism, it is important to begin with an understanding of Taiwan's uniquely complex colonial experience, a history whose structural legacies and psychic effects are integral factors in the evolution of the island's self-image. While Taiwan has not generally been discussed in terms of colonialism, its history in fact presents a fascinating example of the forms of structural domination that characterize the colonial relationship.[1] Despite the "one China" rhetoric subscribed to by the governments of both the People's Republic of China and Taiwan, the island has not always been considered part of China and has often been governed by non-Chinese.[2] Indeed, with its long history of being ruled by "outsiders"—the Dutch (1624–62); a warlord of mixed ancestry (1662–83); the Manchu dynasty (1683–1850); the Japanese (1895–1947); and, since the Communist victory on the mainland in 1949, Chiang Kai-shek's exiled Kuomintang regime—the small island one hundred miles off the southeastern coast of China has suffered centuries of marginalization and subjugation by a succession of foreign rulers. Those who hold that Taiwan's 1945 return to Chinese rule under the KMT marked the end of its colonial experience ignore not only the historical marginalization of Taiwan by China but also the complexities and peculiarities of its historical development in the more than five decades since the end of World War II. While the vast majority of the island's residents today acknowledge their primarily Chinese heritage, certain linguistic, cultural, and experiential differences between the Taiwanese and the mainland Chinese have led many Taiwanese to think of their island as a unique entity that is in many ways distinct from the mainland.[3] Mainland China and Taiwan may share a common linguistic and cultural heritage, but, like the two halves of the formerly divided Germany, their modern identities have been shaped by very different historical experiences.[4] Although it might be problematic to call Taiwan a modern nation-state in the legal-political sense of the term, one can certainly speak of a Taiwanese nation in the sense proposed by Anderson and others—a sense of collective identity, of belonging to some sort of "imagined community." Over the years, many Taiwanese have sought to differentiate themselves and their island from the constructions of political authority imposed by a Chinese government that has sought to subsume regional differences under a unified national "Chinese" culture.[5]

Indeed, Taiwan has a historical separatist tradition that dates back hundreds of years. Its earliest inhabitants were not Chinese at all but of Malayo-Polynesian origin.[6] Beginning in the centuries before Christ, these peoples—now referred to as the island's aborigines—drifted north from the South Seas through Southeast Asia to the island that Portuguese merchants, arriving in the sixteenth century, dubbed Ilha Formosa, the Beautiful Isle. Although Chinese governments had known of the island's existence centuries before the arrival of European explorers, they made no attempt to chart its coasts, establish trade with its inhabitants, or do anything to make it part of China. It was the Dutch who opened the island to settlement, instituting basic government, establishing schools, introducing new forms of agriculture, recruiting Chinese laborers from the coastal villages in Fukien Province across the strait, and building maritime trade with Japan and Europe. It was also during the period of Dutch control that the island came to be known by its current name, T'ai-wan.[7] The Dutch were forced to abandon their flourishing island colony in 1662 when a Japanese-born sea baron of mixed ancestry, Cheng Ch'eng-kung (鄭成功; better known as Koxinga the Pirate), invaded Taiwan, which he ruled as an independent principality until 1683, when his annoying buccaneering raids on the Fukien coast finally prompted Peking to assert some control over the island. Even then, the island was simply declared a dependency of Fukien Province. The first significant wave of Chinese immigrants did not arrive until the late seventeenth century, and these were mostly bandits, pirates, itinerant seamen, and others fleeing discrimination and persecution on the mainland. At that time, crossing the strait to Taiwan was in clear defiance of Peking's ban on cross-channel migration.[8] These people had no aspirations to ever return to the continent, and they distrusted mainlanders and disdained mainland rule. Between 1714 and 1833, the island's people launched three "great rebellions" and innumerable smaller revolts against the Ch'ing (清) imperial government, all of which were brutally crushed—further reinforcing the islanders' resentment and disrespect for continental authority.[9] The central Chinese government, for its part, showed little interest in Taiwan or its inhabitants, dismissing the island as a hopelessly remote and uncivilized outpost, a barbaric land of criminals, pirates, and savages who could not be considered true Chinese.[10] China's noncommittal attitude toward Taiwan was evidenced by its refusal, until 1875, to take any official responsibility for the island and its inhabitants. Even then, the Ch'ing government was merely bowing reluctantly to international pressure: in 1871, Japan complained to Peking about the murder of Japanese sailors by Formosans, and China responded by claiming that its sovereignty over Taiwan extended only to the "civilized" western lowlands—in effect denying responsibility for over two-thirds of the island.[11] When China finally declared Taiwan a full-fledged province in 1887, it was only because Japanese, English, and French forces were threatening to occupy the island. Since the Ch'ing government clearly viewed Taiwan and its inhabitants as more of a troublesome liability than an asset, it is not surprising that, in accepting the terms of the Treaty of Shimonoseki in 1895, it quite willingly ceded Taiwan to Japan in exchange for Japanese withdrawal from Manchuria. Many of the island's inhabitants felt deeply betrayed by China's decision and considered any remaining obligations of loyalty to China to be dissolved.[12] In the early part of the twentieth century, Chinese authorities on the mainland also had little interest in reclaiming the island for China. Mao Zedong, in a lengthy interview about China's war with Japan, even expressed his support for an independent Taiwanese nation: "It is the immediate task of China to regain all our lost territories. . . . We do not, however, include Korea, formerly a Chinese colony, but when we have reestablished the independence of the lost territories of China, if the Koreans want to break away from the chains of Japanese imperialism, we will extend them our enthusiastic help in their struggle for independence. The same thing applies for Formosa."[13]

When the victorious Allies decreed in 1945 that Taiwan be taken from the defeated Japanese and "restored" to Chiang Kai-shek's Republic of China, they failed to take into account this unhappy historical relationship between the Taiwanese and the continental Chinese. Moreover, to think of the Kuomintang's assumption of power over Taiwan in 1945 as a simple reunion of one people elides the dynamics of the colonizer/colonized relationship that characterized the historical interaction between the Nationalist Chinese government and the Taiwanese people. It is true that during the Japanese Occupation, when the Taiwanese were forced to use the Japanese language and were discriminated against based on their identity as "Chinese," resentment of the Japanese colonizers led some among the indigenous population to identify with the Chinese homeland. Intellectuals and leaders of resistance groups, in particular, looked to the anti-imperialist arguments of the May Fourth Movement for inspiration, and many of the songs and poems composed during this period expressed a wistful longing for China.[14] When the Occupation ended in 1945, therefore, the Taiwanese populace initially welcomed the KMT government and celebrated the island's return to the motherland. However, as the disorderly Nationalist soldiers arrived and KMT advance men began preparations for governing the island, the Taiwanese people's hopes for the restoration of peace and self-determination faded within weeks.[15] Chiang Kai-shek's government had long had a reputation for brutality, greed, and corruption, and the man appointed to be the new administrator general of Taiwan—an old Chiang crony named Ch'en Yi (陳儀)—epitomized the KMT's worst faults. As governor of Fukien Province during the 1930s, Ch'en had been notorious for his harsh treatment of locals and for the tight economic grip he held through a system of monopolies. People in Taiwan were also well aware of his history of brutality and quiet collaboration with the Japanese.[16] Hence, even before the arrival of Chiang's government the Taiwanese viewed the KMT with suspicion and distrust.

Despite the fact that they were a tiny minority (between 10 percent and 15 percent of the island's population), the KMT quickly established an ironfisted authority over the indigenous people. Just as the Japanese occupiers had discriminated against the Taiwanese and excluded native islanders from high-ranking jobs in the government, military, state-run industries, and schools, the Nationalist Chinese immediately seized monopolistic control of the island's natural and agricultural resources, its transportation and shipping networks, the banks, the courts, the schools, the media, and other institutional structures abandoned by the Japanese colonial government. Thousands upon thousands of native Taiwanese were forced out of their jobs to make way for the incoming continental Chinese. The island's war-damaged economic infrastructure was dealt a crippling blow as rapacious and unscrupulous carpetbaggers streamed in from the mainland to loot the island—even dismantling entire factories and shipping them to China.[17] In short, rather than welcoming its Taiwanese brethren back into the "warm embrace of the Chinese motherland" the Nationalist regime treated the island as vanquished territory and offered its people little respect. Many Taiwanese understandably ceased to view the Chinese mainlanders as brothers and began to resent their presence as imperialist invaders. A failed rebellion on February 28, 1947, resulted in a retaliatory massacre by the KMT that left some ten thousand Taiwanese dead—including an entire generation of the island's social and intellectual elite, whom the regime viewed as potential leaders of Taiwanese nationalism.[18] In the aftermath of the failed revolt and slaughter, martial law was declared and one-party rule quickly established—a KMT dictatorship that stripped the Taiwanese of sociopolitical power for nearly five decades. The February 28, 1947 incident was a critical turning point in Taiwanese history, a bloody beginning to KMT rule that split its residents into hostile camps and poisoned islander-mainlander relationships for generations. An indigenous Taiwanese consciousness received a giant boost from the incident, however, resulting in the birth of a separate sense of national identity, which, until the reforms that followed the end of martial law continued to be fed by the KMT discriminatory political and cultural practices.[19]

Political nationalism, as Benedict Anderson has noted, relies on the imagination to create a nation, and spreads its vision to the populace by means of intense socialization. Upon assuming control of Taiwan from the Japanese, the KMT regime immediately launched policies aimed at "resinicizing" the Taiwanese. One of the first steps it took was to articulate a common goal, a "sacred mission": the defeat of communism and "the recovery of the mainland" (反攻大陸)—"the *consensus* of aspiration burning in the hearts of 600 million *compatriots*."[20] Since the "myth of nation" is constructed through a sense of continuity with an "immemorial past,"[21] Chiang Kai-shek insisted that "the promotion of civic education must pay special attention to the teaching of 'Chinese History' and 'Chinese Geography.'"[22] Through what Anderson has called the "political museumization" of the mainland Chinese heritage,[23] the Nationalist government attempted to construct spatial and temporal continuity between the island and the continent, consecrating Taiwan as the rightful heir to China's imperial tradition—a "national culture" based on Confucian teachings that emphasized knowledge of China's geography, and monuments, historical heroes, and achievements and valued the literature and arts of the educated elite.[24] While seeking to establish unbroken continuity with "five thousand years of Chinese history (中國五千年),"[25] the KMT conveniently omitted the "interruptions" of the civil war with the Communists, the retreat of the KMT to Taiwan, and its violent imposition of control on the island. Hence, the institutionalized remembrance and careful preservation of a "Chinese" tradition by the Nationalist Chinese government was coupled with "organized forgetting,"[26] which included the systematic suppression of not only the violent conflicts between the KMT and the island's natives but also of Taiwan's aboriginal past and its development under the Dutch and Japanese—that is, any historical experience that would mark the island's difference from China. While these sorts of efforts to strengthen a Chinese identity and assimilate the Taiwanese may have been effective at some level, they also created deep resentments, which ironically contributed to the growth of an indigenous consciousness.[27]

Chiang's government also proved to be skillful at manipulating such icons of nationhood as the national flag (brought over from the mainland and displayed ubiquitously), the national anthem (sung at schools and at the start of all cultural events),[28] and the personification of the nation in the figure of Chiang Kai-shek.[29] The KMT's efforts to integrate the Taiwanese into the Chinese fold also included a strict language policy. Like the Japanese before them, the Nationalists instituted their own official language, Mandarin Chinese (kuo-yu [國語], literally "national language"), as the official medium of government, business, education, literature, and all public discourse.[30] The frustration that the Taiwanese felt at having to learn yet another foreign tongue was further compounded by the government's active discouragement of the use of Taiwanese, the island's indigenous dialect. Not only were laws passed to restrict the use of Taiwanese to the home and the marketplace and children punished for speaking even a word of Taiwanese in school, but government campaigns often lauded the mellifluous grace of Mandarin while dismissing Taiwanese as vulgar and impure.[31] As the government sought to consolidate its authority, the native language as well as indigenous literature, arts, and music were devalued as inferior to the cultural products of the mainland.

In short, from the first days of its arrival on the island in 1945, the Nationalist dictatorship on Taiwan behaved like a colonizer, dominating all political, educational, and cultural institutions on the island and rendering the local population politically impotent while burdening them with a sense of sociocultural inferiority. The emergence of a Taiwanese identity distinct and separate from China is inextricably tied to this history of discrimination, persecution, and repression. While it certainly can be argued that Taiwanese culture and society are simply regional variants of Chinese culture rather than separate national traditions,[32] it is also impossible to ignore the legacy of victimization, frustration, and resentment that has allowed provincial distinctions and historical divergences to become potent symbols of difference around which a Taiwanese consciousness has been built. Over the course of its fifty-year rule on Taiwan, the KMT's brutalities and militaristic repression, its political and social discrimination, as well as its policies of forced assimilation and cultural condescension, all contributed to the sense of us versus them that pervaded Taiwanese society for decades, dividing the island's inhabitants into mainlanders and Taiwanese, and cementing deeply ingrained prejudices and animosity between them. While not everyone on the island fits into these two neat groups[33] and their relevance has diminished in the wake of liberalization, for many years political debate and ideological struggle in Taiwan were framed in terms of these categories. It is a binary pairing that has exerted enormous influence on the Taiwanese cultural imagination and hence represents a crucial tool for any analysis of the island's sense of self.

Hsiang-t'u Literature and Taiwanese Nationalism

As Benedict Anderson and others have emphasized, the rise and spread of "nationalisms" are specifically dependent on the development of forms of mass media. In the nineteenth century, it was the growth of print capitalism and the creation of a literary public sphere—"imagined communities" of authors and readers produced and maintained by cultural implements such as newspapers and literary journals, as well as by cultural institutions such as salons and literary societies—that made nationalisms possible. In contemporary times, other forms of public media, such as television, cinema, and the Internet, have increasingly assumed that mantle. Taiwan's liberalization may have opened the door for public discussion of Taiwanese identity in the chambers of the legislature and on the campaign trail, but the call for the formation of an indigenous national consciousness had long been articulated through a variety of cultural forms, whose rise and fall are tied to specific sociopolitical imperatives, as well as to the fates of particular public media and cultural institutions. The most important of these nativist cultural forms, Taiwanese hsiang-t'u literature (the term 鄉土 literally means something like "country-soil") is generally associated with works by Taiwanese authors written in the late 1960s and 1970s, but it actually originated during the period of the Japanese Occupation (1895–1945) and the Sino-Japanese War (1937–45), when Taiwan was being absorbed both economically and culturally by the Japanese regime.[34] Conceived of by patriotic Taiwanese intellectuals as a nationalistic effort to resist forced assimilation into Japanese culture and to preserve the local tradition, the hsiang-t'u literature of this period sought to realistically depict the social and economic conflicts precipitated by the clash of traditional Chinese feudalism with the capitalist modes of production introduced by the Japanese colonizers.[35] Important native writers of the Occupation era included Yang Kuei (楊逵), Wu Cho-liu (吳濁流), Chung Chao-cheng (鍾肇政) and Chung Li-ho (鍾理和).[36] Their works focused predominantly on the Taiwanese countryside, the area perceived to be most threatened by industrialization and whose inhabitants suffered most under Japanese colonial domination. They celebrated the Taiwanese village as a source and stronghold of authentic indigenous culture and sought to resist Japanese cultural imperialism by advocating use of the Taiwanese dialect—in place of Japanese, the official language—as the language of literary creativity.[37] The fifty-year period of Japanese rule is considered a crucial era for the growth of Taiwanese nationalism, as it put into place the essential social, economic, political, and cultural preconditions for the emergence of a sense of common Taiwanese identity.[38] Chief among these conditions was the clear presence of a foreign other—the Japanese colonizers—against which the native residents of the island could define a self. The discourse that emerged from these dynamics of interaction and reaction was characterized by those narrative structures of exclusion and inclusion and idioms of dichotomy that are so often associated with nationalism:[39] we, the Taiwanese, versus them, the Japanese enemy; Taiwanese dialect versus Japanese language; and the authentic indigenous culture of the rural village versus the foreign influences in the metropolitan city—critical binary structures that would reappear in the hsiang-t'u movement of the 1960s and 1970s.

Postwar Modernization and Neocolonialism

By the time the Nationalist Chinese government assumed the reins of power in 1945, then, the conditions for the flowering of a distinctly Taiwanese consciousness were already established.[40] During the Japanese Occupation, not only had the discriminatory political and socioeconomic structures put into place by the Japanese program of modernization helped to foster feelings of solidarity among the Taiwanese, but the effective isolation of the island from fifty years of political and cultural history on the mainland—combined with the repression and violence that accompanied the KMT's establishment of power—had paved the way for a Taiwanese perception of the Chinese mainlanders as one more hegemonic other.[41] When the hsiang-t'u literary movement reemerged under the KMT regime during the 1960s and 1970s, it drew on the heritage of its anti-Japanese origins, particularly in its adoption of the idiom of dichotomy. Once again, Taiwanese writers sought to preserve the experiences and voices of native culture in the face of domination by a foreign other. By the 1970s, however, the sociocultural situation in Taiwan had been complicated by multiple phenomena—political, economic, social, and cultural. Rather than a singular other, there were now multiple foreign cultural presences threatening to overshadow indigenous culture. On the one hand, there was the official Mandarin-language culture of the KMT government, which continued to dominate Taiwanese society. On the other hand, there were lingering cultural remnants from the Japanese Occupation whose persistent influence on Taiwanese culture was further compounded by the increasing influx of Japanese capital and consumer products into the local economy.[42] Perhaps most problematically, the postwar American presence in Taiwan—through so-called military and economic cooperation—helped to spur rapid industrial growth and modernization on the island, which culminated in the "economic miracle" of the 1970s that earned Taiwan its reputation as one of Asia's "Four Dragons."[43]

The island's spectacular economic boom was not without its costs, however. As Taiwan evolved from a primarily rural, agrarian nation to a predominantly urban, industrial one, Taiwanese society underwent dramatic and traumatic changes, which shook its traditional orders to the core. Economic prosperity and industrialization were accompanied by a host of new problems: social inequities, conflicts between capitalists and laborers, conspicuous consumption, and cultural alienation. As foreign investments grew and the Japanese and American consumer cultures penetrated further into the island's society, many began to question the social and cultural costs of Taiwan's continued military dependence and its increasingly complex economic ties. Intellectuals wondered whether Taiwan was once again being enslaved and exploited by foreign powers— becoming an economic and cultural colony of Japan and the West.[44]

Political Crisis in the 1970s and the Call for Nationalism

In addition to the alarming social transformations that accompanied rapid industrialization and economic growth, a series of embarrassing political setbacks and frustrations also mark the 1970s as a crucial era of transition and change for Taiwan and help to explain the emergence during those years of an intensified native cultural awareness movement in the form of nativist literature. Without question, the first politically trying incident for Taiwan was its 1970 conflict with Japan over the disputed Tiao-yu T'ai (釣魚臺) islands. The unilateral decision by the United States to turn over Okinawa and the Tiao-yu T'ai islands to Japan sparked angry protests among Taiwanese students living in the United States—outrage that spilled over first to Hong Kong and then to Taiwan itself, where heretofore apathetic residents suddenly found their nationalist pride rekindled by this insulting reminder of China's past humiliations by Western powers.[45] This revived "Chinese" nationalism, moreover, was complicated by Taiwan's subsequent diplomatic setbacks. The first of these was, of course, Richard Nixon's visit to Peking, which paved the way for the Carter administration's decision to break formal diplomatic ties with the KMT in order to normalize relations with the People's Republic of China. The political blows suffered by Taiwan in rapid succession—the severance of diplomatic ties with most major nations, including Japan; expulsion from the United Nations; and exclusion from the Olympic Games—were deeply humiliating.[46] The KMT government responded to the political crisis by accelerating the modernization process, determined to strengthen Taiwan's global position by building it into an economic powerhouse. Many intellectuals, on the other hand, had just the opposite response. The crisis prompted them to pause, for the first time, and question Taiwan's zealous race toward modernization, to ponder where exactly the island might be headed.

Abruptly confronted with the delicate problem of the "two Chinas," the Taiwanese people were forced to examine the island's relationship with the mainland and its people. Those who considered themselves patriots suddenly had to ask themselves: "Love of country? Which country?"[47] Abandoned by the United States and many of the world's economic and political powers, they pondered the growing complexities of Taiwan's economic and cultural relationships with Japan and the West and worried over its future within the global order of nations. In short, Taiwan turned inward, entering a period of self-reflection and national soul searching that resulted in the awakening of anti-imperialist nationalistic sentiments, a renewed interest in indigenous cultural traditions, and a general heightening of social consciousness. In the arts, this new critical attitude kindled the passion of humanitarianism. The rise of hsiang-t'u literature, which sought to critically examine the sociohistorical realities of life in modern-day Taiwan and to address the complex changes and antagonisms that had accompanied the island's rapid industrial growth and modernization, was a crucial part of this blossoming sociopolitical awareness.

The Impact of Western Modernism
on Taiwanese Literature, 1950–71

The emergence of a Taiwanese politico-cultural consciousness can be seen not only as a product of events in Taiwan's political development but also as an outcome of its literary history. The first decade of KMT rule is often perceived, from a literary point of view, as something of a cultural desert.[48] The native tradition of resistance literature under the Japanese was unfortunately stifled after the KMT takeover of the island, since many of the nativist authors were either executed or imprisoned by the government.[49] In addition, writers in Taiwan were largely cut off from the humanistic tradition of modern Chinese literature, as the richly varied and socially conscious literature of the May Fourth period was banned by the government because most of its major authors—writers like Lu Hsun (魯迅), Lao She (老舍), and Pa Chin (巴金)—were affiliated with the Chinese Communists.[50] Hence, the literature taught in Taiwan's schools was limited primarily to the Confucian classics and traditional Chinese poetry from the dynastic era. Popular literature consisted largely of escapist entertainment—historical romances and swordsmen epics—far removed from the quotidian realities of Taiwan. The literature of this early period also tended to be monopolized by refugee writers from the mainland, most of whom saw themselves as only temporary visitors on the island.[51] Their writing was dominated by the nostalgic literature of exile, love stories and spy novels set in Shanghai, Nanking, Peking, and other cities in China, which were unfamiliar to the vast majority of Taiwanese readers, who had never set foot on the mainland.[52] Even the few works that acknowledged the existence of Taiwan were obsessed with the Chinese mainland and suffused with a sentimental longing for the homeland across the strait. As Chiang Meng-lin (蔣夢麟) complained in a 1961 essay, the vast majority of the literary works produced in Taiwan during the 1950s avoided confronting contemporary sociopolitical realities and "relied on personal memories to tell only stories of life on the mainland."[53] The time had come, he argued, for writers in Taiwan to "broaden their perspectives and work with the material of the here and now—to closely examine Taiwanese society and discover the needs, desires, frustrations, and hopes of today's youth."

Many critics mark the late 1950s and early 1960s as the beginning of the revitalization of literature in Taiwan, though not yet in a nativist vein. A new generation of young writers, many of them university students, began to publish critical and creative works in newly established literary journals such as *Blue Star* (藍星, 1957–1965), *Contemporary Poetry* (現代詩, 1953–63), *Epoch* (創世紀, 1954–70), *Literary Review* (文學雜誌, 1956–60), and *Modern Literature* (現代文學, 1960–73).[54] The first two journals were devoted to promoting "new poetry" (新詩), while the latter two focused exclusively on fiction. All were marked by an intense interest in European and American modernist literature, which for many young intellectuals had begun to fill the void left by Taiwan's alienation from modern Chinese literary traditions. *Contemporary Poetry* was founded in 1953 by Chi Hsien (紀弦), a poet from the mainland, who in the 1930s had been involved with Tai Wang-shu's (戴望舒) journal *New Poetry*.[55] The subsequently formed Contemporary Poetry Society boasted eighty members, who dedicated themselves to learning from the West: promulgating the "spirit" and "basic elements of all new schools of Western poetry since Baudelaire," emphasizing "horizontal transplantation" rather than "vertical inheritance" in their creative writing, and seeking "the purity of poetry."[56] The group's emphasis on "new forms, new contents, new tools and new techniques" is reminiscent of the professed principles of Chi Hsien's earlier journal, *New Poetry*, but the open advocacy of direct borrowing from foreign modernist models (horizontal transplantation) reflected a rejection of native traditions and marked a further step toward westernization in poetry. *Epoch* was the publication of a poetry society of the same name, whose members, mostly former Nationalist servicemen and university students, enthusiastically translated and introduced the works of Baudelaire, Valéry, Rilke, Verlaine, Yeats, Auden, Eliot, Thomas, and others. Their own attempts at original poetry experimented with imagery and techniques learned from these Western modernist poets.[57]

In fiction, the development of Taiwanese literature was similarly characterized by a fascination with Western ideas and techniques. The two primary journals of the new movement in fiction, *Literary Review* and *Modern Literature*, were both inspired by Hsia Tsi-an (夏濟安), a professor in the Department of Foreign Languages and Literatures at the National Taiwan University (known as T'ai-ta [臺大]). The former was edited by Professor Hsia himself, who in the inaugural issue, proclaimed realism as the journal's guiding principle: "Though we live in a time of great chaos . . . we do not intend to dodge reality. . . . Our conviction is: a serious writer must be the one who can reflect for us the zeitgeist of our time. We are not after the beauty of language for its own sake, for we feel that it is more important for us to speak the truth."[58] Despite the proclaimed commitment to realism, however, the journal became better known for its nurturing of young writers far more interested in formalist experimentation and "the beauty of language for its own sake" than in critical examinations of the complexities of Taiwan's sociopolitical reality.[59] Even more instrumental than *Literary Review* for the development of literary modernism in Taiwan was the magazine *Modern Literature*, which was launched by a group of Professor Hsia's students at T'ai-ta. Like the poetry journals, *Modern Literature* was dedicated to introducing an array of nineteenth- and twentieth-century Western authors to Taiwanese audiences. The authors featured in the journal included the giants of Western modernism: D. H. Lawrence, James Joyce, Virginia Woolf, Franz Kafka, Thomas Mann, Jean-Paul Sartre, William Faulkner, John Steinbeck, Katherine Anne Porter, Eugene O'Neill, and numerous others. In addition, the editors offered translations of articles by American scholars and critics such as Robert Penn Warren, Alfred Kazin, and Edmund Wilson. In their own creative work, the contributors to *Modern Literature* sought to experiment with and create "new artistic forms and styles," engaging, as the manifesto in the journal's inaugural issue stated, in the task of "constructive destruction" vis-à-vis the Chinese literary tradition.[60]

The Western orientation of the *Modern Literature* writers is evident in the short stories and novels of representative authors such as Wang Wen-hsing (王文興) and Pai Hsien-yung (白先勇). Wang, for example, experimented heavily with a wide variety of forms and techniques learned from European and American writers, attempting, with varying degrees of success, to write short stories, sketches, and lyrical essays, as well as novels. He consciously played with unconventional language and unusual imagery, often employing such borrowed strategies as the use of Freudian symbolism. The content of Wang's fiction also addressed themes typical of Western modernism: psychological turmoil, adolescent confrontation, existential angst, sexual desire, frustration, and disillusionment. Pai Hsien-yung's short stories are similarly notable for their fascination with individual psychology. His earliest works, collected in *New Yorkers* (紐約客), depicted the inner struggles of alienated and self-absorbed young Chinese intellectuals living in America. Like Wang's fiction, Pai's writing was marked by radical formal experimentation, particularly Freudian symbolism and stream of consciousness narration. After 1966, Pai's focus shifted somewhat as he turned his attention away from overseas Chinese to write stories about the older generation of mainlanders stranded in Taiwan. Still, even these stories, which were collected in the ironically named *Taipei People* (臺北人), depict people who, trapped in their inner worlds of nostalgic memory, are unable to connect with the realities of the Taiwanese world around them. Pai's stories about mainlanders in Taiwan shared with the earlier generation of refugee writing a preoccupation with the Chinese mainland and personal memories, so the Western modernist obsession with interiority served his creative purpose particularly well.[61]

The enthusiasm shown by the modernist writers for Western thought and experimental literary techniques has often been cited by critics as evidence of their solipsism and abdication of social and political responsibility. One might argue, however, that by embracing the West the modernists were in their own way responding to the specific political and cultural pressures of the time. Deprived of the modern Chinese literary heritage by the ongoing political enmity between the Kuomintang and the mainland government, writers in Taiwan found themselves in a sort of forced isolation. Strict government censorship also made it impossible for them to express directly their anxieties over the possibility—or impossibility—of returning to the mainland. Literatures and philosophies from the West helped to fill this cultural void, while experimentation with new formal techniques provided an outlet for their suppressed creative energies. Just as importantly, the modernist interest in interiority became a vehicle through which the writers could express their feelings of political frustration and cultural loss indirectly through stories of individual psychological turmoil and existential angst. Nevertheless, the modernists' willing embrace of Western literature and philosophies during the 1950s and 1960s made them particularly vulnerable to criticism during the rise of nativist sentiment in the following decade.

Back to the Earth (回歸鄉土):
The Rise of Hsiang-t'u

The vulnerability of the modernist writers became immediately apparent in the wake of Taiwan's political crises of the early 1970s, when some of their more radical pronouncements—such as Chi Hsien's insistence on horizontal transplantation from the West rather than vertical inheritance from Chinese traditions—became easy targets for those caught up in the anti-Western mood of the moment. In their most successful works, the modernist writers actually demonstrated a creative synthesis of both classical Chinese traditions and modern Western techniques, yet in an atmosphere of heated anti-imperialist polemics it was their flirtations with Western ideologies that were most frequently highlighted. Hence, despite the technical brilliance of the new literature and the energy and variety that the young authors of *Literary Review* and *Modern Literature* brought to the Taiwanese literary scene, their efforts were painted by nativist critics as contributing little to the shaping of a native cultural consciousness. Since the focus of the modernist writers was on the private interior world of individual psyches rather than the public external world of social interaction, their works have more frequently been valued for their timeless or universal attributes than for any historically or culturally specific understanding of Taiwan. While theirs is undoubtedly an important contribution to literature in Taiwan, the modernist writers have seldom been credited with taking any significant steps toward the creation of a specifically Taiwanese "national literature" (民族文學). The relative failure of modernist literature to address adequately the contemporary sociopolitical realities of the island was apparent even to some of the contributors to *Modern Literature*. Lucy Chen (Chen Jo-hsi, 陳若曦), for example, acknowledged as early as 1963 that the truly important social issues facing modern Taiwan had yet to be tackled.

> Formosa is not the place it was 10 years ago. But there is little sign of this in the new books that compete for readers' dollars in Formosan bookstores. Most established literary men are afraid or too lazy to expose and analyze either their own inner selves or the changing society around them. Why do they not write about the changes in the cities with their new factories and the thousands of young men and women who come in from the farms to work in them? Or about the armies of government clerks in city and provincial governments and their numb hopelessness as the cost of living climbs further out of reach of their salaries? Or about the farmers who must still stoop to push every individual shoot of rice into the mud but who now wear blue plastic raincoats from Japan instead of the old straw cloak? Or about what happens to a farm family now when it is expected that a marrying daughter take with her as her dowry, a radio, an electric fan, and a sewing machine? Or about Formosa's merchants, cursing official regulations but with enough money to support a growing number of "wine-houses" with Hong Kong-styled furnishings and swarms of pretty "waitresses?" Or about youth, caught up in a fierce competition for places in the universities and subject to all the crosscurrents of new and old ideas?
>
> Formosa has a great many things to write about. And sooner or later Formosan writers will have to take up the challenge.[62]

After the political humiliations and frustrations suffered by Taiwan in the early 1970s, the subsequent sense of cultural crisis that gripped the island underscored more than ever the need to take up this challenge and critically examine the state of the nation. The burst of anti-imperialism that followed these political setbacks was manifested in part by the emergence of a "back to the earth" (回歸鄉土) movement, which began to question the values and ideas of the West and advocated a return to the island's Chinese cultural roots. Among writers and other intellectuals, the mood shifted from disengagement to engagement with immediate sociopolitical issues. The modernist poets and fiction writers, with their Western themes and borrowed techniques, held less and less appeal for a public thirsty for nationalism. Popular and critical attention was gradually turning to other writers, who began working in the late 1960s and were active throughout the 1970s. Known collectively as the hsiang-t'u writers (鄉土作家), these authors engaged the details of the here and now and sought to capture the specifically Taiwanese experience of postwar sociocultural change.

Unlike most of the *Modern Literature* writers, Wang T'o (王拓), Yang Ch'ing-ch'u (楊青矗), Ch'en Ying-chen (陳映真), Wang Chen-ho (王禎和) and Hwang Chun-ming (黃春明) were native islanders who wrote about the kinds of contemporary Taiwanese people and concrete societal problems that many felt had been ignored by literature. Yang, for example, is best known for his examination of daily life in the new industrial manufacturing plants that dotted the island's landscape. Drawing on his own experiences and observations as a refinery worker in the southern Taiwanese city of Kaohsiung, he depicted the abuse suffered by factory workers and examined its bitter consequences. Wang T'o was similarly concerned with economic exploitation, not only in the new manufacturing industries but also in more traditional modes of production such as farming and fishing, which he perceived to have been permanently altered by the introduction of capitalist systems of wholesale marketing, organized distribution, and retailing. His work is particularly critical of the materialist values associated with urban industrialism. As one of the more politically active of the hsiang-t'u writers, Ch'en Ying-chen wrote stories addressing the problems created by the multinational companies (particularly American corporations) that had set up branches in Taipei and in his view were exploiting and enslaving armies of Taiwanese white-collar workers.[63] Wang Chen-ho and Hwang Chun-ming—the two most popular and critically acclaimed of the hsiang-t'u writers—both examined the traumatic changes that modernization and urbanization brought to traditional Taiwanese village life.[64] Their stories, filled with dark but earthy humor, depict the poverty-stricken lives of Taiwan's lower classes, the "little people" (小人物)—peasants, street peddlers, prostitutes, and laborers—in their native counties of Hua-lien (花蓮) and I-lan (宜蘭), who struggle to survive with dignity in a world that is changing with bewildering speed.

Like the modernist writers, the hsiang-t'u writers were loosely affiliated with particular newspapers and literary journals. Many of Hwang's earliest short stories, for example, were published in the literary supplement to the *United Daily News*, one of the island's leading newspapers, as well as in the literary journals *Writer's Forum* (筆匯), *Young Lion Monthly* (幼獅文藝), and *Literature Quarterly* (文學季刊). They also relied on frequent public lectures and literary forums—carefully publicized on college campuses and generously covered by the major newspapers—to build an audience and broaden their appeal. By the mid-1970s, the hsiang-t'u writers succeeded in winning considerable popular and critical support. The new focus on local and contemporary subject matter by these writers was championed not only as a break from the tired nostalgic fiction of the refugee mainland writers who had dominated Taiwanese fiction throughout the 1950s and 1960s but also as a more serious-minded and socially relevant alternative to the escapist literature—teen love stories, historical romances, and swordplay sagas—popular at the time.[65] The works of the hsiang-t'u writers readily lent themselves to the purposes of constructing a national consciousness because of their focus on specifically Taiwanese sociohistorical problems but also because they were perceived as representing a positive shift away from the Western-influenced modernist experimentation and individualistic tendencies of writers associated with the literary magazines of the early 1960s and toward more traditionally realist narratives.

The Hsiang-t'u Literary Debates of 1977–78

Like the nativist literature of the Japanese Occupation, Taiwanese hsiang-t'u literature of the late 1960s and the 1970s was an expression of nationalism in its most classic form, envisioning a nation constructed on the dualism of self and other. Both the fictional works of this period and the subsequent surrounding critical discourse are structured on numerous and sometimes overlapping pairs of binary oppositions: native versus foreign cultures, islanders versus mainlanders, Taiwanese dialect versus Chinese language, experiential versus cognitive knowledge, tradition versus modernity, age versus youth, village versus city, rural agrarianism versus industrial capitalism, and so on. The theoreticians of hsiang-t'u, the most important of whom include Wang T'o, Ch'en Ying-chen, and Yu T'ien-ts'ung (尉天聰), were particularly prone to the pitfalls of dichotomous thinking, often dogmatically reducing the complicated changes in Taiwanese society to a binary struggle between the negative values of an industrial capitalism imposed by foreigners and the positive values of indigenous agrarian society. In their efforts to reassert a native consciousness, the ideologues of hsiang-t'u, most notably Wang T'o, drew heavily for inspiration on the heritage of the anti-Japanese hsiang-t'u literature of the Occupation.[66] Some of these legacies include a focus on the lower classes and an interest in local landscapes, folk traditions, and oral culture—including the deliberate use of the Taiwanese dialect. Just as the use of the local dialect during the Japanese Occupation was a politically provocative choice, hsiang-t'u literature's rehabilitation of the indigenous Taiwanese language in the 1970s proved to be its most distinctive—and controversial—characteristic. Not only did the liberal incorporation of the Taiwanese dialect pose a direct challenge to Mandarin-speaking mainlanders,[67] but its use evoked what Mikhail Bakhtin called a "socio-ideological complex" that was perceived as a potential threat to dominant culture.[68] After all, the native dialect—the collective memory bank of local history—had long been devalued, and even suppressed, by the KMT government. Moreover, it was associated with the island's rural areas, where ordinary Taiwanese people, not the official authorities, lived. A related strategy adopted from Japanese era nativist literature was the idealization of the Taiwanese village as the repository of traditional culture and local folk customs.[69] The village became a symbol of resistance against modernization and urbanization—symbolized by the city— which had been forced on the island by the imperialist powers. Hence, the dichotomy of the urban metropolis versus the rural village became for the hsiang-t'u advocates a foundation on which other binaries in the rhetoric of nationalism were constructed. In the literatures of many colonizers of the imperialist era, the modernity and cultural sophistication of the metropolis (the European homeland) is contrasted favorably and nostalgically with the developmental backwardness of the villages in the colony. In the anti-imperialist discourse of the colonized, the binarism is reversed; the city becomes the source of all of society's increasingly complex troubles, while the village is seen through misty eyes as a symbol of a simpler and more harmonious existence in the rural past. The emphatically anticolonial nationalism of the hsiang-t'u theorists similarly sought to replace the nostalgic stories produced by the mainland colonizers with their own literature of nostalgia.[70]

In their eagerness to satisfy the thirst for nationalism aroused by the political blows of the early 1970s, the advocates of hsiang-t'u literature embraced antiforeign rhetoric against economic and cultural imperialism with such ardent fervor that by 1977–78 Taiwanese cultural circles had become embroiled in the discursive battles known as the "hsiang-t'u literary debates" (鄉土文學論戰).[71] Characterized by increasingly polemical and sometimes bitter attacks, the debates, considered by many to be a watershed event in the development of Taiwanese literature, divided writers into two groups and pitted them against each other, polarizing the Taiwanese literary world into two antagonistic camps. In the beginning, at least, the disputes centered on disagreements between the West-leaning "modernists" (現代派) and the hsiang-t'u nativists (鄉土派), which seemed to be a replay of the tensions between Chinese and Western cultures that have sparked debate throughout modern Chinese history and remain largely an unresolved question. Indeed, the controversy over the relationship between modernization and Westernization can be traced to the early decades of this century, to the May Fourth era (1917–21) and the so-called New Culture Movement (新文化運動),[72] which has been characterized as "the beginning of modern Chinese nationalism."[73] A cultural movement simmering since China's humiliation in the Opium Wars (1840–42) and galvanized by the imperial government's capitulation to the terms of the Treaty of Versailles (1919), the New Culture Movement was from the start profoundly ambivalent in its attitudes toward the West. On the one hand, the driving force behind the movement was the anti-imperialist anger born out of China's embarrassing military and political defeats at the hands of Japan and the Western powers. On the other hand, the advocates of the new culture paradoxically saw Western culture as the key to China's salvation and its integration into the modern world. In the earliest years of the May Fourth era, in particular, Chinese writers and intellectuals fervently called for a complete reevaluation and overhaul of a Chinese tradition that in their eyes had become stagnant and decrepit. As Confucian traditions came under blistering attack, Western political institutions, laws, and scientific technology, as well as Western philosophies, social theories, literatures, and arts, were held up as models for building a new, modern Chinese nation. In literature, for instance, reformists such as Hu Shih (胡適) avidly devoured western literature and aesthetic theories while calling for a total rejection of the Chinese literary tradition, categorically arguing that "Chinese literature produced by the literary men during the last two thousand years is a dead literature, written in a dead language."[74]

The reformers who believed that modernization necessarily meant Westernization, however, were not without their critics. Initially, resistance came primarily from regressive elements in Chinese society—Confucian bureaucrats, old gentry, local warlords—whose opposition to change was dismissed as insignificant. However, in the later years of the May Fourth era—particularly after the horrors and ravages of World War I had left Europe in ruins—even reformists and intellectuals began to reconsider their ardent advocacy of Western culture. In the postwar atmosphere of doubt and pessimism, serious debates arose over the comparative advantages of Eastern versus Western civilization.[75] One of the first influential figures to question the omnipotence of Western science and technology and to defend traditional Chinese civilization was Liang Ch'i-ch'ao (梁啟超), whose meeting in 1918 with disillusioned European intellectuals marked what he called "a major turning-point in current world thought."[76] While the Chinese reformers were exalting Western scientific progress and culture as the keys to successful modernization, the Europeans saw World War I as the tragic manifestation of the bankruptcy of a modern Western civilization that valued technological development and material wealth over spiritual and moral growth. Upon his return to China, Liang articulated these doubts in a series of provocative articles that not only criticized the materialism and moral vacuity of Western industrial civilization but also encouraged the youth of China to respect their own cultural traditions. Liang's challenge to the Western orientation of the New Culture Movement was followed by numerous essays intensifying the controversy over the problem of Eastern and Western civilizations, which, during the 1920s and 1930s and up to the outbreak of the Sino-Japanese War, continued to rage in terms of competing slogans calling for such things as a "national form" (民族形式) and condemning "wholesale Westernization" (全盤西化).[77]

The basic parallels between the May Fourth era on the mainland and the situation in Taiwan of the 1970s are apparent: a string of political humiliations at the hands of Japan and the West precipitated national soul-searching, while the paradoxical embrace of foreign ideas as the key to national revitalization eventually gave way to a desire to return to indigenous cultural roots. As Ch'en Ying-chen notes, Taiwan was a Japanese colony during the years of the May Fourth Movement and after, and therefore it was largely cut off from the debate over the problem of Eastern versus Western civilizations that was taking place among mainland writers and intellectuals.[78] As a consequence of its isolation from the controversy, Taiwan was destined to replay the debates at a later date. According to Ch'en, it was this unresolved tension between native and Western cultures that manifested itself in the Taiwanese literary debates of the 1970s.

A more immediate but equally significant precursor to the hsiang-t'u debates of 1977–78 can be found in the so-called modern poetry debates (現代詩論戰) of 1972.[79] In the wave of cultural nationalism that followed the Tiao-yu T'ai and United Nations incidents, the poets of the Contemporary and Epoch societies became targets of criticism, attacked for their overeager experimentation with techniques and ideas borrowed from symbolism, surrealism, existentialism, and other schools of Western literary modernism. Their embrace of Western thought was widely interpreted as a betrayal of the Chinese cultural tradition, and they were condemned as victims of cultural and intellectual colonization. Moreover, their use of obscure, unconventional language and their obsession with formal stylization elicited charges of hollow aestheticism, elitist decadence, and abdication of social responsibility. Critics such as Kuan Chieh-ming (關傑明) raised the question of the "resinicization" (中國化) of modern Chinese poetry, calling on poets to forget their borrowed Western ideas and techniques and turn their attention to the Taiwanese reality around them, to the daily struggles of ordinary people. His was one of the earliest appeals for a "national style" (民族風格) in Taiwanese literature.[80] The modernist poets, of course, defended their imitation of Western modernist techniques as the healthy creative experimentation necessary for the modernization and revitalization of Chinese literature. They pointed out that despite the learning they had acquired from the West their poetry continued to be shaped by a fundamentally Chinese sensibility. As Yang Mu (楊牧), one of the poets of the Epoch group and a scholar of classical Chinese literature, argued: the impact of the Chinese literary tradition on modern Taiwanese literature is "invisible, yet thicker than blood; a born Chinese can never shake off this traditional literary heritage from his consciousness."[81] The best of the modern poetry did indeed draw on traditional poetic images and themes, but in the ideological heat of the debates the traditional dimensions of the New Poetry were conveniently ignored. In the aftermath of Taiwan's political humiliations, it seems, the moment was right for cultural nationalism and hence for the anti-Western rhetoric of the critics of New Poetry.

The attack on Western modernism initiated by the modern poetry debates eventually evolved into a broader and more constructive discussion of the function of literature and the arts. As the aestheticism of literary modernism fell increasingly out of favor, the historical and social roles of literature were reemphasized. It was during this period of introspective inquiry and cultural renaissance that writers and scholars rediscovered the native Taiwanese literature of the Occupation period. It was also during these years that the works of hsiang-t'u writers like Hwang Chun-ming and Wang Chen-ho skyrocketed in popularity. Their simple, humanist realism provided the perfect counterbalance to the excessive aesthetic formalism of the modernist writers, while their critical view of the sweeping social and cultural effects of modernization on traditional Taiwanese society appealed to the anti-Western, anti-Japanese spirit of the times. The arguments over hsiang-t'u literature therefore must be seen within the larger context of widespread anti-imperialist sentiment. Much of the anger was directed at Japan and the United States, whose growing economic presence and power was perceived to be a serious threat to Taiwanese economic self-determination. For the most ideological of the hsiang-t'u theorists, Wang T'o and Ch'en Ying-chen, their advocacy of hsiang-t'u literature was inseparable from their condemnation of American and Japanese economic exploitation and cultural colonization. Wang T'o, for instance, argues that the cultural and political movements of the 1970s signaled Taiwan's sudden awakening to "the true face of imperialist aggression" (帝國主義侵略者的真面貌). The movements, he writes, "serve an important educational and provocative function vis-a-vis our longtime existence under American and Japanese economic incursions masquerading under the guise of 'economic cooperation.' They sound an urgent wake-up call to our dormant national consciousness, which has for so long been slumbering under the spell of American and Japanese exploitation. At last, we are able to see clearly the ugly conspiracy between these two nations to invade our country and control our economy."[82]

Similarly, Ch'en Ying-chen explicitly connects Taiwan's modern history to the shared experiences of other Third World nations under Western imperialism. He argues that while American military and economic aid was offered ostensibly to help Taiwan rebuild and achieve economic autonomy after World War II, the true motives of the United States were purely selfish and imperialist.[83] In Ch'en's view, America's primary objective was to establish a stable government that would become a pawn in the battle against communism. Its other goals in providing economic aid were to exploit the abundance of cheap labor and to create a new market for American consumer products. In other words, postwar American policies toward Taiwan had forced the island into a classic neocolonial relationship of dependence.

With their antiforeign attitudes and adamant opposition to the growing neocolonial infiltration of Taiwan by the Americans and Japanese, it is not surprising that the hsiang-t'u theorists praised the fiction of Wang Chen-ho and Hwang Chun-ming as exemplary. A number of their works explicitly address the problem of economic and cultural colonization by both the United States and Japan. Wang's satirical "Hsiao Lin in Taipei" (小林來臺北), for example, reveals how much Taipei's businesses and entertainments cater to Americans and Japanese, and it mocks the city dwellers who try to Americanize their names, speech, dress, tastes, and behavior.[84] A later work, *Rose, Rose, I Love You* (玫瑰玫瑰我愛你), is a pointed critique of Taiwan's flourishing sex trade, which was providing native women to satisfy the appetites of American soldiers on leave from their tours of duty in Vietnam.[85] Hwang Chun-ming's stories also attack the neocolonial presence of Japan and the United States from various angles. "Hsiao-ch'i's Hat" (小琪的那一頂帽子) follows a Taiwanese traveling salesman as he tries to market his Japanese pressure-cookers to villagers throughout the countryside.[86] The story suggests the tragic consequences that Japan's economic invasion of Taiwan—spreading throughout society like the cancerous growth hidden under Hsiao-ch'i's hat—has in store for the Taiwanese people. "The Taste of Apples" (蘋果的滋味) uses the comic and fantastical story of a Taiwanese laborer whose rickety old bicycle is run over by an American general's shiny Mercedes limousine to raise serious questions about the American military presence in Taiwan and the degree to which the penetration of American culture has led to blind admiration of all things Western.[87]

Like Wang Chen-ho, Hwang Chun-ming is highly critical of Taiwan's burgeoning sex industry, which caters heavily to foreigners. In "Sayonara, Tsai-chien" (莎喲娜啦, 再見),[88] as well as "Little Widows" (小寡婦),[89] two stories frequently cited as exemplary by hsiang-t'u critics,[90] Hwang uses the metaphor of prostitution to underscore the economic exploitation and geopolitical domination of Taiwan by Japan and the West. The intersection of gender and colonial discourse has been explored in numerous recent writings in cultural studies and postcolonial theory.[91] As Joan Wallach Scott notes, the discourse of gender has been "a persistent and recurrent way of enabling the signification of power in the West" and is not always or necessarily "literally about gender itself."[92] In the imagery of colonialism, the dominant Western powers are most frequently represented as masculine warriors or explorers, while the territories and peoples of colonized non-Western countries are inevitably imagined as feminine: mysterious, passive, virginal, and implicitly available for conquest and domination.[93] Fittingly, in Hwang's "Sayonara, Tsai-chien" seven Japanese businessmen calling themselves the Seven Samurai have traveled throughout the Third World—South America, Southeast Asia, and Korea—checking on their investments and frequenting brothels in each country.[94] On their journeys, they each keep a detailed diary of their many conquests, competing to be the first to have slept with a thousand women. When the seven Japanese arrive to do business in Taiwan, a young man named Mr. Hwang, a clerk in a company with intimate business ties to Japan, is assigned the unsavory task of taking the men on the requisite "whoring tour" of the island. This degrading duty angers and humiliates Mr. Hwang, whose swelling patriotism compels him to curse—if only to himself—Japanese economic imperialism and its casual exploitation of the bodies of Taiwanese women.

The "samurai" who purchase the services of the Taiwanese prostitutes in "Little Widows" are literal warriors: soldiers on leave from another American imperialist venture in Asia, the fighting in Vietnam. In a club called Little Widows,[95] the "bar girls" (扒哥兒吧女) know that they are competing with women all over Asia—in the Philippines, Thailand,

Okinawa, Hong Kong, and Korea—for the American dollars the soldiers carry.[96] To attract the soldiers, the women have Americanized themselves, dyeing their hair reddish-brown; wearing heavy makeup; learning some rudimentary English; adopting American names[97] such as Anna (安娜), Julie (茱麗), Josephine (約瑟芬), and Christine (克麗斯丁); and even undergoing plastic surgery to make their eyes and noses look more Western.[98] However, Mr. Ma, the new manager of the club, proposes a different marketing strategy. Mr. Ma is a humorous figure, a man who has studied marketing and hotel management in the United States and who, like so many West-worshiping urbanites, drinks coffee, smokes American cigarettes, and loves to casually drop English words and phrases into his speech. Claiming that his years in America have given him a better insight into the Western imagination, he proposes that the club be given a Chinese name—Hsiao Kua-fu or Little Widows—and that the girls use their own names, dress in traditional Chinese costumes (borrowed from the wardrobe department of a television studio), and behave in a demure, obedient, and self-effacing manner.[99] In short, he wants them to act as traditionally "Chinese" as possible, playing to the most stereotypical orientalist fantasies of the West. Western colonialist fantasies of seduction typically begin with an element of "unveiling"—a metaphor for imperialist opening and discovery—so Mr. Ma has the women hide themselves behind bamboo partitions.[100] Moreover, he wants them to pretend that they are recent widows, loyal to the memory of their husbands, further reinforcing their image as exotic, forbidden fruit for the American soldiers to pick and consume. As Mr. Ma explains to the women: "For those macho American soldiers, not only are we offering up Chinese maidens, but chaste widows to boot! There's the exotic otherness of it, plus the sense of the 'taboo.' . . . I'll be damned if the GIs don't fall for it!"[101] Here, the figure of the "widow" might also be seen as a variation on the colonialist notion of "virgin territory": an inviolate female body ready for the imperialist project of "exploration, conquest and settlement."[102]

In addition to their criticism of American and Japanese economic exploitation, the hsiang-t'u theorists also attacked what they perceived to be encroaching cultural colonialism by the West, not just in literature but in all aspects of culture. The problem of "wholesale westernization" (全盤西化), which many understood to mean "wholesale Americanization" (全盤美國化), was raised repeatedly.[103] Ch'en Ying-chen, for example, questions the prevalence of Western languages—particularly English— which for three decades have dominated Taiwan's technological and medical scientific discourse. He cites the words of a woman doctor who wants to "save medicine from its colonized status": "Chinese doctors caring for Chinese patients in a Chinese nation find themselves forced to use awkward foreign terminology to describe their medical conditions. Chinese scientists using Chinese materials in a Chinese setting nevertheless compose their research reports in a stilted, unnatural foreign tongue." Why, she wonders, is it that "no one seems to recognize how laughable and humiliating a situation this is?"[104] As Ch'en goes on to note, Taiwanese academia was similarly marked by a discriminatory privileging of Western ideas and foreign learning. In the island's universities, textbooks were all too often in English or another Western language, making it impossible for students to learn anything without constantly flipping through their dictionaries. With the sole exception of the Chinese department, Ch'en complains, university faculty and department heads are far too frequently foreigners. The problem, as Ch'en eloquently argues, is that since 1949 Taiwanese have been so blinded by the uncontested power and global authority of the West that they no longer have faith in homegrown ideas and indigenous traditions of learning. An academic degree of any sort from even the most obscure of foreign universities automatically carries more prestige than an entire wall of diplomas from native institutions. The tragic result of this colonized mentality, Ch'en writes, is that "the entire Taiwanese educational system is ultimately reduced to being nothing more than preparation for higher education abroad."[105]

The issues of cultural nationalism raised by the hsiang-t'u literary debates must therefore be seen within this broader context of a general call for economic and cultural self-determination. The call was not for a chauvinistic rejection of all things Western but for a more balanced and critical assessment of Western civilization, a reevaluation and reaffirmation of native cultural traditions, and a shift from neocolonial dependency to economic and cultural autonomy.[106] Often harkening back to the tradition of May Fourth era anti-imperialism,[107] advocates of hsiang-t'u literature saw the cultural movement as a necessary corrective (修正) to the excessive Westernization of the 1960s.[108] In language strongly reminiscent of the attack on the New Poetry during the modern poetry debates,[109] they attacked the modernist writers—often singling out Wang Wen-hsing, Pai Hsien-yung, Ch'en Jo-hsi, and Ouyang Tzu for criticism—for their "adulation of the West and exaltation of the foreign" (崇洋媚外).[110] In the eyes of the hsiang-t'u theorists, the greatest offense committed by these writers was their failure to "make Taiwan the center" (臺灣為中心).[111] Too often, their stories tended either to fall into the category of mainland-oriented "nostalgia literature" (回憶文學),[112] or to ignore Taiwanese society by focusing on the individual stories of intellectual "wanderers" in America (流亡文學).[113] Neither type of fiction was acceptable to the nationalistic hsiang-t'u theorists. Wang T'o, for example, faulted the modernist writers for allowing their artistic consciousness to be molded not by indigenous concerns and the living, sensory experiences of modern Taiwanese life but by imported Western notions of individualism, alienation, and sexual obsession, as well as by Western intellectual trends such as Freudianism, existentialism, and imagism.[114] Or, as one critic of modernist fiction put it: "Our writers . . . have unthinkingly accepted foreign problems and experiences—most of which are still absent from our experience here in Taiwan—as their own. They mistakenly see the symptoms of other people's illnesses as ours; someone else has the cold, but we're the ones sneezing! Herein lies the reason for contemporary Taiwanese literature's alienation from the realities of Taiwanese life. So much of our modern fiction, whether consciously or unconsciously, is completely removed from our living reality."[115] In the (admittedly reductive) view of hsiang-t'u literature's most vocal advocates, the modernist infatuation with the West bordered on treason. The detachment from Taiwanese reality and the slavish imitation of Western styles were viewed as a deliberate denial of recent Chinese history and a refusal to acknowledge and address the repeated miseries and humiliations inflicted on China by imperialist incursions of all sorts.[116]

By the time the theoretical battles of the literary debates began heating up in late 1977, hsiang-t'u literature was clearly being positioned as the very antithesis of Taiwanese modernism. Among theorists on both sides, simplistic binary logic was the rule. From the perspective of the hsiang-t'u advocates, the short stories of Hwang Chun-ming and Wang Chen-ho represented "not just a pointed contrast, but a direct challenge" to the fiction of Pai Hsien-yung and Wang Wen-hsing.[117] Ch'en Ying-chen's tendency to place the two camps in oppositional pairings is typical of the rhetorical strategy of hsiang-t'u advocates: while modernist literature slavishly looked to the West for inspiration and validation, hsiang-t'u literature was firmly and proudly rooted in the native soil of the East.[118] The modernists were interested only in the solipsistic pursuit of pure aestheticism, while the hsiang-t'u writers sought to produce realistic, socially responsible art. Modernism was elitist and self-indulgent, while hsiang-t'u was popular and compassionate. Modernist literature was the expression of a colonized mentality, while hsiang-t'u embodied a genuine nationalist spirit. In short, according to the ideologues of hsiang-t'u, modernism is characterized by all that is "decadent" (頹廢), while hsiang-t'u represents all that is "healthy" (健康).[119]

Nationalism or Separatism?
The Modernist Response

The modernists, for their part, were similarly prone to simplistic binary thinking and extremist rhetoric. One of the most bitterly antagonistic articles in the debates was written by Wang Wen-hsing, a frequent target of the hsiang-t'u supporters. Wang has actually been quite receptive to hsiang-t'u literature itself—particularly to the works of Hwang Chun-ming—but he has nothing but the harshest criticism for its theorists. Perhaps caught up in the heat of the debate and eager to take on his favored role as provocateur, he adopts a particularly extremist and vitriolic tone in his attack. He appears to relish his role as a deliberately outrageous and, one hopes, sharply ironic voice, as he embraces a position that is in near total disagreement with that of the hsiang-t'u advocates. On the most fundamental level of dispute, he argues that literature has no obligation to reflect social reality; for him, the only purpose of literature is to "make people happy—nothing more, nothing less."[120] He unapologetically defends the difficulty and opacity of the modernists, arguing that literature need not appeal to the lowest common denominator in society. In his fervor to justify his own fiction and the works of his *Modern Literature* colleagues, he misrepresents the hsiang-t'u argument against elitism and obscurity in literature, unfairly suggesting that the nativists want only a crude and simple-minded literature for the inarticulate masses (《一種咿咿啞啞的文學》).[121] His dismissive characterization of hsiang-t'u literature does not acknowledge, for example, the narrative sophistication of much of Hwang Chun-ming's and Wang Chen-ho's work. Most striking is his staunch defense of Japan and the West. While Wang's warning against the resurrection of chauvinistic nationalism, what he refers to as a "neo–Boxer Rebellion mentality" (新義和團思想),[122] is hardly startling, he is being deliberately provocative when he categorically rejects the suggestion that Taiwan might be suffering from a neocolonial cultural and economic invasion by America and Japan.[123] Ignoring the sometimes exploitative structure of transnational capitalism, Wang blithely argues that American and Japanese investments in Taiwan are an expression of the "generosity and goodwill" of those nations and have been only beneficial to the island and its people. He follows this claim with a rhetorical question: "If American and Japanese imperialism is asked to leave, how will we continue to survive?" (把美，日帝國主義請出去我們靠什麼來過活?).[124] This is nothing more or less than a double-edged underlining of common misconceptions of the dynamics of neocolonial dependency. Most outrageous and inflammatory, however, is his pronouncement that "to reject Western culture" is to reject culture (反對西化便是反對文化). He argues, in a perhaps intentional and ironic display of the classic mentality of the colonized, that the growing popularity in Taiwan of American movies, music, and consumer products like Coca-Cola have nothing to do with cultural imperialism but are simply popular due to their inherent and obvious superiority.[125]

Wang Wen-hsing's essay is, of course, suffused with irony and a deliberate extremism; nevertheless, its antagonistic and often defensive tone also reveals the degree to which the centers of authority in Taiwan—the KMT government as well as the refugee writers who had, until the challenge of hsiang-t'u, shaped the established literary canon—felt threatened by the vigor and popularity of the hsiang-t'u movement and were wary of its sociopolitical implications. The KMT's relationship with the native people, after all, had been characterized by distrust and suspicion since the bloody beginnings of its rule on the island. The hsiang-t'u authors were native Taiwanese, whose depictions of Taiwanese life and use of the local dialect, mainlanders feared, were forging a new, possibly subversive kind of connection with their readers. The official response to the rise of nativist fiction, therefore, was a sort of retrenchment in which the binary structures of classic nationalistic thinking were manipulated to reaffirm the KMT's vision of China. In late August of 1977, the government organized a three-day conference called the Symposium of Literary Workers. The ostensible purpose of the conference was to celebrate the creative freedom enjoyed by writers in Taiwan and to condemn the censorship and persecution suffered by writers and artists in Communist China. As many have pointed out, however, it soon became obvious that the true objective of the meeting was to criticize, censure, and ultimately suppress the development of hsiang-t'u literature.[126] The strategy of the government and its apologists was simply to paint the hsiang-t'u camp as traitorous, insinuating that its particular brand of sociopolitical consciousness in literature and art was an invitation to subversion and a threat to the national security and unity of the Republic of China. By mobilizing the politically loaded terminology of "proletarian literature," "literature of the workers, peasants, and soldiers" (工農兵文藝), and "class struggle" (階級鬥爭),[127] the opponents of hsiang-t'u literature sought to link it to the Communist enemy—specifically the rigidly defined socialist realism advocated by Mao Zedong in his famous talks on literature and the arts in Yenan (延安).[128]

The debate over hsiang-t'u literature and its role in the emergence of a "Taiwanese consciousness" (臺灣意識) was even further polarized by the attempts of the government and its cultural apologists to accuse the hsiang-t'u writers of promoting separatism (臺灣分離主義).[129] A cultural debate that had begun as a struggle between Eastern and Western cultures was therefore transformed into a tense opposition between Chinese and Taiwanese. This was a watershed shift, as it brought nativist sentiments that had been simmering beneath the surface bubbling forcefully to the top. Again, it was the hsiang-t'u movement's advocacy of the Taiwanese dialect as the preferred language of creative expression that became a focal point, perceived by the government as evidence that Taiwanese intellectuals were aiming to sever all ties, cultural and political, with China and its traditions.[130] The tension between refugee mainlanders and native islanders created by these accusations was exacerbated in December 1979 with the outbreak of the Kaohsiung riots, also known as the Formosa Incident (美麗島事件),[131] and the subsequent arrest of, among others, Wang T'o and Yang Ch'ing-ch'u. While the charges of Taiwanese separatism were perhaps unnecessarily inflammatory, they clearly touched a nerve for the hsiang-t'u theorists. Many of them made an effort to deny any separatist intentions and to reassert their devotion to China. Yu T'ien-ts'ung, for example, emphatically affirmed his allegiance to the "Three Principles of the People" (三民主義)—the guiding tenets of the Republic of China under the KMT—insisting that hsiang-t'u literature is "necessarily opposed to separatist localisms."[132] In a pseudonymous essay entitled "The Blind Spot of Hsiang-t'u Literature" (鄉土文學的盲點), Ch'en Ying-chen performed an exercise in self-criticism, outlining the position of those who call for Taiwanese cultural nationalism and then dismissing it as the rhetoric of separatism.[133] Instead, Ch'en insists on the continuity between the anti-imperialist spirit of hsiang-t'u literature and earlier resistance movements in China, arguing that the Taiwanese consciousness of which hsiang-t'u authors speak is an inseparable part of a broader "Chinese consciousness" (中國意識), an inherited struggle in pursuit of Chinese self-determination. Indeed, as one observer notes, Taiwanese writers may be the only true heirs to a nationalistic Chinese consciousness, since the Communists on the mainland, with their embrace of Marxist internationalism, have all but destroyed the Chinese cultural tradition.[134]

These pronouncements by the hsiang-t'u theorists of devotion to an all-embracing Chinese nationalism, however, often appeared to be little more than lip service. Even as they proclaimed their allegiance to a unified Chinese consciousness, their fictional works continued to manifest a strong and distinctive regional consciousness, and in their critical writing, they continued to assert Taiwan's differences from the Chinese center. Ch'en Ying-chen, writing under his pseudonym, discusses the Taiwanese world in his fictional works, a world he views as being shaped by a history of not only physical but also political and emotional separation from mainland China; peopled by mainland refugees who, trapped in memories, fail to connect with the Taiwanese society around them; and inhabited by a Taiwanese populace that has long felt abandoned by the Chinese motherland.[135] In another essay, he points an accusing finger at the KMT government of mainland refugees when he notes that "some people, regardless of how long they have lived in Taiwan, have never, in the deepest part of their soul, really considered Taiwan to be a precious part of their homeland; nor have they ever treated the hardworking masses of Taiwanese citizens as their brothers and comrades."[136] Similarly, Yeh Shih-t'ao makes the obligatory assertion that "Taiwanese culture must be considered a mere branch of a larger Chinese cultural tradition,"[137] yet in the paragraphs preceding and following this claim he articulates an elaborate and forceful argument for the uniqueness of Taiwanese culture, a product not only of the island's geographic isolation, distinctive landscape, and tumultuous history but also of its exposure to multiple cultural traditions—Chinese, Polynesian, Melanesian, Malay, European, and Japanese—whose impact in many cases predate Han Chinese influences. All these factors, he argues, have given Taiwan a distinctive cultural identity that differs from the Chinese tradition.

Hwang Chun-ming and the Hsiang-t'u Debates

The binary structures through which the hsiang-t'u theorists articulated their arguments—modernity versus tradition, city versus country, Western modernism versus nativist realism—offer, of course, a rather crudely reductionist view of the Taiwanese cultural scene that effaces the diversity and subtle complexities of the literary texts themselves. Nevertheless, the validity of their classically nationalist model lies in its strategic efficacy for the struggle for sociopolitical power and cultural self-definition in which the hsiang-t'u critics were engaged. Hwang Chun-ming, whose fictional world depicts a Taiwan in the midst of a difficult transition, a predominantly rural society whose traditional lifestyles are being threatened by modernization and foreign influences, has been championed by hsiang-t'u critics as the master of nativist writing precisely because so many of his stories lend themselves to nationalist interpretations. Not only do his stories raise important questions about economic exploitation by Japan, the American military presence in Taiwan, and the growing influence of both Japanese and American culture on the island's youth, but they also tend to be built around the very types of binary confrontations characteristic of the discourse of colonial nationalism—between city and village, the modern and the traditional, the younger and older generations, and the literate official culture of Mandarin (the language of the government) and the dialect and oral folk culture of the Taiwanese people.[138]

Hwang Chun-ming's role in the hsiang-t'u literary debates is a curious one. While his works were repeatedly cited by the hsiang-t'u theorists as model expressions of Taiwanese consciousness, he was relatively detached from the ideological phase of the debate, choosing to stay safely above the polemical fray. Despite the critical praise heaped on his short stories and his status as a literary celebrity, Hwang does not generally think of himself as being first and foremost a writer or intellectual, and he has never lived on his earnings as a writer. Born in the Taiwanese countryside near I-lan in the northern part of the island, he has been a restless wanderer since his schooldays, when he had to be transferred several times from one school to another. Since his vagabond's spirit of adventure took him from home at an early age, he has worked at a wide variety of jobs: as a lunch box vendor, an apprentice at an electrical appliance shop, as an elementary school teacher, as a television reporter, and an executive in an athletic shoe company. He characterizes himself as someone who likes to dabble in all kinds of cultural activities—television, documentary filmmaking, and children's theater and literature in addition to fiction writing—and just happens to have written a few stories that were well received.[139] Unlike Wang T'o, Ch'en Ying-chen, and some of the other hsiang-t'u writers, he did not write any articles theorizing the relationship between hsiang-t'u and Taiwanese nationalism, nor did he become directly involved in Taiwanese politics.[140] He concentrated on his creative works and generally let his fiction speak for itself. He has, however, sometimes employed the rhetoric of nation to discuss his work. For instance, he is well aware that his writing and the renewed interest in Taiwanese language and culture shared by his fellow hsiang-t'u writers must be seen as a part of a more widespread rejuvenation of native consciousness and nationalism. Moreover, he clearly recognizes the potential political implications of the literary movement, comparing the inevitable emergence of regionalist literature in Taiwan to the growth of native literatures in African nations seeking to reestablish a national cultural identity after liberation from colonial rule.[141] Nevertheless, he remains rather bemused by the intensity of the debate surrounding his work and even a bit embarrassed by the lavish praise that has enshrined him as a great man of compassion, the "heartfelt voice for Taiwan's forgotten commonfolk."[142] He writes, he humbly insists, with neither a sociopolitical agenda nor any preconceived aesthetic goals but quite simply from the heart, drawing from the immediate experiences of his life. The colorful rural characters in his stories are all modeled on people he has known— people whose dreams and frustrations have moved him and who haunt his imagination.[143]

Like the hsiang-t'u theorists, Hwang's view of the role of literature emphasizes its human and social rather than its formal or aesthetic aspects. Having assimilated some modernist techniques into his own fiction writing, Hwang was not as antimodernist as the rhetoric of the hsiang-t'u theorists might suggest, and he did not participate in their harsh attack on the Western-influenced modernist writers. Some of his analyses of his own career as a writer, however, clearly illuminate his appeal for those in the antimodernist camp. He jokes, for instance, about his futile attempts to write, as numerous friends had advised him, about the intellectuals and businesspeople in Taipei rather than about simple country folk.[144] Despite his best efforts to banish those "country bumpkins" (鄉巴佬) from his mind, he found that their personalities and their lives remained the most vivid, compelling, and relevant. Another example of Hwang's disillusionment with the excesses of modernist experimentation can be found in his critical evaluation of a story he wrote very early in his career (1962–63), "A Man and His Knife" (男人與小刀). In this psychological story about an anxious and alienated young schoolteacher, Hwang experimented with interior monologue and toyed with Freudian symbolism and such themes as death, Oedipal anxiety, and sexual frustration. When he reprinted this early work in the preface to a later collection, he offered it not as an example of formal sophistication but as the shameful work of an immature and self-absorbed young writer.[145] He criticizes the story for its excessive bleakness, emotional vacuity, and studied nihilism.[146] It represents a stage in his writing, he says, that he is glad to have put behind him. Hence, for Hwang Chun-ming, as for the hsiang-t'u theorists, the transition from the modernist fiction of the 1960s to the nativist literature of the 1970s marks a healthy movement from escapist individualism and youthful irresponsibility to a more mature, compassionate, and reflective social awareness. This movement—and the emergence of a Taiwanese hsiang-t'u consciousness—was inevitable. As Hwang Chun-ming observes, the "varied and colorful voices" of the Taiwanese people simply cannot be silenced. No matter how hard one tries to erase the indigenous cultural consciousness with "capitalist lifestyles, trendy Western ideas and American rock and roll, in the end the Taiwanese voices will always be there, refusing to disappear, clamoring to be heard."[147]

The Ascendency of Taiwanese Consciousness: Political Liberalization and the Rise of Neonativist "Taiwan Literature"

In many respects, the accusations of Taiwanese cultural separatism that the KMT apologists leveled at the hsiang-t'u advocates during the debates of 1977–78 were not completely off the mark. If the debates themselves marked the turning point that brought the long-submerged conflict between China-centered and Taiwan-centered cultural interpretations to the fore, the political liberalization of the 1980s polarized the factions even further. Even at the zenith of the hsiang-t'u debates, nativist writers, whatever their political sympathies, at least professed their belief in a unified Chinese consciousness. As the KMT began to loosen its authoritarian grip and the social and political power of native Taiwanese began to grow, however, the increasingly liberal cultural atmosphere emboldened writers to be ever more assertive of their ideological allegiances. Hsiang-t'u writers who had been imprisoned by the KMT for excessive nativist consciousness were released into the brave new world of Taiwan's fledgling democracy, where they found they could openly declare their political and cultural separatism. Wang T'o, for example, joined the Democratic Progressive Party and ran for office on its ticket. Released from prison at about the same time, Yang Ch'ing-ch'u worked to promote a separate Taiwanese consciousness in the cultural realm, founding a Taiwanese branch of the International PEN literary society to rival the existing Chinese PEN, as well as advocating bilingual education in order to break the domination of Mandarin Chinese on the island.[148] Hence, the literary world of postliberalization Taiwan quickly split into two opposing groups, each, significantly, with separate media alliances. At one end of the ideological spectrum was a mainland-oriented group of writers who were affiliated with the San-san Bookstore (三三書坊, Double Three Bookstore) and its publication, San-san Series (三三季刊), both of which were established at the end of the 1970s. The young writers in this group include the sisters Chu T'ien-wen (朱天文) and Chu T'ien-hsin (朱天心), Ma Shu-li (馬叔禮), Ting Ya-min (丁亞民), and others.[149] At the other end was a neonativist movement that no longer espoused the hsiang-t'u literature of old but the more provocatively named Taiwanese indigenous literature (臺灣本土文學). Led by a younger generation of Taiwanese writers, including Sung Tse-lai (宋澤萊), Hsiang Yang (向陽), and Sung Tung-yang (宋冬陽, the pen name of 陳芳明), this group is associated with the magazine Taiwan Literature (臺灣文藝).[150] This journal is only one of many established during the 1980s that were specifically devoted to Taiwanese literature—a clear sign that many nativist writers were indeed moving down the road towards a kind of cultural separatism.[151]

Among the most radical of the young nativist writers, cultural separatism has become a logical and necessary counterpart of political separatism. For writers like Sung Tse-lai and the poet Lin Tsung-yuan (林宗源), advocacy of an autonomous Taiwanese literature—which is emphatically not "Chinese literature from Taiwan"—goes hand in hand with the political struggle for Taiwanese independence. Fiercely separatist, Sung and Lin have taken extremist positions, dramatically politicizing, for example, the issue of language. While the hsiang-t'u writers of the 1960s and 1970s advocated the use of the Taiwanese dialect in their stories, their promotion of the native tongue never approached the uncompromising militancy with which the neonativists—particularly Lin Tsung-yuan—insist on the use of Taiwanese as a literary medium. Lin, who has published ten volumes of poetry written in Taiwanese, is adamant in his view that the true Taiwanese consciousness can be expressed only in Taiwanese. He also believes that Taiwanese is not simply a dialect of Chinese but a separate language altogether; it follows, of course, that Taiwanese literature is a cultural entity distinct from and independent of Chinese literature.[152] Sung Tse-lai is similarly radicalized in his separatist views; he sees the Taiwanese people as a separate race unrelated to the Chinese and considers his stories in Taiwanese to be part of a "human rights literature" aimed at the founding of an "independent and separate state."[153]

While the radical separatism of nativist writers Lin Tsung-yuan and Sung Tse-lai does not represent the cultural mainstream, there is no question that in the post-Chiang era a vigorous and assertive Taiwanese consciousness is on the rise, rivaling and even dominating the sinocentric cultural interpretations of past decades. The dramatic sociopolitical and cultural changes of the 1980s also rendered many of the old categories of Taiwanese sociocultural debate less reliable than before. In the literary realm, for example, even though most of the writers associated with the Taiwanese indigenous literature group were native islanders and the majority of the San-san writers were second-generation mainlanders, family background or "provincial identity" (chi-kuan, 籍貫) is no longer a predictable or meaningful indicator of a writer's political sympathies.[154] There are Taiwanese who are in favor of Chinese reunification, just as there are people from mainland Chinese families who support the island's independence. In other words, the tension between Chinese and Taiwanese visions of nation can no longer be analyzed in terms of a simple conflict between mainlanders and natives. Far more often the division lies between the older and younger generations of the island's residents—between those old enough to have personal memories of the Chinese mainland and those too young to have experienced anything other than life in Taiwan.

In a recent article, for example, Sung-sheng Yvonne Chang focuses on the writer Chu T'ien-wen, a leading member of the San-san group and a second-generation mainlander, in order to illustrate how the ascendancy of a Taiwanese consciousness is reflected in the cultural productions of the baby boom generation of writers and artists.[155] Chu is a critical figure for two reasons. First, as a respected author of novels and short stories as well as one of the most important screenwriters of the New Cinema (known primarily for her work with Hou Hsiao-hsien), she is a concrete link between Taiwan's literary and cinema circles.[156] Second, the evolution of her own career reflects the ways in which cultural identification in Taiwan has shifted over the last fifteen years, with the gradual decline of a China-centered vision of nation and the ascent of a Taiwan-centered interpretation. The daughter of Chu Hsi-ning (朱西寧), a former military officer and a famous writer in his own right, Chu was raised in the family housing complexes (chuan-ts'un, 眷村) built by the KMT authorities for the troops that followed them to Taiwan. Depicting the lives of refugee mainlander families in these communities, Chu T'ien-wen and her sister Chu T'ien-hsin were among the first writers of chuan-ts'un literature. As Chang notes, this type of literature is characterized by the kind of sentimentality and naive patriotism that one might expect from the children of mainlanders, whose cultural imaginations were shaped by the political interpretations of the KMT as well as by the nostalgic memories of their parents. Chu T'ien-wen's early works as a member of the San-san group therefore displayed not only a romantic obsession with a mythical image of China but also a linguistic classicism and stylistic traditionalism that, as Chang puts it, "served the purpose of reinforcing the hegemony of the orthodox language, an emblem of the 'Central Plain' Chinese culture."[157]

However, as Chu T'ien-wen grew older (as well as wiser and more sophisticated, suggests Chang), she began to examine her once uncritical faith in the Nationalist government's political myths.[158] Moreover, her interactions and collaborations with progressive young intellectuals, including those in the New Cinema Movement, awakened her interest in contemporary social and political issues. Hence, her later works are marked by a gradual shift from a romanticized China-centered vision to more realistic, neonativist portrayals of contemporary Taiwan. In both her fiction and her screenplays for Hou Hsiao-hsien's films, Chu not only turns her attention from the romantic idyll of Chinese history to the more immediate experiences of postwar Taiwan, she begins to express doubts and criticisms of the political status quo.

Chu T'ien-wen's abandonment of her "China complex" and the gradual awakening of her Taiwanese consciousness are depicted by Chang as a process of maturation—a process in which an entire generation of writers and artists in Taiwan shared. Like Chu, many baby boomers born in Taiwan to mainlander families have sought to emphasize the fact that their experiences, too, are historically and emotionally rooted in the contemporary realities of Taiwan. By asserting their own Taiwanese consciousness in their art, they are laying claim to their share of contemporary Taiwanese history and articulating their own visions of a Taiwanese identity. For the postwar generation of Taiwanese—whether mainland Chinese or native islanders—cultural parameters are increasingly being determined by physical geography: the world they know is the immediate reality of Taiwan. If anything, their cultural imaginations are more likely to extend across the oceans to Japan and the West than across the strait to the Chinese motherland. For many decades, "China" had been rapidly receding into the background, no longer part of tangible experience and, with the government's ban on communication with the mainland, gradually fading from memory. It was becoming little more than a distant, mythical place found on maps and in history books. Ironically, the 1987 lifting of the travel ban, which has allowed mainlanders to return to China, not only failed to bridge the gap but even reinforced a sense of distance, as mainlanders returning home after four decades in Taiwan encountered unexpected culture shock—a bracing dose of reality that forced them to reexamine their idealized memories of their homeland. For second-generation mainlanders, whose nostalgic vision of China was inherited and hence already once removed, the shattering of the romantic myth of cultural origin only strengthened their allegiance to Taiwan.[159] As the recent political and sociocultural changes suggest, separation breeds separatism. Given the reality of Taiwan's longtime isolation from the Chinese mainland and its successful independent development, it seems that the emergence of a Taiwanese consciousness distinct from China was a historical inevitability. Taiwanese literature, too, was destined to find its own path, one that depicted the daily struggles and triumphs of people whose lives and experiences were firmly rooted in the soil—the hsiang-t'u—of the island.

2

Toward the Postmodern:
Taiwanese New Cinema and Alternative
Visions of Nation

Throughout the 1970s, the hsiang-t'u spirit of returning to the island's cultural roots manifested itself not only in the Taiwanese literature of the period but in many other arts as well. The world of painting, for example, was swept by a movement away from formalized academic painting—whether based on classical Chinese training or influenced by Western styles and techniques—toward plein air paintings that captured the experiences, energies, and textures of daily Taiwanese life.[1] At the same time, folk art and local motifs enjoyed renewed attention, as art journals and galleries sought out and actively promoted native folk artists and craftsmen such as the painter Hong T'ong (洪通) and the wood sculptor Chu Ming (朱銘).[2] Preservation of the local architectural heritage became a cultural priority, as traditional towns such as Lu Kang (鹿港), in the central part of the island, became the focus of intensive study and restoration efforts.[3] One popular journal of the period, *Echo (of Things Chinese)* (漢聲), was devoted primarily to introducing local folk art traditions—from aboriginal weaving and tattoo art to candy making, doll carving, and puppetry. The performing arts saw a similar revival of interest in folk traditions,[4] while in music Taiwanese folk songs (臺灣民歌) came into vogue and previously unknown folk musicians such as Ch'en Ta (陳達) were discovered and enthusiastically celebrated in the island's cultural media. Perhaps one of the best examples of the newly emerging Taiwanese artistic consciousness is the work of the modern dance group Cloud Gate Troupe (雲門舞集). Under the leadership of Lin Huai-min (林懷民), a dancer and choreographer trained in America, the group's works were creative reinterpretations of Taiwan's legendary and historical past and were characterized by an experimental attempt to combine Western mod-

ern dance techniques with indigenous folk gestures, local theatrical traditions, and native ritual practices. Despite its pervasive influence across
a broad spectrum of arts, however, the nationalistic hsiang-t'u fever of
the 1970s somehow managed to bypass the local film industry. While the
hsiang-t'u spirit was transforming literature, painting, and performing
arts, Taiwanese cinema during this period failed to answer the call for a
native cultural awareness. There are, of course, political and institutional
reasons why a Taiwanese consciousness did not begin to surface in the
cinema until a much later date, reasons tied not only to the particularities of Taiwanese film history but also to the complex, and sometimes
volatile, relationship between cinema and the idea of nationhood.

Cinema and the National

[National cinema] must be read against the local/global interface,
which has become increasingly important in the new world order of
the 1980s and 1990s. This interface operates in every national cinema,
primarily because the film medium has always been an important
vehicle for constructing images of a unified national identity out of
regional and ethnic diversity and for transmitting them both within
and beyond its national borders and also because, from its inception,
the history of cinema has always involved a fierce international competition for world markets.[5]

For much of the modern age, the formation of a national consciousness
and the creation of strong horizontal bonds of comradeship have been, as
Benedict Anderson argues, the domain of the print media—newspapers,
novels, and other literary forms whose unifying and legitimizing narratives of community have been important tools for generating images of
the nation for its citizens. Since the end of the nineteenth century, however, an understanding of the nation as a discursive entity has become increasingly dependent on analyses of visual rather than print media.[6] This
was particularly true in the latter half of the twentieth century, since,
along with television, cinema became a dominant mode of communication, with enormous power to both conjure and sustain "imagined communities." Cinema carries even greater potential for nation building than
literature does because it speaks to a broader audience. As a medium that
relies primarily on visual images and the spoken word, it reaches out
to both literate and illiterate segments of a community. Moreover, because verbal language—a crucial signifier of difference—is only one aspect of cinema, films are more transportable across cultural borders. The

visual images that constitute most "film language" are ontologically more universal. With fewer problems of translation, therefore, cinema has un-rivaled potential for articulating images of nation not only to those within the community but to the rest of the world as well. The photographic base of cinema also endows it with special powers of representation: film can construct a national space—depicting landscapes, peoples, details of be-havior, and dress—that is instantly "real" and recognizable in a way that is unavailable to literary narratives. Cinema's iconic condensation of images can evoke unusually strong feelings of identification in its audience—an instance of what Louis Althusser called the interpellation of the (national) subject.[7]

Another facet of the complex intertwining of cinema and nation is its close alliance in many countries with the institutions of the nation-state. Cinema is an art but also, after all, an industrial one. Hence, its history in any country is unusually dependent—certainly far more than literature—on the level of a nation's industrial and technological development. As an industry, it is also subject to numerous financial imperatives and eco-nomic considerations that do not impact other arts or do so to a far lesser degree. Simply put, films generally cost a lot of money to make, requir-ing adequate financing (often secured through complex arrangements be-tween institutions and individuals) on the front end and proper marketing of the film, in the hope of achieving a respectable return on investment, on the back end. Both ends of the filmmaking process require reaching out to a large community of people, sometimes even a global commu-nity. Cinema is therefore inextricably tied to a vast array of domestic and global commercial networks—arrangements between financial institu-tions; elaborate systems of production, distribution, and exhibition; com-plex international trade agreements; questions of import/export quotas; and so on—all of which have some connection to the political activi-ties of the nation-state. In some countries—and certainly in many Asian nations—there is the additional issue of content control by government agencies.

The history of filmmaking in Taiwan has always been characterized by active government involvement. Compared to its history in other parts of Asia, cinema arrived in Taiwan relatively late. Toward the end of the Japa-nese Occupation, the colonial government founded the Taiwan Motion Picture Association and the Taipei News Picture Association, two enti-ties that merged in 1945 to form the Taiwan Film Studio, which was under the direct control of the Taiwan Provincial Department of Information.[8] In the years that followed, filmmakers and other movie industry types began to migrate to the island from China and more studios were established. Four studios dominated filmmaking in Taiwan throughout the 1950s: the Taiwan Film Studio, the China Movie Studio, the China Educational Film Studio, and the Central Motion Picture Corporation (CMPC). All were owned by the government and, not surprisingly, were devoted to making films that "concentrated on the crimes of communism and the development of Taiwan as the Republic of China."[9] The CMPC, in particular, functioned as the propaganda arm of the Kuomintang, producing mostly documentaries for the party or the armed forces, though also making a number of feature-length movies toward the end of the decade.

During the 1960s, the government took an active role in trying to build up the island's film industry. In order to encourage private filmmakers and fledgling civilian studios to produce more feature films and upgrade quality, for example, the Government Information Office (GIO) made money available for loans. As an added incentive, it agreed to allow local film producers who made a certain number of films each year to share in the highly profitable importation and distribution of foreign films. Aiming to foster a healthy sense of competition and to acknowledge artistic achievements in cinema, it inaugurated the annual Golden Horse Awards (金馬獎). Although it had only limited success, the government also turned its attention to foreign markets, signing a number of coproduction agreements with Japanese companies and sending a few locally produced feature films to international festivals. At the same time, however, the GIO made clear its intention to continue monitoring film production in Taiwan, decreeing, for instance, that movies needed to be cultural and educational in a "positive way" in order to win the required approval of the government censorship board.[10] Indeed, Taiwan has a whole array of complex and forbidding regulatory laws that encompass nearly every aspect of the motion picture process, from scripting and fundraising to distribution and exhibition.[11]

Whether or not active government support of the industry can be credited for it is debatable, but the historical facts are that filmmaking in Taiwan flourished throughout the late 1960s and into the 1970s. Film studios grew large and profitable, signing veteran directors to long-term contracts and nurturing stables of carefully groomed and marketed stars. Throughout most of the 1970s, Taiwanese studios produced over two hundred films annually, most of which were notable for their production standards and entertainment value but not for any cultural or artistic significance. Instead, films of the 1970s stagnated at two extremes: anticommunist and anti-Japanese propaganda films on the one hand and, on the other, films of pure escapism that avoided politics and contemporary sociocultural problems altogether.[12] In those years, Taiwanese cinema was indisputably dominated by fantasy entertainment films: Chinese swordsmen epics (武俠片) and martial arts films (武打片) set in the distant past, along with melodramas and teen romance films based on the wildly popular fiction of Ch'iung Yao (瓊瑤).[13] Both genres tended to be monotonously formulaic thematically as well as stylistically. The conservatism and creative timidity of this period were in part driven by economic imperatives, of course, but they were also attributable to the tight control exercised by the government through its continued involvement in the major film studios, as well as through its censorship board.

The rejuvenation of Taiwanese cinema in the 1980s began, significantly, with small changes in moviemaking policy that eventually led to a loosening of government cultural controls. The most critical change was the ascension of a new director at the GIO in the early 1980s. James Soong (Sung Ch'u-yu, 宋楚瑜) was a film buff who offered many innovative suggestions for rebuilding the stagnant film industry. Among the changes he helped to implement were the following.

1. Reorganizing of the Golden Horse Awards to honor artistic achievement rather than thematic content. Rather than continuing to have government representatives judge the films, Soong insisted that the jury be composed of film professionals.

2. Creating the Golden Horse Awards International Film Festival. By bringing in award-winning foreign films, Soong hoped to increase cinematic literacy in filmmakers and audiences alike, which would in turn raise the standards of local cinematic production.

3. Encouraging Taiwanese film entries in high-profile international competitions.

4. Updating the infrastructure of film law in order to lift the medium to a higher cultural level.[14]

Together, these changes indicated a positive change in the government's view of cinema, reflecting a newfound respect for film as a serious art form and a medium for cultural expression.

A number of other important factors also helped to awaken the local film industry from its moribund state. At the end of the 1970s, the most dangerous threats to the health of the Taiwanese film industry came from two sources.[15] One serious challenge came from the rapidly growing availability of imported or smuggled videotapes of foreign films from America, Japan, and Europe. These pirated tapes were convenient and inexpensive to rent, extremely current, and, because many were illegally imported, usually uncensored.[16] The other source of increased competition was Hong Kong, whose better equipped and financially flush powerhouse studios were producing thematically more diverse and stylistically more sophisticated films. At the same time, the vibrant and innovative work of the group of young directors who made up the Hong Kong New Wave (香港新浪潮) was also attracting a great deal of attention in both Asia and the West.[17] The popularity of the Hong Kong films and foreign videotapes crushed domestic films at the box office and, more ominously, seriously undermined public confidence in the native film industry. By the early 1980s, therefore, the desire to win back both commercial success and critical respect for Taiwanese cinema finally prompted the government to encourage less rigid modes of filmmaking. The innovations initiated by the GIO made possible important thematic, stylistic, and methodological changes in the movie industry that eventually led to the emergence—at last—of a new trend that came to be known as Taiwanese New Cinema (臺灣新電影).

What is Taiwanese New Cinema?

The chief beneficiaries of the government's first steps toward cultural liberalization were a group of young men and women, mostly born in the late 1940s and the 1950s, who in the early 1980s were just beginning their careers in filmmaking. Generally, this group is said to include the directors Tseng Chuang-hsiang (曾壯祥), K'o Yi-cheng (柯一正), Yang Te-ch'ang (楊德昌, known as Edward Yang), Chang Yi (張毅), Li You-ning (李祐寧), T'ao Te-ch'en (陶德辰), Wan Jen (萬仁), Ch'en K'un-hou (陳坤厚), and Hou Hsiao-hsien (侯孝賢); screenwriters Hsiao Yeh (小野), Wu Nien-chen (吳念真), Chu T'ien-wen (朱天文), and Ting Ya-min (丁亞民); cinematographers Li P'ing-pin (李屏賓) and Yang Wei-han (楊渭漢); editor Liao Ch'ing-sung (廖慶松); and producer Chang Hua-k'un (張華坤).[18] As Edward Yang points out, one important factor that set these young film-makers apart from their predecessors was that they came to filmmaking not by climbing the usual apprenticeship steps within the established studio system but on their own terms. Even Ch'en K'un-hou and Hou Hsiao-hsien, who did get their start working for major studios,[19] were quick to free themselves of the rigid constraints of the institutional status quo, bringing a badly needed infusion of new blood to the stagnant local film industry.[20] Seven of these young directors made their feature debuts in the two watershed films that heralded the birth of Taiwanese New Cinema. The first, *In Our Time* (光陰的故事, 1982), was an anthology film with four short segments directed by, respectively, T'ao Te-ch'en, Edward Yang, K'o Yi-cheng, and Chang Yi. The second, *His Son's Big Doll* (兒子的大玩偶, 1983), was released the following year.[21] Also an anthology film, it presented cinematic interpretations of three popu-

1. *His Son's Big Doll*, an anthology film whose title segment was directed by Hou Hsiao-hsien, was one of two watershed films that heralded the birth of Taiwanese New Cinema.

lar short stories by Hwang Chun-ming and introduced three more new-comers: Tseng Chuang-hsiang, who directed "Hsiao-ch'i's Hat" (小琪的那一頂帽子); Wan Jen, who directed "The Taste of Apples" (蘋果的滋味); and, most notably, Hou Hsiao-hsien, who directed the film's title segment, "His Son's Big Doll." Given that both films present harshly critical views of contemporary social conditions and various aspects of government policy, it is quite remarkable that they were produced under the auspices of the state-owned CMPC.[22] Wu Nien-chen remembers the initial reaction of his friends in Taiwan's literary circles when he accepted, in 1980, a job as a screenwriter at the CMPC: shock and disbelief. After considerable soul-searching, he was able to justify his decision to himself and others because he truly believed that under the guidance of a new, more enlightened studio head the CMPC was offering unprecedented opportunities to young filmmakers—many of them newly returned from the United States with professional degrees in film. Wu saw this as a once in a lifetime chance to work with talented and eager artists in a medium that he was convinced was becoming more effective than literature for reaching young people and promoting social change.[23]

These two portmanteau films are considered breakthroughs for a number of reasons. First, the unusually low budget films broke from studio tradition by refusing to use established directors or well-known actors. Rather than building their films around a bankable star, the young directors insisted on being faithful to the stories and characters, only casting actors whom they felt could truly capture the essence of each personality. Most often, the actors used were relative unknowns or even nonprofessionals.[24] The flexibility of the portmanteau form also liberated the filmmakers from the tired old "formula films" (模式電影) of the established commercial cinema, allowing each director the freedom to develop his own individual style within each short segment.[25] The work of the young directors was marked by stylistic innovation and technical sophistication that was new to Taiwanese cinema. Not only did the makers of these two films experiment with different styles of camera work, lighting, color, and editing, they also helped to improve equipment standards.[26] The new directors also eschewed the fast action and melodramatic narrative techniques of the commercial cinema, choosing detail over drama. Most importantly, the two films diverged from the escapist fantasies of the commercial cinema by addressing social, economic, and political issues, bringing to the screen fresh and realistic images of contemporary Taiwan, and daring to explore with an unblinkingly critical eye the rapid and confusing changes sweeping modern Taiwanese society. Indeed, the open pessimism about Taiwanese society expressed in *His Son's Big Doll*—its frank depiction of the poverty and humiliations suffered by the lower classes, for example—along with its explicitly anti-Japanese and anti-American tone, alarmed the conservative forces in the government and the studios to such a degree that they immediately demanded that the film be drastically reedited. The ensuing controversy—dubbed "the Apple-Paring Incident" (削蘋果事件)—prompted large numbers of writers, artists, and critics to rally around the film and argue against government censorship and for freedom of expression.[27] It was during this period of public debate that the term *Taiwanese New Cinema* emerged, coined by critics to describe this young generation of directors and the new direction in which they were taking Taiwanese filmmaking.

There remains much disagreement over whether or not Taiwanese New Cinema constitutes a coherent cinematic movement, particularly among the participants themselves.[28] Some, like directors Ch'en K'un-hou, screenwriter Wu Nien-chen, and producer Chang Hua-k'un, are quite dismissive of the term; they think that the categorization of Taiwanese cinema into "old" and "new" is divisive and counterproductive. Others, like screenwriter Hsiao Yeh, cinematographer Li P'ing-ping, and director Edward Yang, are strongly supportive of the term, believing that the New

Cinema marked an emphatic break with the past and that their generation of filmmakers brought dramatic and lasting changes to all aspects
of Taiwanese cinema. Still others, like Chu T'ien-wen, Tseng Chuang-
hsiang, and T'ao Te-ch'en, believe that the emergence of a so-called new
direction in Taiwanese filmmaking was less a matter of collective conscious effort than of fortuitous timing, and they emphasize the role that
the critical apparatus of the media played in defining the movement. As
T'ao puts it: "In reality, 'New Cinema' came about in the early 1980s
because a number of us with similar backgrounds just happened to get
into filmmaking at approximately the same time. Well, you know that it's
human nature to categorize everything! Anyway, journalists and critics
soon began to group our works together, calling them 'New Cinema,' even
though they really weren't meant to be. Journalists seem to love to refer
to us as 'cutting-edge directors,' even though we never refer to ourselves
that way. [The creation of Taiwanese New Cinema] has all been the work
of journalists and critics."[29]

Regardless of whether one believes Taiwanese New Cinema to be an
aesthetically and ideologically coherent movement or a critically fabri-
cated category, there is no question that these young screenwriters, directors, and cinematographers were united by their frequent collaborations
on films throughout the 1980s, often working closely together in coali-
tion style.[30] Furthermore, they share an attitude toward the cinema that
separates them from many of their predecessors in the established film
industry—a serious and earnest dedication to cinema as a mode of cultural expression that is as significant and worthy of critical attention as
is an established "art" such as literature or painting.

In a clear departure from the slapdash, formulaic, commercial filmmaking of the 1970s, the approach of the Taiwanese New Cinema filmmakers was both intellectual and meticulous. Even though he dislikes the
bipolar categorization of Taiwanese cinema into old and new, Wu Nien-
chen admits that working with the new generation of directors is a radically different experience from studio filmmaking. The New Cinema directors come to their films with a more comprehensive vision of what
they hope to achieve. Consequently, at every stage of production—from
writing the screenplay to choosing locations, character development and
casting, and the actual filming and editing—there are lengthy and serious
discussions among all the collaborators.[31] Hou Hsiao-hsien, for example,
has described in detail his usual working method.[32] He begins by jotting
down the images, characters, ideas, and rough sketches of scenes that he
hopes will become the bare bones of a story. Then he meets with Chu
T'ien-wen and Wu Nien-chen, his chief writers, and spends long hours

brainstorming and going over his notebooks with them before Chu and Wu sit down to write a screenplay. All three of them emphasize that nothing in the screenplay they produce is etched in stone; it is nothing more than a preliminary sketch that evolves throughout each step of the filmmaking process. A particularly inspiring location, the individual personality of an actor, a moving piece of music—almost anything is open to discussion and can change the shape and direction of the film. Hou notes that he thrives on improvisation; he avoids rehearsals because they tend to deaden the dialogue and undermine the naturalism of the film. As Wu Nien-chen says, their highly collaborative approach is incredibly time consuming but also infinitely more stimulating.[33]

This elevation of cinema to the level of serious art, along with the development of an appreciative audience for film, were important objectives for Taiwanese New Cinema. Just as the building of a community of readers depends on the institutionalized support of print media such as books, journals, and newspapers, so, too, the bonding of a community of spectators for film requires the aid of related cultural institutions. In order for Taiwanese cinema to reach its full potential, argues K'o Yi-cheng, it will be necessary to educate and nurture a knowledgeable audience, not only by encouraging new filmmaking talent but also by establishing new standards for film criticism and theory in Taiwan.[34] At the beginning of the 1980s, cinema began reaching for a higher cultural profile, as a new foundation for the development of the motion picture industry was created with help from the forty-year-old Motion Picture Association of Taiwan. Besides providing scholarships for film study and grants for young directors, the foundation sponsors the Film Library (電影圖書館), which acts as a center for the research and exhibition of films, both international and domestic. In addition to providing a gathering place for cinephiles, it sponsors weekly screenings and offers seminars where directors discuss their work with audiences. It also has sponsored the Golden Horse International Film Festival since its inception in 1980. By attracting over a hundred entries from around the world, the annual festival has sought to educate Taiwanese filmmakers and local audiences about quality filmmaking. In addition, the Film Library publishes numerous books and journals dedicated to cinema.[35] The popular media also contributed to the improvement of film literacy on the island, as many major newspapers introduced columns devoted exclusively to serious film criticism rather than the usual entertainment industry gossip. As a result, the status of a relatively new cultural player—the film critic—rose, as writers like Chiao Hsiung-p'ing (焦雄屏) and Huang Chien-yeh (黃建業) began to make a name for themselves.[36] The controversies surrounding early New Cinema films such as *His Son's Big Doll* caught the attention of cultural critics as well as the general media and initiated the critical interest that continued throughout the 1980s. Therefore, one of New Cinema's most significant contributions was reviving, after a decade of declining enthusiasm in the 1970s, the interest of a new generation of college students and intellectuals in domestic films.[37]

The New Cinema directors were further united in their firm commitment to the idea that, like literature and the other established arts, the cinema plays a crucial role in the sociocultural development of a nation—not only because it can hold up a mirror to contemporary society but also because of its potential for actively shaping a nation's self-image and cultural sensibility. As screenwriter Ting Ya-min notes: "The New Cinema directors restored cinema to the status that it deserves, to its proper place in our cultural fabric. Future filmmakers must never forget the powerful influence and stimulating effect that the cinema has on our outlook. The New Cinema directors revitalized cinema by bringing it back to our roots, back to this piece of earth called "Taiwan." They brought its field of vision home to our native soil, to everyday realities, to the people and events that surround us—a refocusing of attention that has definitely had a positive impact on Taiwanese film."[38] It is through cinematic representations, argues director K'o Yi-cheng, that a people envisions itself. Equally important, it is often through the cinema that a nation presents itself—its society, political structures, lifestyles, and culture—to the rest of the world.[39] In the eyes of the New Cinema directors, then, Taiwanese cinema is a potent form of cultural intervention actively engaged in defining the nation's identity within the international community.

Significantly, several of the young directors, including Wan Jen,[40] identify important precedents in the earlier, "new wave" cinematic movements that struggled to rejuvenate their local film industries and redefine national cinemas, often in response to the threat of cultural imperialism posed by the flood of American films and Hollywood-style filmmaking. These include the nationalist cinematic movements that emerged in France,[41] Germany,[42] and Latin America during the 1960s—a decade that has been called the golden age of national cinemas.[43] As with Taiwanese New Cinema, the participants in these movements were mostly young, intellectually minded filmmakers who worked outside the commercial mainstream and whose popularity rode larger waves of political protest and cultural nationalism. A more immediate inspiration for Taiwanese New Cinema was the Hong Kong New Wave Movement of the 1970s, which, as director Tsui Hark (徐克) notes, emerged as a response to Hong Kong's growing awareness and anxiety over its imminent reunification with China in 1997 and was increasingly marked by a preoccupation with questions of "the nation."[44] As the shadow of 1997 loomed ever larger, Hong Kong filmmakers struggled to define a local identity in relation to both their Chinese heritage and Western colonial cultures. Among the works of the Hong Kong New Wave directors, the docudramas of Allen Fong (方育平), which address a number of social problems in contemporary Hong Kong, made a particularly deep impression on the Taiwanese New Cinema directors.[45] Like other new wave movements before them, the Taiwanese filmmakers hoped that by bringing Taiwan's cinema back to its sociocultural roots they could not only provide "an authentic expression" of modern Taiwanese society but also could give it the kind of distinctive shape and character that would win it respect both at home and abroad.

A Sense of Place: Taiwanese New Cinema and the Hsiang-t'u Heritage

In addition to drawing inspiration from these cinematic precedents, Taiwanese New Cinema of the 1980s is also widely considered to be a direct heir to the hsiang-t'u literary movement of the previous decade.[46] The New Cinema directors are linked to the hsiang-t'u writers of the 1970s not only by the seriousness with which they approach their filmmaking and the emphasis that they place on the sociohistorical role of cinema but also by their unwavering commitment to exploring the world and the immediate experiences that they know best—that is, to "making Taiwan the center" (臺灣為中心).[47] In this regard, Taiwanese New Cinema marks a clear departure from the island's mainstream commercial cinema, which either concentrated on "the development of Taiwan as the Republic of China" or escaped into romantic fantasy. Like its literary predecessor, Taiwanese New Cinema is animated by a nationalist impulse in its devotion to capturing, with sociocultural specificity, the lived experiences of the native Taiwanese people as they try to navigate the tides of historical change. The coming of age of the New Cinema filmmakers, however, also marks a significant moment of change in the political and sociocultural landscape, as their generation embodies the blurring of the mainlander versus Taiwanese distinction that for so many years was the starting point for any discussion of Taiwanese society. While the directors of the New Cinema come from both mainland Chinese and native families,[48] they all belong to a generation for which the only real home they have ever known is Taiwan. Born in the late 1940s and 1950s, their childhoods and early adulthoods coincided with the island's own growth and maturation and its most dramatic decades of change. Hou Hsiao-hsien, whose family is from the mainland, spoke for many of the New Cinema filmmakers when he said that all his films have sought, first and foremost, to bring out "the dignity of Taiwan" (臺灣的尊嚴).[49] His autobiographical *A Time to Live and a Time to Die* (童年往事, 1985) vividly and poignantly captures the experiences of the "first-generation Taiwanese" (臺生第一代) children of mainland refugee families, asserting their own claim to the island's contemporary history. Hou's luminous film transcends its personal coming of age story to become an examination of the origins of modern Taiwanese life, a graceful and elegaic tracing of Taiwan's history from the KMT government's exile to Taiwan in 1949 to its decades of quasi-colonial rule on the island and the gradual relinquishment of the dream of returning to the mainland.

It is critical to recognize here how extremely influential the literature of the hsiang-t'u writers was for Hou's generation of Taiwanese youth, all of whom grew up during the peak of its popularity, and particularly for the young men and women who became part of the New Cinema Movement. Indeed, the ties between the literary and cinematic worlds in Taiwan have always been unusually intimate and strong, and many of the important screenwriters of the New Cinema, including Hsiao Yeh, Wu Nien-chen, Ting Ya-ming, and Chu T'ien-wen, began their careers as writers and continued to write fiction as well as criticism even after they began working in film. Chu T'ien-wen's experiences collaborating with New Cinema directors like Hou Hsiao-hsien had a direct impact on her fiction writing. While her early short stories were characterized by a romantic and sentimental nostalgia for China, her later fiction reflects the neonativist spirit of Hou's films, offering more complex and realistic portrayals of contemporary life in Taiwan. All of the Taiwanese New Cinema directors and screenwriters have acknowledged the impact that the hsiang-t'u writers have had,[50] not only on their creative work but also on their worldview in general.[51] Of all the hsiang-t'u authors, Hwang Chun-ming enjoys a unique status that is especially noteworthy. His significance for the New Cinema filmmakers is evidenced by Hou Hsiao-hsien's lengthy discussion about his decision to participate in the making of the anthology film *His Son's Big Doll*, the landmark work that brought three of Hwang Chun-ming's short stories to the screen. According to Hou: "I chose to film 'His Son's Big Doll' precisely because it was a story by Hwang Chun-ming. The fiction of Hwang and other hsiang-t'u writers has been extremely influential to all of us [the New Cinema directors] because theirs are the works that we read during our formative years, our years of schooling. The world described in Hwang's stories is the very world in which we grew up—a world that is intimately familiar to all of us. Moreover, this is a world that hadn't, up to that point, been given any representation on film. When the opportunity arose to bring this world to the screen, therefore, we were all eager to do it."[52] The deep respect and admiration that these young filmmakers felt for Hwang's fiction is apparent in Hou's account of their serious-minded preparations for making the film, which included attending a public lecture by the hsiang-t'u writer. Hou recalled that "we all wanted very much to hear Hwang Chun-ming speak. The day of the lecture was wet and stormy, but we nevertheless rushed through the rain to the National Art Institute, where as usual Hwang had attracted a full house. In making the film, I felt that I had to be very, very careful to be as loyal as possible to the literary text."[53]

The controversy that arose over *His Son's Big Doll* also highlights other aspects of the hsiang-t'u connection. The film raised eyebrows not only for its openly critical view of the social contradictions engendered by rapid modernization in Taiwan but also because for many government cultural authorities it resurrected many of the sensitive issues initially raised by the hsiang-t'u literary debates of 1977–78. For instance, the film-makers' insistence on dubbing all the dialogue in Taiwanese (it was one of the first films to be widely distributed in the local dialect), was once again interpreted as a potentially subversive rejection of the cultural authority of Mandarin Chinese officialdom.[54] Taiwanese New Cinema took up the project initiated by hsiang-t'u literature of rehabilitating the Taiwanese dialect—along with the entire socioideological complex it embodies—and making it even more potent. While the difficulty of writing Taiwanese dialect made its incorporation into hsiang-t'u literature slightly artificial, the orality/aurality of cinema eliminated that problem, and truly gave the native tongue new life and vigor. Government authorities and critics of *His Son's Big Doll* were alarmed by the strong "native consciousness" (本土意識) of the film. That consciousness was also the guiding spirit behind Hou Hsiao-hsien's next two films, *The Boys from Feng Kuei* (風櫃來的人, 1983) and *Summer at Grandpa's* (冬冬的假期, 1984). Both drew from his own experiences growing up in the countryside and brought vivid images of life in Taiwan's rural villages to the screen, further cementing the critical perception of Hou as the hsiang-t'u tradition's chief heir, a filmmaker whose creative vision was inextricably tied to the very soil of the Taiwanese countryside.

There is no doubt that attachment to the land—a pronounced and geographically specific sense of place—is central to the vision of Taiwan constructed by both Hwang Chun-ming's hsiang-t'u fiction and Hou Hsiao-hsien's films. Hwang's stories are set primarily in the rural villages of his native county, I-lan (宜蘭), in the northern part of the island. The villagers in his tales, like old Uncle Ah-sheng in "The Drowning of an Old Cat" (溺死一隻老貓),[55] and the old farmer in "Ch'ing Fan Kung's Story" (青番公的故事),[56] share a worldview that is shaped by the very geography of their villages. They view their relationship to the earth as organic. For example, in a section called "The Lay of the Land" (小地理), Uncle Ah-sheng explains why he refuses to allow the developers from the city to replace the village well with a swimming pool: "As for the lay of the land, Clear Spring is a dragon's head. The village exit leading to the town is the mouth of the dragon, and the well beside the school is the eye, which is why we call it Dragon-Eye Well. Ever since the days of our ancestors, the people in Clear Spring have been protected by this dragon, which is why we've been able to live our lives in peace. Now suddenly someone wants to bring harm to our dragon's eye, and the people of Clear Spring are not going to stand by and let it happen" (26–7).

Hou Hsiao-hsien demonstrates a similar understanding of the organic unity of the land and its inhabitants. Film critic Huang Chien-yeh sees in Hou's films a special emotional connection with village life (鄉鎮感情), particularly in his sensitivity to the specific geographical characteristics of rural locations.[57] Indeed, when preparing to shoot a film Hou usually seeks out a location first, allowing the stories and characters to grow out of the physical environment. *The Boys from Feng Kuei*, for example, came together after a visit Hou made to the island of P'eng Hu (澎湖) off the southern coast of Taiwan. Inspired by the tiny fishing villages on the island, he brought Chu T'ien-wen and his other collaborators there to spend time "researching" the area; from their experiences on the island, they put together the script for *Boys*.[58] The meticulous and loving care with which Hou tries to capture a sense of place is apparent in all of his films, which are often filled with shots of rural landscapes that emphasize the "lay of the land" and serve to contextualize the characters within their physical environment. Hou Hsiao-hsien depicts the rural settings of his cinematic world in such vivid and intimate detail that the geography of the many small Taiwanese villages featured in his films—Feng-shan (鳳山), P'eng-hu, Chin-kua-shih (金瓜石), and Chiu-fen (九份)—seems utterly real and familiar to many of his admirers.[59]

Hou's deep emotional attachment to the rural landscapes of Taiwan constitutes one of the strongest bonds linking New Cinema to the heritage of hsiang-t'u literature, and it certainly played a role in his emergence as a leading figure of the movement. In the critical discourse surrounding Taiwanese New Cinema, however, these associations with hsiang-t'u literature have resulted in some instances in an unfortunate misrepresentation. During the literary debates of the 1970s, the ruralism of Hwang Chun-ming and Wang Chen-ho's fiction was used by the opponents of hsiang-t'u, who wanted to dismiss the nativist literature as nostalgic pastoralism, to launch generalized attacks on all hsiang-t'u writing. Similarly, the high critical profile of Hou Hsiao-hsien's rural films led to the widespread and oversimplified misconception that Taiwanese New Cinema was nothing more than "hsiang-t'u cinema" (鄉土文學電影).[60] In reality, neither hsiang-t'u nor New Cinema is solely about rural life; many of the fictional works and the films are set in cities and address urban issues as well. What they do share, however, is a strong sense of place and a common interest in describing the peculiarities of the changing modern Taiwanese landscape and examining the sociocultural contradictions that have accompanied the island's transformation from a predominantly rural, agrarian society to an increasingly urbanized nation.

The Ideological Phase: Taiwanese New Cinema and Third Cinema

It is important to note here another factor that binds Taiwanese New Cinema with its literary predecessor: the flourishing of an impressive body of critical literature in its wake. During the 1970s, a critical battle over the value and meaning of hsiang-t'u literature broke out, a debate conducted largely among the Taiwanese intelligentsia that had little impact on general audiences. Similarly, despite its nationalist rhetoric and populist concerns, Taiwanese New Cinema was not a cinema of or for the masses.[61] Instead, like the European new wave film movements from which it draws inspiration, and like the nationalistic cinemas that emerged in Latin American and Africa during the 1960s,[62] Taiwanese New Cinema is produced primarily by urban intellectuals.[63] Unlike the majority of earlier filmmakers, who worked in the studio system, the chief figures of the Taiwanese New Cinema are distinguished by their high level of education. Most have college degrees, including specialized university training in film studies. Many of the key figures are conversant with Western film theory and alternative film practices and are committed not only to opening a critical dialogue on issues facing society and Taiwanese cinema but also in connecting that dialogue with intellectual and cultural movements worldwide.[64] For instance, Taiwanese New Cinema entered a more self-conscious, ideological phase when in 1987 fifty signatories—directors, actors, writers, and critics associated with Taiwanese New Cinema—issued a proclamation declaring their dedication to a new, artistically progressive cinema that is "critically self-reflective, historically aware, and conscious of cinema's potential as a national cultural form."[65] The nationalism they embraced employed, to a large degree, the oppositional vocabulary of self and other not only inherited from the native hsiang-t'u tradition but also learned from the Third World nationalisms with which many of the New Cinema proponents were familiar. One of the chief problems that the advocates of New Cinema specifically addressed, for example, was the growing hegemony of American culture in Taiwan, particularly the powerful influence of Hollywood's cinematic tradition on local studios. Calling on the government, cultural institutions, and the public media to support their efforts to revitalize native culture in order to reestablish "cultural self-determination" (民族的自主文化), they positioned themselves as an alternative to the established institutions of Taiwan's commercial film industry,[66] which, like the national film industries of so many Third World countries, is closely modeled on Hollywood—from its institutional and economic structures, to its promotion of the star system and its reliance on escapist romances, comedies, and action films.[67] The signatories of the proclamation argue for a Taiwanese cinema that does not always look to Hollywood or the bottom line. Insisting on the revolutionary "newness" of Taiwanese New Cinema, they call for the creation of a space outside of the commercial industry for the development of an "alternative cinema" (另一種電影). By choosing these words to position itself as an alternative to Hollywood commercialism, Taiwanese New Cinema consciously and explicitly linked itself with Third Cinema movements in Africa and Latin America—movements with which New Cinema proponents clearly felt a strong affinity.[68] Like New Cinema, which seeks to make Taiwan the "center," Third Cinema departs from commercial cinemas with its insistence on a "more focused address of the 'national.'"[69] Third Cinema is additionally relevant for an understanding of Taiwanese New Cinema because over its many decades of theory and practice its view of the national has evolved in directions that illuminate important ways in which the visions of a Taiwanese nation offered by New Cinema directors differ from those of their hsiang-t'u literary predecessors.

From its inception in the late 1960s, Third Cinema was conceived of as an anti-imperialist and counterhegemonic movement,[70] and its early practitioners and theorists embraced the essentialist dichotomies—past versus present, foreign versus native, urban industrial versus rural agrarian society, print versus oral culture, and the West versus the non-West—that best enabled it to distinguish itself from imperialist cultures and the dominance of Hollywood. As the practice evolved, however, it began to move toward a more complex, less essentialist conception of the national.

Paul Willemen, for example, notes that in its later incarnations Third Cinema was above all a call for acknowledging and exploring the multi-cultural complexity of postcolonial societies; he characterizes the aim of the makers of Third Cinema as a "recognition of the many-layeredness of their own cultural-historical formations, with each layer being shaped by complex connections between intra- as well as inter-national forces and traditions."[71] Third Cinema rejects the homogeneity of Hollywood-style filmmaking; hence, it seeks to subvert the commercial cinema's mono-lithic view of society by foregrounding the differences within contem-porary society, "revealing divisions and stratifications within a national formation, ranging from regional dialects to class and political antago-nisms."[72]

Taiwanese New Cinema likewise begins with the binary oppositions inherited from the anti-imperialist nationalist rhetoric of hsiang-t'u lit-erature. However, what distinguishes Taiwanese New Cinema from its literary predecessor is a more evident shift away from the binarisms of classical nationalism toward a more postcolonial or postmodern under-standing of nation that is neither essentialist nor caught up in notions of cultural authenticity. Instead, it attempts to move beyond the anticolo-nial strategy of defining a native self against a dominant foreign other, which merely reverses the terms of an existing binary opposition, to-ward a more radical questioning of the dichotomy itself. If hsiang-t'u questioned the simple unity of a single Chinese nation by foreground-ing Taiwan's differences from the presumed center of Chinese culture, the critical discourse surrounding it also attempted to construct a co-herent Taiwanese nation in its place. New Cinema, on the other hand, moves toward a more radical interrogation of the very possibility of such transcendent wholes. Its neonativism recognizes the intricacy and slip-periness of the ties between the social and the cultural and attempts to transcend the binarism of China versus Taiwan in order to more fully acknowledge the complexity of Taiwanese society.[73] If commercial cine-mas around the world have tended to reinforce the idea of an essential-ized and unitary nation-state, the artistic and experimental films of the new cinema movements have sought to undermine those unities, open-ing up, as one cultural theorist has put it, "fissures and fault lines in the nationalist discourse" and "setting in motion a de-totalizing dialectic."[74] In Taiwanese New Cinema, Hou Hsiao-hsien's films exemplify this tran-sition from a homogenizing conception of nation to one that acknowl-edges the divisions, stratifications, and antagonisms that constantly frag-ment and redefine not only societies but even individuals. His filmic representations of Taiwan reflect a mode of understanding that shifts away from essentialist thinking toward a recognition that in the modern global system of mass migrations and intersecting cultures individuals and nations can no longer be seen as unified, stable entities but are instead constantly shaped and reshaped by all of the many cultures and value systems with which they come into contact. Hou Hsiao-hsien, himself a second-generation mainlander and a hybrid product of mainland Chinese heritage, Taiwanese upbringing, and Western and Japanese influences, refuses to simplify, reduce, or deny any of the complicated and multifarious elements that make up Taiwanese identity and history. Unlike many of the hsiang-t'u writers, Hou's politics defy simple classification; in no way could he be easily labeled pro-Taiwan or anti-Mandarin.[75] In his critically acclaimed reexamination of Taiwanese history, the 1989 film *City of Sadness* (悲情城市), for example, Hou does not adopt the oppositional strategy of constructing a single indigenous counternarrative to challenge the KMT government's official history. Instead, the ambivalence and heterogeneous texture of the film questions the limitations of such binary oppositions themselves. Rather than reducing the complexities of human existence into a single authoritative truth, Hou opens history up to include multiple voices, multiple narratives, and multiple forces that coexist and are in constant contention.

Similarly, Hou's films begin to break down the very binary oppositions that they set up between Taiwan's Chinese past and its more Westernized present, its rural traditions and its industrialized future. Although he follows the hsiang-t'u writers in exploring the profound sociocultural differences between the country and the city in *Summer at Grandpa's*, *The Boys from Feng Kuei*, and *Dust in the Wind* (戀戀風塵, 1986), his is not a simple black and white view that glorifies the rural past and condemns the urban present. Hou's films do not seem to be searching, as so many nationalistic films do, for an authentic or pure Taiwanese identity that must be saved from the destructive forces of modernization and cultural imperialism. Instead, he seems much more interested in the dynamic tension between the many different forces that shape modern Taiwanese society and in the way individuals are able to grow by creating and re-creating themselves as they move between multiple cultures. This is particularly evident in *Daughter of the Nile* (尼羅河女兒, 1987), whose young protagonist finds herself caught between Chinese cultural traditions, native Taiwanese beliefs, American consumerism, and Japanese popular culture. Hou's film refrains from judging too hastily the relative merits of these different cultural influences; rather, he acknowledges them all as factors that shape modern Taiwanese identity. Perhaps more than his hsiang-t'u predecessors, he is able to see the positive dimensions of postcolonial society, recognizing that it is precisely from this modern intermingling of diverse cultures that, as Salman Rushdie has said, "new and unexpected combinations of human beings, ideas, politics, movies, [and] songs emerge."[76]

3

Remembering and Forgetting, Part I:
History, Memory, and the Autobiographical
Impulse

Popular Memory and the History of the Everyday

One of the most crucial factors that binds a group of people together to form a nation is "the possession in common of a rich legacy of memories," a shared heritage, which through repeated articulations creates and reinforces a sense of historical continuity and community.[1] During the decades of martial rule under the Kuomintang, much of Taiwan's historical past and local experience was systematically suppressed through an "organized forgetting" that sought to maintain the myth of a coherent Chinese nation unified with the mainland.[2] Since the end of martial law, however, the Taiwanese people have accelerated their attempts, through political as well as cultural efforts, to challenge the narrow perspectives of the KMT's official view of the island's modern history in order to resurrect forgotten memories and reclaim the island's historical past. In the cultural realm, both hsiang-t'u literature and New Cinema saw as one of their chief objectives the restoration of Taiwan's "popular memory" (大眾記憶)—images of modern Taiwanese people and their diverse experiences—to the island's cultural consciousness.

The tension between official history and popular memory is very much at the heart of any struggle to define a sense of nation. Contemporary cultural studies have emphasized that the various social groups that make up postcolonial societies are shaped by different historical experiences and varying degrees of subjugation and hence enjoy different degrees of accessibility to power and representation. Participation in privileged narratives such as historical writing—articulating and giving authoritative shape to the past—is a self-affirming act that enables one to comprehend and control the present and promises a culturally empowered subjectivity. This is something that dominant social groups have long understood and exploited. For the colonized or otherwise marginalized subject, then, the act of narrating the past can become the key to securing cultural and political recognition, "the coinage that purchases entry into the social and discursive economy."[3] Hence, it is not surprising that the desire to reexamine history has been a central impulse animating the discourses of class, gender, and ethnicity in the First World, as well as liberational nationalisms and postcolonial discourse throughout the Third World. In his studies of Third World cinemas, Teshome Gabriel has envisioned "official history" and "popular memory" as two historiographical forces locked in a constant battle for access to power and representation.[4] Official history is the kind of monologic, totalizing narrative that is written by a dominant culture (the colonizer) and is characterized by atemporal fixity and the suppression of alternative views. Notes Gabriel: "Official history tends to arrest the future by means of the past . . . . [It] claims a 'center' which continually marginalizes others. In this way its ideology inhibits people from constructing their own history or histories" (53). It also tends to focus on public, political events. Popular memory, in contrast, opens a window to the private sphere of the common people and gives voice to the multifarious experiences of the colonized—experiences that have been suppressed or denied by the dominant culture. It reassesses the past, "ordering the past not only as a reference point but as a theme of struggle; it is a *look back to the future*, necessarily dissident and partisan, wedded to constant change" (54). The treatment of history in anticolonial discourse, then, is necessarily interventionist and revisionist. Cultural efforts to recuperate history for the marginalized and oppressed seek to "wrest control of the . . . past from its scribes and curators in the present."[5] They also constitute a form of counterdiscourse that speaks for "subaltern peoples on the periphery or the margin of the colonial situation."[6]

Modern efforts to rewrite national histories, therefore, have sought to restore voices and perspectives ignored by traditional historiography, often turning to previously neglected sources of information such as popular songs, oral histories, diaries, testimonials, confessions, and even photo albums—that is, personal rather than public narratives.[7] One such effort that has particular resonance for Taiwan can be found in Germany, a country that is unusually preoccupied with matters of collective memory and national identity.[8] The movement known as *Alltagsgeschichte*, "the historiography of everyday life,"[9] aims to challenge the primacy of political history by turning away from public narratives (*Geschichte*) towards private stories (*Geschichten*).[10] Seeking to rewrite history "from below," Alltagsgeschichte subverts the traditional nation-state model of historical discourse by rejecting conventional narratives of "great men and great deeds" and hopes instead to capture the subjective experiences of everyday life at a regional, local, or even individual level.[11] It concerns itself primarily with the stories of workers, peasants, and the rest of the "nameless masses," and with oral culture and native traditions, and is less interested in articulating the cause and effect structures of history than in evoking mood and atmosphere—presenting the "texture of everyday life . . . working, eating, drinking, celebrating, falling in love, marrying, raising children, worrying and rejoicing: . . . everyday experiences below the surface of ideology and political events."[12]

This desire to rediscover the experiences of ordinary people and to present the complexly textured realities of their everyday lives resonates deeply with the objectives of both hsiang-t'u literature and Taiwanese New Cinema. The 1970s "back to the earth" (回歸鄉土) movement, of which hsiang-t'u literature was a critical part, was precisely such an attempt to reenvision Taiwan from below, to restore native perspectives to cultural and historical discourse by focusing on the quotidian struggles of ordinary people in modern Taiwan. Supporters of hsiang-t'u literature pointed out that during the Japanese Occupation, as well as the Kuomintang era, indigenous residents and scenes of local life were conspicuously absent from the island's art and literature. When native Taiwanese did appear, they were silent, picturesque objects in the background, included only to provide a folkloric bit of local color.[13] Hsiang-t'u advocates were critical of traditional methods of teaching history for similar reasons, faulting them for dwelling on the Chinese dynastic past while ignoring the everyday experiences of the Taiwanese masses.

> For so many years our teaching of history has been nothing more than "historiography for the sake of historiography" (為歷史而歷史); the Three Principles of the People tell us to focus on the lives of the people, yet the "lives" that conventional historiography has concerned itself with are the lives of emperors and aristocrats, not the lives of the populace at large. Emperors and aristocrats constitute only a miniscule segment of society, hence all that history offers us seems to be strange tales and amusing occurrences from a distant and fabulous past—nothing that has any tangible connection to our experiences today. Under this system, even if a person can recite historical time lines forward and backward what good will it do him?[14]

Hwang Chun-ming and his fellow hsiang-t'u writers introduced into the literary landscape precisely the kinds of contemporary individuals who exist outside of the mainstream of political, social, and economic "progress" and whose life experiences had for so long been left out of the narrative of Taiwanese historical development. In the work of writers such as Hwang Chun-ming and Wang Chen-ho, the kind of marginalized figures who previously appeared only as one-dimensional country bump-kins were given depth and humanity. Their stories resonate with voices from the fringes of Taiwanese society: impoverished farmers and fisher-men toiling in the island's tiny villages, fighting to keep their traditional ways of life alive in the face of industrialization and growing competition; small town workers trying to adapt to new labor practices and modern technologies; prostitutes struggling for self-determination and dignity in an increasingly exploitative society; day laborers who have come from the countryside to the city in search of opportunity; and elderly villagers try-ing to come to terms with the new values and attitudes of a Westernized society. More important, the daily experiences of these previously anony-mous common folk are told from their perspectives and for the first time in their own language.[15]

Cinema and History: The Politics of Representation

As a medium that is both visual and aural, cinema in Taiwan has been even more instrumental than fiction in restoring images of everyday life to the island's cultural imagination and in giving voice to the many stories that make up modern Taiwanese history. Since this chapter and the next focus primarily on historical representation in recent Taiwanese films, a brief discussion of the complex ties that bind cinema and the writing of history might be helpful. The special relationship between history and the filmic medium has been well-recognized and effectively exploited from the earliest days of cinema.[16] With its photographically accurate, larger than life images and its realistic sound and action, the motion pic-ture is uniquely equipped to sweep viewers into the past and cause them to experience people, places, and events as if they were really there. The persuasive power of the photographic image is such that in the mind of the viewer it can become as vivid and authentic as the memory of a lived experience.[17] In today's world of audiovisual saturation, historical knowl-edge—social memory—of past events comes primarily from film, tele-vision, and other popular media.[18] The cinema's potential for national mythmaking was recognized from its inception, and totalitarian govern-ments—from German and Italian Fascists to Chinese and Stalinist Com-munists—have been particularly sensitive to the power of the cinematic image to shape public memory.[19] The Nazi Third Reich, perhaps more than any other ruling regime, was acutely aware of the demogogic power of images and obsessed with controlling filmic representations of the regime and the German nation.[20] Indeed, Nazi mythmaking was so effective and the images and sounds put on film by Hitler's propaganda machinery so deeply ingrained in the German collective memory that the obsession of young filmmakers of the last twenty-five years has been to find alternative images of German life and history to counter the audiovisual legacy of the national socialist era,[21] a primary reason for the keen interest that Taiwanese filmmakers, cinema enthusiasts, and scholars have shown in German cinema.[22]

Taiwanese New Cinema has likewise been eager to find alternative representations of modern Taiwanese history. Like the hsiang-t'u writers from whom they drew inspiration, many of the young directors have dedicated themselves to challenging the narrow view of modern history institutionalized by schools and official culture by acknowledging the multiplicity of historically subordinated groups in Taiwanese society and attempting to describe the great diversity of experiences in contemporary life. In a number of recent essays, Wu Ch'i-yen (吳其諺) has noted that the single most significant contribution of New Cinema to the definition of a Taiwanese cultural identity is its ground-breaking attempts to construct historical representations of the "Taiwanese experience" (臺灣經驗) in filmic form, to claim cinematic space for "popular memory" (大眾記憶).[23] The breakthrough film *In Our Time* (光陰的故事, 1982) traced four decades of Taiwan's postwar social and economic evolution through four portraits: a child in the 1950s, an adolescent in the 1960s, a university student in the 1970s, and two young adults in the 1980s. It is no coincidence that the chronology of the four stories and the ages of their protagonists provide a parallel to the personal growth and maturation of the young directors themselves, who, like the island itself, were coming of age in the 1980s. With increasing attention to temporal, geographical, and social specificity, Taiwanese New Cinema brought to the screen distinctly Taiwanese stories of social, economic, and political change that had rarely if ever received cinematic representation.[24] *His Son's Big Doll* (1982) and *Taipei Story* (青梅竹馬, 1985), for example, trace the rapid economic transformation of both a small town and a major urban center, examining the impact of modernization on people of many different social classes and raising questions about the social and human cost of economic imperialism by multinational corporations. Films like *Summer at Grandpa's, The Boys from Feng Kuei, Dust in the Wind, Daughter of the Nile, Super Citizen* (超級市民, 1985), and *The Terrorizer* (恐怖份子, 1986) address the problems arising from rapid urbanization and the collapse of traditional societal values.

Taiwanese New Cinema also acknowledges the multiple strata within Taiwanese society by bringing to the screen the stories of previously marginalized social groups:[25] women (*You Ma Ts'ai Tzu* [油麻菜子], 1983, and *Kuei-mei, a Life* [我這樣過了一生], 1985);[26] the island's aborigines (Huang Ming-chuan's [黃明川] *The Man from Island West* [西部來的人], 1990), whose previous representations in film had been largely folkloric in nature; and another long-neglected segment of Taiwanese society, ordinary refugee families from the mainland (*A Time to Live and a Time to Die, Long Live Youth* [童黨萬歲], 1989, and *Banana Paradise* [香蕉天堂], 1989). The inclusion of this last group was an important development because native Taiwanese have long thought of the mainland Chinese as a monolithic group, blurring the distinction between the experiences of KMT officials and other upper class mainlanders, who retreated to Taiwan—most of them representing the cream of the crop from China's political, intellectual, and business worlds—and those of lower class refugees and the soldiers, who came to the island as part of the KMT's ragtag army. While members of the mainland elite often continued to enjoy lives of power and privilege on Taiwan, ordinary refugees and soldiers frequently led isolated, impoverished lives[27]—experiences that have been worlds apart.[28] Until the arrival of Taiwanese New Cinema, very little attention had been paid to the lives of ordinary mainlanders. Films like *Banana Paradise* and *Long Live Youth* gave their experiences representation and took important first steps toward exploring the complicated political and emotional ties between Taiwan and China. They attempted to examine, for instance, some of the historical origins of the uneasy relationship between mainlanders and native Taiwanese by turning to a historical era long considered taboo: the 1950s reign of "white terror" (白色恐怖)—the KMT government's paranoid witch hunt for communist spies.[29]

Edward Yang's complex epic *A Brighter Summer Day* (牯嶺街少年殺人事件, 1991) offers a broader but also more detailed portrait of this turbulent period, when the island was thrown into turmoil both by the massive influx of KMT soldiers and refugees from the mainland and by the cultural confusion precipitated by the postwar presence of American military personnel. Yang's film examines the difficulties faced by mainlanders adjusting to a life in exile in the aftermath of war, political upheaval, and cultural dislocation. At the same time, the tense relationships between mainlanders and islanders are played out in the film through the interactions between rival gangs of disaffected youth, who, severed from traditional familial structures and moral guidance, fill their lives with mindless violence and American popular culture.

Indeed, the nostalgic imagination of much of recent Taiwanese literature and film has focused on the 1950s and 1960s—decades that, as Sung-sheng Yvonne Chang has noted, are critical to Taiwan's current generation of writers and filmmakers for two reasons.[30] Many of this generation were born just after World War II, and revisiting their childhood and adolescence fills a need to better understand their own personal growth and emotional development. At the same time, the look backward also responds to sociopolitical needs in Taiwan's current climate, raising broader questions of identity and identification during a period in which the island's past, present, and future relationships with China are being openly debated. The surge of stories by and about the group variously called "first-generation Taiwanese"[31] or "second-generation mainlanders"[32] is significant because for this group—as well as for those of mixed Taiwanese and mainlander parentage—issues of identity have always been particularly thorny, tied as they are to the difficult relationship between the island and the mainland and to the political question of Chinese unity.[33] Native Taiwanese have traditionally grouped them with the mainlander other, yet most Taiwan-born mainlanders have no firsthand knowledge of and feel little emotional attachment to China. Many believe that they are just as Taiwanese as the native islanders.[34] As the liberalization that followed martial law has strengthened the cultural and political power of native Taiwanese and the trend towards indigenization has gained momentum, many second-generation mainlanders worry that they will be increasingly marginalized by, and even excluded from, Taiwanese society. Their anxiety over their place in Taiwanese society has led, as Sung-sheng Yvonne Chang has observed, to a proliferation of works that foreground this group's geographical and historical rootedness in Taiwan—a declaration of their identification with the island rather than the mainland and a claim to their legitimate share of Taiwan's modern history.[35]

History, Autobiography, and Cultural Crisis
A Time to Live and a Time to Die

> Is [autobiography] the model for imperializing the consciousness of colonized peoples, replacing their collective potential for resistance with a cult of individuality and even loneliness? Or is it a medium of resistance and counterdiscourse, the legitimate space for producing that excess which throws doubt on the coherence and power of an exclusive historiography?[36]

Hou Hsiao-hsien is a perfect example of a second-generation mainlander who through his films has sought to articulate his place in Taiwanese history and to affirm his identification with the island on which he has

lived his entire life. Of all the Taiwanese New Cinema directors, no one
has been more concerned with Taiwanese history and identity than Hou.
All of his films revolve around a central question: What does it mean to
be not Chinese but a modern Taiwanese? Like other directors of the postwar generation, Hou began his search for the origins of modern Taiwanese identity with a retrospective look at his own childhood and youth.[37]
Among the thousands of ordinary Chinese families who followed KMT
forces into exile from the mainland was Hou Hsiao-hsien's own family.
Their experience in Taiwan is the subject of the highly personal *A Time
to Live and a Time to Die* (1985)—a film whose title could more accurately
be translated as *Childhood Memories*. It is frequently cited as one of the
great masterpieces of Taiwanese New Cinema.[38]

As in the film, Hou's family came to Taiwan from Mei County in
Kwangtung Province. Like so many refugee mainlanders, they viewed
themselves as transient visitors, yearning for the day when they can return to the mainland. To a large extent, the Nationalist government's official myth of "recapturing the mainland"—a slogan only recently abandoned—deepened the sense of dislocation and alienation experienced by
these exiles; by keeping alive the dream of an eventual return to the
motherland, the government allowed the mainlanders to avoid facing the
realities of life in Taiwan. For the members of Hou's family, who are
Hakka (客家), the experience of exile was further complicated by the
fact that, unlike the KMT officials and powerful families who supported
Chiang Kai-shek's government, they were outside the realm of power.[39]
Their position was one of extreme marginalization and their experience
one of double exile.[40]

Writing the Self into History

Hou's cinematic exploration of his childhood and adolescence is only
one of many personal narratives that have recently been brought to the
screen in Taiwan. Indeed, autobiography has been an extremely important form for Taiwanese New Cinema and for Hou Hsiao-hsien in particular. In addition to the autobiographical *A Time to Live and a Time to
Die*, two of his other films, *Dust in the Wind* and *Summer at Grandpa's*,
are the autobiographies of their respective screenwriters, Wu Nien-chen
and Chu T'ien-wen. The homeward journey that these works represent
were in some cases quite literal: many of the scenes in *A Time to Live and
a Time to Die* were filmed at Hou Hsiao-hsien's childhood home, while
Summer at Grandpa's was shot on location at the home of Chu T'ien-
wen's grandfather.[41] It has often been noted that narrative re-creations

of the past often take the form of autobiography, since personal narratives are the most meaningful and coherent centers of reference for ethnicity and place, particularly in times of sociocultural crisis. As traditional sources of stability and identification crumble, "autobiographers make repeated efforts to recollect their past and discover whatever continuity may establish their identity in a pluralistic universe."[42] Critical writing about the autobiographical form in the West, for example, has frequently located the genesis of the genre in the radical transition to the romantic age, when the agency of the rational, unitary self was celebrated as something that could give shape to the chaos of external reality and the vagaries of historical experience.[43] Because of this emphasis on the rational self, the autobiographical genre has conventionally been assigned a relatively narrow definition: a self-narrated, retrospective story that encapsulates the life of a unique individual and somehow captures his or her "essence." Recent critical reevaluations of the genre, however, have questioned traditional conceptions of autobiography as self-defining narratives of individuals, examining instead a diversity of autobiographical practices as potential forms of collective self-storytelling. In postmodern, postcolonial conceptions of autobiography, explorations of a personal past can also be seen as ongoing quests for a cultural or regional identity.[44] In the words of Phillipe Lejeune, "autobiographical narratives . . . are the place where a collective identity is elaborated, reproduced, and transformed,"[45] particularly, he argues, "at the point [in history] where traditional civilization cracks."[46] Hence, while the conventional view of self-narration emphasized the unity and uniqueness of the autobiographical subject, autobiographical writing, as reconceptualized by postmodern theory, recognizes the heterogeneity and instability of the discourses of identity.

Many theorists have suggested that autobiographical writing is a crucial form for groups who have been marginalized and whose perspectives have been systematically erased from history.[47] In her essay "Writing Autobiography," for example, bell hooks says that it was her concern over the "rapid disintegration of black folk experience" that led her to examine different forms of life writing and undertake the complicated process of rethinking the autobiographical genre. For hooks, using autobiography to preserve and transmit the experiences of black southern life is a necessary act; remembering experiences that differ from dominant culture, she argues, is a matter of personal and cultural survival.[48] Marginalized subjects have had almost no say in the construction of their own socially acknowledged identities, individual or collective. Their identities and experiences are far more likely to have been narrated and defined (through stereotypes and other myths) by those with greater access to power and representation. For subjugated groups, then, the act of autobiography is a multidimensional process that involves both the *deformation* and *reformation* of identity, offering the marginalized subject the opportunity to both challenge stereotypes and dominant narratives and make his or her long-suppressed voice heard. It allows the marginalized subject to write the self into history.

The critique of dominant social structure implicit in the autobiographical acts of minority or subordinated subjects is often paralleled by the deconstruction of traditional paradigms of genre and identity.[49] Just as the authority of official history is undermined by multiple alternative versions of "popular memory," so, too, are the conventions of the autobiographical genre—based on the concept of a coherent unitary self— challenged by the heterogeneity of forms that postmodern/postcolonial self-writing takes. A key feature of Phillipe Lejeune's conception of autobiography, for example, is a shift of focus from the past to the present. It is not the past as preconstituted in autobiographical experience that is of interest but the remembrance and imaginative re-creation of that past in the present unfolding of the autobiographical act—in the act of writing itself.[50] As James Olney puts it, the autobiographic focus has shifted from "autos" and "bios" to "graphe."[51] This emphasis on the discursive nature of autobiography has allowed the emergence of the genre-stretching term *autobiographical fiction* and for the recognition that autobiographical writing is above all an act of human narrative creation.[52] It is a way of constructing identity that serves the emotional, social, cultural, and political needs of the present. Understanding the autobiographical occasion as a socially and historically contingent act also undermines the conventional view of the autobiographical subject as stable and autonomous. Instead, it suggests that identity is forever shifting, that each act of autobiographical narration gives it only temporary shape.

In *A Time to Live and a Time to Die*, Hou's cinematic quest for his own identity and the cultural identity of his parents' generation is structured precisely by such creative acts of autobiography—storytelling occasions that are consistently italicized as such. Since film is usually considered a mimetic rather than a diegetic art (it shows rather than tells), the deliberate foregrounding of narrative acts in the film is significant; its effect is to call attention to the film's own constructedness. As Avrom Fleishman has argued: "While the motivation ascribed to film practices has almost universally been connected to realism, empathy and other forms of intensified conviction by the audience, the effect of storytelling situations is to encourage a sense of fictiveness. . . . Narrated stories seen and to some degree believed are also perceived to be stories told, and thus marked as created by the thought and speech of men and women."[53]

A Time to Live and a Time to Die highlights numerous forms of autobiographical narration. In addition to the first-person voice-over narration,[54] which frames the film and marks its images as the present-day (adult) Hou's reconstruction of his childhood memories, it also inscribes multiple discursive acts of recollection within those memories, as the older members of Hou's family—his father, mother, and grandmother—repeatedly articulate their memories as a way of coping with their painful experience of exile in Taiwan. Again, the emphasis on the past as memory underscores the subjectivity (and hence the instability) of historical knowledge. At the same time, the film's multiplicity of narratives—which intersect, illuminate, and interrogate each other—presents a challenge to the traditional view of autobiography as the story of a single individual. While the internal voice-over that frames the film suggests that it is first and foremost Hou's own story, the dramatized narrations that incorporate multiple stories introduce the notion of film structured as a medley of voices, moving it away from traditional autobiography and toward the extended form of autobiography that Teshome Gabriel has termed *heterobiography*: a multigenerational, transindividual autobiography in which (the) collective subject(s) is/are the focus.[55]

In the film, the despair of exile is represented by the older generation: the parents and grandmother of Ah-Hao (阿孝), one of four brothers and the character understood to be Hou's boyhood self. As war refugees who followed the KMT from the mainland to Taiwan, the older members of the family are unwilling and unable to adjust to their new home. In Ah-Hao's memory, his parents live in isolation—in part self-imposed—from the surrounding presence of Taiwanese village life. The father is mostly remembered as silent and sickly, an invalid who never leaves the dark confines of their Japanese-style house (a remnant of the Japanese Occupation), which is furnished with flimsy rattan furniture. On several occasions, the father is seen writing at his desk. It is only after his death, toward the end of the film, that it becomes clear that he has been writing in his diary—a form of personal narrative whose characteristic sense of discontinuity and impermanence, interestingly enough, reflects his experience of exile.[56] The father's story of exile emerges as Ah-Hao's older sister reads excerpts from his journal. Her difficulty in holding back her sobs as she reads and the quiet respect with which everyone listens to the father's narrative suggest a moment of revelation and connection: the father's words finally help the children to understand his emotional distance, his lack of connection to their daily lives. Mourning his displace-

2. *A Time to Live and a Time to Die*. For mainlanders like Ah-Hao's grandmother, the lost mainland remains the "structuring absence" that anchors their sense of self.

3. *A Time to Live and a Time to Die*. Ah-Hao's grandmother searches for her lost homeland in the Taiwanese countryside, poignantly illustrating how the lonely yearnings of an exile produce an "imaginative geography."

ment from the mainland and convinced that his stay in Taiwan will be temporary, the father was never able to set down roots on the island—a sense of impermanence poignantly signified by the inexpensive furnishings in the house, intentionally bought to be easily thrown away when it came time to return to the mainland.

The mother is, in her own way, equally alienated from the life of the village. As Ah-Hao remembers her, she spent much of her time indoors, cooking and caring for her children and sickly husband. Her brief and infrequent forays out of the house were strictly to run household errands rather than to socialize. What Ah-Hao remembers most about his mother, however, is her need to continually, almost obsessively, fill her children's ears with her recollections of the family's life on the mainland—stories about the early years of their marriage, about their friends, and most of all about the son they had left behind. Speaking in Hakka, the dialect of their native region, she narrates her past in vivid detail, struggling to cling to what Salman Rushdie has called, poetically, "a lost home in a lost city in the mists of a lost time."[57] Her almost compulsive autobiographical impulse underscores not only the need for memory but also the need to narrate oneself in order to construct a sense of identity.[58]

For these exiles, the world that is most real is not the one that lies outside their windows and doors but the one that lives in their memories and dreams—the Chinese mainland that lies somewhere across the waters of the Taiwan Strait. For them, the lost mainland of China remains the cen-

4. In Hou's autobiographical *A Time to Live and a Time to Die*, as each member of the older generation dies another link to the mainland Chinese past is severed.

ter, the place most tied up with their sense of self and history; it is the "structuring absence" that shapes their collective consciousness.[59] The haunting power that the homeland holds over the imagination of these exiles is most poignantly articulated in the scenes between Ah-Hao and his grandmother. The film opens with the old woman wandering through the streets of the village, talking to herself and searching for her beloved grandson. As she does almost every day, she wants to ask the boy to accompany her on a journey back to the old family village in Kwangtung Province "to pray to the ancestors"—her way of instilling in the boy a sense of origin, of teaching him who he is. When Ah-Hao accompanies his grandmother on these long walks through the Taiwanese village, he is alternately amused and embarrassed by her behavior, but he understands that she is searching for the road back to the mainland. On one such walk, the old woman becomes so completely absorbed in her memories that her nostalgia for her motherland transforms the alien landscape into the more familiar roads and waterways of her home on the mainland. She asks the owner of a snack shop how far it is to Meikong Bridge, a landmark in her native village. The shop owner, who doesn't understand Hakka, can only smile and shake her head in puzzlement. As grandmother and grandson resume their walk, the old woman continues talking, certain that she recognizes the way: "It's not far . . . we just follow the main road, go past the dam, and we'll be at Meikong Bridge." It is as if she believes that the force of her memory, her act of narration, can transform the landscape and lead her home. The tragicomic moment poignantly captures how the lonely yearnings of an exile produce what has been called an "imaginative geography."[60] It is also the moment that Ah-Hao, as the narrator of the film, recalls as a definitive memory of his childhood.

Ah-Hao's childhood memories tell the collective story of an entire generation of Taiwanese for whom the Chinese homeland has no tangible reality or authoritative meaning; it exists only as an imaginary world constructed in textbooks; in the official political rhetoric of the government; and, for the children of exiled mainlanders like Hou's family, in the memories and dreams of the older generation. The story of the mainland is only one of the many cultural discourses that shape their identities. Ah-Hao and his siblings inhabit three cultural-linguistic worlds and move between the different dialects with ease and fluency: Hakka at home in the nostalgic world of family memories, Taiwanese in the concrete world of life in their village, and Mandarin in the official world of their schools. The children's unselfconscious use of the different dialects and the film's incorporation of all three tongues constitute an important acknowledgment of the polyglot and multicultural nature of contemporary Taiwanese society. Their choice of Taiwanese and Mandarin over the Hakka spoken by their parents, moreover, underscores the film's recognition of the need to let go of a nostalgic vision of the past in order to participate fully in the present. As each member of the older generation of mainlanders dies—first the father, then the mother, and finally the grandmother—their memories of the mainland disappear with them. When the father dies, the story of the family's arrival from the mainland and dreams of going home, so carefully kept in his handwritten journal, die too. The mother, whose nostalgic storytelling kept alive the memories of those across the strait, is literally silenced when she loses her tongue to oral cancer before her death. Each death marks the severance of yet another of the children's links with the Chinese past; together they chronicle Taiwan's gradual relinquishment of the dream of returning to the mainland.[61] The film ends with the frozen image of the four brothers silently staring at the dead body of their grandmother, a powerful final image that marks for Hou's generation the closing of one era and the transition to the next. Like the brothers, Taiwan stands poised on the brink of tremendous change. In 1991, after four decades of stubbornly upholding its official slogan of "recapturing the mainland" and clinging to a unitary Chinese identity, the Taiwanese government finally abandoned its nostalgic dream and tacitly acknowledged its autonomous role in the global order of nations. Although Taiwan's future remains uncertain, its people, like the children in Hou's film, have begun to come to terms with the past. As the film suggests, Taiwanese of Hou's generation—including Taiwan-born mainlanders—neither blindly accept the authority of the KMT government nor subscribe to the monologic narrative of history it has imposed.[62] Rather than remain the silent objects of someone else's history, they accept the challenge of writing their own and becoming the narrators of their own futures.

4

Remembering and Forgetting, Part II:
Hou Hsiao-hsien's Taiwan Trilogy

Interweaving Past and Present:
Critical Historiography or the Uses of the Past

Like contemporary theories of autobiography, recent critical reconsiderations of other forms of historical writing have witnessed a shift away from conventional notions of recovering the truth of the past toward analyses of the various attitudes and motivations that shape discursive acts of memory in the present. In a famous passage from his "Theses on the Philosophy of History," for example, Walter Benjamin writes that "to articulate the past historically does not mean to recognize it 'the way it really was' (Ranke). It means to seize hold of a memory as it flashes up at a moment of danger."[1] Like much of modern historiography, Benjamin's philosophy of history rejects the claims to authority and objectivity that typified nineteenth-century historical writing. Instead, it is emphatically critical and interventionist. Benjaminian historiography, his idiosyncratic form of historical materialism, is further notable for its departure from traditional linear models that see history as an inexorable progression through time. While conventional modes of historical writing seek to construct a single coherent and chronological narrative—what Benjamin describes as a "sequence of events like beads on a rosary" (263)—he aims to "blast open the continuum of history" (261) in a "Messianic cessation of happening" (263). His is a historiography based on rupture and fragmentation; it stops time dead in its tracks by wrenching specific moments or events out of the homogeneous order of history and reconfiguring them into monads "pregnant with tension" (262). The classical historical narrative passively offers up a fixed "'eternal' image of the past," but Benjaminian historiography is based on a constructive, interactive principle (262) that recognizes a dialectical relationship between past and present. Benjamin's historical materialist "grasps the constellation which his own era has formed with a definite earlier one" (263), and actively engages in the constant construction and reconstruction of the past.[2] If history is an ongoing process generated by an ever-changing dynamic between past and present, the writing of history, then, is itself historical. All representations of the past, Benjamin would argue, are inevitably shaped and defined by the political and cultural concerns of the specific moment from which they emerge.

The complex system of modern global society has put many developing countries precisely into Benjaminan "moments of danger." Already burdened by colonial histories, the nations of Africa, Latin America, and Asia have been further plunged into cultural crisis as rapid modernization and integration into the world order are bringing a flood of foreign cultural media into contention with indigenous cultures. Taiwan's modern history has certainly been colored by a sense of cultural crisis, and many of the noteworthy literary and cinematic works that have emerged in the last few decades are characterized precisely by a preoccupation with the past that suggests an underlying sensitivity toward the transitional moment of danger in which the island finds itself. The body of films that Hou Hsiao-hsien has made during the 1980s and 1990s, in particular, are marked by a deep historical consciousness that might readily be seen in Benjaminian terms. His cinematic constructions of the personal and collective past illuminate the dialectic of past and present, attempting to find a sense of the past that might be usable in comprehending and coping with the crises of the present moment in Taiwanese history. His films seek to articulate the specific historical experiences of Taiwan over the last forty years, while at the same time reassessing the island's past, present, and future relationships with the West, Japan, and mainland China.

Taiwan after Martial Law:
Hou Hsiao-hsien's Taiwan Trilogy

All of Hou's films are permeated with a historical awareness shaped by the present-day realities of Taiwanese society, and nowhere is this more apparent than in the most overtly historical of his films—the three works that form his ambitious "Taiwan Trilogy" (臺灣三部曲):[3] *City of Sadness* (1989), *The Puppetmaster* (戲夢人生, 1993), and *Good Men, Good Women* (好男好女, 1995). More than any of his previous films, these three works are very much the products of the specific sociopolitical moment

86 Envisioning Taiwan

in which they were made. Each examines long-"forgotten" topics in Taiwanese history: respectively, the infamous February 28 Incident of 1947, the Japanese Occupation, and the "white terror" political persecutions of the 1950s. Discussions of these periods in local history were considered taboo under the iron-fisted rule of the KMT, so it is not likely that Hou's films could have been made prior to the current liberalization of cultural policy.[4] The first film of the trilogy, *City of Sadness*, has frequently been characterized as Hou's "post-martial-law film,"[5] his response and contribution to the remarkable democratization process in Taiwan that was launched by the lifting of martial law in 1987 and has steadily gathered momentum since the death of Chiang Ching-kuo (eldest son and successor of Chiang Kai-shek) in 1988. After enduring four decades of authoritarian rule by Chiang's Kuomintang, Taiwan now finds itself in a "golden age" that at last combines economic prosperity with the beginnings of both cultural and political liberalization.[6] Decades of strict censorship and tight control by the government have been loosened, allowing for spirited debates over social, cultural, and political matters in the newspapers, magazines, and other forms of public media. The island is also undergoing a political rebirth unprecedented in its history. After martial law was lifted, the ruling Nationalists allowed, for the first time, the formation of rival political parties.[7] Former "enemies" of the regime were given their freedom, as political prisoners were released and political exiles allowed to return home. The presidents who succeeded Chiang, Lee Teng-hui and Chen Shui-bian, are both native-born Taiwanese, as are many cabinet members. After centuries of rule by a long succession of outsiders, the Taiwanese people are at last being given an opportunity to actively participate in their own government and are clamoring to make their voices heard. Protests and street demonstrations have become common, and legislative sessions are often raucous and lively.

Decolonization and the Recuperation
of History: *City of Sadness*

The present moment marks a critical transition in the island's history. As Taiwan begins to step toward democratization, it is edging closer and closer to a potentially bright but as yet uncertain future. The Taiwanese people are exhilarated by the novelty and dizzying pace of current cultural-political change, but their exuberant hopes for the future are accompanied by the fear of a conservative backlash. This was especially true in the wake of the violent retaliation and subsequent repression that shut down the pro-democracy movement in Beijing in June of 1989 and is reflected in Taiwan's concern over China's management of the Hong Kong takeover. Indeed, the shadow of Tiananmen looms large over the contemporary Taiwanese psyche and lurks behind *City of Sadness* as well.[8] It is no accident, therefore, that the historical period depicted in Hou's first film after the lifting of martial law is another era of transition—from Japanese Occupation to rule by the Nationalist government—that saw a brief moment of hope for political liberalization followed by disillusionment and harsh repression. In an interview, Hou made clear his conviction that a reexamination of this crucial period is fundamental to an understanding of contemporary Taiwanese society, of the antagonistic relationship between the government and the people, and of the tensions between mainlanders and native Taiwanese. Says Hou: "The years between 1946 and 1949 constitute a special period in history because they have important implications for political, cultural, and social change in Taiwan. Amid change, people have tremendous survival instincts and determination to face the challenges that arise."[9] Hou's reexamination of history, then, is a Benjaminian attempt to "seize hold of a memory as it flashes up in a moment of danger," to illuminate the "constellation" between the Taiwanese past and the Taiwanese present, and to write, as it were, a "history of the present."[10] As Taiwan faces the challenges of today, it can—and indeed must—learn from historical experience. Hou's deliberate articulations of the "forgotten" past in *City of Sadness* and the other films in his trilogy of Taiwanese history orders the experiences of the past into, as Teshome Gabriel put it, "not only a reference point but . . . a theme of struggle."[11]

The notion of struggle is central to an understanding of the role of history and historiography in Hou's films. In interviews, Hou has asserted his belief that after centuries of invasion and colonial rule by the Spanish, Portuguese, Manchus, Japanese, and Nationalist Chinese Taiwan is finally in the process of decolonization.[12] The recuperation of native history is a crucial component of decolonization, for, as Albert Memmi has noted "the most serious blow suffered by the colonized is being removed from history." The colonized is "condemned to lose his memory," only to have it replaced by one that is "not of his people. . . . The history which is taught to him is not his own."[13] In Memmi's view, one of the most important steps the colonized can take toward liberation must be the restoration of memory and the reclamation of his or her place as a subject—rather than a mere object—of history. Walter Benjamin's philosophy of history similarly valorizes interventionist historiography as an important tool in the struggle against oppression by the ruling classes. "In every era," he writes in "Theses on the Philosophy of History," "the attempt must be made anew to wrest tradition away from a conformism that is about to overpower it" (255). The task of the historical materialist is to "brush history against the grain" (257) and challenge official histories—those "documents of civilization" that are inevitably "documents of barbarism" (256)—written by the victors. Like Alltagsgeschichte, therefore, historical materialism valorizes the everyday. It is not interested in the lives of "the great minds and talents" of an era or their participation in major political events but in "the anonymous toil of their contemporaries" (256).

The notion of popular memory that lies at the core of Teshome Gabriel's conception of Third Cinema promotes a similarly deconstructive project; like Benjaminian historiography, popular memory aims to "brush history against the grain." Many important works of Third Cinema from Latin America, for example, have challenged official accounts of slavery and the slave rebellions by recounting historical experiences from the slave's point of view.[14] Humberto Solas's *Lucia* (1968), a three-part history of revolutionary consciousness in Cuba, depicts revolution from the perspectives of three different classes, beginning with the aristocrat, moving on to the bourgeois intellectual, and ending with the peasant-worker. The film leaves no doubt that its three phases trace a progression from the least to the most enlightened class. Solas, a devoted student of Cuban history, has offered some insights into his motivations for making Lucia that echo the sociopolitical climate surrounding the genesis of *City of Sadness*. Latin America witnessed much spirited revolutionary activity in 1968–70, with student movements rising everywhere and social upheaval from Mexico to Brazil. Says Solas: "It was a beautiful time. The whole continent was reasserting itself." At the time, Cuba was celebrating what was called the Hundred Years of Struggle, referring to the "century-long search for genuine independence" that began with the fight for independence from Spain and continued through the Socialist Revolution of 1959. Says Solas: "I wanted to view our history in phases, to show how apparent frustrations and setbacks—such as the decade of the Thirties—led us to a higher stage of national life"; this, he states, "was the underlying principle of *Lucia*." The parallels with Hou's impetus for making *City of Sadness* are striking. Taiwan, too, has reached a critical moment in its history, a "beautiful time" of political fervor that has the potential to become the culmination of a long "search for genuine independence." Hou Hsiao-hsien shares Humberto Solas's recognition of the need in such "moments of danger" to turn to the past in order to understand the challenges of the contemporary situation. Both understand that the past and present are inextricably intertwined. As Solas puts it: "Whenever you make a historical film, whether it is set two decades or two centuries ago, you are referring to the present."[15]

As the appearance of Hou's Taiwan Trilogy attests, Taiwan's writers and filmmakers are taking full advantage of these heady days of cultural liberalization and political pluralism, seizing the opportunity to probe the island's history with increasing attention to details and specificity, and striving to restore suppressed perspectives. This feverish, almost obsessive, digging into the past is evidenced by the recent proliferation of books about local history—volumes and volumes of historical research, which include collections of suppressed documents, oral histories, victims' biographies, and the like.[16] The late 1980s and early 1990s also saw the emergence of "political fiction" (政治小說), a new genre of writing best represented by Chang Ta-ch'un (張大春), whose works include *The Great Prevaricator* (大說謊家) and *The General's Monument* (將軍碑); Shih Ming-cheng (施明正), author of *One Who Longed For Death* (渴死者); and Yang Chao (楊照), who wrote *Lost Souls* (黯魂).[17] While the hsiang-t'u literature of earlier decades was as frequently politicized as political, these works intentionally took on provocative political themes.[18] Shih's novel, for example, was one of several that dealt with the experiences of political prisoners in Taiwan, detailing their physical and psychological suffering behind bars, as well as their social maladjustment on release. In Yang's *Lost Souls*, themes of historical disentitlement and national guilt are woven through the story of three generations of a Taiwanese family haunted by the terror of political persecution.

At the heart of many of these works of political fiction was the infamous February 28 Incident of 1947. Actually a series of protests triggered by resentment of KMT corruption and repression, the uprising was violently suppressed by Nationalist government officials, whose massacres killed eight to ten thousand Taiwanese—among them an entire generation of the island's social and intellectual elite. While the massacre was a critical turning point whose repercussions have been felt in Taiwanese society ever since, it was effectively erased from public memory by the KMT. Until the mid-1980s, any mention of the incident was strictly prohibited. The newly liberalized political climate, however, was signaled by an unprecedented public commemoration of the incident on February 28, 1988, the year Lee Teng-hui took office. Large street demonstrations took place in the island's major cities, and President Lee himself spoke to the nation about the "tragedy," acknowledging that it needed to be "treated with sincere understanding."[19] Even before the official lifting of Taiwan's state of emergency, however, many books and articles about the incident had begun to appear. With President Lee's official sanctioning of public discussion, research into this critical event accelerated. Drawing on oral histories, diaries, personal letters, and interviews, writers compiled victims' biographies and other alternative histories.[20] Throughout the late

1980s, the reexamination and retelling of the incident became an integral part of the Taiwanese struggle for political and cultural empowerment.

Hou Hsiao-hsien's *City of Sadness* was a milestone in this process of decolonization. As part of the larger effort to recuperate Taiwan's lost history, its contributions cannot be overestimated. Its box office success in the domestic market and the critical acclaim it won on the international circuit made it—and its portrayal of the circumstances surrounding the incident—the topic of heated discussions in private conversations as well as the public cultural media. After four decades of enforced silence on the topic, the Taiwanese people were finally given the opportunity to air their views about this critical event. Hou's film is noteworthy not only because it dared to bring its retelling of the controversial event to the big screen but also because it attempted to undermine official interpretations of the incident by deliberately telling history "from below." As Wu Ch'i-yen noted in his essay on Taiwanese New Cinema and historical representation, for the first time, the history of the past four decades is not being told from the vantage point of the KMT rulers and does not focus exclusively on public, political events.[21] Instead, he emphasizes, the films of 1980s Taiwanese New Cinema adopted the perspective of the "common people" (庶民), the lower classes and the socially marginalized. Milestones of political history are pushed away from the centers of these films to become their backdrop; what comes to the fore are the daily experiences—the miracles, tragedies, hopes, fears, hard work, and determination—of ordinary Taiwanese families. *City of Sadness* explicitly denies the KMT government representation and subjectivity by giving it no visual presence. Officialdom exists in the film only as a disembodied voice heard in a radio broadcast or as offscreen dialogue, a faceless police uniform shot from behind, a pair of heavy military boots echoing down a prison hallway, or a shadowy figure brandishing a rifle in the dark. Instead, the film gives names and voices to those anonymous toilers who are unacknowledged by official history, to the common folk whose stories together make up Taiwanese popular memory.

Interweaving Public and Private: Narrative and the Open Texture of History

The challenge to dominant sociopolitical structures that Hou's film represents is paralleled in the film's very form by a deconstruction of the textual authority and generic conventions traditionally associated with the writing of history. Over the last two decades, it has become commonplace to discuss historical writing in terms of *narrative*.[22] Consider, for example, the definition of history offered by French critic Jean-François Lyotard: "History is made up of wisps of narratives, stories that one tells, that one hears, that one acts out; the people do not exist as a subject but as a mass of millions of insignificant and serious little stories that sometimes let themselves be collected together to constitute big stories and sometimes disperse into digressive elements."[23] History, then, is no longer conceived of as a univocal, seamless narrative. Instead, it emerges from a complex and intricately textured web of multiple, heterogeneous, and fragmentary stories that by chance touch, intersect, overlap, and sometimes contradict each other.

At this juncture, a brief examination of Soviet literary theorist Mikhail Bakhtin's notion of the dialogic novel might prove fruitful because it offers not only illuminating parallels to Lyotard's conception of historical narrative but also provides a handle for understanding the narrative strategies Hou employs in his complex film. Bakhtin's idiosyncratic theory of the novel is developed primarily in the four essays collected in *The Dialogic Imagination*,[24] but it is also discussed to some extent in his *Problems of Dostoevsky's Poetics*.[25] To begin with, it must be noted that Bakhtin is distinguished by, as one of his American translators has it, his "extraordinary sensitivity to the immense plurality of experience."[26] His theoretical writing, therefore, is deliberately antisystematic and opposed to strict formalization. It is for this reason, perhaps, that he has been most attracted to the novel, that "baggy monster" of a genre that he explicitly contrasts with more ordered forms such as poetry or the epic. Unlike more traditional theorists, Bakhtin is not at all interested in the novel as a genre in the usual sense of the term—that is, as a specific literary form with identifiable characteristics that is historically thought to have come into being in the West with Cervantes or Richardson. He has little patience for historical periodization, canon definition, or generic purity. Indeed, his conception of the novel is distinctly antiformalistic and antigeneric. In "Epic and Novel," for example, Bakhtin celebrates the novel as the only literary genre that is still young, vital, and hence relevant to modern existence "in all its openendedness" (11). All other genres—and here he singles out the epic as exemplary—are "already antiquated," having "lived as already completed genres, with a hardened and no longer flexible skeleton." The novel, in contrast, continues to develop; it remains in a state of flux so fluid, Bakhtin asserts, with a certain degree of excitement, that "we cannot foresee all its plastic possibilities" (3). In distinguishing between the epic and the novel, he evokes "the national" in ways that are particularly relevant to our current arguments. Although he does not adhere to the kind of historical periodization typical of traditional literary criticism, he does associate certain distinctive characteristics of the novel with "a specific rupture in the history of European civilization": the age of imperialism, when Europe emerged from "a socially isolated and culturally deaf semipatriarchal society" (11) to encounter a multitude of different languages and cultures. For Bakhtin, the moment Europe became aware of its existence as part of an international and, more importantly, polyglot world marked an irreversible change in its cultural and creative consciousness. As he remarks, "the period of *national* languages, coexisting but closed and deaf to each other, comes to an end" (12, my emphasis). The epic, in his mind, is directly associated with this closed and immutable idea of the national, which he sees as incompatible with the modern, openended world of the novel. For example, he argues (13) that the epic form is characterized by (1) its concern with "a national epic past"—in Goethe's and Schillers's terminology the "absolute past"; (2) its obsession with a univocal national tradition rather than "personal experience and the free [and diverse] thought that grows out of it"; and (3) "an absolute epic distance that separates the epic world from contemporary reality."[27] The novel, in contrast, is characterized by its polyglot consciousness, by its fascination with the multiplicity and diversity of experience, and by its "maximal zone of contact" with "the spontaneity of the inconclusive present" (12, 27).

Protean flexibility, multiplicity, and an affinity for the ever-changing and inconclusive present—these are some of the ideas that lie at the heart of Bakhtin's theory of the novel. It is probably more useful, then, to speak of "the phenomenon of novelization" (7) than of "the novel." In his introduction to *The Dialogical Imagination*, for instance, Michael Holquist suggests that Bakhtin's novel is less an identifiable form than a deconstructive process or subversive force. In his words, the novel "is the name Bakhtin gives to whatever force is at work within a given literary system to reveal the limits, the artificial constraints of that system. Literary systems are comprised of canons, and 'novelization' is fundamentally anti-canonical. It will not permit generic monologue. Always it will insist on the dialogue between what a given system will admit as literature and those texts that are otherwise excluded from such a definition of literature. What is conventionally thought of as a novel is simply the most complex and distilled expression of this impulse."[28] Novelization, then, can be seen as a subversive impulse that is not limited to the novel per se but can insert itself into any text—a poem, a play, a film or (one might argue) a historical text. It is a not even limited to a particular historical period. In eras that, in the traditional periodization of literary genres, predate the novel, the subversive force of novelization could be found in the

noncanonical low genres—those "genres of everyday life" (33) that represented the "contemporaneous, flowing and transitory" (20).

If we take as a starting point Bakhtin's idea of novelization, or dialogism, as a subversive, antigeneric force, then it gradually becomes clear
how successfully Hou Hsiao-hsien's film dialogizes not only official history as narrated by the KMT but also the very genre of the historical film—
particularly the kind of historical epic so prominent in cinematic history. It does so by exposing the generic expectations and limitations of
the historical film and, to use Bakhtin's words, by inserting "an indeter-
minancy, a certain semantic openendedness, a living contact with un-
finished still-evolving contemporary reality (the openended present)" (7).
Hou Hsiao-hsien, for example, has invited discussion of the film's status
as a "historical narrative" by repeatedly insisting that *City of Sadness*—
despite a high-profile publicity campaign that constantly evokes history[29]
—is not a historical film. While he acknowledges that history provides
an important backdrop for the film, he insists that he intended it to be,
as most of his previous films have been, primarily a family saga.[30] The
film also challenges conventional assumptions about the historical film
because it presents not a sweeping view of great men and great deeds—
the epic "world of 'beginnings' and 'peak times' in the national history, a
world of fathers and of founders of families, a world of 'firsts' and 'bests'"
(13)—but intimate and simple stories of the "challenges and difficulties"
faced by an ordinary Taiwanese family and their circle of friends and
acquaintances.[31]

Finally, Hou does not narrate history in the classical sense, that is,
he does not offer a coherent and logical explanation of a chronology of
events.[32] Here Bakhtin's notion of novelization or dialogism and Lyotard's
definition of history as intertwining fragments or wisps of narratives intersect and become particularly useful for illuminating the ways in which
an alternative sense of history emerges from the overlapping stories of the
individuals who inhabit *City of Sadness*. The subversive forces of novelization in Hou's film challenge the system of history by forcing a dialogue
between the texts admitted by the system—public accounts of political
history—and those that are normally excluded from historical discourse
—the private stories of the Lim family and its friends. There are, to begin
with, the personal narratives of the four Lim brothers, sons of an old Taiwanese hoodlum called Ah-luk-sai (阿祿師).[33] The eldest son, Bun-heung
(文雄), is carrying on the family businesses, running a nightclub and gam-
bling establishment called Little Shanghai and shipping goods between
the Taiwanese port of Chilung (基隆) and Shanghai on the mainland. His
involvement with the underworld in shipping illegal goods eventually

gets him killed by the Shanghai bosses. The second son, Bun-Hsim (文森), family members recount, is a doctor who loves Beethoven but has disappeared after being conscripted by the Japanese and sent to the South Seas. Most of the family has given him up for dead, but his wife clings to her hopes and patiently awaits his return. Bun-leong (文良), the third son, was sent to Shanghai by the Japanese and returns from the battles there shell-shocked and traumatized. After he recovers, he becomes enmeshed in underworld activities, which leads to his arrest by the government authorities. The beating he receives at the hands of the KMT leaves him a physical and mental cripple. Much of the film focuses on the youngest son Bun-ch'ing (文清), a deaf-mute who works as a photographer and is the family intellectual.[34] He often functions as a silent observer of events and is the family's chief witness to the political upheavals of the era. His friends include Hiroe (寬榮),[35] an idealistic young schoolteacher, Hiroe's circle of intellectual friends, and Hiroe's sister Hiromi (寬美), a nurse who comes to the mining village of Kim-Kuei-chiu (金瓜石) to work in the hospital, and who eventually becomes Bun-ch'ing's wife.[36] Significantly, most of the film's events are told from the perspectives of Bun-ch'ing and Hiromi—two individuals who stand on the margins, he because of his physical handicap, she because of her gender. Their narratives, together with those of the Lim brothers, weave a complex web of stories that offers a densely textured portrait of Taiwanese life during the period of transition from Japanese Occupation to KMT rule.

Significantly, these personal stories are told in neither a chronological nor a carefully emplotted manner but are gradually revealed in "wisps": snippets of conversation, fragments of diaries and letters, and seemingly unrelated images and sequences of action that a viewer must attempt to piece together. Unlike many historical films, *City of Sadness* does not have a single authoritative narratorial voice—whether in the form of an external voice-over (as in the March of Time films) or intertitles—to give its images shape and definitive meaning. Nor does it offer the kind of guidance and direction that the "narrator effect" of a more conventionally coded film might provide.[37] Instead, Hou's film is full of temporal disjunctions, gaps, and discontinuities that leave audiences with a rich and complex, though ambivalent and incomplete, sense of history. History is not so much narrated as evoked; it does not unfold as a logical, univocal sequence of events but emerges as a complicated Benjaminian constellation that brings together fragments of individual life stories and a multitude of perspectives into a monad that remains open, ambiguous, and pregnant with tension. Hou acts not as historian but as *bricoleur*, gathering together a heterogeneous collection of texts, images, songs, anecdotes,

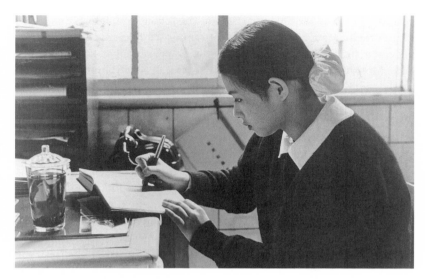

5. In *City of Sadness*, Hiromi's diary is one of the many fragmentary, nonpolitical "voices" that subvert the monologic narrative of "official history" and together weave a complex web of stories offering a densely textured portrait of Taiwanese life during the period of transition from Japanese to KMT rule.

and fragments of life stories and presenting them without internal coherence.[38]

The way in which major events of public and political history are introduced into this network of personal narratives suggests that the fates of the Lim family members and their friends are meant to represent the fate of Taiwan as a nation.[39] Private and public events are woven together from the film's very first scene: images of an extremely personal event, the birth of a child in the Lim family,[40] are accompanied by the voice of the Showa Emperor emanating from the radio.[41] An intertitle—stark white characters against a black background—explains both the visual image and the Japanese soundtrack: "On August 15, 1945, the Showa Emperor declared Japan's unconditional surrender, bringing an end to Japan's fifty-one-year occupation of Taiwan. Lim Bun-heung's woman in Ba-dou-ah gave birth to a son, who was given the name Lim Kong-ming." The film closes with a similar juxtaposition of private and public events: a long freeze-frame of Bun-ch'ing's new little family—himself, Hiromi, and their infant son—is followed by a nearly-silent and by this time familiar shot of dinnertime in the Lim household. The visible changes in the family members who gather around the table and move in and out of the frame remind us of the tragic toll that the events of history have taken on this family. The intertitle that follows signals another major event in Taiwanese political history: "December 1949. The mainland is lost and the Nationalist government relocates to Taiwan, establishing its temporary capital in Taipei." This interweaving of private and public narratives in the sequences that frame the film suggests that each marks the beginning of a new era in history for both the Lim family and Taiwan.

The film's opening intertitle, with its straightforward reference to the end of the Japanese Occupation, establishes the narrative mode of a historical chronicle and raises expectations for a conventional telling of Taiwanese political history.[42] What *City of Sadness* delivers, however, is something altogether different. It is important to note here the contrast between the way political evolution is depicted and the way the experiences of the Lim family are conveyed. While the events of public history are marked by abstract temporal markers—August 15, 1945, and December 1949, the two dates that frame the action—the body of the film operates within the private sphere and is shaped by the material human experiences that mark the passage of time, not only births, reunions, mar-

6. The "public" and "private" spheres are interwoven from the very first scene of *City of Sadness*, as the Showa emperor's announcement of Japan's unconditional surrender is juxtaposed with an extremely private event: the birth of a child in the Lim family.

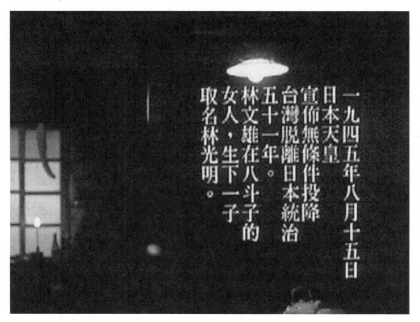

7. While the events of public history are marked by abstract temporal markers, *City of Sadness* operates primarily within the private sphere, marking the passage of time through personal events that chronicle growth and change within the family: births, deaths, reunions, and marriages.

riages, and deaths—intensely personal experiences that chronicle growth and major changes in the family—but also scenes of working, eating, drinking, loving, arguing, and worrying, the experiences that make up the texture of everyday life.

The focus on the private moments of everyday life is in itself, of course, nothing revolutionary; both the East and the West have well-established traditions of intertwining family saga and historical epic. What is most striking, however, is that, unlike what occurs in a narrative such as *War and Peace* or *Gone with the Wind*, for example, the events of public history that impinge on the lives of the Lim family do not even briefly take center stage. Indeed, the presence of history in *City of Sadness* is nearly imperceptible because it enters the narrative primarily as verbal rather than visual information. The use of intertitles and radio broadcasts in the opening sequence of the film establishes a strategy that continues throughout: the major political developments of this period in Taiwanese history are introduced into the narrative not through visual representation but primarily through language, both spoken and written. The activities of the government and its direct interactions with the Taiwanese people are rarely if ever depicted on the screen. Instead, public history enters the space of the film—and invades the private space of the family—through intertitles, the soundtrack (radio announcements, music, and Hiromi's voice-over narration of her diary entries), and the dialogue. There are, of course, the many serious political discussions in which Hiroe and his friends engage, but a great deal of political history also finds its way into the film through Ah-luk-sai's rambling monologues, through humorous anecdotes, through the casual conversations Bun-heung has with friends in his nightclub, through the songs they sing, and through the written notes (intertitles for the film audience) that Bun-ch'ing and Hiromi use to communicate with each other.

The significance of Hou's suppression of the visual in his filmic representation of history cannot be overestimated. As has often been noted, the rapid flow of images that constitutes film makes it a particularly powerful ideological tool, one that hinders rather than stimulates the critical faculties of the viewer.[43] The "reality effect" and "visual pleasure" associated with the cinematic image make it an especially persuasive—and hence dangerous—medium for historical representation.[44] Film has the power to render the past visible, to make viewers feel that they are eyewitnesses who can look directly at historical events. Film audiences for whom "seeing is believing" tend to forget that cinematic visualizations of history are not transparent windows on the past or mirror reflections but are, like verbal narratives, constructed re-presentations. The convincing realism of the cinematic image also lends the historical film a special authority that tends to dominate or altogether obliterate alternative versions of the past. Historical representation in *City of Sadness* is decidedly unfilmic: the voice-over commentary, intertitles, and written texts that contain most of the historical information are presented in an openly unrealistic manner. The effect of Hou's insistence on filtering all public historical events through language, as well as through the subjectivities of individual characters, therefore, is to remind us that all historical knowledge is mediated through human acts of narration and to underscore the idea that the history is, after all, storytelling.[45] This emphasis on the discursive and ultimately indeterminate nature of historical truth, consistent with Walter Benjamin's conception of historiography, is an idea that Hou and his scriptwriters have frequently invoked as a response to those Taiwanese film critics and cultural pundits who stubbornly insist on treating *City of Sadness* as semidocumentary, endlessly debating the accuracy of its historical representations.[46] Coscriptwriter Chu T'ien-wen seems fully attuned to Benjaminian historiography when she reminds her critics that the "representation of an historical era can never be more than what an author chooses to see in that era. It is always circumscribed by the author's own attitudes and motivations. A completely objective and comprehensive account of an era—whether in historical writing or fictional writing—simply does not exist."[47]

By allowing history to emerge from multiple and heterogeneous wisps of narratives, Hou's film avoids the limitations of conventional historiography, which insists on reducing the complexities of human experience to a single authoritative narrative. Like the Bakhtinian novel, *City of Sadness* is opened up by the forces of heteroglossia to accommodate the sometimes dissonant polyphony of voices that make up Taiwanese society. History is understood as an ongoing process, a continual interplay among heterogeneous forces that present options for different histories and potential futures.[48]

The Transition to Nationalist Rule: 1945–49

Every narrative, however seemingly "full," is constructed on the basis of a set of events which *might have been included but were left out.*[49]

Until very recently, the four years that elapsed between the end of the Japanese Occupation in 1945 and the relocation of the Nationalist government from the mainland to Taiwan in 1949 have been almost completely elided—intentionally forgotten—from official versions of Chinese history. Under the Nationalist government's educational system, history classes were devoted entirely to mainland Chinese history. Very little of the Taiwanese experience, let alone the controversial period 1945–49, has been permitted a place in the official curriculum.[50] Hou Hsiao-hsien's cinematic evocation of these chaotic years is one of the first attempts to examine this missing period, and it presents a clear challenge to official versions of Taiwanese history. From the KMT perspective, the Japanese surrender and the end of the Occupation was a great victory, which "liberated" the Taiwanese from oppression and exploitation by the imperialists and returned them to the "warm embrace of the Chinese motherland." It was to be the start of a new era of peace and prosperity for the Taiwanese people. Indeed, that initial sense of hope and expectation for the future is reflected in the sequence that opens *City of Sadness*. After a number of shots in a dark house filled with the agonizing cries of a woman in labor, a burst of light fills the screen as electricity is restored in the Lim family home and a son—symbolically named Kong-ming (光明), or Brilliance—is born. The sequence that follows depicts the festive opening of the family's new nightclub, named Little Shanghai in honor of the great city on the Chinese mainland.

8. As the celebratory opening of the Little Shanghai nightclub suggests, the Taiwanese initially welcomed the mainlanders with a sense of jubilant expectation, a hopeful optimism that was quickly extinguished by the brutal behavior of the KMT government.

Taiwanese jubilation and optimism, however, was short-lived, as the behavior and attitudes of the Nationalist officials sent to govern the island began to alienate and antagonize the native population. *City of Sadness* traces the gradual disillusionment, the growing discontent, and ultimately the anger that the Taiwanese people come to feel. Dominant historiography has of course perpetuated the myth that the transition to Chinese rule was a joyous reunion of one people. While the ancestors of those who consider themselves native to Taiwan did come from China centuries ago, interaction between the island and the mainland was in fact extremely limited throughout the eighteenth and nineteenth centuries, as Taiwan was virtually ignored by the central Chinese government. The island's sense of separateness and difference was aggravated by a half century of Japanese rule and again by the Nationalist government's arrogant behavior when it took over. Chinese officials did not welcome the Taiwanese populace as their own; instead, they adopted the attitude of a conquerer. In his first public address, Lieutenant General Ko Ching-en (葛敬恩), head of the KMT's "advance team," which arrived in October

1945 to begin the transfer of power, unabashedly expressed his contempt for the island, which he considered to be "beyond the passes" (關外), at best on the margins of true Chinese civilization. He publically characterized Taiwan as "degraded territory" and the Taiwanese as a "degraded people,"[51] an insistence on the inferiority and savagery of native peoples that is typical of a colonizing force.[52]

Nor did the Taiwanese welcome the new arrivals as their Chinese brothers and sisters.[53] In *City of Sadness*, the profound cultural, linguistic, and experiential differences that separate Taiwanese and mainlanders are underscored by the babel of mutually incomprehensible tongues—Japanese, Taiwanese, Cantonese, Mandarin, Shanghainese, and Hakka—spoken by the characters. A number of scenes foreground the multiple levels of translation necessary for Taiwanese and mainlanders to communicate with each other,[54] an obstacle that clearly raises the potential for mutual misunderstanding between the two groups. In the eyes of many Taiwanese, Chinese from the mainland share no particular kinship with native islanders; their linguistic, cultural, historical, and experiential differences position them, like the Japanese, as foreigners.[55] Walter Benjamin has said that "all rulers are the heirs of those who conquered before them," an observation with which many Taiwanese might well agree. To them, the KMT government was the alien power that replaced the Japanese forces as a colonizer and therefore could hardly be considered an improvement.[56] In Hou's film, this idea is first suggested in a humorous and irreverent conversation between Hiroe and his friends. Enjoying an evening of food and drink at the Little Shanghai, the men joke about the confusion caused by the changing of national flags that accompanied Taiwan's "glorious recovery" (光復). The Japanese flag—taken down and made into children's clothing and diapers by thrifty Taiwanese villagers—had been easy to display; no matter how it was hung, it was always right side up, with the sun always centered. The Nationalist flag, they laugh, is too much trouble; no one can agree on whether the sun should be rising or setting! Beneath their humor lie ambivalent feelings toward the new regime and uncertainty about the future. Will KMT rule bring a bright new day for Taiwan or does it forecast a night of eternal darkness?

Later in the conversation, the jovial tone gives way to a more serious and embittered expression of the Taiwanese people's disillusionment with KMT rule. Hiroe speaks for many Taiwanese when he complains about the new governor-general assigned by the Nationalist Party to take over from the Japanese: "How could they give such responsibilities to a bandit like Ch'en Yi (陳儀)? We shouldn't have any high hopes for the Nationalist government." According to George Kerr, Chiang Kai-shek's appointment of the controversial Ch'en to the top position in the new administration was a revealing decision that demonstrated Chiang's utter lack of concern for the future of Taiwan and its people.[57] Ch'en's reputation both within China and abroad was that of an unscrupulous opportunist, who, like Chiang Kai-shek himself, had extensive associations with the Shanghai underworld. In his eight years as governor of Fukien, the mainland province closest to Taiwan and that from which the ancestors of many Taiwanese families came, Ch'en was known to have "systematically looted" the province, squelching protests and demonstrations with unparalleled brutality.[58] For the Taiwanese, then, his appointment promised not the peace, order, and prosperity they had hoped for in the initial euphoria of liberation but continued oppression and exploitation.

Like all colonizing forces, the Nationalist government perpetuated the myth that the Taiwanese people welcomed KMT leadership on the island. However, just as there had been native resistance to the Japanese so there was discontent with KMT rule. According to Kerr, as early as six weeks after Taiwan's liberation, protest posters began appearing here and there, lampooning Nationalist soldiers and caricaturing Ch'en as a fat pig. They were accompanied by the captions "Dogs go and pigs come!" and "At least the Japanese dogs protected the property!"[59] From its earliest days, Ch'en's administration epitomized corruption and greed. In addition to seizing control of the banks, schools, hospitals, railroads, shipping, and all other major forms of transportation and communication, KMT officials — both military and civilian — indiscriminately confiscated industrial raw materials, agricultural stockpiles, and all of the real properties surrendered to them by the Japanese.[60] They left almost nothing for the astonished Taiwanese, who had been looking forward to regaining at least a fair share of the property recovered from the Showa empire.

Even more devastating than this government-sanctioned looting was the extreme system of monopolies Ch'en Yi imposed in order to bring the island's entire economy under his control. Following a plan he had implemented while governor of Fukien, he established a number of commissions — Mining and Industry, Agriculture and Forestry, Finance, and so on — that effectively gave the KMT government a stranglehold on production, trade, and transport of goods. The commissioners, as well as the directors, managers, and operating personnel below them, were all mainland Chinese, of course. The Taiwanese had no place in this giant economic monopoly. One of the disgruntled Taiwanese intellectuals in *City of Sadness* summarizes Ch'en's strategy succinctly: "To put it harshly, this is no government. This is a company, and Ch'en Yi is the Boss. It's so convenient; all the profits go straight into his own pocket!"

Ch'en's system of "necessary state socialism" resulted in unrelieved economic disaster for Taiwan.[61] Unemployment soared among the native people as mainland Chinese nepotism displaced thousands upon thousands from jobs in education, law, government, and medicine. In *City of Sadness*, Hiroe and his friends tell the story of a friend who lost his job at a courthouse when a mainlander took over and "replaced all the Taiwanese employees with his wife, his uncles, and his nephews. Now the whole courthouse is run by his family!" They also allude to the social problems created by Taiwanese soldiers conscripted by the Japanese who returned from the South Seas only to find that there was no work for them at home. Like the deeply troubled Lim Bun-leung, many of these ex-soldiers were walking time bombs. The government monopolies that had the most immediate and far-reaching effects on the Taiwanese people were those on tobacco and alcohol and such staples as rice and sugar. Again, the conversations between Hiroe and his friends reveal the corruption of government officials and the suffering of the Taiwanese populace. Government officers, they complain, had seized control of the island's rice and sugar supplies and were shipping the stockpiles to the mainland: "They're selling them for a good price. The officials here don't care if we have enough to eat; they take everything and ship it to Shanghai for a good profit on both ends." The economic hardships under KMT rule made even the Japanese seem preferable. Says one man bitterly: "When the Japanese were here, even in the toughest of times, even during the air raids, we still had enough rice rations. How long has Ch'en Yi been in charge now? The price of rice has gone up fifty-two times! But have our salaries gone up even one cent?"

These disillusioned Taiwanese intellectuals demonstrate both an understanding of colonial strategies of oppression and a determination to resist them. One man mocks the Nationalist Party rhetoric that all Taiwanese resisters are "Japanese collaborators." The KMT officials "have their own logic. For example, someone like you . . . [he points to one of his friends] the Japanese taught you to have a 'slave mentality' and you must learn to change." He feigns contempt as he imitates a KMT official, scolding, "You can't even speak Mandarin!" They all laugh, but their laughter cannot hide their bitterness and anger: "Slave mentality? Fuck that! Are we so cheap that we become slaves so easily?" Not only did the Taiwanese people express their discontentment in private conversations, but they actively protested and sought reform. Although Hiroe's and Bun-ch'ing's involvement with Taiwanese patriots is not depicted on-screen until the latter half of the film, even their early conversations allude to the activists in Taipei—particularly a certain Teacher Lin (林老師)—with whom both are in contact. Their remarks suggest that Teacher Lin and others in the capital city are actively pushing for Taiwanese representation and involvement in the new government. *City of Sadness* also reveals that the disillusionment and discontent expressed by these Taiwanese intellectuals were shared by all sectors of the native population because everyone was suffering from the economic and social chaos that resulted from Ch'en Yi's authoritarian and exploitative rule.[62] The Taiwanese people in the film bemoan their tragic history, angry that they have never had a voice in determining their fates. Says one of the intellectuals: "The Ch'ing court sold us out in the first place. Who ever asked us Taiwanese if we agreed to the Treaty of Shimonoseki?" Lim Bun-heung puts it in simpler words but with equal eloquence: "We Taiwanese are the most pitiful. First come the Japanese, then come the Chinese. We're eaten by everyone, ridden by everyone, but cared for by no one." Hou's film captures the rising tide of Taiwanese resentment during those chaotic years of transition. Hiroe and his friends articulate the rapidly spreading sentiment that the Taiwanese people must rise up and assert their rights: "It all comes down to this: if the KMT government doesn't change, even though we won the war with Japan, the people will still have to suffer for a long time. The way I see it, waiting for change is of no use. If we want to have a future, the suffering multitudes must stand up courageously. If the Nationalist government keeps letting Ch'en Yi have his way, sooner or later there'll be trouble in Taiwan."

The February Incident and the March Massacres

"Trouble" came to Taiwan in early 1947, less than two years after the Chinese Nationalists took over the island. Tensions between the KMT government and the Taiwanese populace reached a fever pitch and finally exploded on February 28, 1947, in the violent confrontation that has come to be known as the Two-two-eight Incident (二二八事件).[63] Once again, KMT corruption and monopolistic control over the island's economy precipitated the crisis; this time, the tobacco monopoly provided the immediate spark. On the evening of February 27, a woman called Lin Chiang-mai (林江邁) and her two children set up a portable stand in a park in Taipei, hoping to sell a few packs of cigarettes. Monopoly Bureau agents soon appeared, accompanied by a dozen policemen, and immediately proceeded to confiscate the vendor's goods and her small supply of cash. When she resisted, she was beaten and pistol-whipped by the agents. A crowd of bystanders gathered and, angered by the brutality of the government agents, moved in to attack. Chaos erupted as the agents and police fired wildly into the crowd to clear a path for their escape. The confrontation left a bystander named Ch'en Wen-hsi (陳文溪) dead and the vendor gravely injured.

The next morning, February 28, a crowd of two thousand or more angry Taiwanese marched from the park where the clash had occurred to the Monopoly Bureau headquarters. They carried protest banners and placards. Among their demands were appropriate punishment for the agents who had killed an innocent citizen the night before; the immediate resignation of the bureau chief; and, most important, reform of the government's monopoly system. Rioting erupted, and the Nationalist soldiers guarding the bureau headquarters sprayed the crowd with machine-gun fire, killing an unknown number of the unarmed civilians and wounding scores more.[64] The brutal response of the government ignited the Taiwanese populace, tapping into the frustration and resentment that had been building over eighteen months of KMT rule. In the days and weeks that followed, demonstrations and riots erupted all over Taipei and eventually reached cities and villages throughout the island. Taiwanese patriots grew bolder and louder in their demands for economic and political reform.[65] Ch'en Yi's government, reinforced by troops sent clandestinely from the mainland by Chiang Kai-shek on March 8, retaliated with characteristic swiftness and brutality. Taiwanese activists were treated not as protesters against maladministration in the provincial government but as insurgent rebels who threatened Nationalist rule—hence justifying, in the government's view, their subsequent campaign to eradicate Taiwanese resistance throughout the island. Though no one knows the exact death toll, it is widely believed that ten, twenty, or even thirty thousand Taiwanese may have died as Nationalist soldiers swarmed the island, arresting and executing people thought capable of resistance. Kerr related eyewitness accounts, his own and those of other foreigners in Taiwan, of random shooting and bayoneting, with machine-gun squads driving into villages and firing wildly as they stormed through. Students and other intellectuals were often singled out as targets, rounded up by the thousands, and imprisoned or executed. Kerr describes seeing groups of students tied together and driven to execution grounds in and around Taipei and the northern port of Chilung. Two students, he writes, were beheaded near the front gate of his house.[66]

Ch'en Yi's government succeeded in suppressing the Taiwanese uprising, but the result of the bloody clash between mainland rulers and native people was a deep and bitter emnity that poisoned Taiwanese politics and society for four or five decades. For many, the February 28 Incident is *the* symbol of the KMT's "foreign domination" (外來政權) of Taiwan's "native people" (本土族群), the defining event dividing China and Taiwan into separate and irreconcilable entities.[67] From the beginning, the Nationalist government sought to suppress the facts surrounding the incident and, under the martial law that was imposed on the island following the confrontation, any discussion of the incident was taboo. While older Taiwanese remember and carry deep resentment over its aftermath, they were afraid to discuss the massacres with anyone but family—and even then, only in hushed tones. Since the incident was eradicated from official history and was not discussed in the public media, the younger generation of Taiwanese had only the sketchiest knowledge of what occurred. For many, Hou Hsiao-hsien's *City of Sadness* was their only source of historical knowledge, their introduction to the historical event. Some critics of the film have argued, therefore, that anyone—historian or filmmaker—taking on such a politically sensitive subject has a special responsibility to Taiwanese society.[68] It is no surprise, therefore, that even though the February 28 Incident is kept in the background in the film, much of the discussion surrounding *City of Sadness* has focused on its representation of this particular historical event.

Like other major events in political history, the incident itself is never given visual representation on-screen in Hou's film. Instead, it enters the film's narrative in purely verbal form by means of Ch'en Yi's radio broadcast officially reporting the confrontation between the cigarette vendor and the Monopoly Bureau agents. Ch'en's Shanghai-accented Mandarin is heard in the hospital in Kim-kuei-ah.[69] The governor-general clearly seeks to downplay the incident and placate the Taiwanese people with the use of soothing and conciliatory words that belie the ruthlessness of his response to the incident: "Compatriots, on the evening of the twenty-seventh, someone unfortunately was killed during an investigation. I have already taken care of the matter. As for those who killed others in the incident, I have sent them to court to be tried severely and sentenced accordingly. There is one woman who, although she was not seriously wounded, has had her medical needs taken care of. I've arranged for proper compensation."

As the film demonstrates, however, the Taiwanese people were well aware that a major political crisis was at hand. Hiromi's response to the radio broadcast, as she narrates her diary entry in voice-over, reveals Taiwanese anxiety over the implications of the event: "The radio today reported an incident in Taipei: killing between Taiwanese and mainlanders. Taipei is under martial law. . . . Everyone is afraid. A war just ended; how can another start again?"

The official KMT interpretation of the February 28 Incident has always been that Taiwanese rebels under the influence of communist agitators instigated the confrontation.[70] In *City of Sadness*, Ch'en Yi is the voice of official history as he broadcasts over the radio to the Taiwanese population: "Compatriots of Taiwan, yesterday temporary martial law was again announced. I here reemphasize with 120 percent sincerity to the majority of peace-loving people that my announcement of martial law is *totally* for your protection. You must not heed the rumours of spies, for from an ounce of suspicion comes an ounce of fear. You must believe that no harm will come to law-abiding citizens. My announcement of martial law is directed toward a tiny handful of traitorous rebels. For each day that they are not eradicated, peace-loving compatriots must endure another day of unrest." Throughout the rest of the film, however, this monologic official representation of history is subverted by the forces of Bakhtinian novelization or dialogism. According to Bakhtin, in order for monologic texts to become dialogic, they must first be "embodied. . . . they must enter into another sphere of existence: they must become *discourse*,[71] that is, an utterance, and receive an *author*, that is, a creator of the given utterance whose position it expresses" (*Problems of Dostoevsky's Poetics*, 184). By contextualizing dominant history as an "utterance" produced by a specific person (Ch'en Yi) living in a specific historical period (a time when the KMT was in the process of consolidating power in Taiwan), belonging to a specific social class (the ruling class), and addressing a specific audience (the Taiwanese masses), Hou exposes and underscores the ideological biases of what has long been accepted as the objective truth.

The official interpretation of the February 28 Incident as a purely political struggle is further undermined in Hou's film by the subversive effects of what Bakhtin refers to as the centrifugal forces of heteroglossia. Bakhtin's novelization, we might recall, is a process by which conventional genres become more "free and flexible . . . by incorporating extraliterary heteroglossia" ("Epic," 7).[72] In the case of *City of Sadness*, "extraliterary heteroglossia" refer to those discourses, normally considered to be outside the generic boundaries of historical narrative—nonpolitical voices such as economic and sociological discourses, personal letters and diaries, and so on—that Hou incorporates to interrupt, challenge, complicate, and ultimately explode the monolithic view of Taiwanese history offered by the KMT. Hou suggests, for example, that the February confrontation could also be seen as an economic rather than a political battle, an outcome of deep-seated discontent and resentment provoked by widespread corruption and economic exploitation by KMT officials. References to the tobacco monopoly and the smuggling activities of corrupt government officials are made early in the film, foreshadowing the February 28 Incident and the escalation of violence in its aftermath. The tragic fates of Hiroe and his friends and the experiences of Bun-ch'ing and the rest of the Lim family show that the goal of Ch'en Yi's government was not to eradicate "a tiny handful of traitorous rebels" but to indiscriminately punish the Taiwanese people for daring to resist KMT rule. The Lim family suffers greatly during the chaos and violence of the March massacres. Returning from a trip to Taipei, a wounded Hiroe reports the arrival of Nationalist troops from the mainland: "They're arresting and killing people as they go." The Lim family is forced to shut down its business because of the fear and confusion. Bun-heung's eldest daughter explains to Hiromi that "things are too chaotic. People are getting killed everywhere, and the neighboring houses are being ransacked." The retaliatory reaction of the angry Taiwanese people is violent as well. In a tense scene that captures the irrational and impulsive anger of the Taiwanese toward mainlanders, Bun-ch'ing is approached by a group of Taiwanese youths on a train.[73] Unaware that he cannot hear them, they angrily ask him where he is from. When he fails to answer, they ask again in Japanese. Since a Taiwanese would understand Japanese and Bun-ch'ing does not respond, one of the men yells "He must be a mainlander!" and they surge forward to beat him up. Hiroe arrives just in time to tell them that Bun-ch'ing is a deaf-mute.

Both Bun-ch'ing and Hiroe personally experience the brutalities of the government crackdown. Arrested for his association with Teacher Lin, Bun-ch'ing sees his prison mates taken away one by one and escorted to the execution grounds by KMT soldiers. Although he cannot hear them, the gunshots fired by the executioners echo on the film's soundtrack. Bun-ch'ing also has the sad task of taking a cell mate's belongings and his last will and testament to the man's widow and small children. A poignant note, scrawled in the dead man's blood and addressed to his children, reads: "You must live with dignity. Father has committed no wrong." Writes another dying man: "Separated from the motherland in life, I am reunited with her in death. Life and death are determined by fate, so there is no need to think or worry about them."[74] Hiroe and his friends, like so many Taiwanese intellectuals and students at the time, are forced to hide out in the mountains. They, too, are tracked down and summarily executed by Nationalist soldiers. By the end of the film, the interpenetration of public history and private stories is total, as the tides of political change completely disrupt the Lim family order and their normal rituals of life. With almost no dialogue, the final dinner scene reveals the toll that political history has exacted on the family: the bustling activity that characterized earlier family meals is replaced by a poignant silence. The Lim family men are all either dead, missing, or in KMT prisons; the only ones left to carry on are an old man, a mental cripple, small children, and the women of the family.[75] The film ends in limbo, as Bun-ch'ing is arrested again, leaving Hiromi and their young son alone to face an uncertain future. Hiromi's final voice-over, a letter to Bun-heung's daughter, expresses her hope for the future—embodied in her growing young son—but also reveals her doubts and fears, as she describes the rapidly approaching winter.

> This picture [the family portrait that is the penultimate sequence of the film] was taken three days before your Fourth Uncle was arrested. The day they took him, he was taking pictures for someone. He insisted on finishing his work and then was quietly taken away. I have inquired everywhere in Taipei but have no news. Ah-chien has teeth already and a beautiful smile. His eyes are very much like your Fourth Uncle's. Please come and visit me if you have time. It has already begun to grow chilly. The wild grasses have begun to flower, blanketing the whole mountain in white. It looks like snow.

A Look Back to the Future

Today, more than fifty years after the violent events of 1947, Taiwan seems finally ready to search for a better understanding of this controversial chapter in its history. Lee Teng-hui's government initiated the reexamination of the episode in order to move toward easing tensions between the government and the people, between mainlanders and native islanders. His interior minister, Wu Po-hsiung (吳伯雄), a native-born Taiwanese whose uncle was killed in the March massacres, declared that it was time "to heal the wounds of history," and on the weekend of February 22–23, 1992, the Taiwanese government at last broke its official silence on the topic of the February 28 Incident, issuing a lengthy report on the events.[76] In the report, the government contradicted its longtime official interpretation of events by acknowledging that corruption and misrule were the fundamental causes of the uprising and by admitting to killing an estimated eighteen to twenty-eight thousand native-born Taiwanese in the 1947 incident and the massacres that followed. The government fulfilled its promise to erect a monument to the victims of the massacres; a memorial was dedicated in February of 1995, accompanied by an official apology from President Lee. The Democratic Progressive Party has vowed to push forward with legislation to provide compensation for their families.

For Walter Benjamin, the writing of history is inextricably tied to the possibilities of redemption, for "only a redeemed mankind receives the fullness of its past" ("Theses," 254). This is particularly true in transitional eras and periods of sociocultural crisis. Hou Hsiao-hsien similarly sees the exploration of the past in *City of Sadness* as a necessary catharsis for the Taiwanese people, without which the tensions and conflicts of society cannot be put to rest. He wants the healing process to begin and envisions his film as a "look back to the future"—a new start for Taiwanese-mainlander relations and the beginning of a new phase in Taiwanese history: "I hope that a renewed understanding of 'Two-two-eight' will help everyone to finally cast away its dark shadow and to go on living with energy and vitality. What I most desire is for people who see my film to leave the theater not only with tears in their eyes but with a new sense of pride, of empowerment, and with the determination to move toward the future."[77]

Play/Dream/Life: *The Puppetmaster* and the Theater of History

Hou Hsiao-hsien has said that he knew very little about Taiwanese history until he began work on *City of Sadness*.[78] The research he did for the film captivated his imagination and motivated him to investigate further the historical origins of contemporary Taiwanese society. Hou sees his filmmaking—and particularly his Taiwan Trilogy—as the process by which he can try to understand the culture and history of the island he calls home. *City of Sadness* may be the best-known film of the trilogy because of its critical success overseas and its role in reviving local debate on the February 28 Incident, but the other two segments of his trilogy are equally worthy of close examination. The film Hou made in 1993, *The Puppetmaster*, is the second installment of the trilogy. While *City of Sadness* depicted the years following the end of the Japanese Occupation, *The Puppetmaster* probes even further into Taiwan's past, focusing on the fifty years of the Occupation itself—a period of the island's history that was also nearly erased by the government's determination to downplay all non-Chinese aspects of Taiwan's heritage. Hou has expressed his belief that, in order to truly understand how Taiwan came to be what it is today and to gain a secure sense of belonging, one must dig beneath the many layers of the island's complex past. He sees the Japanese Occupation as a crucial period to which many of contemporary Taiwan's sociocultural structures and attitudes can be traced.[79] In *The Puppetmaster*, he once again approaches public political history from below, telling the story of Taiwan under Japanese rule through the colorful life story of a figure from

the margins of Taiwanese society: Li T'ien-lu (李天祿), Li T'en-luk in Taiwanese, the aged master of Taiwanese hand puppetry who has appeared
as a grandfather in all of Hou's films since *Dust in the Wind*.

If *A Time to Live and a Time to Die* was autobiography and *City of Sadness* was family saga, *The Puppetmaster* might best be described as an
anecdotal biography.[80] In this respect, the film is very much in line with
the historiographical trend in Taiwan during the late 1980s, when oral
histories and interview-based victims' biographies were considered crucial tools of local history following martial law.[81] The film traces Li's life
and times from his birth in 1910 to the Japanese surrender in 1945, rely-
ing sometimes on vignettes with dramatizations by actors to tell its story,
sometimes on the old master's recollections in his own voice, whether
heard on the soundtrack or spoken directly to the camera. Like *City of
Sadness*, this film begins with the announcement of a political milestone
in Taiwanese history before shifting its focus to Li's personal story. An
opening intertitle defines the historical parameters of the film: "1895,
China loses the war and signs the Treaty of Shimonoseki, ceding Taiwan
and the Pescadores to Japan. Thus, Japan ruled Taiwan for fifty years, until
World War II." The scene that follows is not exactly a birth but a very
similar private moment: a family is seen sitting around a table, where a
proud father and grandfather are toasting the birth of a son, Ah-luk (阿祿).
Into this celebratory scene is suddenly interjected the voice of an old man,
Li T'en-luk himself, who in voice-over tells the story behind this family
gathering. Li, a natural-born storyteller whose colorful, improvisational
monologues have often been the highlight of Hou's previous films, is even
more animated talking about his own life. Shortly after his birth, Li tells
us, a fortune-teller predicted that he was destined to have a hard life. The
difficulties began almost immediately, with his father and grandfather
quarreling over which surname the baby should bear. The father thought
it logical that the baby should share his surname, Hsu (許), K'o in Taiwanese, but the superstitious grandfather insisted that Ah-luk call his parents
Auntie and Uncle and take the surname Li, after the matchmaker who
had brought his parents together. "And so," explains Li wrily, "That's how
I was born." This pronouncement is followed by a shot of a hand puppet
theater set up in a field, then a shot of the performance itself. No dialogue or expository narration accompanies the images, only the songs and
music of the puppet show. As the show ends and the puppets disappear
behind the theater curtains, the screen fades to black and the film's title —
literally *Play, Dream, Life* — appears in bold red characters.

It is worth noting that in the opening scene of *City of Sadness* it is the voice of the emperor announcing Japan's surrender in a radio broadcast—the voice of public political history—that penetrates the private sphere of the Lim family. In this film, in contrast, there is only personal narrative on the soundtrack, the recollections of an old man looking back on the beginning of his life. Hence, despite the politically significant historical markers that open the film, *The Puppetmaster* deliberately pushes political history far into the background. Even more than *City of Sadness*, it valorizes the apolitical lives of the common masses by refracting major events in political history through the limited consciousnesses of ordinary people. While *City of Sadness* devotes significant screen time to the political discussions and debates of intellectuals, *The Puppetmaster* leaves that public world behind. There is, however, one scene in *City of Sadness* that foreshadows the deliberately apolitical attitude later embraced in *The Puppetmaster*:[82] In this scene, Hiroe and his fellow Taiwanese patriots are at Bun-ch'ing's house, heatedly debating Taiwan's political future. While these would-be movers and shakers of history talk around a table in the center of the room, Bun-ch'ing and Hiromi are off to one side, listening to romantic music and writing notes to each other about the legend of Lorelei. Oblivious to the political debate going on in the room, they are far from the center of public history, immersed in subjective experience.

Over the course of this scene, the attention of the film shifts from Hiroe and his compatriots to linger on the exchange between the deaf-mute and the woman, choosing the private over the public, the margins over the center. As puppetmaster, opera actor, and itinerant folk artist, Li T'en-luk is someone who truly lives on the fringes of Chinese society (江湖人物). By choosing Li's life experiences as the prism through which to view the Taiwanese past, Hou has said, he meant to search for the essential elements of Taiwanese culture that lie beneath the surface of publicly acknowledged history and beyond ideology. Li's story is less about the politics of the Japanese era than about the common person's adaptability in the face of historical events that are beyond his or her control or comprehension.[83] Fifth-generation Chinese director Zhang Yimou (張藝謀) has made a similar observation about his film *To Live* (活著, 1994),[84] which follows an ordinary Chinese family through nearly forty years of political turmoil on the mainland, from the civil war between Chiang Kai-shek's KMT and Mao Zedong's Communists through the establishment of the People's Republic, the failed experiments of the Great Leap Forward, and the insanity of the Cultural Revolution. History, says Zhang, is full of stories about heroes and great deeds; what are missing are the stories about ordinary Chinese, who, whatever the political drama of the moment, quietly go about the business of everyday living.[85] His film is less about China's turbulent modern political history, which only provides a backdrop, than it is about the stubborn perserverence of Xu Fugui (徐富貴) and Jiazhen (家珍), two "little people" who are politically uncommitted and unreflective. Their only concern is to face the challenges that each day brings, simply "to live."

From a private perspective, then, political history appears merely as a series of hurdles to overcome, pragmatic adjustments to be made in order to survive. In *The Puppetmaster*, the massive and dramatic changes that marked the early stages of the Japanese takeover—a radical restructuring that overhauled every aspect of life on the island, from its political institutions, economic organizations, health, education, and transportation systems to the physical appearance of its cities and villages[86]—cause barely a ripple in Li T'en-luk's daily life. His memories of those years focus on ordinary things: his boredom with traditional schooling, the punishment he suffered at the hands of his parents, and finally his teenage rebellion, when he left his family to apprentice with a traveling puppet theater troupe. Early in the film, the political reality of the Japanese Occupation invades the private sphere of Li's family in a brief scene in which the drama and political significance of the moment is notably underplayed: as part of the Occupation's efforts to modernize and "Japanize" (Kominka, 皇民化) the Taiwanese, soldiers ask members of the family to cut off their traditional Chinese pigtails. The family does not even question the order let alone reject it as a colonizer's act of forced cultural assimilation. For them, it is only a minor annoyance, alleviated by the soldiers' offer of opera tickets in exchange for their compliance. The entire episode is probably most significant for the fact that the family is given tickets to the opera, perhaps planting the seeds for Li's future career.

Throughout the film, the impact of Japanese colonization on Taiwanese life makes itself felt very gradually, without unusual drama or commentary and largely without conflict. As Li recounts his memories or scenes from his life are reenacted on-screen, here and there a Japanese word or phrase slips into the dialogue, a casual comment is made about a visit to a Japanese doctor, a Japanese song is heard on the soundtrack, or a Japanese-style house appears on the screen. There are, of course, instances when major political events have a direct impact on Li's life, but the events themselves are not given visual representation but only referred to in passing in Li's voice-overs. Li tells us, for example, that in the wake of the 1937 Marco Polo Bridge Incident, the clash in northern China that precipitated the eight-year Sino-Japanese War, life was very difficult for traveling puppet troupes. Ever fearful of spies and subversive activity, Japanese police censors felt it necessary in 1938 to ban popular puppet shows, which they found were caricaturing the Japanese and mocking their government.[87] It was during this period that Li joined an opera troupe as an actor. Later, when the Japanese colonial government began heavily conscripting Taiwanese for military duty to fight the Chinese and, as the Pacific War escalated, the Americans and the British, Li was recruited to help in the war effort and participate in the government's assimilation program by performing Japanese propaganda puppet shows. The vignettes depicted in the film include the funeral of a Taiwanese soldier who had died fighting for Japan and a puppet show dramatizing the hero's final battle, in which he dies valiantly defending the imperial forces from the American and British devils.

As in *City of Sadness*, Hou's depictions of the relationships between ordinary Taiwanese and the Japanese colonials living on the island during the Occupation reveal a human side of Japan seldom acknowledged by official history. Even today, the Taiwanese attitude toward Japan and Japanese culture is deeply ambivalent, a mixture of wary antagonism and repressed nostalgia. It is a love-hate relationship that can only be understood by looking back to its roots in the Occupation. While Japanese brutalities and discrimination against the Taiwanese were undeniable, the colonial government also laid the foundations of an infrastructure that made Taiwan's postwar economic boom possible. Moreover, although Japan was the political enemy during the Occupation, at a personal level many solid working relationships—even friendships—developed between Japanese colonials and Taiwanese natives. Some of the most poignant scenes in *City of Sadness* capture the sorrow of Japanese colonials being repatriated, forced to leave behind the Taiwanese places they have called home for many years. In *The Puppetmaster*, some of the Japanese soldiers and officials are insensitive bullies, but there are also those who help Li and his family and feel genuine affection for Taiwan, their second home. For ordinary Taiwanese dealing with the everyday reality of living under the Occupation, political antagonism rarely comes into play. For a poor commoner like Li, moreover, political resistance is simply impractical. Flexibility and a cooperative spirit are often necessary for survival. Li, for example, agrees to join the Japanese government's propaganda puppet troupe because in the uncertainty of wartime he is grateful for the promise of a nice apartment, a good salary, and most importantly security for his family.[88]

On the other hand, Japan's imperialist ambitions and her eight-year war with China and then the Western Allies took its toll on the native Taiwanese population, not only on the youth who were conscripted and

9. *The Puppetmaster*. For Taiwan's ordinary citizens, the dramas of public political history have little meaning. Intent on salvaging the metal from abandoned airplanes, they are too busy with the everyday task of living to contemplate the end of the Japanese Occupations.

sent into battle but also on the island's civilians. One of the casualties of the prolonged war, for example, was the public health system. As funds, supplies, and personnel were taken away from public services and put into the war effort, disease—particularly malaria—spread throughout the island. In *The Puppetmaster*, the war forces Li and his family to move around constantly, and eventually they are stricken with malaria. Li falls ill but continues to perform puppet shows, resting on a bed behind the stage during his bouts of fever and chills. His father-in-law contracts the most severe case and resorts to sleeping in an empty coffin to relieve his fever. He eventually dies from the disease, as does Li's youngest child. Li is shown making a tiny coffin for his dead child, but it is without visible bitterness or resentment. As his voice-over suggests, Li's attitude toward the personal tragedies he has suffered as a consequence of political events is one of stoic resignation: "One's fate can't be changed." Even after the Japanese are defeated and begin their retreat from the island, he expresses no enmity toward the former colonizers. At the end of film, he even relates how after the surrender he helped to protect a group of Japanese soldiers from an angry Taiwanese mob. The final image of the film shows men, women, and children tearing apart planes that have been abandoned in

10. In *The Puppetmaster*, a deliberate emphasis on autobiographical storytelling by Li T'ien-lu reminds us that the past can only be recaptured as memory and as such can never be fully or accurately reconstructed.

a bombed out airfield; they are salvaging the metal for other uses. It is an eloquent reminder that for ordinary, apolitical citizens the dramas of political history mean very little. They have no time to contemplate the significance of Japan's surrender or Taiwan's "glorious liberation"; they are too busy with the everyday tasks of living. As Heiner Muller notes, "What is history for the elite has always been work for the masses."[89]

History and Memory

As the deliberate emphasis on autobiographical storytelling in *A Time to Live and a Time to Die* and *City of Sadness* repeatedly remind us, the past can only be recaptured as memory and as such can never be fully or accurately reconstructed. The processes of memory always seize hold of the past selectively, emphasizing and lingering over only those images and events that have special significance to the recollecting subject at that particular moment in time. In *The Puppetmaster*, the life story of Li T'en-luk is shaped by the intensely personal, unpredictable, and often unreliable operations of memory, by the particular concerns and sensitivities of the present self. Hence, while the film presents the experiences of Li's childhood and youth in more or less chronological order, it remains extremely elliptical and impressionistic, full of gaps and discontinuities. Li's retrospective look at his past seems to center primarily on the various women in his life. Early in the film there are dramatizations of his childhood conflicts with his cold and indifferent father, but the stories he narrates in voice-over or directly into the camera are mostly about the women in his life. There are recollections of his mother and the filial daughter-in-law who was willing to exchange her own health—and ultimately her life—to save Li's gravely ill grandmother. Then there is the stepmother who made Li's childhood miserable. One of the longest, most colorful stories he tells is about his grandmother, who came to live with him after all the other relatives decided she was hexed, for everywhere the old woman went someone fell ill and died. Li, of course, escapes her "curse" and buries her when she dies. Surprisingly little is said about Li's wife and children, who are scarcely seen. Their entry into his life is suggested through brief, wordless vignettes: the sound of firecrackers and music in the distance hint at a marriage, and a woman screaming in pain and a servant scurrying by with a pan of water suggest the birth of a child. In contrast, Li tells a number of elaborate tales about a prostitute, Li-chu (麗珠), whom he met, lived with, and finally left during the war.

The film is also filled with nonnarrative images and suggestive details —a second-floor balcony, a tree towering over a temple, a puppet theater in an open field, a dirt road winding through rice fields, a fishing boat gliding silently across the water—that seem to take on almost Proustian significance. The memory-laden details provide the texture of Li's recollected life, but because they are often presented without exposition or commentary they do not narrate it in the conventional sense. As in *City of Sadness*, in which the personal stories of the Lim family members were revealed in "wisps of narratives" that the viewer is forced to weave together, *The Puppetmaster* offers only fragments, perhaps raising more questions about Li's life and times than it answers.[90] In the end, the film underscores the indeterminacy of identity, emphasizing the impossibility of fully reconstructing a life or of really knowing the man called Li T'en-luk.[91]

Deconstructing the Past: The Illusion of History, the Inscrutability of the Self

One of the most persistent themes in classical Chinese literature and philosophy—from Chuang-Tzu's famous dream of the butterfly to Ts'ao Hsueh-ch'in's *Dream of the Red Chamber*—has been the interplay between illusion and reality. Hou Hsiao-hsien's *The Puppetmaster* is one of two recent Chinese films (Chen Kaige's *Farewell My Concubine* is the other) that once again takes up this theme. Hou's film has been described as a blend of documentary and fiction, with *documentary* referring to the sequences in which Li T'en-luk speaks directly to the camera and *fiction* referring to the dramatic reenactments by the actors.[92] The film is actually much more complex, as it ultimately questions the very distinction between the two modes. Like *City of Sadness*, the film is a bricolage that juxtaposes a polyphony of heterogeneous discourses and multiple perspectives in an attempt to undermine conventional paradigms of historical and personal narrative. In addition to the discourse of official history—whether information presented through the intertitles or knowledge that the viewer is assumed to bring to the film—there are Li T'en-luk's memories, which he narrates in voice-over and direct address to the camera; Hou's restagings with actors of the events in Li's life; and the many performances of opera and puppetry included in the film. All four of these voices are introduced in the pretitle sequence and interact with each other throughout the rest of the film. Sometimes they complement each other: in one instance, a puppet show about the sorrow of leaving home precedes Li's recounting, in voice-over, his decision to leave his family and apprentice with a traveling puppet troupe. Another example occurs when an opera performance about a young gentleman's chance encounter with two ladies is followed by Li's memories concerning his first meeting with the prostitute Li-chu, who later becomes his mistress: she and a her friend boldly introduce themselves to him after a show. More often, however, the different voices contradict each other. The best example involves the characterization of the stepmother. The dramatic vignette that depicts her introduction into Li's life is very poetic and suffused with nostalgia: the child Ah-luk is summoned to meet his new mother, who solemnly performs a belt-changing ritual to join her life to his. Li's impression of the woman, however, is quite different. In his words, it is a "life made miserable by my stepmother" that drives him away from home.

The questions arising from the contradictions between visual image and verbal narration are: Which representation is more "real" and which version tells the truth about Li's past? The title of the film translates literally as "Play, Dream, Life." *Play* most likely refers to the puppet shows and opera performances in the film, but the associations of the other two are not so clear. One could argue, for example, that visual images are more real than words; hence, the dramatic vignettes must correspond to life while Li's narrated memories, colored by his concerns and desires of the moment, are associated with dreams.[93] On the other hand, one could just as easily argue the opposite, that the actors, speaking dialogue written by Hou and his screenwriters, are reconstructing an illusion of the past within a closed fictional space while Li T'en-luk as raconteur is real, with the camera simply documenting him telling his story. If the actors re-enacting Li's life are mere performers mouthing the words of others, are the dramatic vignettes in which they appear any more real than the play of the hand puppets? Hou offers no answers to these questions; the tensions and dynamic interplay between the different voices simply serve to undermine and blur conventional distinctions between life and dream, reality and illusion, document and fiction.

The disjunction between the perspectives and voices in the film—image versus text, the narrating "I" (Li's voice-over commentary) versus the narrated I (the actors who portray Li in his childhood and youth)—creates an ironic distance, which challenges both the narrative continuity and naive referentiality associated with conventional historical representation. It forces the viewer into an active, critical stance and reminds us of the constructedness of all forms of representation. This is particularly apparent when the dramatization of an episode in Li's youth—the episode in the coffin shop, for instance—is jarringly interrupted by a shot of the old man Li has become sitting on the set where the action has been taking place. Li tells his story directly to the camera, further breaking the diegetic illusion.[94] Hou's distanciation techniques are not unlike the strategies of Jean-Marie Straub and Danielle Huillet, radical filmmakers who also sought to challenge the conventional assumptions of historical representation,[95] to whom European film critics have often compared Hou.[96] With his long sequences of puppetry and folk opera and his many shots of audiences and puppeteers working backstage, Hou further emphasizes the performative and presentational, again reminding viewers of their role as spectators of a constructed film image, an illusion.[97]

Finally, the metaphor of puppetry raises a host of interesting questions about history, identity, and the possibility of apprehending truth. Puppets, after all, have no life of their own; they depend on someone to manipulate them and put words into their mouths. In Hou's film, the actors dramatizing scenes from Li's life can clearly be seen as puppets, but who exactly is the puppetmaster of the film's title? The most obvious answer would be Li T'en-luk, since it is his memories that are being reenacted. Yet, as the contradictions between the dramatic vignettes and Li's narrated recollections remind us, the words spoken by the actors are not necessarily part of Li's memories but were written by the screenwriters Wu Nien-chen and Chu T'ien-wen. Li has even less control over the reconstruction of his past than it first seems, as even his monologues are subject to the whims of Hou Hsiao-hsien and his editors. So is Hou the puppetmaster responsible for producing this portrait of a life, this performance of Taiwanese history? The very unanswerability of such a question points to the central lesson of Hou's cinematic explorations of Taiwanese history: that transparent documentation of historical truth is impossible. Knowledge of the past—whether personal or collective—is always subjective, shaped by the needs and concerns of the individual writing in the present moment. As the film's English subtitle reminds us, "There is always someone pulling the strings . . ."

Memory and Imagination: *Good Men, Good Women* and the White Terror

Once upon a Time: that means, as in a fairy tale, not only something past, but also a brighter or happier someplace else.[98]

The work of memory situates experience in a sequence that keeps it alive, a story which can open out into free storytelling, greater life, invention.[99]

Hou's original plan for the final installment of his Taiwan Trilogy was a film entitled *Once upon a Time There Was a Man Named P'u-tao T'ai-lang* (從前從前有個浦島太郎), a Rip Van Winkle kind of tale about a political prisoner, jailed since the February 28 Incident, who suddenly finds himself released into the liberalized Taiwanese society of the 1980s. The story of the difficulties he faces trying to adjust to the island's modern, materialistic, and multicultural society was intended to bring Hou's cultural history of Taiwan up to date. The title of the proposed project, which suggests a connection between history and fairy tales, promised to continue the deconstruction of realistic historical representation begun in *City of Sadness* and *The Puppetmaster*.[100] While Hou did not make the film he originally proposed, its story was brought to the screen by his New Cinema colleague Wan Jen (萬仁) in the 1995 *Supercitizen K'o* (超級大國民). The film was produced and directed by Wan, but it was written by Wan together with two of Hou Hsiao-hsien's core collaborators, Wu Nien-jen and Liao Ch'ing-sung. Through the personal remembrances of an old man named K'o (許), a victim of political persecution by the KMT, Wan's film examines the white terror years of the 1950s—the political aftermath of the February 28 Incident in which thousands of Taiwanese intellectuals disappeared, either killed by the KMT or imprisoned on Green Island (綠島), an isolated speck of land off the coast of Taiwan. His melancholic memories, intensified by lingering grief and regrets over friends and relatives who suffered because of his activities, paint a portrait of a repressive but in some ways more noble past that contrasts sharply with present-day Taiwanese society.

As the film begins, K'o is a frail old man attempting to reenter society after a nearly thirty-year absence: sixteen years in KMT prisons, followed by twelve years of self-imposed isolation in a nursing home. As he moves back into his daughter's large and well-appointed home and begins to explore the new Taiwan, he sadly comes to realize that he, who had always thought of himself as a progressive youth, is now an out-of-step old man. Alternating between the present (filmed in color) and K'o's memories of his past (filmed in black and white), the film depicts him as a lonely old man lost in time and desperately trying to connect with history. The old man wanders around Taipei—a city at once vaguely familiar and utterly alien to him—searching for the recognizable landmarks that are for him signposts of his memories of political persecution. As he visits each site, he is dismayed to find its history of pain and injustice erased, replaced by landmarks of Taiwan's materialistic new consumer society. The martial court where he and his friends were imprisoned and tortured by the KMT is now a glitzy shopping mall. The military storehouse where the Japanese, and after them the Nationalist Chinese, stored their guns, knives, and other instruments of enforcement is now an elegant five-star hotel. Most disconcertingly for K'o, the execution field where so many of his friends were put to death by KMT soldiers is now a public park—Youth Park (青年公園)—filled with pleasure-seeking young men and women who have no knowledge of the atrocities committed there only a generation ago. As the old man contemplates the lush green park, he sadly notes that "the sound of gunshots still echo as if it were just last night, the screams of my friends still ring in my ears. . . . I looked out and saw only green grass where there once was fresh blood, laughter and youth, singing and dancing. . . . They say no one even remembers Ma-ch'ang-ting [馬場町, the execution grounds] anymore."

Old man K'o also tries to tie his past to the present by seeking out old friends and colleagues—those who were members of his political study group and were with him when KMT soldiers broke down their doors, confiscated the forbidden books they were reading, and arrested them all. The fate of his fellow patriots is no less sad and discouraging. Once vibrant, energetic, and full of youthful optimism for Taiwan's future, they are now old, tired, and forgotten in the wake of progress. One of them, known as Foggy, lives in a small shack hidden in the shadows of Taipei's gleaming new skyscrapers. K'o's flashbacks tell us that during the Japanese Occupation Foggy was a proud member of a military band; now he barely scrapes by, playing his sax in funeral processions and taking odd jobs. When K'o inquires how he's been since being released from prison, he shrugs and replies, "Just filling my belly and waiting to die." Another of the colleagues whom K'o locates, Old Wu, was so traumatized by the persecution he suffered that he is completely paranoid. When K'o visits him, Wu scarcely nods acknowledgment before putting on the headphones of the Walkman he is clutching and tuning out. His wife explains: "He doesn't realize that martial law has been lifted and that times have changed. He thinks that the government implanted a transmitter in his brain and can pick up any political thoughts he might have. . . . That's why he drowns out his thoughts with music all day." K'o gently lifts the headphones to hear what Wu is listening to: Kuomintang military music, complete with such lyrics as "The mainland is our national soil. . . . We'll reclaim it in victorious battle!" The last colleague K'o seeks out, Lin, has withdrawn from contemporary life in another way, by seeking refuge in a quiet corner of the countryside, far from the chaotic activity of the city.

K'o is determined to seek out his former colleagues because he desperately needs to find closure for an event in his past that haunts his memory: the execution of his friend Ch'en Chen-yi (陳政一). Ch'en was the only member of their group to receive the death penalty—a fate for which K'o feels personally responsible. It was he who, unable to bear the torture by KMT soldiers, gave them Ch'en's name and whereabouts. Images of Ch'en's execution—a military truck and jeep driving to the middle of a vast, empty field in the dark of night, the shouting of KMT soldiers as they drag Ch'en and two other prisoners out of the trucks and force them to their knees, the loud echo of the gunshots, and Ch'en's proud and defiant face as he falls, blood spreading across his white shirt—open the film and wake the old man K'o from a tense and fitful sleep. This "memory"—really an imagined memory since K'o was not present at the execution—recurs throughout the film, as K'o will never be at peace until he finds Ch'en's grave and asks his forgiveness. While his former colleagues are reluctant to revisit those years of persecution, K'o is compelled to look backwards. Almost everything he sees or hears in modern-day Taipei triggers his memories of the past. Though often recalling painful events, those memories are nevertheless romanticized, infused with nostalgia (the black-and-white images of the film's memory segments are often tinted with sepia tones). This constant alternating between modern-day Taiwan and Ko's memories of the 1950s not only strengthens the contrast the film draws between the Taiwanese past and the island's present, it also calls attention to the necessary dialectic of past and present that underlies all processes of remembrance. When one feels nostalgia, it is usually because one feels dissatisfied or anxious about the present. In K'o's case, his experiences of 1990s Taiwanese society—politically liberated but increasingly plagued by materialism, corruption, and opportunism—cause him to yearn for his youth, when social ideals, political passions, and personal loyalties flourished despite (or perhaps due to) a harshly repressive atmosphere. K'o watches the street demonstrations and legislative debates made possible by liberalization and can't help but notice the distracted demeanor and listless attitude of many of the protesters. The political debates in the legislature—which K'o watches on television—inevitably seem to degenerate into shouting matches and slugfests. Most disillusioning of all, K'o discovers that while political involvement in his day was about social ideals, ideological commitment, and a heartfelt desire for representation today it is about a different kind of power: media access, social recognition, and most of all money. His own son-in-law, a wealthy businessman who decides to run for elected office to increase his social stature and influence, is the very embodiment of political opportunism. His cynicism is made clear when he scoffs at his wife's reluctance to let him get involved in politics: "Times are different now. Haven't you heard the saying? 'Electoral politics know no master. All you need is money.' Of course we can win the election! Things aren't like they were in your parents' day. They just bumbled stupidly along, clinging to 'ideals.' Politics is business! What are you afraid of?" Even when he is arrested for buying votes and his house is ransacked, he shrugs it off as just part of doing business. For an old Taiwanese patriot like K'o, the corrupt and chaotic political atmosphere is disheartening. Can this mess be what they fought so hard for? Why they spent so many years in prison? For which they sacrificed their lives?

While the past may be romanticized as a deliberate contrast with the present in Wan Jen's film, its depictions of 1950s Taiwanese intellectuals is not completely rosy either. Toward the end of the film it becomes clear, for instance, that old man K'o's wife and daughter paid a high price for his single-minded dedication to his social and political ideals. K'o's memories of his family (significantly few compared to his remembrances of his political colleagues, which dominate his memory) consist primarily of sentimentalized images of his smiling wife playing the piano while K'o and his young daughter waltz in their living room, but his daughter remembers the impact of his activities on their lives very differently. Now grown and bitter after years of estrangement, she angrily reminds him how he cared only about his friends and their ideals, never once—not even now—

showing any concern for the well-being of his family. She reminds him (and the film includes flashbacks that depict her version of the past) how much her mother suffered during his long years in prison, struggling to hold the family together and faithfully enduring the long and difficult trip (via two trains and a fishing boat) to visit him on Green Island—only to be met with a few minutes of silent indifference and, on her final trip, divorce papers. K'o's wife killed herself immediately after that visit, leaving his daughter to be passed around, as she bitterly recalls, from relative to relative, none of whom wanted to be burdened with a child from a "rebel's family" (叛亂家庭). In school, she was regularly taunted and humiliated in front of the class and interrogated by school and government officials after each visit she made to Green Island. Even after his daughter's tearful efforts to reach out to him and broaden his perspective, old K'o remains locked in his narrow and obsessive view of the past. Without saying a word to comfort his daughter, he leaves the house and continues on his mission to find Ch'en Chen-yi's grave and pay his last respects. The final images of the film, however, hint at a possible reconciliation between father and daughter, who—with both having reexamined and retold their pasts—are perhaps able to make peace with each other at last. K'o's daughter is asleep in bed when the old man returns from his vigil at Ch'en's grave, but she wakes and goes downstairs when she hears him come in and collapse in exhaustion by the door. Without a word, she helps him to his room and into bed. As he sleeps, she begins to read through his diary. The film's last image is a flashback, this time in color rather than black and white. Is it memory or fantasy? Does it belong to father or daughter? Whatever one decides, the closing image is a beautiful one, picturing the young K'o family—father, mother, and daughter—walking hand in hand across a mountaintop at sunset. As they approach the camera, they stop, put their arms around one another, and smile. The image fades to black and white, then finally to black as the film ends.

The film Hou finally made as the concluding installment of his Taiwan Trilogy was released the same year as *Supercitizen K'o* and is called *Good Men, Good Women*. Like Wan Jen's work, Hou's film also focuses on the political witch hunts of the 1950s and romanticizes Taiwanese intellectuals of that earlier era—individuals whose political passions, social ideals, and committed relationships contrast with the material decadence and cynical opportunism of modern Taiwanese. In this respect, the two films represent the cinematic equivalent of an important trend in fictional and nonfictional Taiwanese literature of the years following martial law:[101] a fascination with oral histories and compiled biographies of victims of KMT persecution—Taiwanese political martyrs, the good men and good women to which the title of Hou's film refers.[102] Indeed, the film may have been inspired by one of the most significant of these "martyr biographies" (烈士的傳說): Lan Po-chou's (藍博洲) *Song of the Swinging Chariot* (幌馬車之歌). First published in 1988 in the journal *Humanity* (人間雜志) as part of its Taiwanese Popular History (臺灣民眾史) series, it tells the story of Chung Hao-tong (鍾浩東)—also known as Chung Ho-ming (鍾和鳴)—through a patchwork of diary entries by his widow, Chiang Pi-yu (蔣碧玉), his brother, and other friends, relatives, and political colleagues. It was later published in book form, complete with photographs and additional interviews with other political victims of the period—a configuration of the past through the juxtaposition of verbal and visual texts that is not unlike the kind of bricolage Hou attempted in all his historical films.[103]

Like *Supercitizen K'o*, *Good Men, Good Women* explores the dialectical interplay between the past and the present and emphasizes the notion of history as memory and imagination. While both films alternate between scenes set in 1990s Taiwan and depictions of the past, Wan Jen's film is the more conventional in form. Most of the film uses relatively straightforward flashbacks and internal voice-overs to delve into the personal memories and reflections of a single individual—old man K'o. Even though his daughter's recollections provide an alternate, contrasting view of K'o's past toward the end of the film, it is clearly his nostalgic longing that dominates *Supercitizen K'o* and sets its tone. Hou's film, on the other hand, has an extremely complex structure, which juxtaposes multiple layers of time and perspective. Even more than Wan, Hou envisions historical knowledge as the work of the imagination, a creative construct shaped and colored by the present. The modern-day protagonist of *Good Men, Good Women* is a young film actress named Liang Ching (梁靜), who is preparing to play the Taiwanese patriot Chiang Pi-yu in a movie about her efforts, and those of her husband Chung Hao-tong, during the anti-Japanese war, as well as their later arrest and persecution by the KMT during the white terror. While the young woman prepares for the role, she is suffering her own sort of persecution, as an anonymous caller who has stolen her diary harasses her over the phone and faxes her pages from the diary. The faxes unnerve her not only because they represent a double invasion of her privacy but also because they forcibly remind her of her own recent past, when she was a drug-addicted bar girl involved in a tempestuous relationship with a gangster named Ah-wei (阿威), now gone, shot dead in her arms one night.[104] She also is trying to work through her complicated relationships with her sister and brother-in-law, with whom she may or may not have been overly intimate. The film weaves together fragmentary and discontinuous scenes from multiple moments in time and diverse perspectives. While it deliberately plays with notions of reality and illusion, so that it is not always easy to differentiate between the different layers of the film, the scenes may be broken down into four basic categories. First are the present-day scenes of Liang Ching's daily life: Liang in her apartment, sleeping, bathing, and reacting to the anonymous phone calls and faxes she receives; and Liang interacting with her sister and brother-in-law at the little restaurant they own, arguing and scuffling with her sister in an indoor badminton court, and dancing with her in a discotheque, crying and falling into her arms. All of these scenes are shot in color and usually take place in dark, cramped spaces. The second category includes scenes that depict her memories of her love affair with Ah-Wei—a period in her life characterized by the headlong pursuit of instant gratification: days and nights filled with drinking and dancing, crazy flirtations, and impassioned lovemaking, as well as arguments and violence. Shot in highly saturated color, these scenes have a kind of surreal, intoxicated quality, particularly the blue-tinted scenes of Liang Ching and Ah-Wei in their love nest.

Standing in stark contrast to these scenes are those that portray events in Taiwan's past, for example, the crisp and austere black-and-white images that trace, in almost documentary fashion, the story of Chiang Pi-yu and Chung Hao-tong's patriotism, social commitment, and eventual martyrdom. These scenes depict their decision to travel to the mainland to join the anti-Japanese guerrillas fighting there, the interrogations they had to endure before they were welcomed to join the mainland fighters (who suspected their motives simply because they had come from Occupied Taiwan), their return to Taiwan and their dedication to education, their disillusionment with the KMT government and involvement in an underground dissident journal called *Brilliance* (光明報), their subsequent arrest and detention, Chung's death at the hands of the KMT, and his widow's dignified efforts to collect money from her neighbors in order to claim the body for burial. Although they are documentary in style, these "film within the film" scenes seem to portray the historical past as it is constructed in Liang Ching's imagination—created in her mind, perhaps, as she reads about the couple and prepares for the role she is to play.[105] Mixed with these black and white images are other depictions of past events, scenes from the lives of the patriots set apart by the fact that they are in color, albeit in extremely muted tones. Most of these depict Liang Ching and the other actors rehearsing scenes from the film about Chiang and Chung. While the black and white scenes of the past could conceivably be read as transparent depictions of historical events, the scenes of acting are clearly marked as fictive reenactments—present-day construc-

11. By intercutting scenes depicting the lives of Taiwanese patriots Chiang Pi-yu and Chung Hao-tong with scenes of the actors who portray them, *Good Men, Good Women* offers a complex interplay of past and present, character and actor, and illusion and reality.

tions of the past. Even in their visual qualities, they lie somewhere between black-and-white and color, between past and present. The polyphony of the film's many layers is further complicated by Liang Ching's numerous voice-overs, which serve different functions at different points in the film. Sometimes they are internal to the action depicted on screen, as when she reads the diary entries that are coming in by fax. At other times, her words take on a more impersonal and authoritative tone, as when she narrates events from the lives of Chiang Pi-yu and Chung Hao-tong. At still other moments, she reflects on her preparations for her role as Chiang Pi-yu—such as her meeting with the real Chiang, now a very old woman.[106] Indeed, the interplay of past and present, character and actress, and illusion and reality is even more complex in this film than in *The Puppetmaster* or *City of Sadness*.

In its retelling of Chiang Pi-yu's and Chung Hao-tong's story, *Good Men, Good Women* also revisits many of the themes explored in the two previous films of Hou's trilogy. One of these is the mutual distrust and suspicion with which Taiwanese and mainlanders began their association and which inevitably fed into the historical tragedies—the February 28 Incident and the white terror—that have impacted their relationships to this very day. When Chiang, Chung, and their compatriots from Taiwan arrive on the mainland after a long and difficult journey, determined to help fight the Japanese, they are surprised to be greeted with suspicion

12. As the numerous interrogation scenes in *Good Men, Good Women* make clear, the mutual distrust between Taiwanese and mainlanders was aggravated by misunderstandings arising from the linguistic gap separating the two groups.

and interrogated like criminals. The mainland Chinese were understandably wary of these arrivals from Taiwan, which was, after all, occupied by the Japanese. As the numerous scenes of interrogation make clear, this mutual distrust was further aggravated by the misunderstandings that arose from the linguistic gap that separated the Taiwanese and the mainlanders. Forced by the mutual incomprehensibility of multiple dialects to tediously repeat questions as well as answers and to rely on several layers of translation simply to communicate, both sides must have felt frustration and exasperation. As *Good Men, Good Women* suggests and *Supercitizen K'o* explicitly articulates, the misunderstandings and suspicions that tainted these initial interactions between Taiwanese and mainlanders contributed directly to the white terror, when the KMT's lingering doubts about Taiwanese loyalties and paranoia about communist spies led them to arrest Taiwanese indiscriminately, determined to spare no communists, even if that meant killing a hundred innocents.[107]

Most importantly, however, the concluding segment of Hou Hsiao-hsien's Taiwan Trilogy continues to build on the new historical awareness developed in the first two films. Together, they are an important contribution to current efforts to restore lost passages of Taiwanese history to the island's cultural consciousness. Films such as Hou Hsiao-hsien's and Wan Jen's are also significant because they emphasize the fact that historical imagination—the very act of memory, of actively constructing and creatively retelling the past—can be a critical tool for empowering one-self to deal with the crises of the present moment. Today's newly liberalized Taiwan finds itself at a critical crossroads—a Benjaminian moment of danger that could lead to disaster as easily as to a brilliant future. On the one hand, it is moment of golden opportunity for Taiwan, as the island's economic prosperity has finally been matched by cultural and political pluralism, opening up seemingly limitless and unprecedented possibilities, which could lead to a truly democratic society. At the same time, there is a definite sense of impending doom and disaster, as the enthusiastic and often uncritical embrace of newfound freedoms and opportunities threatens to degenerate into social chaos. The exhilaration of the moment, therefore, seems to be tempered by sadness and anxiety over society's lapsed morals, lost ideals, and forgotten priorities. The verses that open *Supercitizen K'o* capture beautifully this ambivalence over the recent changes in Taiwanese society.

> The fog has lifted, landscapes and objects are finally becoming
> clear . . .
> But then why, why are they all brimming with tears?

By blurring the borders between past and present, public and private, memory and imagination, and reality and illusion, films such as Wan Jen's and those that make up Hou Hsiao-hsien's historical trilogy pose a challenge to viewers, asking them to awaken their own historical imagination, to cast a retrospective glance at Taiwanese history and their own past in order to better comprehend the complexity of the current cultural moment. They challenge today's Taiwanese to take control of their own destiny, to "seize hold of a memory" in the hopes of creating a better and brighter future.

5

Language and Nationhood: Culture as Social Contestation

Culture embodies those moral, ethical, and aesthetic values, the spiritual eyeglasses, through which [human beings] come to view themselves and their place in the universe. Values are the basis of a people's identity, their sense of particularity as members of the human race. All is carried by language. Language is the collective memory bank of a people's experience in history. Culture is almost indistinguishable from the language that makes possible its genesis. — Ngugi wa Thiong'o

It is always a mistake to treat languages in the way that certain nationalist ideologues treat them, as *emblems* of nation-ness, like flags, costumes, folk-dances, and the rest. Much the most important thing about language is its capacity for generating imagined communities, building in effect *particular solidarities.* — Benedict Anderson

Decolonizing the Word:
Language, Culture, and the Building of Nations

Contemporary cultural theorists have taught us that the word is a sensitive gauge of the dynamics of social intercourse and that language is inextricably enmeshed in hierarchies of power. Mikhail Bakhtin, in particular, has argued that all language is deeply socioideological, that it comes into being only in the unpredictable heterogeneity of human social interaction and is therefore inseparable from the dynamics and particularities of actual sociopolitical conditions.[1] What interests him most is the tense, oppositional nature of human communication—that is, the struggle for power and authority that lies at the heart of all human linguistic practice. Every verbal utterance, he asserts, is "a contradiction-ridden, tension-filled unity of two-embattled tendencies in the life of language," that is, every utterance is shaped by an ongoing battle between the powerful centripetal forces that try to unify and centralize sociopolitical and cultural understanding and the centrifugal forces of social heteroglossia that simultaneously attempt to decentralize and diversify experience.[2] Bakhtin points to the emergence of standardized national languages as a principle illustration of this conjunction of language and power. For him, the establishment of a national language is a centripetal force that attempts to create within a heteroglot linguistic environment "the firm, stable nucleus of an officially recognized literary language" that can unify a diverse population into a community and can centralize verbal-ideological thought.[3]

Benedict Anderson has similarly noted that the emergence of a national language capable of unifying a diverse population into an imagined community has little to do with the inherent characteristics of any given language but depends primarily on the ways in which it is used in concrete social, cultural, and political situations. For him, the key component that determines a language's functions as a historical agent of nation formation is its relationship to the technologies and institutions of *writing*, specifically in its printed form. Thus, "print-language is what invents nationalism, not a particular language per se."[4] These languages, which Anderson alternately refers to as administrative languages, print-vernaculars, and languages-of-state, become powerful precisely because of their complex alliances with institutions of law, politics, commerce, and (most importantly) education that lay the basis for imagining national communities by creating a literate public bound together in a unified field of exchange and communication.[5]

Whenever there is an asymmetrical arrangement of power—whether along ethnic, class, gender, or territorial lines—language becomes a potent symbol of group identity and can therefore become an even more crucial tool in the struggle for authority.[6] The colonial situation provides a particularly pronounced illustration of this kind of linguistic contestation. As the history of European imperialism attests, the encounter between the language of a colonizing nation and the language of its colonized territory precipitates, more often than not, a linguistic drama in which the psychic and cultural worlds represented by the two tongues are in constant conflict.[7] Colonial bilingualism is never a simple linguistic dualism in which each language is equally valued. Instead, the imperial language of the colonizer is institutionalized as the language of official public discourse,[8] and its legitimacy and authority over the colonized population is reinforced through a simultaneous degradation and devaluation of the "mother" tongue of the colonized natives.[9] In many colonial situations, indigenous languages were primarily oral, with no standardized scripts of their own, and the introduction of the colonizer's language into a colonized territory coincided with the introduction of writing, print, and institutions of education. Hence, as John Beverly has observed, the authority of imperial languages was based in large part on an ideology, developed simultaneously with nineteenth-century European conceptions of the national, that privileges writing over orality, for "it is not so much as technology that writing and the culture of the book functioned . . . but rather as an ideology of the enterprise of conquest."[10] Thus, it "makes literature and literary values the key signifiers of identity for a national-bourgeois intelligentsia."[11] This colonial legacy, he argues, lies at the heart of Latin America's idealization of literature and the literary, as well as its underappreciation for or even disdain of nonliterary (specifically oral) indigenous cultural forms. He cites as evidence of this colonial and oligarchic cultural heritage the conjunctural coincidence of the boom in Latin American literature represented by writers such as García Márquez and the political agitation for national liberation generated by the Cuban Revolution in the 1960s—an idealization of the role of literature as an instrument of national liberalization.

While Beverly's analysis focuses exclusively on Latin America, similar examples of national liberation movements that idealize literature and emphasize its centrality as social practice can easily be found elsewhere around the globe. History is filled with sociopolitical conflicts that make language and writing the battleground for cultural self-assertion. Indeed, if the unifying power of an imperial language has been the cornerstone of every official nationalism in the age of empire, so has the reinstatement of native languages been the centerpiece of many of the colonial nationalisms that arose in response.[12] Every writer working in a multilingual colonial or postcolonial environment is faced with a difficult linguistic choice. Does one write in the language of an imperial power and risk absorption into an oppressor's culture or should one choose to write in a native tongue? In the context of decolonization, a writer's selection of one language over another necessarily becomes politicized.[13] Consider, for instance, Kenyan author Ngugi wa Thiong'o's decision in the late 1970s to renounce English and return to his native Gikuyu as his preferred medium for creative expression. "I believe," he explains in *Decolonizing the Mind*, "that my writing in Gikuyu language, a Kenyan language, an African language, is part and parcel of the anti-imperialist struggles of Kenyan and African peoples."[14] Ngugi's fervent appeal for the recuperation of his native language reveals his belief in the primacy of language—particularly a precolonial indigenous tongue—as a powerful rallying point around which the national community can cohere.[15]

Language and Nationhood **133**

The Colonized Writer's Dilemma: Linguistic "Abrogation" and "Appropriation"

One of the central questions that remains to be resolved in the fiercely contested debate over the relation of language to national culture is, as one critic put it, "Does a nation depend on a single unifying language to sustain its identity, or is the national space inherently polyglot?"[16] In Africa, for example, the controversy over language choice has raged for decades, beginning long before Ngugi's dramatic renunciation of English. The theoretical debate over the role of language in the cultural decolonization of Africa attracted such major figures as Chinua Achebe, Gabriel Okara, Leopold Senghor, Ezekiel Mphalele, Wole Soyinka, and Frantz Fanon.[17] Their views on how postcolonial writing can best seize the language of the center and replace it with a more nationalistic discourse vary widely, but they fall along a range of strategies whose polar extremes have been described as the processes of "abrogation" and "appropriation."[18] Abrogation, a strategy structured on binary oppositions, involves the emphatic rejection of the language of the metropolitan power as the preferred means of communication and a return to writing primarily, if not exclusively, in an indigenous tongue. It is a "return to roots" approach that is often colored by sentimentality. Ngugi's deliberate abandonment of English and subsequent embrace of his native Gikuyu, for instance, offer an exemplary illustration of the abrogationist's nostalgic search for an authentic, unadulterated, nativist mode of expression.[19]

The linguistic strategies of writers such as Achebe, Okara, and Soyinka, however, fall closer to the other end of the spectrum. Instead of envisioning an original precolonial, prelapsarian, national culture, strategies of appropriation acknowledge the inevitable syncretism of the postcolonial environment and draw strength from its multicultural reality. Appropriationist writers espouse a less organic and idealist notion of language and therefore do not see the European languages as inherently oppressive and alienating. Rather than negate the foreign tongue altogether, appropriationists take the language of the colonizer and make it their own by hybridizing it with native linguistic and literary traditions. Hence, Achebe, Okara, and Soyinka defend their use of English by demonstrating their ability to inflect their writing with the phrasing, rhythm, and narrative strategies of indigenous African languages.[20]

Language and Power: Taiwanese Encounters Mandarin

Ulf Hannerz has observed that "A language . . . is a dialect with an army."[21] The strategies of linguistic abrogation and appropriation highlighted by the debate in African literature are relevant to the controversy over language and national culture in Taiwan not only because African attempts to grapple with the language question were a direct source of inspiration for many Taiwanese hsiang-t'u writers but also because discussions of the language issue in Taiwan have similarly been marked by the tension between these two conflicting tendencies.[22] Even before the Taiwanese literary debates of the 1970s brought the issue to the fore, a confrontation of languages—a linguistic battle between the languages of a colonizer and a colonized—has always been at the heart of the struggle to define a Taiwanese community. Beginning in 1895, the residents of Taiwan were subjected to the same imperial policies—based on the European model of official nationalism—that Japan used to "Japanify" all of its Asian colonies. This included, of course, the institutionalization of Japanese as the language of authority and nation taught in schools and used in the media and all official discourse.[23] The use of Taiwanese, the indigenous tongue of the island, was discouraged in public and hence limited to the private sphere of home and family. After the end of the Japanese Occupation in 1947, the role of imperial language was assumed by Mandarin, the administrative language used by the Kuomintang. Mandarin and Taiwanese, the two major languages spoken in Taiwan today, are both vernacular dialects of Chinese and are mutually unintelligible when spoken. Mandarin owes its differentiated status as an administrative language and its special relationship with Chinese nationhood, however, to its historical association with the very institutions of officialdom and technologies of literate culture that give it authority and status in society far exceeding those of a purely oral dialect.[24]

In premodern China, of course, the position at the top of the linguistic hierarchy was occupied by Classical Chinese. Literary languages such as Classical Chinese or learned Latin differ from administrative languages, what Walter Ong calls grapholects, in that they have little or no basis in an oral dialect but are purely chirographic from their inception.[25] Patrick Hanan, in his study of Chinese vernacular literature, has observed that Classical Chinese (wen-yen, 文言, literally, "written word") has throughout the history of imperial China "served as the written medium in government and law, and as the vehicle of learning, history, and tradition for the class by whom and for whom it was primarily written, the class which it helped both to create and define."[26] The class to which he refers is the educated class of nobles and officials, who, though constituting a relatively small percentage of the country's population, held the reins of power precisely because of their mastery of Classical Chinese, the language of upward mobility. In the case of imperial China, the connection between language and institutions of power could scarcely have been more explicit. Under the imperial examination system, admission into the mandarin bureaucracy and its community of learning could be gained only by proving one's competency in the literate culture of Classical Chinese—not only a general mastery of the language but also mastery of strictly regulated literary forms such as the lyric poem and the essay.

In modern China, the privileged vernacular that developed into an administrative language is Mandarin. Unlike Classical Chinese, which was rarely if ever spoken, Mandarin is based on one of China's many regional oral dialects, the Peking vernacular. Ever since the May Fourth Movement advocated its use as a replacement for Classical Chinese as an instrument of administrative centralization, however, it has come to be clearly distinguishable from the regional Peking dialect in its spoken form. The divergent social functions and cultural meanings of the Mandarin language and the Peking dialect cause their speakers to relate to them in entirely different ways. Adopted as the official language for all public discourse, Mandarin possesses social, economic, and political power that a mere dialect does not enjoy. Mandarin's status as a language of state is dramatically apparent in present-day Taiwan, where it stands in opposition to the native oral dialect, Taiwanese. While Taiwanese has been spoken on the island for generations and is mother tongue of the majority of the population, Mandarin (*kuo-yu*, 國語, literally "national language") is a relatively new import, brought from the Chinese mainland to Taiwan in 1949 by the Kuomintang regime and imposed on the indigenous population through compulsory education as an integral part of its nation-building strategy of unifying the populace and eliminating cultural differences. With Mandarin as the official language of the island, the use of Taiwanese was officially discouraged.[27] Even though recent political changes on the island have begun to challenge its hegemony, Mandarin continues to dominate most public media, from scholarly journals to newspapers and magazines, as well as television, film, and radio. Although it is rapidly gaining legitimacy as a medium for public discourse, Taiwanese remains largely relegated to interactions in the private sphere. In urban centers, where the influence of the media are most strongly felt, Mandarin continues to be the dominant language. Hence, the socioideological worlds represented by Mandarin include not only the world of officialdom but also the world of modern urban life. In the island's rural areas, Taiwanese remains the language most widely spoken, though younger generations, educated in Mandarin, are beginning to lose contact with the indigenous tongue. Native oral culture still exists in those areas where the spoken dialect reigns, but it is rapidly diminishing as Mandarin, along with the urban official culture it represents, penetrates deeper and deeper into the countryside.

This overlay of the oppositional pairings of Mandarin versus Taiwanese, literate versus oral culture, and city versus countryside is neither coincidental nor insignificant. Indeed, these binarisms can be seen as logical outgrowths of modern European nationalisms that are at heart binary models of conquest: the superiority of technology (writing and print) over nature (speech), of knowledge over ignorance, of urban sophistication over rural backwardness, and in specifically colonial contexts of the metropolitan culture of the colonizer over the indigenous culture of the colonized.[28] In Europe, the rise of cities—and the subsequent shift of human, material, and institutional resources in favor of urban centers— went hand in hand with the emergence of nationalism. Hence, the city, as the center of government, commerce, and education, becomes a crucial image in the rhetoric of nation and empire.[29] The flip side of this cult of the city, however, is a backward-looking nostalgia for the simple life of the countryside, represented in romanticized form by the pastoral: a rose-tinted view of country life from the perspective of the city, a creative "ruralization" of the countryside, which in reality may not have been as exclusively agricultural as imagined. This nostalgia for a simple rural past is often paralleled by an idealization of regional dialects and oral culture— a sentimentalizing tendency that has manifested itself, for instance, in the work of scholars such as Albert B. Lord and Walter Ong, who envision orality and literacy as two fundamentally antithetical states of consciousness.[30] Both Lord and Ong romanticize oral societies as organic communities held together by shared traditions passed on through face-to-face communication—*preliterate* societies still innocent of the exploitative structures and alienating technologies associated with print societies. Intellectuals at the other end of the political spectrum—Marxists such as Walter Benjamin and Georg Lukács—have expressed a similar nostalgia for the integrated world of oral culture, lamenting the isolation and artificial formality of the world of writing and print.[31] Moreover, an idealized vision of oral societies informs much of colonial and postcolonial criticism, the kind of idealization of precolonial indigenous societies that underlies, for example, the binary oppositions between First and Third World cultures laid out by Teshome Gabriel's influential work on Third Cinema.[32]

The problem with these kinds of cultural analyses is that they fail to escape the limitations of binary thinking so typical of European nationalisms. Instead, they merely reverse the binarisms, privileging simplicity over sophistication, nature over technology, rural over urban, oral culture over literate culture, and so on. They also are as vulnerable to xenophobic, racist, and other exclusionary tendencies as colonial ideologies are. Nevertheless, it is important to note that, reductive, sentimental, and idealistic though they may be, the emotional pull and strategic efficacy of binary models like these have made them an undeniably important part of the polemics of national liberation in postcolonial struggles around the world. Taiwan, of course, is no exception, as oppositional pairings contrasting city and country, literate and oral culture, and imperial language and native dialect were critical analytical tools for nativist movements such as hsiang-t'u literature and Taiwanese New Cinema.[33]

Much of the discussion surrounding the language issue in Taiwan, for instance, has been framed in binary terms. The status of the Taiwanese dialect has been a central concern in the island's struggle to define its cultural identity since the island was colonized by Japan in 1895. The anti-Japanese hsiang-t'u movement of the Occupation period made the restoration of the Taiwanese dialect a key component of its agenda and the hsiang-t'u writers of the 1960s and 1970s similarly considered the preservation of the native language and local culture from the hegemonic domination of Mandarin a top priority.[34] Hwang Chun-ming has expressed deep concern for the future of the Taiwanese dialect and feels a profound sense of duty to protect his native language from the threat posed by Mandarin. "Each country or region has its own dialect," he writes. "Mandarin was originally a northern dialect, so theoretically once we are outside of Peking, we must consider Mandarin a 'foreign' language. . . . Its history on this island cannot compare with that of the native dialect. Our native language has a life of its own; we cannot extinguish that life."[35] His view of the 'otherness' of Mandarin is underscored in a number of essays in which he explicitly addresses issues of language and culture in Taiwan.[36] For example, he deliberately sets up a diametric opposition between Mandarin, the so-called national language (所謂國家語言), and the island's local dialect. Taiwanese, he argues, is a rich and evocative language organically linked to concrete material living,[37] while Mandarin is a highly abstract, profoundly westernized language that he associates with modern technology, industry, and science,[38] a contrast that clearly echoes the romanticized view of oral versus literate societies imagined by Western thinkers.

Hwang considers the championing of indigenous languages to be a defining characteristic of nativist literary movements not only in Taiwan but in any number of Third World nations where literacy is not the norm or the standard literary language is that of an oppressor. Comparing the Taiwanese hsiang-t'u movement to anticolonial efforts in Africa, he cites parallel developments in Kenya as an example: "Today we see similar phenomena [the emergence of nativist literatures] in Third World nations . . . like Kenya, for instance. Illiteracy rates are extremely high there, and the official language, English, is the language of the ruling sector, not of the people. It would be wrong for a Kenyan writer to write in English. When a Kenyan writer uses his native language to write about indigenous people and local problems, that is hsiang-t'u literature."[39] Though Hwang does not mention Ngugi wa Thiong'o by name, his comments suggest his solidarity with the Kenyan writer's decision to abandon English for his native tongue. Hwang's view of language has much in common with Ngugi's, as he is committed to the preservation and elevation of a native dialect that in his view is the very embodiment of a more authentic indigenous culture. From a theoretical perspective, then, Hwang might be considered an abrogationist, seeking to reject Mandarin, the alien and oppressive linguistic standard imposed by the ruling elite, the language of modernity and Westernization. Indeed, at a polemical level, the abrogationist stance was a critical part of the entire hsiang-t'u movement.

In practice, however, the problem of writing in Taiwanese, an essentially oral language, proved to be far more complicated. Like his fellow hsiang-t'u writers, Hwang is a native islander and considers Taiwanese to be his mother tongue. Nevertheless, all of his formal education, which occurred under KMT rule, was in Mandarin. Moreover, the very act of writing—particularly if he intends to reach the more educated audience that would be likely to buy his books—also requires the use of Mandarin.[40] Hwang, in other words, finds himself in the difficult position familiar to so many colonized writers: in order to participate effectively in "the culture of the book," he must use the language of the other, however awkward the process might be and no matter how strong his emotional allegiance to the native dialect.[41] Despite the abrogationist tendencies of his polemical arguments, therefore, Hwang's stories are actually characterized more by appropriationist linguistic strategies. Like the African writers Chinua Achebe, Gabriel Okara, and Wole Soyinka, who appropriated the language of the colonizer by hybridizing it with native linguistic and literary traditions, Hwang works with a carefully balanced mixture of Mandarin and Taiwanese,[42] consciously and liberally incorporating the native dialect into his writing. The techniques he and other hsiang-t'u writers use to accentuate the indigenous flavor of their narratives include, for example, the deliberate use of untranslated— and hence for Mandarin speakers undecipherable—Taiwanese words and phrases.[43] This strategy is effective in highlighting cross-cultural confrontations in postcolonial situations since, as has been noted, it "not only registers a sense of cultural distinctiveness but forces the reader into an active engagement with the horizons of culture in which these terms have meaning."[44] Sometimes, glosses of the Taiwanese words and phrases are provided.[45] Wang Chen-ho, whose works are heavily laced with the Taiwanese dialect, includes copious footnotes in order to render the dialogue intelligible to nonnative readers. Hwang, on the other hand, chooses to include parenthetical Mandarin translations.[46] In either case, the effect of this hybridized writing is to underscore the cultural differences that separate Taiwanese from Mandarin and, just as importantly, to highlight the subaltern status of the native writer. In many ways, the laborious awkwardness of the reading experience mirrors the internal dissonance experienced by Taiwanese writers, who are forced to write in a language not entirely their own.[47]

From a thematic perspective, the linguistic battle in the oppositional pairing of Mandarin and Taiwanese and the different sociolinguistic worlds they represent is a recurring issue in many of Hwang's stories. Hwang's characters are mostly simple rural men, women, and children who are relatively uneducated and speak only the native Taiwanese dialect. Living in a closed, traditional village society governed by conservative Confucian ways and superstitious beliefs, they are often unwitting victims of changing societal values. Those who move to the city for work are impoverished laborers who live on the margins of urban society, and the gap that separates them from the modern, Westernized world of the city is often underscored by the linguistic chasm that exists between the ordinary Taiwanese populace and the ruling authorities. In "Ah-Ban and the Cop," for example, a middle-aged peasant woman who has come into the city to sell some vegetables is arrested by a policeman for illegal vending.[48] Their encounter is a comedy of miscommunication, as the woman is unable to tell him how to write her name and the policeman, who is trying to fill out a criminal report, cannot understand the name of her village.[49] She tells him she is from Gwei-liao-ah (猓寮仔), near Syou-bi-ah (小埤仔), but he has no idea what she is talking about. As it turns out, he only knows the village by its Mandarin name, Yung-fu-ts'un (永福村), "Eternal Blessings Village."[50] The communications gap between the Chinese authorities and the Taiwanese people is even more clearly illustrated in Hwang's "The Taste of Apples."[51] In this story, when a young foreign affairs policeman helps an American military officer find the family of a Taiwanese laborer struck by the officer's limousine, their conversation involves multiple layers of translation. The Chinese officer, of course, translates the American's account of the accident into Mandarin, but the laborer's wife, Ah-Kuei, remains mystified. Hwang writes: "Since Ah-Kuei didn't understand Mandarin, all she saw was the policeman energetically opening and closing his mouth. The motioning of his hands caused her to look even more apprehensively toward her daughter, Ah-Chu, hoping that she would let her in on what was happening" (161). From Ah-Kuei's point of view, the Mandarin-speaking policeman might just as well be speaking English since for her both languages are equally foreign. Ah-Chu, on the other hand, has learned Mandarin at school and is able to translate the policeman's words into Taiwanese.

The story that thematizes this clash between linguistic life worlds most explicitly is "The Drowning of an Old Cat" (溺死一支老貓).[52] In this story, the fundamental lack of understanding between modern urban and traditional rural culture is neatly underscored by the mutual unintelligibility of Mandarin and Taiwanese. The community described is a traditional agrarian society, and the sixty households of Clear Spring Village are hardworking farm families "as pure and simple as the spring water" (13) for which their village is famous. They love the land and for generations have tilled it diligently. So far, the village has been fairly well insulated from the aspects of urban culture—materialism, miniskirts, go-go dancing, and a fashionable fear of death—that have already infected the town nearby.[53] Change, however, has begun to threaten the village's traditional way of life, as the young people are venturing into the city—the girls marrying townsmen and the boys bringing city girls back to the village (12). The clash of cultures arises when the people of Clear Spring Village find their peaceful lives disrupted by neighboring townspeople, who want to build a swimming pool on the village's most sacred spot: Dragon-Eye Well.[54] Attracted by the healthful qualities of its streams and ponds, urban types—"physicians, senior bank officials, lawyers, school principals, assemblymen, businessmen" and Rotary Club members who go by names such as David and Tom (13)—also begin to invade the village.

The confrontation between city and village cultures erupts when old Uncle Ah-Sheng (阿盛), one of the village's respected elders, learns of the townspeople's plan to construct a swimming pool on the site of the sacred well. Steeped in Confucian traditions, he fears that the intrusion of alien—and in his mind shabby—urban values will pollute the spiritual purity of the village, for "if the pool opens, the people who come from town to go swimming will be mixing with each other, wearing almost nothing. Who knows what'll be going through their minds? Here in Clear Spring we've always been simple decent folk, but this could bring ruin to our sons and daughters and corrupt the entire village!" (21). Deeply superstitious, Uncle Ah-Sheng worries that the dragon god whose eye the well represents might take offense at the desecration of the site and refuse to protect the villagers and the land they love so much.

Uncle Ah-Sheng, along with the other village elders who gather daily in the courtyard of the village temple, represent the oral culture of the Taiwanese countryside.[55] The idea that the transmission of knowledge and history in nonliterate cultures depends primarily on oral repetition is conveyed by the daily gathering of Uncle Ah-Sheng and his cronies at the temple, where they "talked of the past, and even though their talk was very repetitious they never tired of it" (15). As an elder and guardian of traditional values, Uncle Ah-Sheng naturally takes the lead in rallying the villagers to block construction of the swimming pool. The meeting between the villagers and the representatives from town is a comic and revealing illustration of the profound gap that separates urban Mandarin culture and the oral culture of the Taiwanese village. The townspeople try their best to convince the villagers of the benefits the pool will bring, but they fail to elicit any response from the audience—mainly because the country folk, especially the old people, cannot understand Mandarin. Thus, "The village chief opened the meeting with a speech in Mandarin that left our old-timers feeling terribly dissatisfied, simply because they didn't understand a word he said. Next, the three gentlemen [from the town] came up and gave speeches, though in the eyes of the oldsters it was nothing more than an unbearable series of gestures" (25). Even after the village chief translates into Taiwanese the main points of the speeches, the villagers respond with silent indifference. Hence, while the immediate cause for the crowd's failure to appreciate the arguments set forth by the townspeople may be the language barrier that divides them, its inability to grasp the signs of progress and prosperity that the townspeople claim the pool will bring arises from the fact that the villagers do not share urban values. Cars, independence for local schools—these concepts are meaningless to the villagers because they have no place in the rural community's normal frame of reference. When Uncle Ah-Sheng addresses the townsmen, he is accompanied by the deafening cheers and applause of his fellow villagers, whose feelings he eloquently summarizes.

"I would like you to go back and tell the people in town that Uncle Ah-Sheng of Clear Spring says that if they want to go swimming to please go home and take a dip in their bathtubs!" . . .

He continued, "Don't be fooled into thinking that Clear Spring is the place to build your swimming pool—the water in Clear Spring is for our use in the rice fields, not for you townspeople to take baths in!" The waves of applause increased along with the pitch of the excitement in the old man's words: "The people of Clear Spring have no use for your 'vehicular traffic'—all anyone needs is two good legs.

We're concerned only about our fields and our water. As for the lay of the land, Clear Spring is a dragon's head. The village exit leading to the town is the mouth of the dragon, and the well beside the school is the eye, which is why we call it Dragon-Eye Well. Ever since the days of our ancestors, the people of Clear Spring have been protected by this dragon, which is why we've been able to live our lives in peace. Now suddenly someone wants to bring harm to our dragon's eye, and the people of Clear Spring are not going to stand by and let it happen." He turned around. "Isn't that right?" (26–27).

The wild enthusiasm of the villagers for Uncle Ah-Sheng's remarks is in direct contrast to the stony silence with which they greeted the towns-people's arguments. Quite simply put, this is because he speaks their language. Not only do they respond to his colorful Taiwanese, to his direct appeals for support ("Isn't that right?"), and to the homespun wisdom, traditional superstitions, and rustic humor with which he peppers his address, but they fully relate to the shared values that hold their rural community together. The people of Clear Spring are bound to their land in a very traditional manner; they perceive their village as an organic unity, a dragon that cannot be disturbed. They resist the changes imposed from without and hope to keep their village peaceful as it has been since the days of their ancestors. The townspeople, for their part, cannot comprehend why anyone would oppose the progress symbolized by the new pool. Moreover, they are amazed that Uncle Ah-Sheng, who can neither read nor write, can incite the crowd to such fervor. With no conception of the simple love of the land that binds the rural community together, they can only speculate that there must be "someone in the background" goading the old man on (28).

Later, when the battle against the townspeople intensifies and village morale begins to deteriorate, it becomes increasingly evident that the traditional glue holding the community together has already begun to weaken. Newer urban values have begun to infiltrate the consciousnesses of the villagers, particularly the minds of the younger, Mandarin-educated generation. Their personalities having been shaped by Mandarin and the more-self-centered activity of writing,[56] they have lost the strong sense of community that characterizes oral culture and have instead become more individualistic, concerned only with themselves and their own material pleasures. The gap between the Taiwanese-speaking elders of the village and the Mandarin-educated youths is meant here to be symptomatic of the profound differences between oral and literate cultures, a schism neatly dramatized in the scene in which Uncle Ah-Sheng, having lost the support of his fellow villagers, goes to County Chief Chen's office to seek help. County Chief Chen came from a family of farmers, but as a literate man he has apparently lost contact with the oral village culture of his elders. In a scene meant to contrast the personal connectedness of oral communication with the impersonality of print culture, Uncle Ah-Sheng attempts to explain his objections to the pool construction. Chen barely acknowledges his presence. Instead of giving the old man his undivided attention, the young bureaucrat pores over a pile of paperwork: "All the time Uncle Ah-Sheng was talking, the county chief's head was buried in the stack of official documents, as he mechanically affixed his seal to one after another" (34–35).[57]

Given the obvious lack of communication and understanding between the illiterate village elders and the literate village youth, it comes as no surprise that when the pool is finally completed the young people are thrilled by the new luxury brought to their village by the townspeople: "A great many people were gathered outside the chain fence around the swimming pool watching the hilarity and the splashing inside. Many of the local children ran home, raising a big fuss until they were given a dollar to go swimming. Young people who should have been out working in the fields had put their hoes aside and were staring, as though mesmerized, at the bras and short red pants of the swimsuits, their desires aroused" (35–36). Uncle Ah-Sheng, convinced that the townspeople and their pool have indeed begun to "bring ruin to our sons and daughters and corrupt the entire village," is greatly distressed. In one final act of protest and defiance, he drowns himself in the pool. Ironically, even as his coffin passes by the closed pool on the day of his funeral, the laughter of the irreverent and impatient village children, who have crept into the pool and are frolicking in the water, "poured over the walls like waves" (36).

Oral Culture and Native Wisdom: The Storyteller

Hwang Chun-ming's concern for recuperating the indigenous dialect and native oral culture extends beyond thematically highlighting the confrontation between the newer Mandarin-language culture and traditional Taiwanese society; it is reflected in the very style of his writing. Just as Chinua Achebe and Ngugi wa Thiong'o's narratives rely on strategies culled from the African oral heritage to express native resistance to the hegemony of English-language culture, Hwang's stories insistently draw on various aspects of Taiwanese oral tradition—proverbs, traditional tales, conversation, oratory, folk songs—to assert the island's cultural difference from the Chinese center.[58] This syntactic fusion of literary writing and vernacular locutions is apparent not only in the dialogue issuing from the mouths of the characters but also in the narrative itself, which, even when not in the first person, tends to be highly inflected with the rhythms of oral storytelling.[59] The opening passage of "The Drowning of an Old Cat," for instance, owes much to oral tradition. Although there is no identifiable storyteller who introduces himself as "I" in the text, a distinct narratorial presence can be sensed from the rhythm and syntax of the language.

> The out-of-the-way county in this story has been designated by the Taiwanese provincial government as a developing area. Its urban center is a small town of forty or fifty thousand people. When the town youth are in the presence of people from the outlying country-side, they habitually put on airs of self-importance to show that they are urbanites; the somewhat older people, with their greater understanding of humility, will go no further than to nod their heads with slightly superior smiles on their faces. People from the country-side cheerfully and loudly tell anyone within earshot stories of their daughters who have married men from town. And even though the ears of listeners ring with this barrage of talk, they feel it only proper, for were they to have an eligible young daughter, she too would leave the farm and marry a townsman (so they think). Even greater glory comes to someone whose son brings a townswoman back to the farm as his wife, for no matter how their lives turn out together in the end, at least in the beginning there is a great deal of loud, enthusiastic talk. (12)

The tone of the narrative is relaxed and conversational and suggests an oral storyteller attempting to establish a rapport with his or her audience. A mock storyteller's manner[60] is created through the use of emphatic phrases such as "this story" and parenthetical asides—"(so they think)"—to the audience.[61] By addressing the audience in confidential tones, the narrative conveys a sense of the face-to-face intimacy that suggests the dynamic relationship between an oral storyteller and his or her audience. The description of the village meeting provides a further example of this interaction: "That speech in Mandarin which the village chief gave left our old-timers feeling terribly dissatisfied, simply because they didn't understand a word he said. Next, those three gentlemen also came up on stage and gave speeches, but these, in the eyes of the oldsters, were nothing more than unbearable series of gestures" (25).[62] Phrases such as "*that* speech," "*our* old-timers," and "*those* three gentlemen" help to create a sense of voice that suggests the rhythms of vernacular storytelling.

Hwang's casual, conversational style has earned praise from those who describe him as a "balladeer of the Taiwanese countryside."[63] It has also drawn criticism from those who believe his loose narratives are an indication of his lack of artistry and sophistication.[64] Those who dismiss Hwang as a mere storyteller, however, not only reveal their bias in favor of established literary culture, but are also missing the point. Hwang has amply shown in his stories that he is capable of employing such literary refinements as flashback, shifting points of view, interior monologue, and cinematic effects.[65] His mock storyteller style serves to reinforce the importance of oral traditions—particularly storytelling—in his conception of Taiwanese culture.

In the idealized view of oral cultures, the storyteller is a particularly romanticized figure. In his classic study of oral literature, Albert Lord argues that "from the dawn of human consciousness," singers of oral songs or tales "have been a deeply significant group and have contributed abundantly to the spiritual and intellectual growth of man."[66] Every folk group —every family, village, tribe, nation, or culture—has at its center a storyteller.[67] Whether a "resident tiller of the soil" or a "travelling wayfarer,"[68] the storyteller's function is "to combine the lore of the past with the lore of faraway places, to conserve and deposit into popular memory what has transpired in life and everyday social existence."[69] By preserving human experiences and shaping them through oral performance into shared folk traditions, the storyteller plays a significant role in helping to define a sense of cultural or community identity. Not surprisingly, the narratives of decolonizing Third World nations tend to give prominence to storyteller figures, often elderly men and women to whom the community turns for guidance. Reverence and respect for the aged may characterize many cultures around the globe, but they are particularly important values in the predominantly agrarian societies of the Third World. Unlike industrialized societies, which are often characterized as valuing specialized knowledge and skills that are independent of age, agrarian communities are thought to value the broad knowledge and wisdom that can only be accumulated over years of life experience.

The figure of the old storyteller plays a crucial role in a number of Hwang's rural stories, but is featured most prominently in "Ch'ing Fan Kung's Story" (青番公的故事), a beautiful and moving tale about an old man who recognizes that societal change is on the horizon and fears that the new order will disrupt or eliminate the traditions of the past.[70] Although he understands that change is inevitable, he tries to preserve what he can of folk legacies through storytelling and other forms of oral transmission. An old farmer, Ch'ing Fan Kung loves his land, which has provided him with a rewarding if difficult life. He remembers his youthful years in the village of Wai-ah-wai (歪阿歪) with great fondness and hopes to pass on his rural heritage to his adoring young grandson, Ah-Ming (阿明).[71] By relating stories of his own experiences and sharing traditional legends and folktales, Ch'ing Fan Kung imparts to the boy the values he feels are most important in life.

The story opens with the old man leading Ah-Ming through the ripening fields of rice, patiently instructing the boy in the traditional ways of the farmer. Since one of the characteristics that distinguishes oral societies from literate ones is the organic integration of the human and natural worlds, the old farmer in Hwang's tale is depicted as being closely attuned to his physical environment. Rather than living by abstract clock time, he judges time by natural phenomena.[72] The way to recognize when the grain is ripe, he tells Ah-Ming, is to listen to the sound of the wind blowing through the rice fields: when it produces a sound "like the sudden northwest rain" (3), the grain will be ripe in a week. Ch'ing Fan Kung senses that the traditional agrarian ways of the Taiwanese farmer are threatened by the new industrial culture of the cities, which are beginning to lure young people away from the countryside. It is with a sense of urgency, therefore, that he repeatedly admonishes his grandson to remember his words.

Remember! In the future, whenever you hear the wind blowing through the rice fields, sounding like the sudden northwest rain, you'll be able to calculate it exactly: in one week, it will be time to harvest the grain. Don't ever forget! That's the value of experience. In the future, all these fields will be yours. The others don't want the fields; I know they don't. But as long as you're willing to become a farmer, all this land—from the edge of the embankment to the end of the channel—will be yours. For a farmer, experience is the most important thing. Ah-Ming, do you understand what Grandpa is telling you? (3)

The old farmer's deep attachment to nature and his heartfelt belief in local folk legacies are touchingly apparent when he reminds his grandson to call the scarecrows in the fields brothers so that the birds they are meant to keep away do not overhear and realize that they are being tricked.

"Grandpa!" Ah-Ming had fallen behind and was holding a straw hat in his hand. "The scarecrow's hat fell off!"

"Ssssh!" Ch'ing Fan Kung stopped and turned around to scold the boy. "Don't say 'scarecrow' so loudly! If the sparrows hear you, won't all our hard work have been for nothing? Remember, sparrows are clever little devils. From now on, don't say 'scarecrows' anymore; you should call them 'brothers.' To be a good farmer, experience is the most important thing. You have to begin remembering all the things that I tell you now. In the future, they will be very useful." (4)

Ch'ing Fan Kung's respect for nature is again evident when he warns his grandson against killing any "reed-singing birds," lest he offend the gods of nature and bring disaster on the village. Indeed, he tells the boy never to shoot at any kind of bird: "Ah-Ming, you must remember this. When you are grown, don't ever shoot at birds, especially not at reed-singing birds!" (19).[73] The old farmer tells his grandson about these folk practices because, as he says, "they will be very useful." As Walter Benjamin has argued, it is this desire to instruct—to pass on wisdom or truth—that marks the true storyteller. Every real story, he writes, "contains, openly or covertly, something useful. The usefulness may, in one case, consist in a moral; in another, in some practical advice; in a third, in a proverb or maxim. In every case the storyteller is a man who has counsel."[74] Benjamin draws a significant distinction between the "wisdom" transmitted through oral culture and the "information" that circulates in literate cultures. While knowledge in the form of information is impersonal and objectively verifiable, the wisdom that accumulates over years of lived experience can only be transmitted through human interaction, passed on through the oral tradition from one generation to the next.[75] Unlike information, wisdom is inextricably enmeshed in the lives of those who narrate it. It is, as Benjamin describes it, "counsel woven into the fabric of life . . . the epic side of truth."[76]

It is because he feels he has valuable counsel to share that Ch'ing Fan Kung decides to tell his grandson a bedtime story that night: "Ah-Ming, Grandpa is going to tell you a story," he begins. "I'll tell you only one, and then you'll have to go to sleep, okay?" (7). He gets no further than the first line, however, when Ah-Ming complains impatiently, "Oh Grandpa, you've already told that one." Ch'ing Fan Kung has indeed told this story many, many times but precisely because of the very important lessons it contains.

The old man loved to tell this particular story to children. He felt that its educational value was important and correct. Here is the gist of the story: A young king once ordered that all the old people in the country over the age of fifty be rounded up, taken to a faraway place in the mountains, and abandoned there to die of starvation. The young king believed that old people were useless beings and that letting them live would only be a waste of precious food. There was, however, a filial court minister who decided to keep his two aging parents in a secret part of his house. It just so happened that at this time the country was beset by all kinds of troubles and irresolvable dilemmas. The father of the filial court minister was wise and came up with the answers that solved the nation's problems. From this, the young king learned a lesson; he learned that the experience of older people could be extremely valuable. Therefore, he rescinded the order and reunited all the old people of the country with their sons and daughters. (7)[77]

The legend of the king and the old people teaches two traditional beliefs that Ch'ing Fan Kung feels he must pass on to his grandson: first, that one must respect and care for one's elders; and, second, that experience leads to wisdom. As a Confucian, Ch'ing Fan Kung views filial piety as the most important of human virtues; as a farmer, he knows the value of lived experience. Interestingly, even though Ch'ing Fan Kung does not repeat the legend of the king to Ah-Ming—who has no interest in hearing it again— the narrator of Ch'ing Fan Kung's story does, and he begins by telling the reader "Here's the gist of the story." While Ch'ing Fan Kung's storytelling impulses are frustrated by his unresponsive audience, Hwang Chun-ming's are not. The deliberate inclusion of the folk legend at this point in the story—which contributes nothing to the advancement of the plot— underscores Hwang's determination to preserve traditional oral tales and the important lessons and values they impart.[78]

When Ah-Ming finally falls asleep, Ch'ing Fan Kung finds his mind returning to the past. He recalls his youth, when *his* grandfather lovingly instructed him in the ways of the farmer. Specifically, he remembers the time when the floods came without warning,[79] inundating the land, sweeping away the village of Wai-ah-wai, and drowning everyone in his family—including his beloved grandfather, who sacrificed himself to the rising waters so that Ch'ing Fan Kung might live (10–11). He remembers how, left alone with the barren fields, he had struggled to restore the land's productivity. His vivid memories excite him so much that he cannot resist the urge to tell the story of his youth to his sleeping grandson: "The more he thought about [his past] the more excited the old man became. He didn't feel sleepy at all. He had never been as proud of the struggles of his youth as he was at that moment. Ch'ing Fan Kung couldn't help himself; he had to wake Ah-Ming up, even though it had been so difficult to put the child to sleep only moments before. He was eager to tell the boy about the experiences that had made him proud of his life" (14). These acts of memory and storytelling serve an important function. Through his nostalgic reminiscences of his struggles to restore the productivity of his farmland, Ch'ing Fan Kung reaffirms his love for the land and the traditional agrarian way of life. His wish to share his experiences with his grandson reflects his desire to pass on the rural values and lessons of the past.

As in so many of Hwang Ch'un-ming's rural stories, the ending of "Ch'ing Fan Kung's Story" juxtaposes tradition and modernity, rural and urban. The old man and his grandson travel along the Muddy River to town in order to apply for a government farm loan. Afloat on an old-fashioned bamboo raft, they pass beneath a modern, vehicular bridge. The old man, aware of the conveniences that the bridge has brought to the people of the area, speaks of the modern addition to the rural landscape with pride. At the same time, however, he recognizes the negative implications that the bridge, which ties the village of Wai-ah-wai to the unfamiliar urban culture of the city, has for the traditional agrarian community. It is with nostalgic affection, therefore, that the old man tells his grandson about the days before the bridge, when the only way for people on opposite sides of the river to visit one another was to cross by raft (24).

As their raft passes beneath it, grandfather and grandson notice that a traffic light mixup has resulted in a noisy traffic jam and an angry confrontation between two truck drivers in the middle of the bridge. The clamorous scene presents a stark contrast to the quiet rural setting that Ch'ing Fan Kung and Ah-Ming have just left.

> The scene on the bridge had become chaotic. Both drivers stood there arguing, neither willing to back up. To back a vehicle up for almost half a *li* is not an easy thing to do. Water from melting ice was splashing down from the truck that was rushing a load of fish from the port of Nan-fang-ao to the south. The driver of the other truck, who was transporting a group of rescue workers to an avalanche site on the Su-hua Highway, was also frantic. As for the drivers of the cars behind them, some were honking their horns with malicious glee. The drivers near the front were yelling like they were about to come to blows. Below the bridge, the water of the Muddy River flowed silently, unconcerned.
>
> Ch'ing Fan Kung thrust his pole into the water and steadied the raft. Keeping one eye on the argument on the bridge, he began to tell Ah-Ming a story about the water sprites once thought to have inhabited the Muddy River: "Once upon a time, a very long time ago, there were many, many water sprites living here in the Muddy River. In

order to be reincarnated, the water sprites have to find a human to exchange bodies with. So, you see, these water sprites, they . . ."

No one had told the story of the water sprites for a very long time, not since the bridge had been constructed and people had ceased using rafts. But today, from the mouth of Ch'ing Fan Kung, these water sprites were emerging one by one, reappearing in the form of beauties with bound feet, sitting on the banks of the river, waiting for someone to carry them across the water. (24–25)

Ch'ing Fan Kung revives the Taiwanese rural past through his storytelling, but it is not simply an effort to block out the present. Even as he narrates the legend of the water sprites to his grandson, he keeps one curious eye on the bridge above. He recognizes the inevitability of historical change and perhaps even acknowledges some of its benefits. Nevertheless, he remains nostalgic for a simpler communal existence. More important, he continues to believe in the relevance of traditional cultural practices and values and in the wisdom of indigenous legends and superstitions. These he keeps alive through memory and storytelling.

Oral Culture and Carnivalesque Subversion:
"The Gong"

Hwang Chun-ming has noted on several occasions that most of the characters in his rural stories were inspired by real people he met in his hometown and other small villages in northern Taiwan.[80] He speaks most affectionately of an old village gong beater named Han Ch'in-ts'ai (憨欽仔) —Kam Kim-ah in Taiwanese—the hero of the longest of Hwang's rural stories, "The Gong" (鑼).[81] Like Ch'ing Fan Kung, Kam Kim-ah is steeped in Taiwanese oral culture. He knows all the local legends, folk songs, proverbs, and superstitions and is of course a master storyteller. In fact, he is a man whose very survival depends on his oral skills—for he is the gong-beating town crier in his little village. As the story opens, the old man's job has been rendered obsolete by a new fangled pedicab, complete with loudspeaker, undoubtedly brought in from the nearest city. With his livelihood taken from him, Kam Kim-ah is at first forced to beg and borrow from reluctant shop owners, and even to steal yams and papayas from people's gardens. Soon, however, he decides to join a group of old vagrants who congregate near the village coffin shop and earn their livings by serving as professional mourners at funerals, an occupation that is greatly despised.

The central incident in "The Gong" occurs as Kam Kim-ah, despite his pride and overinflated self-opinion, attempts to secure a place among the vagrants without damaging his superior reputation. He insists that his association with the group is only temporary and rebuts their mocking remarks about how the pedicab "took his rice bowl away" by nonchalantly explaining that he quit because he was tired of dealing with deadbeats who failed to pay him for his services. He soon manages not only to secure a place in the group but also to earn his companions' respect and admiration. His status among the vagrants is attributable in large part to his superior skills in oral performance. Every time he speaks, his colorful and expressive style captures the attention and admiration of the others.

> The smiles that Kam Kim-ah had anticipated appeared on the faces of every man present; not only were they interested in what he was saying, they were also feeling respect for him.
> "Old Kam Kim-ah here is no fool. If beating a gong was such a good life, do you think I'd just hand my ricebowl over to someone else?"
> The others all smiled and nodded their heads.
> As he spoke he was always saying "Kam Kim-ah here, this, that, and the other," and he would thrust out his chest or tug on his sleeve—each sentence was accompanied by some sort of action. Scabby Head and the others, feeling that he was something special, were filled with envy. (78)

The old gong beater's elevated position in the group is further cemented when, on learning that the men are hungry because there has not been a funeral in a long time, he recalls an old wives' tale that says hitting a coffin with a broomstick is a surefire way to drum up funeral business. Kam Kim-ah gallantly volunteers to do the deed and immediately wins the wide-eyed admiration of the others.

That night, however, the deeply superstitious Kam Kim-ah is tormented by guilt, terrified that if the old wives' tale is true and somebody really does pass away during the night he will be held responsible for the death. Lying awake nearly the whole night, he struggles to convince himself that no matter what happens he will not be to blame. The next morning brings word that old and wealthy Scholar Yang has finally succumbed. Though Kam Kim-ah is wracked with guilt, the hungry vagrants celebrate the good news. Expecting a lavish funeral banquet, the old men heartily congratulate Kam Kim-ah on his wisdom. When the feast turns out to be meager, however, the fickle old men turn against him. His strained relationship with the vagrants is dealt a crippling blow when the leaders of the group accuse him of impregnating the village lunatic Crazy Ts'ai

(瘋彩), a pretty young woman whom Kam Kim-ah has lusted after but not touched.

Kam Kim-ah's pride is unexpectedly restored when he is summoned to the district headquarters to make a public announcement regarding property and income taxes. Determined to prove that his services are far superior to those of the pedicab and its loudspeaker, Kam Kim-ah musters all his creative skills and energies for an all-out gong-beating performance. In his overzealous enthusiasm, he performs a wildly embellished "gong song," which, though entertaining for his appreciative audience, ultimately mangles the message he was hired to convey. He loses his job again, this time probably for good. As the story ends, the usually eloquent Kam Kim-ah is so shaken by his dismissal that he can barely finish his rounds, stumbling over his words and finally losing his voice altogether.

The casual, vernacular rhythms of the "mock storyteller" style that characterized "The Drowning of an Old Cat" are even more clearly evidenced in "The Gong." The oral quality of the prologue, for example, is apparent even in translation: "Kam Kim-ah hadn't beaten his gong for some time now, probably eight or nine months, or perhaps even as long as a year. He couldn't remember anymore. In any case, it had been a long, long time. Whenever this fact crossed Kam Kim-ah's mind, his belly filled with anger: here he was, the only practitioner of the unique profession of gong-beating, and to think that nobody came to hire him anymore" (61).[82] The final words of this passage—"here he was, the only practitioner of the unique profession of gong-beating"—clearly reflect Kam Kim-ah's own rather hyperbolic estimation of his worth; while the story's narration uses the third person rather than first, therefore, it seems to be consistently focalized through the consciousness of Kam Kim-ah. Hence, the narrative language manages to capture the colorful expressiveness and loose rambling rhythms of the old gong beater's colloquial and sometimes crude manner of speech. The following passage of narrated monologue, for instance, effectively captures Kam Kim-ah's nostalgia for better days, his foolish arrogance, and his overinflated assessment of his fame and importance in the village community.

Back in the days when Kam Kim-ah's gong was still in use, every third day witnessed a minor event, every fifth day a major one. So among the town's old-timers, he drank wine more frequently than all the others, and sometimes when he had a little money he would even splurge and buy some of the more expensive Shao-hsing wine. And in the matter of names, why, even among people of distinction there was no one whose name carried the weight of Kam Kim-ah's. You had only to say three words, *Kam Kim-ah*, and anyone—man, woman, or child—would immediately know of whom you were speaking. But were you to mention the mayor of the town, Brother Fu-tung, or refer to him, more precisely as the old doctor's grandson, well, old doctor's grandson or not, there was no guarantee that everyone would recognize the name. Yes, in those days Kam Kim-ah could truly lay claim to both fame and fortune. (62)

More than in any of Hwang's other stories, the lively oral culture of the Taiwanese dialect finds revitalized creative expression in "The Gong," which generously incorporates a profusion of Taiwanese phrases, idiomatic expressions, figures of speech, and proverbial sayings, particularly in the colorful dialogue and richly entertaining gong songs that Kam Kim-ah performs.[83] For the Chinese reader, the Taiwanese dialect that peppers the text stands out clearly from the passages of standard Mandarin and helps to authenticate the people, places, and general rural feel of the story. Unfortunately, most of the dialect is lost in translation, but it might be informative to point out a sampling of Taiwanese phrases frequently used in the text, as well as their Mandarin equivalents. For example, the Mandarin terms for *boss* and *woman* are, respectively, *lao-pan* (老闆) and *nu-jen* (女人). In "The Gong," the Taiwanese terms *lao-t'ao-kei* (老頭家) and *tsa-po-lang* (查某人) are used instead. The latter term is part of a purely oral vocabulary and has no corresponding written form. The Chinese characters that Hwang uses to transcribe the term are Mandarin phonetic approximations of the Taiwanese pronunciation, and as such their linguistic difference becomes clearly marked within the text.

Hwang's idiomatic usage of the Taiwanese dialect is featured most prominently in Kam Kim-ah's colorful gong-beating songs, which, when read aloud, rhyme best when Taiwanese pronunciations are used. As with many oral dialects, Taiwanese idioms frequently employ interesting metaphors. For example, consider the following passage from one of the story's three gong songs:

> Laugh? You can laugh after you pay your taxes . . .
> Don't you dare take any chances . . .
> If you don't believe me, see what happens when the time comes;
> if I, Kam Kim-ah, am deceiving you with my words . . .
> I, Kam Kim-ah, will gladly let everyone slap my face . . . (141)

The Taiwanese phrase that has been translated as "don't you dare take any chances" means, literally, "don't have iron teeth" (不要鐵齒), or, less colorfully, "don't be stubborn." The expression "deceiving you with my words" is, in Taiwanese, *kung-pei-ts'at* (講白賊), literally, "to tell a 'white thief.'"

The concrete earthiness of these idioms—as well as the curses, oaths, profanities, and other elements of Taiwanese oral culture incorporated in "The Gong"—is extremely important, not only because it adds realism or authenticity to the story but also because it exemplifies what Mikhail Bakhtin calls the carnivalesque.[84] The concept of the carnivalesque is an integral part of the larger Bakhtinian search for centrifugal, subversive forces of liberation, for a radical counterdiscourse aimed at overturning official culture and the languages of authority,[85] and for a "politics and poetics of transgression."[86] Bakhtin is interested in developing a strategy that dissolves boundaries, pits the subversive energies of the margins (the working classes, popular festivities, utterances, and vernacular speech) against the hegemonic forces of centralization (the ruling elite, official institutions, the language system, and literary discourse) and seeks to destabilize the rigid hierarchies that organize society and culture. He hopes to invert existing aesthetic and moral polarities such as heaven versus earth, mind versus body, and the "high" official discourses of the state and the university versus the "low" popular languages of the peasantry and the urban poor. As part of this anti-authoritarian project, Bakhtin seeks to undermine the canon of officially sanctioned—and in his mind, suffocatingly rigid and artificial—high art by privileging the vital and dynamic forms of low folk traditions. Therefore, the cultural forms he celebrates are those that in his view develop amid the base materiality of everyday life: popular songs, curses, oaths, proverbs, anecdotes, comedies, parodies, and satire.

Bakhtin's desire to recuperate the various forms of popular speech normally excluded from official intercourse leads to a special enthusiasm for what he calls "billingsgate"—the cries and shouts of street vendors, the songs and tales sung by marketplace storytellers, proverbial sayings, curses, profanities, jokes, and other forms of folk humor.[87] Hwang Chunming's "The Gong" owes much of its vitality and humor precisely to its generous incorporation of these particular elements of local folk culture—Taiwanese billingsgate, as it were. In his work as an essayist and documentary filmmaker, Hwang has taken a great interest in exploring various forms of Taiwanese oral culture.[88] He does so because, like Bakhtin, he believes that the popular language of the people is the root of a community's culture, and that the songs, proverbs, curses, and even profanities of the common folk are often the "purest expression" of a nation's culture.[89]

It is significant, therefore, that much of the language in "The Gong" is coarse and much of its humor crude—even scatological—in nature. Bakhtin has argued that the transgressive poetics of the carnivalesque follow the logic of what he calls the "grotesque body"; this he associates with all that is marginal and base, rejecting the spiritual for the physical and deemphasizing the upper body (head and heart) in favor of the "lower bodily-stratum": "the genital organs, the anus and the buttocks, the belly."[90] According to Bakhtin, "the essential principle of grotesque realism is degradation, that is, the lowering of all that is high, spiritual, ideal and abstract; it is a transfer to the material level, to the sphere of earth and body."[91] Carnivalesque literature, therefore, celebrates the body, as well as acts of *carne-lavare*,—eating, drinking, and enjoying sexual pleasures, as well as farting, urinating, and defecating. Much of the humor in Hwang's story centers on physical characteristics and bodily functions. The names by which most of the old vagrants are known, for example, are open acknowledgments of physical or mental disabilities: Scabby Head (臭頭), Blockhead (大呆), One-Eye (獨眼), and Hernia (大囊包). Their conversations are raunchy, full of *shits* and *fucks* and *your mother's*. In addition, several of the scenes are concerned with eating and defecating: Kam Kim-ah tries to ignore the rumbling and growling of his empty belly, he attempts to steal yams and papayas to appease his gnawing hunger, and he squats over a giant cesspool and nearly falls in. When he contemplates taking an indirect route to get where he is going and then rejects the plan, he exclaims: "Taking such a roundabout route just to get to the southgate was like taking your pants off to fart!" (64). As he sheepishly scurries away from one of his debtors and pretends to ignore the shopkeeper, the man yells at him: "You didn't hear me? Hah! Are your ears plugged with shit? . . . You want me to clean them out with a manure spade? Huh?" (81). Sexual desire is also emphasized, as when Kam Kim-ah lustfully daydreams about Crazy Ts'ai. Sometimes acts of bodily elimination and copulation are even confused, as in the scene that finds the old vagrants laughing hysterically when they inadvertently discover who has impregnated the town lunatic.

"Tell us, what did you do with Crazy Ts'ai?"
"Don't. What did I do?" Blockhead stammered. "I . . . I only . . . I only took a piss in her, that's all." (130)

The humor is earthy and coarse but in keeping with an oral folk culture and, according to Bakhtin, the source of the carnivalesque's subversive power.

Another notable feature of "The Gong" is the profusion of proverbs and folk sayings, which are said to be the vessels through which members of an oral community can explain, comprehend, and cope with the problems they encounter in life. Kam Kim-ah and the other old men are all familiar with traditional proverbs, so no matter what situation or topic of conversation should arise they are always ready with a suitable proverbial comment. The old gong beater is particularly adroit in his use of proverbs, and he seems to have an appropriate local saying to respond to any question or situation. In the story, Kam Kim-ah is first inspired to proverbial wisdom when he ventures into Mr. Lam's vegetable patch to steal some papayas. Terrified that the female ghost said to haunt the garden will appear, the old man tries to protect himself by repeating, over and over, a popular saying: "The hungry ghost is king of the ghosts; the full-bellied ghost is startled by the wind" (65). Amusingly enough, after he has stolen the papayas to fill his belly, it is Kam Kim-ah who finds himself "startled by the wind": thinking that the ghost has appeared, he runs screaming from the garden.

While proverbs and folk sayings are often idealized as golden "nuggets of wisdom," this is not the case in Hwang's story. Kam Kim-ah's fondness for proverbial sayings reveals not only his deeply superstitious nature but also the complacent fatalism with which he tends to face life and which ultimately contributes to his downfall. Rather than facing his difficulties and trying to solve the problem at hand, Kam Kim-ah always has a proverbial saying to rationalize the unpleasant situation in which he finds himself.[92] When one of the men to whom he owes money roughs him up, for example, Kam Kim-ah consoles himself by observing: "There's truth to the saying that lightning only strikes good men" (84). After losing his job, the old gong beater is forced to survive on stolen fruits and vegetables. One day when he succeeds, thanks to some fast talking, in buying six pastries and three packs of fancy Long Life cigarettes on credit, he summons up an old Taiwanese expression to account for his good fortune: "He rubbed his slightly protruding belly, now stuffed with pastries and several cups of tea. . . . 'Hai! The old saying is right on the mark: A blade of grass, a drop of dew. Damned if it isn't true—A blade of grass, a drop of dew'" (74). The expression means that there is subsistence for everyone; even a blade of grass will have its drop of dew. Rather than admitting that he will have to find a new job and earn some money to pay his debts and buy food, Kam Kim-ah deludes himself into believing that he will be well taken care of naturally.

Kam Kim-ah also proves to be quite skilled at using proverbs to communicate with other people. When one of the old men asks him for one of his expensive Long Life cigarettes, for instance, he smiles wryly, pats his empty pocket, and asks rhetorically, "Does a chicken with a crooked beak get any of the good feed?" (85). His most adroit applications of proverbial sayings, however, usually concern himself. He outdoes himself, for example, when he cites proverbs to relieve himself of any guilt over the death of Scholar Yang. His guilt is precipitated, of course, by his belief in a local old wives' tale: "If there's no business at the coffin shop, all you have to do is strike a coffin three times with a broom, and the next day someone will come over to buy a coffin" (91–92). Having done the deed, Kam Kim-ah tosses and turns half the night until he finally comforts himself with yet another saying: "A happy thought suddenly struck him: if it's not the first watch, it must be the second by now, and I haven't heard the crow of a rooster. 'The first and second watches signal death, the third and fourth signal happy events,' and that's right. That thought led to another: I haven't killed anyone, I haven't" (107).

There are other instances in which Kam Kim-ah employs proverbial sayings not to comfort himself but in order to lend an air of authority to the things he says. As communally shared beliefs, proverbs are thought to convey a greater degree of truth. When asked by the old vagrants why he no longer beats his gong, for example, he tries to gain acceptance by flattering them while complaining about the ingratitude of his former customers: "'If everyone was as good as you fellows, we'd never have to talk about conscience,' Kam Kim-ah said to the others. 'There's nothing false about what the ancients said: There are two men of conscience: he who has died and he who hasn't been born'" (77).

This particular scene is one of many interesting moments in "The Gong" when the act of oral performance is highlighted. Kam Kim-ah is an excellent storyteller who takes pride in his oral skills and always relishes having the attention and admiration of an enthusiastic audience. He knows that it is his oral creativity and idiosyncratic storytelling style that has won him respect among the old vagrants and that his status in the village as a whole is also tied to his linguistic virtuosity. After his encounter with the ghost in Mr. Lam's garden, for instance, the old gong beater's popularity soars for a time. The townspeople gather nightly at his home in the air raid shelter to listen to his story. Each time he repeats it, he embroiders and embellishes the tale in response to questions from his audience. He proves his improvisational skills in the following lively and animated account of his ghostly encounter, which he performs for a group of excited young children.

"Was her tongue this long?" a child asked, sticking his tongue as far out as it would go.

"That's nothin'!" Kam Kim-ah put his hand on a level with his navel and said: "It came down to here, all the way down to her belly button."

"Wow!" The child's face grew pinched and small, though his staring eyes were larger than ever.

"Her . . . her . . ." Another child wanted to ask something. "Whew! I'm afraid to say it."

"He wants to know what the ghost's eyes looked like." One of the other kids said it for him.

"Her eyes! Wa! They were this big." He made circles with his fingers the size of eyeglass lenses. "But I couldn't see the pupils—the eyes were all white, with blood-red lines running through them."

"When she walked, did she float above the ground?"

"Of course she did!"

"Were her nails long?"

"This long. And there was poison on every one of them. Any place they touched a person it turned to blood."

"Aiyo! Weren't you scared?"

"Me? Not too scared. If I had been, she would have snatched me away then and there!" (69)

The description of Kam Kim-ah's interactive give-and-take with his audience highlights one of the primary differences between oral storytelling and written narrative—that storytelling necessitates communication and face-to-face contact while both writing and reading are activities that can be done in isolation. The bond between storyteller and audience reinforces the strong sense of community that characterizes oral cultures and that so many mourn as lacking in literate societies.

Kam Kim-ah's greatest oral performances are the gong songs he composes as he walks up and down the village streets. Two of the three performances included in the story are the old gong beater's memories of better times, before the village began to be urbanized and when his oral skills were still appreciated. He is proud of his performances and the vital services he performed for the village community, such as helping an anxious mother find her lost child.

Bong! Bong! Bong!
   "The gong-beater's coming your way . . .
   "Listen everyone, here's what I have to say . . .
   "A child, his name is Ah-Hsiung . . .
   "Three years old, but really only two . . .

"His eyes big as flower buds, cute as a bug's ear; barefoot, black open-crotch pants, a white shirt . . .

"Anyone seeing him take him to the police station right away . . .

"Or to the quilt shop beside the Temple of the Patriarch . . .

"Ah-Hsiung's mother is on pins and needles . . ."

Bong! Bong! Bong! (96)

Another time, Kam Kim-ah was responsible for making sure the whole village heard about an important religious festival at the local temple:

Bong! Bong! Bong!

"The gong-beater's coming your way . . .

"Listen everyone, here's what I have to say . . .

"A call for all pilgrims at the Ch'i-ting Temple of the Patriarch . . .

"Tomorrow afternoon at two o'clock . . .

"Fire dancers will be there, tallies will be drawn . . ."

Bong! Bong! Bong! (114–15)

Kam Kim-ah's final assignment, to alert the villagers that property and income taxes are due, does not seem to him nearly as important a contribution as helping to find a lost child or announcing a Buddhist festival. After all, the simple country folk of the village have little comprehension of the importance of paying income taxes (140). Nevertheless, Kam Kim-ah is grateful for the opportunity to resume his position as the town crier and carries out the task with extra enthusiasm. Determined to prove once and for all that the impersonal broadcasting of the pedicab is no match for his intimate delivery and oral flair, the old gong beater gives it his all, stretching his imagination to the limits to give this oral performance added color and zest.

"The gong-beater's coming your way . . .

"Listen everyone, here's what I have to say . . .

"This year's propriety tax and income tax . . .

"Are due at the end of the month . . .

"If it has not been paid . . .

"You know how this government office is: they'll come down on you like a chicken butcher . . ."

"You people may have never slaughtered a chicken, but you've seen others do it . . . it's no laughing matter . . .

"When the time comes, if I, Kam Kim-ah, have lied to you . . ."

Bong! Bong! Bong! Three more beats of the gong.

"I, Kam Kim-ah, will let you cut off my head and use it as a chair . . ."

(141–42)

The villagers love Kam Kim-ah's comic announcement. A cheering, laughing crowd soon gathers around him, and the old gong beater's heart nearly bursts with joy. Much to his surprise, however, the official from the district headquarters angrily orders him to stop his gong beating. The implication here, of course, is that the young bureaucrat, already too far removed from the life world of oral culture, cares only about the concise and efficient delivery of government information. He has little appreciation for Kam Kim-ah's entertainingly creative digressions and earthy humor. Stunned by the official's reprimand, Kam Kim-ah can barely stammer out the rest of the announcement, then loses his voice altogether.

The inability of the government official to appreciate the value of Kam Kim-ah's improvisational performance again underscores the distance separating the Mandarin-language culture of Chinese officialdom and the traditional oral culture of the Taiwanese country folk. This clash of cultural values can be seen, for example, in Kam Kim-ah's miscomprehension of the announcement he is hired to make. The official from the district headquarters gives him his instructions.

> "Okay, then you just announce that this year's property tax and income tax are due by the end of the month."
> "Yes, yes, I understand: the propriety tax and . . ." (137)

The misunderstood words are slightly different in the Chinese original, but Howard Goldblatt's translation provides an excellent illustration of the fundamental differences between modern urban values and traditional rural concepts. The idea of a property tax may be comprehensible to an urbanite who understands the concept of individual ownership, but it has little relevance to village folk such as Kam Kim-ah. The concept of propriety, on the other hand, is readily understood by someone steeped in traditional Confucian beliefs.

Kam Kim-ah's defeat by the modern, loudspeaker-equipped pedicab—which in the old man's mind is destined to "destroy the social fabric" of the village (62)—represents a tragedy commonplace in traditional societies threatened by the forces of modernization and urbanization.[93] His ultimate failure can also be seen as a sad comment on the fate of indigenous oral cultures in the modern world of technology. Kam Kim-ah, once so proud and articulate, is reduced to unintelligible mumblings after being scolded by the government official. By now his voice "had become a wail. He fought hard to enunciate each and every word, but it was impossible. . . . His voice was quivering so badly that the words were unintelligible, although his mouth continued to move as if he were still speaking, he opened and closed it with great effort. Before long there were no more sounds, but by reading his lips, the onlookers could pretty much tell that he was saying, over and over: 'I, Kam Kim-ah . . . I, Kam Kim-ah'" (145). Kam Kim-ah's loss of voice portends the decline of the native Taiwanese dialect and its rich oral culture. Like him, it must struggle to maintain and assert its unique identity—"I, Kam Kim-ah . . . I, Kam Kim-ah." It is precisely this desire to forestall the decline of Taiwanese oral culture in the face of foreign influences that compels Hwang Chun-ming, like so many other hsiang-t'u writers, to incorporate the vocabulary and rhythms of the native dialect, as well as its widely varied forms of oral expression, into his writing.

Speaking in Tongues: Bilingualism, Translation, and Postcoloniality

For a bilingual writer like Hwang Chun-ming, whose polyglot linguistic status is a by-product of the forces of colonialism, the choice of language always involves both personal and political considerations. On the one hand, the personal concerns of commercial viability—the need to reach a broad book-buying readership—may compel him to write in the dominant, officially sanctioned language. On the other hand, he might be drawn by his emotional attachment and political commitment to his native culture to use his mother tongue. As a result, the bilingual subject is often depicted as a divided voice, perpetually adrift between competing languages and hence characterized by "linguistic madness."[94] The problem with this oppositional binary conception of bilingualism, however, is that it marginalizes the writer from the center of both language cultures, leaving him or her in a state of paralysis and powerlessness. Within the colonial hierarchy, the writer who chooses his or her native tongue exclusively is shut off from mainstream culture and made to feel inferior and inadequate. One who chooses to write in the dominant language, on the other hand, experiences the guilt of political compromise and often feels like a traitor to his or her native culture and people.

The hero of Hwang Chun-ming's "Sayonara, Ts'ai-chien" (莎喲哪啦, 再見), is a bilingual subject who finds himself in precisely such a predicament.[95] This bitingly satirical story is Hwang Chun-ming's most polemical attack on colonial and neocolonial forces in Taiwan; the target of his critique is historical Japanese colonial oppression of the island and its continuing economic and cultural imperialism. The protagonist, a certain Mr. Hwang, is a young man employed by a Taiwanese company that has close business ties with the Japanese. Because of his fluency in Japanese, Hwang is asked by his superiors to help entertain seven visiting Japanese businessmen. The job he is assigned to do, however, is an "onerous affair" (17) that precipitates Hwang's internal agony, a "painful psychological struggle" (218) that fills him with shame and guilt: much to his dismay, he is asked to take the Japanese men "whoring around with some of my countrywomen" (217). As if playing the pimp were not degrading enough, Hwang is asked to take the Japanese to the hot springs in Chiao-hsi (礁溪), his hometown (220). The entire narrative is in the first person, the bitter and angry confession of a self-described Taiwanese patriot who feels that his actions constitute a betrayal of his family and his nation.[96]

Hwang is particularly ashamed to be prostituting his own country-women because in his view such actions only help to perpetuate the subordination of the Taiwanese nation and reinforce the superiority and power of imperialist nations like Japan. In fact, his theory is that the cheap availability of a country's women is an indisputable indication of its backwardness and inferior status (223). To underscore his point, he cites examples of countries in South America where fourteen-year-old girls can be bought for the "exact price of a cup of coffee in one of those big hotels."[97] On a psychological level, he argues, Taiwan is still a Japanese colony, not only because its women are sold cheaply to Japanese men but also because of the deep penetration into Taiwanese society and culture of Japan's economic and cultural imperialism. As they drive through the countryside on their way to Chiao-hsi, for instance, the Japanese men note how similar the Taiwanese landscape is to Japan's while the song on the radio is "yet another Chinese rendition of a popular Japanese tune" (234). Finally, as one of the men points out to a chagrined Mr. Hwang, the effects of cultural imperialism are evidenced in the young man's "perfectly fluent Japanese."

The bilingual young man's guilt and embarrassment over his fluency in an oppressor's language at first causes him terrible discomfort in his role as translator. Even though he knows it is his job to translate for the Japanese businessmen and the Taiwanese prostitutes they hire, he finds it unbearable to have to translate everything they say—every lewd comment, every inane piece of small talk. When he finally becomes fed up, he refuses to translate any more and instead teaches the Japanese and the girls a few selected phrases of the others' language and tells them to fend for themselves. The comical exchanges that ensue, as the girls mock and insult the Japanese without their knowing it, make Mr. Hwang realize for the first time that his bilingualism puts him not in a position of submission and ambivalent loyalty but in a position of power. He takes full advantage of this opportunity to turn the tables on the imperialist exploiters. Assuring the prostitutes that the Japanese cannot understand a word they are saying, he encourages them to charge more for their services. When the girls set their price at four hundred dollars for the Japanese, Hwang translates their request, saying loudly to the men, "One thousand for the night," adding, "and that's not a bad price!" (247).

At the end of the story, Mr. Hwang parlays his fluency in two languages into an opportunity to lecture and shame not only the Japanese businessmen but also a Chinese university student they meet on the train. Hwang is annoyed at the young student's blind admiration for and deference toward the Japanese and is suddenly inspired to use his position as a linguistic intermediary "to hurl a few barbs at the Japanese and teach my young friend a lesson at the same time" (262). Rather than being faithful in his translations, therefore, he launches his own attacks. Hwang tells the student, who is hoping to travel to Japan to study Chinese literature, that the Japanese are college professors and "translates" their astonishment that he would want to study Chinese culture in Japan. He further conveys their disappointment that young Chinese continue to view their own country as inferior to Japan and America: "It's strange that if your own people say something, it's like a fart in the wind, but if a foreigner says the same thing, it's like a message from the gods" (268). To the Japanese businessmen, he says that the student is researching Chinese history and wants to ask them about the eight-year war of resistance against Japan. By doing so, he forces the Japanese into a discussion of Japanese atrocities against the Chinese people and an acknowledgment of their own participation in the violence. In the end, Hwang manages to shame both parties into an uncomfortable silence. Even though he remains guilty of pimping his countrywomen to the Japanese, he scores a minor victory by finding, through his bilingualism, the subversive potential in a difficult predicament. Rather than limiting himself to choosing one language or the other, Hwang embraces both and plays their linguistic differences against one another to the advantage of his countrymen. He exemplifies the postcolonial subject who has discovered, as one critic put it, "how to write two languages simultaneously, how to write a life lived between languages."[98]

Toward Heteroglossia: Taiwanese New Cinema and the Language Issue

This possibility of embracing multiple languages rather than being subservient to one is an idea that is taken up and further explored by Taiwanese New Cinema. Like the hsiang-t'u literature from which it drew inspiration, Taiwanese cinema of the 1980s was also deeply concerned with the island's colonial heritage and the resultant polyglot nature of contemporary society. The transposition of linguistic issues from the medium of literature to that of film, however, altered the debate over the relationship between language, power, and national identity in significant ways. For example, Taiwanese New Cinema's assumption of the linguistic battles waged by hsiang-t'u literature against the island's dominant literary culture offered many advantages. As a medium that is both aural and visual, the cinema greatly facilitated hsiang-t'u's project of rejuvenating the Taiwanese dialect and recapturing elements of indigenous oral culture, restoring some of the concrete immediacy of communication that champions of oral culture value so highly. While Hwang Chun-ming and other hsiang-t'u authors had to struggle with the difficulties of attempting to write in a dialect that is primarily oral, Taiwanese filmmakers—who could record spoken dialect or any type of oral performance, whether songs, operas, or storytelling, directly onto a film's soundtrack—largely avoided such complications. As a medium with multiple channels of communication, film is also far more conducive than written literature to foregrounding the dynamic interplay of languages in a heteroglossic postcolonial society such as Taiwan's. In addition to incorporating multiple languages within the diegetic world of a film (including dialogue in Mandarin and Taiwanese, for example), the tension between different sociolinguistic worlds can further be conveyed through the use of Chinese subtitles—which create a kind of dissonance in the viewing experience comparable to the glossing of Taiwanese phrases in hsiang-t'u literature. The advantage of having both an aural soundtrack and written subtitles to work with enabled Taiwanese New Cinema filmmakers to reach a far broader and linguistically diverse audience than Hwang and his colleagues ever could. While the impact of hsiang-t'u literature was limited to a relatively small and educated readership, Taiwanese New Cinema, by virtue of its direct visual mode of signification as well as its use of Taiwanese on the soundtrack, was accessible to a wider range of socioeconomic groups.

As was true of hsiang-t'u literature, the incorporation of the Taiwanese dialect and other regional tongues into filmmaking is considered to be one of New Cinema's major breakthroughs. Until the release of the watershed film *His Son's Big Doll* in 1983, the local dialect was seldom if ever used in cinematic dialogue.[99] Instead, all characters—regardless of age, region, class, occupation, or educational level—spoke in standard Mandarin. Indeed, characters whose Mandarin was thickly accented with Taiwanese inflections (臺灣國語) were automatically understood to be socially inferior, buffoonish figures.[100] If Taiwanese dialect was used at all, it was used sparingly and invariably only for comic effect. *His Son's Big*

Doll was the first film to be distributed with its dialogue dubbed entirely in Taiwanese. The ideological significance of this choice was not lost on the government or cultural critics. While vast numbers of liberal-minded Taiwanese intellectuals rushed to support the film and praise the realism of its dialogue, the film had trouble passing the government censorship board and drew criticism from those who felt the use of Taiwanese was a thinly veiled attack on Mandarin and hence an attack on all mainlanders.

Language preference and political affiliation, of course, are not clearly and inevitably linked,[101] so use of the Taiwanese dialect in hsiang-t'u literature and Taiwanese New Cinema need not be read as an expression of anti-Mandarin or antimainland sentiments. On the other hand, this type of interpretation, which reduces the island's linguistic situation to a simple binary of opposites, has in fact been encouraged by many of hsiang-t'u literature's most ardent polemicists. The militant neonativists of the 1990s, in particular, have uncompromisingly linked their promotion of an autonomous literature in Taiwanese with the island's political independence.[102] The Taiwanese New Cinema directors influenced by hsiang-t'u literature of the 1960s and 1970s, however, adopted a less exclusionary, more complex view of language, challenging the essentialist idea of a linguistically defined nation through a more careful examination of the diversity of linguistic usage within the particulars of social interaction. The incorporation of Taiwanese and other dialects in New Cinema might better be seen as an acknowledgment of the linguistic and cultural complexity of a modern society shaped by a history of colonization, political turmoil, mass migration, and rapid socioeconomic change. The characters in Hou Hsiao-hsien's films, for instance, do not speak Taiwanese exclusively. Rather, they use several Chinese dialects—Mandarin, Taiwanese, Hakka, Cantonese, and Shanghainese—naturalistically and in a manner appropriate to the specific social context of the dialogue, as well as to the age, occupation, and educational level of each character. In *A Time to Live and a Time to Die*, for example, the three different dialects spoken by the characters correspond to three socio-ideological worlds and to three phases in the lives of the young protagonists, three different stages in their social and civic education. As young children, they speak Hakka (客家, the dialect of their mainlander parents) in the intimacy of the familial environment. As they get a bit older and begin to venture outside the home, they speak Taiwanese with their friends in the village. The schools, however, teach them Mandarin—the unifying official language that inaugurates them into society and molds them into cultured, civilized citizens. The further along the children are in the educational system, therefore, the more they seem to be shaped by Mandarin-language culture. Nearly without exception, the children use

Mandarin whenever they discuss their progress in school with their parents. The oldest child, a daughter of high-school age, speaks Mandarin almost exclusively. Mandarin, then, functions as the language of maturity, the mark of one's entrance into the symbolic order of Taiwanese society. It is, notably, the language used by the adult protagonist, who narrates his childhood memories in the voice-overs that frame the film.

The effects of both political and cultural colonization on linguistic practice in Taiwan are also addressed in several of Hou's other films. *City of Sadness* is particularly explicit in its commentary. Early in the film, the colonial education system under the Japanese is highlighted by a scene in which young Taiwanese schoolchildren join their Japanese teacher, Shizuko (靜子), in singing a traditional Japanese folk song, "Akatonbo," which expresses a yearning for motherly love and a nostalgic longing for home. The bitter irony of the scene, of course, is that the homeland to which the song refers is Japan, a country that is not home at all to the Taiwanese children but a country they have never even visited. Postliberation residues of Japanese colonial education are apparent throughout the film. For example, several Taiwanese continue to use the Japanese names they were given during the Occupation, and even the less educated characters instinctively use many Japanese words and phrases—especially polite social niceties—in their everyday conversation. Hou himself has said that one of his chief objectives in incorporating so many different languages and dialects—Mandarin, Taiwanese, Cantonese, Shanghainese, and Japanese—into the film was to realistically capture the linguistic confusion and complexity of those immediate postwar years, as mainlanders from many regions of China converged on Taiwan and threw the island's sociolinguistic world into chaos.[103]

Taiwan's subsequent colonization by Mandarin-language culture is similarly underscored in several of Hou's films. After the Kuomintang takeover in 1945, Mandarin took the place of Japanese as the official language of the island, a fact alluded to in a revealing scene from *Dust in the Wind* when the father of the young male protagonist urges him to continue his education and laments his own lack of educational opportunity. He was in elementary school, he says, when the "liberation" came, and the subsequent change of government ruined his chances for a decent education. He complains that "Japanese syllables changed to Chinese syllables (あいうえお碰到ㄅㄆㄇㄈ) . . . and my whole education was suddenly a total waste (讀了跟沒讀一樣)!" Linguistic difference also becomes the mark of political antagonism, as the Taiwanese rebels depicted in *City of Sadness* use the test of language to identify their mainland Chinese enemies. Unlike native islanders, mainlanders were distinguished by their inability to speak either Taiwanese or Japanese, and Taiwanese

13. In *City of Sadness*, Taiwanese rebels use the test of language to identify their mainland Chinese enemies, who can speak neither Taiwanese nor Japanese.

rebels frequently interrogated their captives in those languages to determine their backgrounds. As in a number of Hwang Chun-ming's stories,[104] many of Hou's films are critical of the growing influence of American culture and the English language—which has been taught as a mandatory second language in Taiwanese schools since just after World War II —in Taiwanese society. The children in *A Time to Live and a Time to Die*, for example, sing an amusing song as a way of memorizing English words and phrases such as "come," "go," "one dollar," "I love you," and "I don't know." They represent a generation of Taiwanese whose cultural consciousness is increasingly being molded by American pop music— which dominates the soundtrack of *Daughter of the Nile*—and by American consumer brands such as Timex (*Dust in the Wind*) and Kentucky Fried Chicken (*Daughter of the Nile*).[105]

Like their counterparts in literature, many Third World filmmakers have responded to the threat of American cultural imperialism with a renewed interest not only in indigenous dialects but also in traditional oral culture. Diverse forms of oral folk culture—storytelling, folk wisdom, and traditional music and ritual—are frequently highlighted in Third World films as alternatives to the modes of knowledge and communication engendered by colonization and modernization.[106] Examples from Afro-Caribbean filmmaking include Sergio Giral's *The Other Francisco*, Tomas Gutierrez Alea's *The Last Supper*, and Euzhan Palcy's *Sugar Cane Alley*, which all incorporate African music and dance and the telling of traditional African proverbs and stories as part of their strategy to challenge and subvert Western interpretations of slavery. Hou Hsiao-hsien similarly foregrounds indigenous folk culture and the oral tradition in his films, devoting a great deal of attention to the depiction of traditional ritualistic practices. *City of Sadness*, for instance, features long and detailed sequences depicting numerous folk rituals. Near the beginning of the film, an elaborate celebration—complete with incense, firecrackers, and a bountiful feast—marks the opening of a new business. Later the wedding of Bun-ching and Hiromi and the funeral of Bun-heung are depicted with equally loving and meticulous attention to ceremonial details. Another film, *Dust in the Wind*, contains a brief exorcism scene. In many of his films, Hou also incorporates folk songs to great emotional and symbolic effect. Most notably, he highlights oral performance itself, not only in his frequent use of intimate voice-over narration but also in the long passages of storytelling and improvisational monologues in which he allows his characters—particularly the grandparent figures—to indulge. His 1993 *The Puppetmaster*, which relies almost wholly on Taiwanese puppeteer Li T'ien-lu's oral recollections of his life (narrated in both in voice-over and directly to the camera) to paint a portrait of Taiwan during the Japanese Occupation, is the best example of this strategy. From the seemingly aimless ramblings of the grandfathers and grandmothers in Hou's films come tales of ancestry, anecdotes of history, proverbs, and nuggets of folk wisdom that together constitute the strength and wealth of Taiwanese popular memory and are meant to represent an alternative to modern modes of understanding.[107] Hou's interest in folk traditions and oral culture is nostalgic, to be sure, but not entirely uncritical, demonstrating that resisting domination by Western culture is not simply a matter of embracing tradition over modernity or of choosing a native language and culture over a foreign tongue but of striving toward a more critical understanding of the complex dynamics that shape their relationship.

Third Cinema and the Search for an Alternative Visual Language

In the Taiwanese struggle for cultural self-definition, the transposition of linguistic issues from the written medium of hsiang-t'u literature to the visual medium of Taiwanese New Cinema had other, more complex ramifications as well. If modern thinking about national and cultural boundaries has traditionally been dominated by the differences between verbal languages, then postmodern conceptions of nationhood will undoubtedly need to take into account other symbolic modes, particularly the audiovisual media technologies that are radically reconfiguring the globe and changing the ways communities are imagined. It has commonly been observed, for example, that ours is an era increasingly grounded in *visuality*, where our imaginings of ourselves and others are dominated less by the written word than by the visual image—movies, advertising imagery, music videos, and simultaneously broadcast news images. In her recent study of contemporary cinema from the People's Republic of China, Rey Chow describes the modern/postmodern era in which we live as a world in which the literary is on the wane and in which "the discourse of technologized visuality" has become increasingly important.[108] More specifically, Chow sees the centralizing power and position of authority traditionally associated with the written word and literary culture now shifting dramatically to technologies of the visual. She writes, for instance, of the growing "menace of vision and visuality" and "the foreboding of the soon-to-be-realized, all-encompassing force of the visual image in modern and post-modern culture, when entire nations, histories, and peoples are to be exposed, revealed, captured on the screen, made visible as images; when visuality is to become the law of knowledge and the universal form of epistemological coercion."[109] In other words, visual languages are becoming the new hegemonies of our age. Moreover, their positions of authority in the postcolonial world are reflected in their inheritance of structures of power established by the (verbal) imperial languages of an earlier era. As Chow points out, contemporary studies of the visual culture of postcoloniality tend to reinforce those traditional models of European cultural hegemony that set up First World/Third World relationships in binary models of conquest and possession.[110] Such models define the visual "gaze" as fundamentally Western (the "spectator,") and the object of that gaze (the "spectacle") as fundamentally non-Western.[111]

Again, while binary cultural paradigms like these are flawed by reductive thinking and deeply ingrained biases, they have proven to be very useful from both the practical and polemical points of view and have been extremely influential among First World cultural theorists and Third World cultural practitioners alike. Binarisms like these often produce, as we have seen, models of resistance that also rely on oppositional pairings. Hence, Chow argues that the new global hegemonies of specifically Western forms of visuality—the visual language of Western cinema, for instance—have given rise in non-Western cultures to forms of resistance that attempt to counter, repudiate, or deny that dominant visuality.[112] It is not surprising, then, that since resistance to linguistic homogenization is a central theme of Taiwanese New Cinema the search for film languages that resist the dominant visual language of Western cinema has also been an important concern. This quest for alternative cinematic languages has of course been a critical objective of "new" cinematic movements elsewhere in the world as well. In cinema studies, the hegemonic visual language against which "alternative" film movements worldwide have reacted is widely understood to refer to the type of cinematic articulation codified by Hollywood during its golden age (between 1930 and 1960) and by its national-industrial imitations around the world: "American-style movie-making at its most orthodox commercial manifestation as mainstream studio entertainment."[113] Whether described as the "institutional mode of Representation"[114] or "classical Hollywood cinema,"[115] it is an almost universally understood and globally replicated code of moving imagery, production process, and industrial organization. The Hollywood film, then, is generally understood to be a studio-based production that adheres, by and large, to an established filmic syntax whose origins can be traced back to D. W. Griffith's codification of continuity editing. Usually, it is a high-budget spectacle aimed at a mass audience that features big stars, insists on the rapid and complicated manipulation of time and space through "transparent" editing conventions, emphasizes the logical and concise linear progression of dramatic action, and encourages the emotional identification of the audience with the characters—especially an individual hero or heroine. Its institutionalization as a standard of cinematic discourse worldwide puts it in a position of power directly comparable to that of an imperial language. As one film historian notes, "Hollywood, the supranational institutionalized discourse of economic, representational, and social exchange, functions and is recognized as a language of central administration. That is to say, it is a language of power. . . . It is functionally analogous to the King's English, High German, Central Thai, and Examination Chinese in their respective periods and, following this analogy, we might call this discourse the royal code of moving pictures."[116]

Theories of "resistance" cinema, therefore, tend to support modes of filmmaking that deliberately reject the institutional structures, production practices, and cinematic syntax associated with Hollywood. These include, of course, most national cinema movements, which, like Teshome Gabriel's notion of Third Cinema, tend to fall back on binary models to identify characteristics that distinguish the language of Third Cinema from the dominant language of commercial filmmaking. Gabriel's rigorous model exemplifies both the advantages and the pitfalls of such dichotomous cultural paradigms. Intended primarily as a descriptive rather than a prescriptive model, his dichotomy is founded on a belief that Western cultures (based on print or literate cultural forms) and non-Western ones (based on folk or oral cultural traditions) are characterized by fundamentally different conceptions of time and space and of how the human, the social, and the natural worlds coexist within these dimensions. These different time-space articulations result, he argues,[117] in fundamentally oppositional narrative rhythms and visual images in Western and non-Western cinemas: "Where western films manipulate time over space, Third World films seem to emphasize space over time."[118]

Reductive though it may be, Gabriel's binary model is alluring precisely because it is so simple and concise. It also happens to offer many useful insights that can lead to a better understanding of Third World films, as an impressive number of works of non-Western cinema can be found to provide convincing illustrations for his arguments. This is not to disregard, of course, the number of difficulties his proposal for a unifying "Third Aesthetics" raises. First, of course, is the problem of defining Third Cinema exclusively in terms of its difference from Euro-American cinema—Third Cinema is *non*-Western cinema. In Gabriel's paradigm, the West retains its centrality as the standard by which the Third World's otherness is measured. Again, Hollywood may be the primary other against which national cinema movements in the Third World are reacting, but by no means is it the only one. National cinemas are also shaped by their relationships with other arts—past or present—within their own cultures. Another problem with a model like Gabriel's is the consequent homogenization of Third World films into a single unified aesthetic. Not only are differences between the many nations and cultural traditions of the Third World elided but the diversity of cultural production within each nation is left unrecognized. As Paul Willemen has pointed out, the original Latin American manifestos of Third Cinema refused to prescribe a specific aesthetics or identify a particular formal strategy as the correct mode for socially conscious filmmaking, insisting that Third Cinema is "an open category," an "experimental cinema."[119] It "can make use of the documentary or the fictional mode, or both. It can use whatever genre, or all genres."[120] Their main criterion for Third Cinema was that it lead to an analytically informed understanding of social formations and hence open the way toward change.

Nevertheless, Third Cinema theorists also fell into the trap of defining the aesthetics of Third Cinema primarily in terms of their opposition to the dominant cinemas of Europe and America. Like the new cinema movements in Brazil and other Latin American countries associated with Third Cinema, Taiwanese New Cinema also has been considered new precisely because it challenges the Hollywood-style conventions of Taiwanese commercial cinema, opening filmmaking up to more daring formal experimentation.[121] Director Edward Yang, for example, took an explicitly oppositional stance vis-à-vis institutionalized filmmaking when he declared: "I want to challenge contemporary Taiwanese cinema, to shatter the ossified traditions of filmmaking."[122]

Italian Neorealism and Third Cinema

This notion of "oppositional" filmmaking is important because from the beginning Third Cinema in Latin America was influenced by revolutionary cinematic currents in Europe that also were, in part, precipitated by anxieties over encroachments by foreign—notably American—cultures: movements such as Italian neorealism and British ideas about the social documentary.[123] The parallels that Italian neorealism offers to Third Cinema in general and Taiwanese New Cinema in particular are striking, both in terms of its historical significance as a cinematic movement and in terms of its stylistic characteristics. Italian neorealism flourished, after all, during a turbulent period in Italian history when the country was occupied by a succession of foreigners—first German Fascists and then the Allied troops that came to liberate Italy.[124] These experiences and the sociocultural upheavals that accompanied Italy's postwar modernization set the stage for the emergence of a cinematic trend that sought to capture the specific social, moral, and psychological atmosphere of its historical moment. Like Taiwanese New Cinema—and like the Third Cinemas of Latin America and Africa—Italian neorealism remained primarily an art cinema, favored by intellectuals but not by the mass public.[125] Its rise during the postwar period was also aided—ironically for a cinema insistently focused on Italian realities—by a creative encounter with films and film theory from foreign countries, particularly France and the Soviet Union.[126]

The typical list of production and stylistic innovations associated with Italian neorealism has by now become familiar: eschewing the glamour and glossy perfection of big-budget commercial filmmaking in favor of a sparer and low-cost artisanal cinema, removing the economic pressure and hence increasing the director's creative freedom, shooting on location rather than on studio soundstages, using lesser-known actors or even nonprofessionals to tell ordinary stories about ordinary people doing everyday things, using the long take rather than conventional editing in order to maintain spatial integrity and allow events to unfold at their own pace, and using the visual complexity of deep focus to exploit the possibilities of the mise-en-scène. What is illuminating about this list is how deeply it resonates with discussions of Third Cinema in general and Taiwanese New Cinema in particular. Teshome Gabriel, for instance, has identified the use of nonprofessional actors, location shooting, and the long take as some of the most significant stylistic markers of Third Cinema.[127] Nearly all of these aesthetic strategies are also among the innovative and unconventional formal characteristics that separate Taiwanese New Cinema from Taiwanese commercial films.[128] While their departure from established Hollywood techniques marks these characteristics as strategies of resistance, many of the formal strategies associated with Taiwanese New Cinema were also, as both Hou Hsiao-hsien and his frequent collaborator Chu T'ien-wen attest, partly pragmatic decisions; lack of access to and funding for studio facilities, proper equipment and trained actors, for example, led to the use of location shooting and non-professionals.[129] Eventually, however, a strategy born of necessity developed into an aesthetics increasingly articulated by filmmakers and critics alike.

In one of the earliest theoretical essays associated with Italian neorealist filmmaking, Luchino Visconti made an eloquent plea for a new, humanistic cinema in which "the most humble gesture of a man, his face, his hesitations and his impulses, impart poetry and life to the things which surround him and to the setting in which they take place."[130] It is a description that might well be used to characterize the cinema of Hou Hsiao-hsien. Like the Italian neorealists, Hou is interested in discovering the human drama and poignancy of banal objects and daily incidents. His films exhibit a faith in the inherent beauty of simple gestures, glances, or even no significant action at all—allowing for the emergence of the poetry of the everyday. Unlike commercial action films and romances, Hou's films contain little drama in the conventional sense of the word. Since they seldom follow a single dramatic action through a logical progression of exposition, development, climax, and denouement, there are no tense chase scenes, no meaningful love scenes, no cathartic emotional confrontations, and no climactic fights. Human events that have the greatest potential for drama—such as birth and death—are handled quietly and in long shots or take place completely offscreen.[131] Instead of exciting action and emotional drama, Hou's films offer up little vignettes of quotidian activities: a mother shops for vegetables in the village market, a grandmother and her grandson go for a walk, a mother and daughter prepare dinner together, a family shares a meal (there are many meals in

Hou's movies), a grandfather tries to coax his grandson to eat his dinner, some friends see a movie together, a group of boys shoot pool at the local hangout, or a group of girls celebrate a birthday in a cafe.

In many of these scenes, dialogue—which in a mainstream film often carries a heavy expository burden—has very little dramatic significance. Quite frequently, there is no dialogue at all. One of Hou Hsiao-hsien's most striking—and for viewers accustomed to Hollywood-style movies most frustrating—contributions to the style of Taiwanese New Cinema is his willingness to use long, evocative stretches of silence.[132] While these scenes of everyday life are undramatic, they are by no means lacking in emotional resonance. One of the most remarkable scenes in *City of Sadness*, for example, is a single long take in which Bun-ch'ing and Hiromi, eating dinner with their infant son, receive a letter bearing news of her brother Hiroe's death. There are no words and virtually no sound—no music, no dialogue, no intertitles—during the entire shot, which lasts well over two minutes. Instead, their pain is conveyed by subtle gestures and glances after each reads the letter in silence: Bun-ch'ing sinks slowly to his knees and covers his face with his hands. Hiromi's response is most moving: after gently holding Bun-ch'ing's hand for support, she puts aside the letter and stoically continues feeding their baby, even as the tears began to fall silently down her cheeks.

Much has been said and written about the lack of narrativity in Hou Hsiao-hsien's films, which have sometimes been characterized as sketches or essays rather than narratives.[133] Hou himself has repeatedly asserted that he cares little for Western narrative logic or the subtleties of classical plot development.[134] What interests him most, he says, are the possibilities for disrupting logical linear narrative construction. It is unimportant, in his mind, whether viewers are able to piece together the many incidents and events of *City of Sadness* into a single comprehensible narrative, or to decipher the complicated relationships of the many characters; what he hopes the audience will come away with is a sense of the mood, the emotional tenor, the moral and psychological atmosphere of that specific moment in Taiwanese history.[135] In order to achieve this, Hou and his editors consciously suppress the conventions of classical Hollywood editing—which fragments the total experience of time and space in order to manipulate it for narrative purposes—in favor of the spatio-temporal unity that can be maintained through the use of the long take, the long shot, and composition in depth. In filming conversations, for instance, Hou seldom relies on conventional shot-reverse-shot structure to follow the dialogue. Nor does he use medium shots and close-ups to underscore dramatic or emotionally significant moments; the fights and scuffles that break out among the men and boys in *City of Sadness* and *The Boys from Feng Kuei*, for example, are always photographed in long shot and often in a single take. The prevalence of the long take in the films is a natural consequence, say both Hou and his editors, of their desire to allow the inherent rhythms and emotional flow of the actions themselves to shape the editing rather than the other way around.[136]

Chinese Aesthetics and Taiwanese New Cinema

Hou's refusal to impose any dramatic structure or hierarchy of signifi-cance on the details and events of the lives of his characters brings to mind the great neorealist works of Vittorio De Sica, particularly the two famous long takes in *Umberto D* that André Bazin singled out for praise: the old pensioner's retirement to bed and the young servant girl's awaken-ing in the morning and working in the kitchen. There is, however, a cru-cial difference between De Sica's long takes and Hou's: the former em-phasize movement, while the latter valorize stasis. In the long takes in *Umberto D*, the camera is in constant movement, restlessly wandering around the bedroom and kitchen. It follows the servant girl's movements around the kitchen and directs the viewer's eye toward her various ac-tivities—closing in on her hands, for instance, as she prepares the cof-fee. In *City of Sadness*, in contrast, the camera seldom moves. Instead, it sits in a fixed and familiar location as the characters move in and out of the framed space. It would be wrong, therefore, to conclude that the aesthetic strategies employed by Hou and other Taiwanese New Cinema filmmakers are simply borrowed from Italian neorealism; that, of course, would be to suggest that the filmic language of New Cinema is merely the substitution of one western cinematic aesthetic for another (the classical Hollywood film). Hou has said that his use of a static camera, which is usually placed at a distance, evolved primarily out of practical concerns: the inexperience of his technical crew necessitated simpler camera work, while his nonprofessional actors felt more comfortable when the camera was kept at a less-intrusive distance.[137] At the same time, many of his sty-listic hallmarks that could be identified as generically non-Western can in fact be traced to aesthetic traditions that are specifically Chinese. Hou cites, for instance, a number of indigenous arts and traditional Chinese values as significant factors in the development of his visual style.[138] The dark lighting and subdued colors of his images, he notes, were born of his desire to capture both the atmosphere and the distinctive architectural style of Taiwan's older homes, as well as to utilize the colors of local folk designs. The static frontal shots particularly evident in *The Puppetmaster*,

Hou asserts, are the result of his attempts to reproduce the perspective of Chinese opera and puppet theater audiences. Furthermore, he attributes his tendency to position the camera in hallways just outside of rooms to traditional Chinese modesty and respect for the privacy and integrity of intimate spaces—particularly bedrooms and bathrooms.

Indeed, there is much in Hou Hsiao-hsien's films to suggest that his is a cinematic language that owes as much to Chinese aesthetics as to Western filmmaking techniques. The disruption of linear narrative development and the preference for the spatio-temporal unity of the long take and the complexity of composition in depth, for example, can readily be traced to the long traditions of Chinese painting and lyric poetry. Hong Kong film critic Lin Nien-t'ong (林年同), who has written extensively on traditional aesthetics and Chinese cinema, argues that while Chinese movies of the 1930s both mastered the techniques and appreciated the expressive possibilities of Eisensteinian montage Chinese filmmaking developed a mature and distinctive cinematic style only in later decades, inspired by native traditions of lyric poetry and classical painting, as well as by ancient Chinese philosophies. The centerpiece of the Chinese cinema aesthetic, in Lin's analysis, is the idea of ching-yu (鏡游), or "wandering in the lens"—a concept derived from landscape poetry and painting whose origins can be found in Taoist philosophy, primarily that of Chuang Tzu (莊子).[139] Lin likens the operations of ching-yu to a Chinese variation on the long take and further breaks down the idea of wandering in the lens into two levels of meaning: "wandering eye" (游目) and "wandering heart/mind" (游心).[140] What he suggests is that, unlike montage-driven Western cinema, which both directs the viewer's visual attention and manipulates his or her emotional and intellectual response, Chinese cinema based on the aesthetic of ching-yu allows the viewer the freedom to see, feel, and think without following a predetermined sequence or having to arrive at any logical conclusions.

This is an aesthetic strategy that is not found in conventional Hollywood filmmaking but can clearly be seen in Hou Hsiao-hsien's work. Hou himself has alluded to Taoist philosophy in noting the obliqueness and ambiguity in his films.[141] His films, he acknowledges, are unlike Western narratives because they neither emphasize action nor rely on precise and logical exposition to create meaning. They also depart, he argues, from Confucian ideals of harmony and order. Instead, he insists, they are closer to Taoist philosophy and Chinese lyric poetry, their meaning(s) emerging from a gradual accumulation of discrete and sometimes contradictory images, incidents, emotions, and sensations that together coalesce to create a complex impression or experience. It has often been observed, for example, that Hou Hsiao-hsien's films are filled with "pillow shots"—cutaway still lifes of landscapes, empty rooms, or objects—which serve no narrative function, neither advancing the action nor explaining character motivation, but create atmosphere, suggest emotional associations, and enrich the overall cinematic experience.[142]

Another aesthetic strategy that Hou draws from the Chinese poetic tradition is the use of natural landscapes as metaphors for human emotions. In the beginning of *City of Sadness*, Hiromi arrives in the little mountain village full of exuberant optimism for the future and describes the landscape in glowing terms: "The autumn air in these mountains is already refreshingly cool and the scenery has been beautiful throughout my journey. To think that from now on I will be able to enjoy such beautiful sights . . . my heart fills with hope." By the end of the film, her mood has darkened considerably. Not surprisingly, so has her perception of the mountain landscape. The village "has already begun to grow chilly. The wild grasses have begun to flower, blanketing the whole mountain in white. . . . It looks like snow." The natural world features more prominently in Hou's films than in most Western ones, primarily because of its central role in Chinese poetry and painting—indeed, in the entire Chinese cultural tradition. Moreover, the traditional Chinese folk religions practiced in Taiwan are animistic and attribute spirituality and emotions to all natural phenomena.

Chinese conceptions of the spatio-temporal relationships between the human, the social, and the natural posit individual human beings as part of the greater fabric of society and the universe at large. Hou's films, therefore, are characterized by an expansive sense of space in which individual human events are clearly rooted in larger realities—in familial relations, social interactions, and the natural world. In *City of Sadness*, for example, a secure sense of spatial orientation is created through repeated shots of the village landscape and identical camera positions depicting familiar spaces: the foyer of a hospital, the dining room of a family home, an ancestral altar room, and so on. The fullness and complexity of the space inhabited by the characters is reinforced by the multiple visual planes created by deep focus, as well as by the creative use of important nonvisual elements—most notably the soundtrack and offscreen space. Hou Hsiao-hsien's films are also marked by a sense of time that is very different from Western notions of temporal progression. Time is not linear and evential but cyclical and ritualistic, based not on numerical abstractions but the familiar rhythms of life. Time is marked by the changing of the seasons in the natural world and by the life rituals that measure human existence: birth, marriage, death, and so on.

Spectatorship and the Potential for Change

Dedramatization, the disruption of linear narrativity, the downplaying or elimination of dialogue, the suppression of conventional dramatic editing in favor of the long take and composition in depth—all of these formal strategies identified with Taiwanese New Cinema in particular and Third Cinema in general pose a challenge to the viewer accustomed to the more conventionally structured films of Hollywood-style commercial cinema. In a classically structured film, it is imperative that everything—shot sequences, dialogue, editing patterns, camera angles, music—works together to seamlessly weave a logical and comprehensible dramatic narrative. A spectator familiar with the conventional language of film need do little more than passively consume the spectacle that is presented; all he or she needs to do is—as they say—sit back, relax, and enjoy the show. The unfamiliar and unconventional stylistic strategies employed by Third Cinema disrupt that comfortable sense of effortless consumption. Films such as Hou Hsiao-hsien's do not present ready-made ideas; they demand a new form of spectatorship that calls on the active and critical participation of the viewer in constructing the meaning of the film. Hou's aesthetic of participation draws, as he has observed, on both Taoist philosophy and traditional Chinese arts. Taoist philosophy provides no neat narratives or simple answers; it is meant to stimulate thought.[143] Chinese landscape painting, Hou points out, is characterized by its use of "empty spaces" (空白)—voids that are meant to allow the viewer to enter, connect, and contemplate.[144] In Hou's films, the narrative gaps and discontinuities, the empty expansive spatial compositions, and the long stretches of silence might be seen as the cinematic equivalent of these voids. Hou's aesthetic strategies bring to mind the type of structure of reception that Teshome Gabriel has suggested is a crucial characteristic of a Third Aesthetics: an aesthetic of interaction based to a large degree on indigenous Third World oral traditions.[145] A cinema of pure entertainment may be appropriate for a society that is already stabilized and settled, but, as Gabriel points out, most societies in the Third World remain engaged in an ongoing struggle for sociopolitical, economic, and cultural autonomy.[146] In these decolonizing societies, he argues, film cannot afford to be mere entertainment but needs to be used discursively toward a critical understanding of the medium itself, of the institutions from which it emerges, and of society and the world at large. Cuban filmmaker Tomás Gutierrez Alea best expresses this new awareness of cinema's role in sociocultural formation and of the need to actively engage film viewers in a critical dialogue.

If we want to serve something higher, if we want to fulfill its function more perfectly (aesthetic, social, ethical, and revolutionary), we ought to guarantee that it constitutes a *factor in spectators' development*. Film will be more fruitful to the degree that it pushes spectators toward a more profound understanding of reality and, consequently, to the degree that it helps viewers live more actively and incites them to stop being mere spectators in the face of reality. To do this, film ought to appeal not only to emotion and feeling but also to reason and intellect. In this case, both instances ought to exist indissolvably united, in such a way that they come to provoke, as Pascal said, authentic "shudderings and tremblings of the mind."[147]

6

The Country and the City:
Modernization and Changing Apprehensions
of Space and Time

It is significant . . . that the common image of the country is now an image of the past, and the common image of the city is an image of the future. That leaves, if we isolate them, an undefined present. The pull of the country is always towards old ways, human ways, natural ways. The pull of the idea of the city is towards progress, modernization, development. In what is then a tension, a present experienced as tension, we use the contrast of the country and city to ratify an unresolved division and conflict of impulses . . . —Raymond Williams

Sociopolitical Development and the Rural/Urban Model

In his classic study of the powerful images of country and city in English literature, Raymond Williams insists not only on the centrality of these two archetypal forms of human settlement and the contrasts they elicit as major categories of sociocultural consciousness but also argues that the English experience of transformation from a traditional rural to an industrialized urban capitalist economy is in many ways paradigmatic of the world at large—the very basis for the idea of global development.[1] It was duplicated, he contends, not only on a global scale with imperialist expansion in the nineteenth century,[2] but also later within societies formerly colonized by Western metropolitan cultures.[3] Throughout the developing nations of the Third World, therefore, "chaotically expanding cities" are growing, uprooting traditional rural laborers from the villages and small towns of the countryside and drawing them into new urban centers of a global industrial economy—the direct result, says Williams, of an "imposed economic development and its internal consequences."[4]

Taiwan's urbanization over the last several decades, for instance, has in many ways been intimately tied to its history of colonization, as well as to the forces of neocolonialism and cultural imperialism. The Japanese occupational government laid the groundwork for Taiwan's modernization in this century, establishing the island's first urban centers and building the infrastructure—railroads, highways, and other networks—necessary for their continued growth. It is, however, due largely to both the post–World War II American military presence on the island and to a rapid infusion of American and Japanese capital investments that modernization in Taiwan has been able, in a few short decades, to completely transform the island's economy from primarily rural agrarian to primarily urban industrial.[5] In addition to Taipei, the economic, cultural, and political center of the island, several cities have developed across Taiwan, including Chilung to the north, Taichung in the middle of the island, and the trading port of Kaohsiung in the south.[6]

Among the most troubling consequences of this rapid modernization in Taiwan, however, are the growing sociocultural gaps—real and imagined—between the island's cities and villages. For example, the growth of urban centers as the focus of political, educational, and commercial development has resulted in a very real shift in human, material, and institutional resources in favor of the cities. As a result of this disproportionate distribution of resources and opportunities, the industrialized urban cities of many developing nations are perceived to be more cosmopolitan, or Westernized, in all aspects of life, while the rural villages of the countryside are seen as places where more traditional indigenous ways of life persist.[7] It is important to reiterate here that the country and the city are best understood as two sides of the same coin, two interdependent, complementary concepts that circumscribe each other's territory and define each other's cultural meaning, as cultural conceptions of rural life come into being only from the perspective of urban experience.[8] Quite frequently, these take the form of pastoral visions of a peasant past—which may or may not coincide with historical reality or personal experience—imagined by urban intellectuals, who, in response to some present-day need, look to the past with nostalgia.

Hence, the dialectic of country and city has been at the heart of the modern experience for many nations, as the crisis of values precipitated by urbanization and capitalist development—and in the ex-colonial and neocolonial world the threat of foreign cultural hegemony—often gives rise to the longing for an ordered, communal, and comfortingly familiar past.[9] In the development of Chinese literature and film in the twentieth century, for example, the landscapes of country and city provided critical symbolic backgrounds against which complex issues of selfhood, nation, and cultural identity were played out. While many national traditions have some kind of idyllic "rural community" at the core of their conceptions of cultural identity, the German idea of *Heimat* is worth a brief exploration not only because it offers particularly compelling points of comparison for Chinese visions of the rural but also because its complex relationship with the nation's political history illustrates both the effective emotional appeal of the pastoral vision and its inherent limitations—including its vulnerability to manipulation by forces of political extremism and sociocultural exclusionism. Heimat has most often been translated as "home" or "homeland," but neither English rendering really captures the multitude of moral connotations, social overtones, and political implications that the term has accrued in German history.[10] New German Cinema filmmaker Edgar Reitz, whose popular but controversial sixteen-hour film *Heimat* (1984) generated intense debates on German history, society, and culture, was once asked to explain the meaning that the word Heimat holds for the German people.[11] Rather than offering a simple definition of the term, Reitz emphasized its emotional dimensions and symbolic importance. "The word is always linked to strong feeling, mostly remembrances and longing. 'Heimat' always invokes in me the feeling of something lost or very far away, something which one cannot easily find or find again. In this respect it is also a German romantic word and a romantic feeling with a particular romantic dialectic. 'Heimat' is such that if one would go closer and closer to it, one would discover that at the moment of arrival it is gone, it has dissolved into nothingness. It seems to me that the more one has a precise idea of 'Heimat' the further one is away from it. This for me is 'Heimat'; it's fiction, and one can arrive there only in poetry, and I include film in poetry."[12] The history of the word *Heimat* provides an illuminating illustration of how the rural idyll can come to play such a critical role in a people's developing sense of nationhood. Said to have roots in ancient German, its role as a way of thinking about Germanness is a relatively modern phenomenon. The origins of its modern usage have been traced to the late eighteenth century, when a small group of writers interested in the idea of the German language as the expression of a German nation resurrected the long-neglected ancient term to express "homey tranquility and happiness."[13] The idea of Heimat gained in popularity throughout the nineteenth century at a time when, significantly, the traditional political structures of the German states were disintegrating and society was entering a period of rapid change and upheaval. Forces of political centralization were threatening to destroy local communities, while industrialization and urbanization were beginning to transform the social landscape of the country. In many German regions, the reaction to these rapid changes was a revival of interest in local history, customs, dialects, and folklore.[14] The literature of the period, which found a large, popular audience, located Heimat in the idyllic villages of the German country- side, where people were depicted as living in ordered, close-knit commu- nities in harmony with nature. In contrast to the new German city, the village was romanticized as a place where folk customs and speech were preserved and old ways of life persisted. Hence, functioning as a defense against these social and political changes, the nostalgic concept of Heimat offered a comforting myth about the possibility of order and community in the face of fragmentation and alienation. By the 1890s, rapid industri- alization and a massive population shift from the German countryside to new urban centers gave rise to numerous neoromantic "Heimat move- ments," which continued to emphasize the rural roots of Heimat, con- structing it to embrace everything that was lost in the twin processes of modernization and urbanization.[15] The emotional connotations of the term increased in weight as it came to be associated with family, lost childhood, secure human relationships, unalienated precapitalist labor, and a comfortingly familiar agrarian German identity.[16] The industrial- ized city became the other, associated with rootlessness, alienation, and superficial values. It was frequently depicted as an anonymous and soul- less concrete jungle filled with hectic but mindless activity, decadent and immoral. As a center of international business and cultural exchange, the city was linked to all that was foreign, unfamiliar, and therefore threat- ening.

During the two world wars of the twentieth century, the rural idyll of Heimat took on an even rosier glow as military invasion by foreign armies and the horrors and chaos of battle made the imagined pastoral beauty and serenity of the rural Heimat more psychologically and culturally ap- pealing than ever,[17] becoming a focal point for German cultural identity and national pride.[18] The explicitly nationalistic colorings that Heimat acquired during World War I continued to intensify throughout the cen- tury, culminating in the ugliest and most controversial period in the his- tory of the term: its eventual appropriation and exploitation by Hitler and his National Socialist revolution.[19] Under Hitler, the Heimat move- ment's originally modest interest in preserving the integrity of local cul- ture and identity was overlaid with militant nationalism and the rhetoric of racial superiority and distorted into a murderously exclusionary ideol- ogy of Germanness.[20] It is largely due to the Nazi exploitation of the term that to this day any discussion of Heimat and ruralism is necessarily emotionally and semantically overdetermined. As Anton Kaes notes, "Scenes of provincial life are never innocent in Germany."[21]

Modernization, the Rural Idyll, and Taiwanese Hsiang-t'u Literature

Similarly, the relationship between rural China and a culturally authentic vision of the nation has been one of the most prominent themes throughout the history of modern Chinese literature, sparking numerous cultural and political debates over the years. Whether we turn our attention to the initial emergence of an urban-rural polarity in the works of the May Fourth writers in the 1920s and the leftist writers who followed in the 1930s, to Mao's utopian image of the Chinese peasantry and his advocacy of an earthy literature for the people in the 1940s, to Taiwanese "native soil" (hsiang-t'u 鄉土) literature of the 1960s and 1970s, or to the rise of a "search for roots" (xungen, 尋根) movement in PRC literature of the mid-1980s, it becomes readily apparent that the problematic of the rural is a recurrent issue in Chinese cultural discourse and carries with it a complex burden of sociocultural connotations and political implications.[22] Scenes of provincial life in the context of modern China, therefore, are seldom innocent either, and terms like *hsiang-t'u* have played a role in Chinese discourse about place, belonging, nation, and cultural identity for much of this century. The idea of a native soil literature extends back to the origins of modern Chinese literature in the May Fourth Movement of the 1920s. While early May Fourth literature has been characterized as predominantly lyrical and urban in nature, the focus of modern Chinese fiction soon shifted toward more humanistic and realist depictions of life in rural China. During the late 1920s and early 1930s, when politically engaged leftist writers began to dominate the mainstream, the contrast between the hardworking and decent Chinese peasantry and the corrupt, immoral, urban-based capitalists who exploit them became a prominent theme in both literature and film. Lu Hsun (魯迅), though not himself a rural writer, took note of the nativist tendency in May Fourth era literature and praised its commitment to bringing to the fore the contemporary social and political issues—whether poverty, ignorance, or exploitation by foreign capitalists—facing China at the time. May Fourth writers such as Lao She (老舍), Mao Dun (茅盾), Shen Congwen (沈從文), and Xiao Hong (蕭紅) shared to varying degrees a distinctly antiurban bias and a sympathetic—even nostalgic—identification with rural China. Lao She's works, for example, may be set in the city, but they are clearly rural in spirit, nostalgic for the simple ways and values of "old Peking," and harshly critical of the modern urban elements that conspire to crush his rural protagonists. Similarly, Mao Dun's works chronicle the decadence, greed, and corruption in Chinese cities like Shanghai, while offering a decidedly more sympathetic view of the Chinese peasants, the hardships they endure, and their resilience in the face of victimization by the twin evils of capitalism and imperialism. The most romanticized visions of rural life came from writers like Shen and Xiao, who wrote with bitter-sweet nostalgia of life in the far-flung provinces of West Hunan and Man-churia—worlds away from the urbanization and foreign influences infil-trating China's coastal regions.

The city in Chinese literature of this period was most frequently repre-sented by Shanghai, the booming port that was China's gateway to the rest of the world. With a local stock market that became one of the leading exchanges in the world and with steady streams of foreign businessmen and capital flowing through it, Shanghai had acquired by the late 1920s many of the characteristics of international cosmopolitan culture. Shang-hai urban culture was strongly affected by the physical presence of nu-merous foreign enclaves (and foreigners) in the city, as well as by the West-ernized tastes and habits of the many foreign-trained Chinese students, who often chose to settle there after returning from abroad. Hence, in all aspects of life—styles of dress, culinary habits, cultural interests, com-mercial entertainment facilities—Shanghai epitomized the encounter be-tween old and new, East and West. It was, in the Chinese imagination, the embodiment of everything that was both fascinating and frightening about the modern West. While the fast-paced cosmopolitan lifestyle of Shanghai was not without its appeal to Chinese writers, the image of the city that stands out in Chinese literature from the 1930s onward is the unrelentingly negative portrait endorsed and continually propagated by Communist ideology: Shanghai as "sin city," tainted by foreign influences and the center of political corruption, economic exploitation, and moral degeneration.[23] Anti-imperialist sentiment was on the rise throughout the 1930s, sparked by the 1931 invasion of Manchuria by the Japanese and fueled by their subsequent bombings of major Chinese cities, so it is not surprising that both the literature and cinema of this era were dominated by leftist ideology, which denigrated the city and celebrated the country-side as the source of China's moral fortitude and the stronghold of resis-tance against foreign invasions—military or cultural. When a full-scale war of resistance against the Japanese broke out in 1937, Chinese litera-ture became even more insistently nationalistic and entered, it can be argued, a rural phase from which it has only recently begun to emerge.

Being fought concurrently with the war of resistance against Japan, of course, was an equally important struggle: the civil war between Chiang Kai-shek's Kuomintang and Mao Tse-tung's Chinese Communist Party (CCP). It is this particular context that gives the urban-rural polarity in modern Chinese literature its specific political overtones. The city —Shanghai—is generally identified with Chiang's KMT, the party that consorts with foreign powers and whose representatives are frequently imagined as personifying political corruption, bourgeois decadence, and capitalist greed. Mao's CCP, on the other hand, presents itself as the party of the people, which in China means the peasantry. Following Mao's victory and the establishment of the People's Republic of China, therefore, the image of the good peasant—honest, hardworking, faithful, and self-sacrificing—gained increasing iconic significance in the self-representation of the Chinese nation. May Fourth writers may have celebrated the traditional virtues of rural China and criticized the processes of modernization and urbanization that victimized the peasantry, but in general they refrained from excessive idealization of the masses. In Mao's China, however, literary and cinematic visions of the peasantry were increasingly utopian. One of the cinematic genres established during the 1950s, for example, was the village film, which featured beautiful rural landscapes and scenes of happy, industrious peasants working together for the good of the local community and the future of the nation.[24] This idealization of Chinese rural life culminated, of course, during the Cultural Revolution (1966–76), when urban youths were forcibly sent to the countryside (*xiafang*, 下放) to learn from the peasants. The depictions of peasant life in this period were supremely ideological, elaborately staged spectacles of rural glory that are in some ways reminiscent of Germany's Nazi era *Heimatfilme*.[25] It is this particular heritage of peasant representation in modern Chinese history that has colored conceptions of the rural in more recent Chinese literature, not only in the literature of the PRC but even in Taiwan.

On the island of Taiwan, the term *hsiang-t'u* first entered the discourse of place and identity during a period of traumatic sociocultural change, emerging under the Japanese Occupation both as a form of local resistance against assimilation into Japanese culture and as an effort to protect traditional agrarian lifestyles from the industrial and capitalist modes imposed on the island by Japan's ambitious program of modernization. Partly influenced by regionalist literature from the May Fourth period on the mainland, Occupation era hsiang-t'u literature idealized the Taiwanese countryside as the repository of indigenous culture and folk customs and constructed the city—the seat of imperialist power and foreign culture—as the evil other. The sociopolitical circumstances surrounding the revival of hsiang-t'u in the late 1960s and early 1970s offer parallels both to this earlier period in Taiwanese history and, strikingly enough, to the renaissance of Heimat regionalism in Germany during those same years. Just as Germany entered a period of soul-searching following a series of political setbacks in the early 1970s, Taiwan's inward-turning search for its cultural roots was similarly prompted by political disillusionment and growing anxiety about the future of the island.[26] By the 1970s, thanks to massive infusions of capital from Japan and the United States after World War II, rapid industrialization and urbanization were already transforming every aspect of Taiwanese life. As Taiwan's new urban centers expanded, families and rural communities were fragmented and traditional social relationships radically altered by the demographic shift from countryside to city. Moreover, the rich diversity of local beliefs and folk traditions was increasingly being undermined by growing enthusiasm for "international" culture and ideologies, largely imported from Japan and the West. The political frustrations precipitated by the Kuomintang's failures and humiliations in the international arena during the 1970s were simply the straw that broke the camel's back.[27] In the face of the challenges posed by these internal changes and external threats, concerned Taiwanese searching for a positive affirmation of the island's communal identity again turned to its rural past as a source of strength and hope.

Like the German idea of Heimat, the Taiwanese notion of hsiang-t'u appealed to a psychological and emotional need for familiarity, order, and coherence during a time of upheaval and uncertainty. Its manifestation in the 1970s shares some of the most romantic aspects of the German Heimat tradition. It was based, for instance, on a nostalgic longing for something—harmony with nature, a familial sense of community, time-honored cultural traditions, a local way of life—thought to have been sacrificed in the island's mad rush toward modernization. All the positive human values that were imagined to have been lost were connected to the Taiwanese countryside, which was celebrated as the last stronghold of authentic indigenous culture, while all that was foreign, distant, and dehumanizing was associated with the city. As in the Heimat tradition, this rural village versus urban metropolis dichotomy formed the basis for all the other pairs of binary oppositions—tradition versus modernity, native versus foreign, local dialect versus national language, peasant masses versus educated elite, youth versus age, nature versus industry, coherence versus fragmentation—mobilized by the supporters of the hsiang-t'u movement.[28] The emotional resonance of the rural idyll clearly appeals to Hwang Chun-ming, whose works, both fictional and nonfictional, are suffused with a poignant nostalgia for Taiwan's rural past. The

reminiscences and anecdotes in essays such as "The Past Can Only Be Savored as Memory" (往事只能回味) and "The Tomato Tree on the Roof"
(屋頂上的番茄樹), for example, typify his romantic affection for the simple world of the peasant.[29] With a touching combination of humor and
sentimentality, Hwang celebrates the natural beauty of the Taiwanese
countryside, the genuine warmth and homegrown wisdom of the rural
characters he remembers from his youth, and the vividness of the dialect
they speak.

The Rural World and the Maternal Sphere

Hwang's affection for figures from his childhood in the Taiwanese countryside points up another characteristic shared by the rural visions of German Heimat and Taiwanese hsiang-t'u: the idealization of one's childhood home and in particular of its associations with the maternal.[30] Like
Heimatfilme, Hwang's fictional works include romantic narratives of redemption. For instance, the motif of a return to the place of one's birth—
to the maternal sphere—plays an important role in the story "A Flower in
the Rainy Night" (看海的日子).[31] The heroine of the story—which is without question the most sentimental and romanticized of Hwang's rural
stories—is a world-weary prostitute named Pai-mei (白梅), who has spent
her life moving from brothel to brothel in the small towns and fishing villages of the island. When Pai-mei was eight, her poverty-stricken family
was forced to give her up to be raised by another family. They in turn sold
her, at the tender age of fourteen, into her current life of misery. For fourteen years, she has suffered the loneliness of life on the road, never staying
in one brothel for very long (for fear of becoming "old merchandise"). Her
rootless existence has been void of any meaningful emotional bonds: few
friends, no family, no sense of past or future—nothing but anonymous
sexual transactions. Pai-mei and the other girls in the brothel dream wistfully of someday returning to their childhood homes in the countryside—
to "raise chickens and geese, and to pick fruit from the orchards in the
shadow of the mountains" (69).

The story traces Pai-mei's efforts to go home, both physically and spiritually. Bitter after years of abuse by her customers and tired of the humiliation of social ostracization, Pai-mei is determined to recover her
roots and rediscover her sense of self. Her salvation, she believes, lies in
motherhood: she allows herself to become pregnant by a shy and gentle
young fisherman. Once she is sure she has conceived, she packs her things
for the journey home—not to her adoptive family but to her natural
mother, who lives in a little farming community in rural I-lan County.

The Country and the City   **189**

The emotional bonds with one's childhood home are special; only by re-turning to the place of her birth, the story suggests, can Pai-mei be reborn. Pai-mei's arrival in her native village is highly romanticized. When she gets off the bus on the dusty dirt road, she leaves her other life—and the stigma of her profession—behind. As she walks between the rice paddies toward her childhood home, she steps into a world that is a classic rural idyll. In the verdant fields, men and women, young and old, work side-by-side, hoeing in unison. Pai-mei, now referred to by her childhood name Mei-tzu (梅子), feels instantly comfortable and secure. As her childhood memories come rushing back, she feels as though she has never left. The close-knit community of the village is envisioned as an extended family, and Mei-tzu immediately renews her bonds with the elderly "aunties" and "uncles" she left so many years ago. As a lively group of young children gather around to greet her, she easily guesses their family affiliations: "You must be Ah-chiao's boy! And you must be Ah-Bak's!" (96–97). The entire village welcomes her with open arms, and she has no trouble settling into the familiar social fabric of the village. No one belittles her because of her past or questions her pregnancy. Indeed, as the birth of her child draws near, all the villagers express their love and concern and pray that she be blessed with a son. When she does deliver—a boy, of course—she is surrounded by family, including the mother with whom she has finally reconciled. Mei-tzu's social rehabilitation is complete and her sense of self finally secure when, on a train with her young son, she is at last treated with kindness and respect. As she gazes out the window to the sea, she feels that she "finally has found a place in this great, expansive world" (124).

From Rural Organicity to Urban Fragmentation: The Spatio-Temporal Structures of the Country and the City

The nostalgic world of the rural idyll, then, is marked by coherence and comprehensibility. It is an imaginary world that offers security and per-manence, where one's relationships with the natural world and society are knowable and unchanging. The contrasts established between the country and the city are frequently expressed in terms of what Mikhail Bakhtin refers to as the chronotopic[32] differences—different conceptions of the spatio-temporal relations among the human, the social, and the natural world—that characterize the rural and urban experiences. The chronotope is just one of many contemporary models that attempt to theorize the impact of sociohistorical development on space-time articulations, most of which are based on some form of the rural/urban, periphery/core binarism.[33] The rural world, in Bakhtin's view, is a place of idyllic unity, where the human experience of time is intimately bound to space, "an organic fastening down, a grafting of life and its events to a place, to a familiar territory with all its nooks and crannies, its familiar mountains, valleys, fields, rivers and forests, and one's home. Idyllic life and its events are inseparable from this concrete, spatial corner of the world where fathers and grandfathers lived and where one's children and their children will live. This little spatial world is limited and sufficient unto itself, not linked in any intrinsic way with other places, with the rest of the world."[34]

The rural communities in Hwang Chun-ming's stories, where families have tilled the same soil for generations, reflect this organic sense of time and place. Uncle Ah-sheng of "The Drowning of an Old Cat," for instance, describes the geographical and social unity of Clear Spring Village in animistic terms: "As for the lay of the land, Clear Spring is a dragon's head. The village exit leading to the town is the mouth of the dragon, and the well beside the school is the eye, which is why we call it Dragon-Eye Well. Ever since the days of our ancestors, the people of Clear Spring have been protected by this dragon, which is why we've been able to live our lives in peace. Now suddenly someone wants to bring harm to our dragon's eye, and the people of Clear Spring are not going to stand by and let it happen" (26–27). Here, the intimate bonds between the peasant and the physical landscape in which he lives are captured in an extremely vivid image: the village and the dragon spirit that protects it are one. If the dragon is harmed or offended in any way, then the physical security and generational continuity of life in the village can no longer be assured.

The coherent sense of space that characterizes the rural idyll is paired with a cyclical view of time that Bakhtin refers to as folkloric time. Life in the countryside is organized around the concrete temporal rhythms of agricultural labor, which, in turn, correspond to the seasonal cycles of nature. The old farmer in Hwang's "The Story of Ch'ing-fan Kung" marks time not with abstract clock or calendar notations but with the lived experiences and accumulated knowledge from generation upon generation of those who have worked the earth and coped with natural phenomena.[35] He knows, for example, to prepare for floods when he hears the warbling of the "reed-singing birds" (9, 19). He can tell from the sound of the wind— "like the sudden northwest rain" (3)—when the grain will be ready for harvesting.

It is precisely this imagined sense of unity—both with nature and with the village community—that underlies the powerful emotional appeal of the rural idyll for a society being transformed by industry and urbanization. For both the German Heimat and the Taiwanese hsiang-t'u movements, the most lamentable loss in the transition from country to city life is this secure sense of one's place within a comprehensible social-spatial-temporal matrix. The world of the modern city is envisioned as an impersonal and alienated place "in which one separates from everything" and is cast adrift, with no tangible bonds to nature, family, work, or society.[36] The familiar organic unities of the rural world are shattered and irretrievably lost. Ruralist movements have attributed the fragmentation of experience in urban life to, among other things, the physical architecture of cities, the alienation of labor in industrial capitalism, and the impact of technological progress and mass media. In his "From 'Confucius Says . . .' to 'According to the Newspaper,'" Hwang laments the disappearance of the kind of person-to-person transmission of knowledge characteristic of traditional agrarian societies.[37] In the age of "Confucius Says," people learned through direct observation and participation—from life experience. In today's "age of mass media" (大眾廣播時代), in contrast, personal human contact is no longer necessary. Instead, people learn by gathering fragments of information from newspapers, books, television, film, and—to update Hwang's list—computer networks. The regrettable result of such technological progress, argues Hwang, is that experience is atomized and people become both physically and spiritually isolated.[38]

The fragmentation of experience in urban life and the alienating effects of modern technology are vividly illustrated in Hwang's "Two Sign Painters" (兩個油漆匠).[39] Like the family in "The Taste of Apples,"[40] Strongman (阿力) and Monkey (猴子), the two sign painters of the story, came from a small village in eastern Taiwan to work in the big city—representative of the trend in urbanizing countries like Taiwan, of rural youth who stream into the city to "try their luck" in hopes of striking it rich in the new capitalist society (82). What they find in the city, of course, is far from what they imagined. After several years, Strongman and Monkey are still stuck doing menial, meaningless labor for exploitatively low wages (72). Although they sometimes feel homesick (Monkey, in particular, sings folk songs from his native village for comfort), they find it impossible to go home to the countryside—partly because they still hope to find an alternative to a life of working the fields, but mostly because of pride. Having boasted to the folks at home of their financial successes in the city, they are too embarrassed to return empty-handed (68, 83).

The city where Strongman and Monkey work is filled with giant new skyscrapers; ten and twenty stories tall, they are cold, gray, and threatening (63–64). On this day, the two painters are working on an enormous advertisement for a soft drink company. The ad, which takes up the entire outside wall of a skyscraper, features the naked torso of "V V," the most popular actress of the moment. Strongman and Monkey are suspended at the seventeenth floor of the building, assigned to paint the actress's two gigantic breasts. Even though they have been painting for several days, they are annoyed because they have no way of telling whether they have made any progress. Like the twenty or so other workers on the mural, each assigned to a different section of the giant woman, they have no overall perspective of the image; all they see is a disjointed fragment.[41] Strong-man finds it extremely frustrating: "They were supposedly painting V V's breast, but who could tell? A pair of breasts several stories high—when you're stuck up close to the wall, just painting stroke, after stroke, after stroke, you finally have to wonder: what in the world am I doing?" (65, translation mine). The two of them work in isolation, without even the opportunity to chat and relax with the other painters. In their nearly three years in the city, they have made few friends, since they move from job to job and workers come and go. It is a lonely, anonymous existence of which they are beginning to tire (84).

As the two painters smoke, lament the abuse they have suffered at the hands of their bosses, and ponder whether to quit their jobs, a sudden gust of wind knocks one of their paint buckets to the street seventeen stories below. The media circus that unexpectedly follows underscores both the emotional alienation of Strongman's and Monkey's urban existence and the specularization of life in modern capitalist society. Even though no one is hit by the falling bucket, a crowd of curious onlookers gathers on the street below, creating a colossal traffic jam. When police cars arrive, Strongman and Monkey suddenly realize that the crowd thinks they are about to jump to their deaths (88–89). They shout to the police that they have no intention of committing suicide, but the press arrives and the media frenzy begins. Before they know it, Monkey and Strongman be-come instant celebrities and are being interviewed by newspaper, radio, and television reporters who blind them with camera flashes, shine harsh spotlights on them, force scary-looking microphones in their faces, and bark questions through bullhorns that distort the human voice (94).[42] All around them, TV technicians are shouting foreign words: "Camera," "Zoom in," "Close-up!" The bewildered sign painters answer reporters' questions for a while, but the press clearly is not satisfied with their re-sponses. Monkey suddenly comes to a realization: "I understand. This is only newsworthy if I jump. Strongman, they are going to be disappointed, you know?" (102). As the cameras and lights close in tighter and tighter around the two, Monkey desperately wants to climb down, to get away.

As the story ends, Monkey falls—the crowd below gasping in unison—and Strongman is reduced to a shaking, whimpering mess, cowering in a corner.

The grotesque images of urban existence evoked in "Two Sign Painters" function, of course, to further reinforce a sense of nostalgia for its opposite—the uncorrupted simplicity of the rural idyll. The emotional and polemical efficacy of such stark contrasts between the city and the country served the nationalistic project of the hsiang-t'u movement well, but the naive reductiveness of the binary opposition was not without its problems. As supporters of Heimat movements in Germany discovered, an overly simplistic romanticization of the rural village and demonization of the city is vulnerable to attack by those alarmed by its regressive tendencies. In Germany, for example, a 1931 essay titled "People Are Returning to the Soil" criticized Heimat literature's embrace of rural themes and polemical opposition to the modern, avant-garde literature associated with the city.[43] Its author expressed anxiety over the reactionary potential of the new agrarian regionalism, seeing it as short-sighted, exclusionary, and dangerously insular. His fears were borne out not long after, as the major themes and motifs of Heimat literature—glorification of the German country and its people, suspicion of the foreign and the urban—were readily assimilated into the blood and soil ideology of national socialism.

Taiwanese hsiang-t'u literature's romanticization of the peasantry was subjected to similar polemical attacks during the 1970s literary debates between Taiwanese "modernists" (現代派) and "regionalists" (鄉土派). Hsiang-t'u writers were repeatedly criticized, for example, for their excessively negative, stereotypical depictions of city folk—inevitably portrayed as shallow, greedy, and corrupt and as blind followers of foreign fashions. Their characterizations of country folk were attacked as being equally one-sided—idealized as lovable, honest, and sincere, guardians of the island's indigenous morality and culture. Such simplistic oppositions, warned one critic, feed into a dangerously narrow and chauvinistic conception of the Taiwanese hsiang-t'u, fostering a naive nationalism that appeals far too much to sentiment.[44] For many, hsiang-t'u's criticism of the urban establishment seemed to be an attack on the KMT, and its glorification of Taiwanese peasant life was uncomfortably reminiscent of the rural utopias associated with Maoist ideology. Indeed, many of the movement's harshest critics specifically invoked Maoist slogans ("worker-peasant-soldier literature," 工農兵文學) in an attempt to discredit Taiwanese nativist literature and blacken all hsiang-t'u writers with the communist label. Hsiang-t'u writers, for their part, were also acutely aware of the dangers of uncritically contrasting the goodness of the country and the evil of the city. Their polemical writings were some-times defensive in tone when dealing with the urban-rural issue, and they often argued for a broader vision of hsiang-t'u that would embrace Tai-wanese urban realities as well.[45]

New German Cinema and the Anti-Heimatfilme/Taiwanese New Cinema's Revised Vision of Hsiang-t'u

In Germany, the excessive romanticization of the rural idyll in the Hei-mat literature of the 1930s and the subsequent appropriation by Hitler's National Socialists of its themes and motifs tainted the concept of Hei-mat for many years. Not until the revival of interest in Heimat during the 1970s was any serious critical reevaluation of the Heimat tradition at-tempted. During the late 1960s and early 1970s, however, a new genre of film emerged, which sought to tackle head on the negative legacy of the Nazi era and 1950s Heimatfilme. Known as critical Heimatfilme or anti-Heimatfilme,[46] they took the country-city dichotomy established by the Heimatfilme and turned it upside down. Instead of idealizing the country-side as a simple and unsullied world of natural beauty where warm human relationships flourish, the critical Heimatfilm revealed the rural village as a false idyll—a place plagued by feudal oppression, reactionary backward-ness, and small-minded intolerance—the breeding ground for a multitude of neuroses.[47] Often the films offered as one-sided and misleading a view of Germany as did the genre they were trying to subvert. New German Cinema filmmaker Edgar Reitz's sixteen-hour *Heimat* is fascinating be-cause it contains elements of both the romantic Heimat tradition of the 1930s and 1950s and the anti-Heimat approach of the 1970s. It was em-broiled in controversy as soon as it was released, attacked as a nostal-gic harkening back to the 1950s romantic Heimatfilme or, even worse, to Nazi products of the genre, but simultaneously linked to the critical Heimatfilmes of the Left.[48] Reitz himself acknowledges the film's deep ambivalence towards the concept of "Heimat." His purpose in making the film was not to offer an abstract definition of the term, but to explore the concept's entire messy history, to directly confront its multiple and often contradictory meanings, and to grapple with all the positive and negative feelings and associations it evokes.[49] Hence, the film is filled with senti-mental scenes of provincial life reminiscent of 1950s Heimatfilme—bu-colic landscapes, smiling children, men and women working and going about their daily routines. It also, however, reveals the less picturesque aspects of village life: the petty jealousies, blind conformity, insularity, and narrow-minded distrust of anything or anyone who is not local.

Interestingly enough, Reitz's film attracted a significant amount of attention in Taiwanese film circles. *Film Appreciation*, probably the leading critical film journal in Taiwan, devoted a large portion of a special issue on "Film, History, and Popular Memory" to discussions of and commentaries on the film, as well as to translations of several related articles on New German Cinema by Thomas Elsaesser, Eric Rentschler, and Anton Kaes.[50] Not coincidentally, the issue also featured a number of important essays on history, politics, and the role of nostalgia in Taiwanese New Cinema. While the title of Reitz's film is translated as "Home" (Chia-yuan, 家園),[51] it is worth noting that the term *Heimatfilm* is translated as "hsiang-t'u film" (鄉土電影),[52] underscoring the affinity between the two ruralist movements.

Of course, Taiwanese New Cinema owes an acknowledged debt to the ruralist traditions of Taiwanese hsiang-t'u literature. The high critical profile of Hou Hsiao-hsien's works—particularly of his rural films—has resulted in the widespread but unfairly simplistic perception of Taiwanese New Cinema as nothing more than "hsiang-t'u cinema" (鄉土文學電影). It is true that Hou's films continue hsiang-t'u literature's interest in the impact of urbanization on Taiwanese life and specifically in examining the contrasts between country and city. The rural-urban dichotomy, however, is a common focus for films from countries still in the throes of modernization. Many of the most powerful works of Third Cinema, for example, explore the tensions and contradictions between the cultures and value systems of the urbanized capital city and the rural villages that surround it.[53] The complexity of the ever-changing relationship between the city and the country is a recurrent theme in a number of Hou Hsiao-hsien's films. Two of his earlier works, *Summer at Grandpa's* and *The Boys from Feng Kuei*, form something of a pair. The former tells the story of a young city boy who spends a summer with his grandfather in the countryside and discovers an older, more traditional way of life— one that honors family, values the community, and appreciates the natural world. The latter depicts the experiences of a group of young men who leave their homes in a small fishing village on a remote outer island to find work in the southern Taiwanese port city of Kaohsiung. There they discover a way of living and working with other people that is entirely different from their rural experience. *Dust in the Wind* moves between the city and the country. The two young protagonists in the film, like so many young people in developing nations, leave their homes in the village to travel to the capital city of Taipei in search of an education and a job.

Hou Hsiao-hsien's films have generally been regarded as the cinematic counterpart to the idealistic rural vision of hsiang-t'u literature, particularly in their treatments of the country-city polarity.[54] A closer look, however, reveals that the films contain contradictions and ambiguities that suggest an ambivalence toward hsiang-t'u ruralism that shares similarities with Edgar Reitz's complex relationship with the German tradition of Heimat. While fundamental contrasts between the country and city persist in Hou's films, they are also notable for their sense of balance. Although there remains, for example, a certain degree of nostalgia for the familiar communal traditions of rural life as an antidote to the uncertainties of modern urban existence, the films mark a departure from the hsiang-t'u literary tradition in their avoidance of excessive sentimentality and idealization of the village. Urbanization is seen in these films as an irreversible global historical reality. Like Raymond Williams, Hou recognizes the importance of moving beyond a mere contrast of the country and the city toward a more thorough examination of their complex interdependency.

The Rural Past: *Summer at Grandpa's*

Raymond Williams emphasized that a cultural conception of rural life comes into being only from the perspective of urban experience; an image of the country exists only in relation to the city. It is usually a backward reference to a traditional way of life that tends to surface in times of traumatic sociocultural change. Often these edenic images of a happier rural past are located in the childhoods of their authors.[55] In Hou Hsiao-hsien's films, childhood and the "knowable community" of village life are indeed often linked. His own childhood memories of the Taiwanese countryside are depicted in *A Time to Live and a Time to Die*, and the childhood of Hou's frequent collaborator, Chu T'ien-wen, is the inspiration for *Summer at Grandpa's*, for which Chu wrote the screenplay.

Tung-tung (冬冬), the protagonist of *Summer at Grandpa's*, is a child of the city. When his mother is hospitalized (in an imposingly large and sterile hospital) for a serious illness, he and his little sister T'ing-t'ing (亭亭) are sent to spend their summer vacation at their grandfather's house in the countryside.[56] From the start of the film, then, the country is established as a sort of refuge from the unpleasantness and complications of modern city life. The train that whisks them from Taipei to the little village of T'ong-luo (銅鑼) takes them from a world of schools, hospitals, and automobiles to a world of trees, rivers, and animals—from a heavily regulated and inanimate world of civilization to the living, spontaneous world of nature. Tung-tung's first act when he arrives in the countryside is emblematic of his passage from an industrialized society to a way of

14. *Summer at Grandpa's.* Tung-tung's first act when he arrives in his grandfather's village is emblematic of his passage from city to country. He exchanges his toy jeep (mechanical, remote-controlled, fast) for a turtle (natural, self-propelled, slow).

life that is closer to nature: he exchanges his toy jeep (mechanical, remote controlled, and fast) for a turtle (natural, self-propelled, and slow).

The little boys in the village welcome the "city kid" enthusiastically. Tung-tung is equally excited about his new friends and immerses himself in this new and beautiful rural world. Through his adventures with the boys, he learns about things he has never experienced in Taipei or read about in the books at his school in the city. He goes from learning from books to learning from nature. He and T'ing-t'ing discover the simpler joys of rural life: instead of playing with toy cars and airplanes, they join the village children in racing turtles. They experience the thrill of riding a bicycle down an empty country road and on the narrow dirt paths that run between the rice and vegetable fields. Tung-tung joins the boys for a swim in the river. Perhaps because his city upbringing has made him more inhibited, he keeps his underwear on; the country boys, though, frolic in the nude, utterly carefree. Tung-tung's sense of wonder and discovery is underscored by his exclamation, from the top of a huge tree he has climbed, that "You can see forever from here!" As a panoramic shot offers Tung-tung's treetop view of the lush green expanses below, the only sounds on the soundtrack are those of nature: the rustling of leaves as the wind blows through the trees and the chirping of cicadas. The tranquil beauty of the scene exemplifies an idyllic vision of rural life, with its "timeless rhythm of agriculture and the seasons."[57]

Another important dimension of the idealized conception of the country is the notion of an organic community based on immediate face-to-face interpersonal relationships. Tung-tung's nuclear familial arrangement in Taipei is a symptom of urbanization, Western individualism, and the consequent dispersal of traditional families.[58] Young people like Tung-tung's mother typically leave their homes in the village to move to the city and seldom return. Most of their communications with their families are mediated through letters or telephone calls. At his grandfather's house, in contrast, Tung-tung experiences the intimacy of direct relationships within a traditional extended family, where three generations live together in the family home (三代同堂). Moreover, he gains a sense of continuity, of family history, as his grandfather sits down to share with him old family photo albums and, on a visit to the ancestral temple, tells him stories about the family's achievements. The close-knit communal feelings of the family seem to extend, moreover, to the village community at large. Tung-tung's grandfather is the village doctor and seems to know and care about everyone personally. When the village "crazy," a mentally disturbed young woman named Han-tzu (寒子) becomes pregnant, Tung-tung's grandparents, aunt, and uncle sit down with her father to discuss what to do about the child. Throughout the discussion, they show genuine concern for the young woman's future and compassion for her father's suffering. When one of Tung-tung's little friends from the village—gone in pursuit of his runaway cow—fails to come home, Tung-tung's whole family joins the search party.

Despite these scenes of natural beauty, simple pleasures, and communal feeling, *Summer at Grandpa's* does not present a wholly idyllic, sentimentalized view of the rural past. Childhood is not depicted as all innocence and joy; human relationships in the country, it turns out, can also be complicated and difficult. Even early in the film, the tranquility of the country morning, filled with the soothing sounds of chirping cicadas and twittering birds, is often shattered by the roar of a train speeding by—a reminder of the technology's inevitable encroachment. By the middle of the film, each time the boys venture out into the fields to play they stumble on scenes of troubling behavior and morality associated with the adult world. Walking through the countryside with their fishing nets and poles, the boys come across a violent scene as two thugs beat a truck driver with rocks and then rob him of all his belongings—even the sunglasses on his face and the chain around his neck. When his youngest uncle Ch'ang-ming (昌明) tries to protect the thugs (his childhood friends) from the police, Tung-tung struggles to understand the complicated loyalties involved.

Another sequence that exemplifies the film's refusal to idealize childhood or the rural past is the sequence depicting the relationship between Han-tzu and the local bird catcher. The sequence begins with lovely shots of the rice fields, accompanied by the chirping of birds. These are followed by close-up shots of a number of little birds tangled up in fine-meshed netting that is set out in the fields. A broad-shouldered and tanned young man comes to collect the birds, gently untangling them from the netting. A portrait of robust rural manhood, the bird catcher traps birds in the traditional, time-honored way. Hoping to steal a few birds from the cage, Tung-tung and the boys follow him to a house. The idyllic tenor of the sequence is unexpectedly shattered by the disturbing scene the boys then witness: the bird catcher, who seems to be drinking, teases Han-tzu, who is in the house. As the sexual flirtation continues, the couple retreats into a back room and out of view. Tung-tung begins to understand the meaning of the encounter he has witnessed only later, when he overhears his grandparents discussing Han-tzu's pregnancy. Tung-tung learns more about human sexuality from his observations of uncle Ch'ang-ming and his girlfriend Pi-yun (碧雲). When the two take Tung-tung to play pool, they spend most of their time making eyes at each other and eventually disappear into a back room, leaving Tung-tung in the awkward position of having to entertain himself while listening to their flirtatious giggling. Tung-tung receives a lesson in the complicated nature of human relationships when Pi-yun and her mother come to his grandfather's house to demand that Ch'ang-ming be held accountable for Pi-yun's pregnancy. Any illusions that Tung-tung (and the audience) might have had about the communal harmony of rural existence are broken by his grandfather's unsympathetic reaction to this development: he chases Ch'ang-ming out of the family home and refuses to see him or speak to him again.

Summer at Grandpa's, then, is perhaps less a nostalgic rural idyll and a story of childhood innocence than it is a tale about growing up, about the inevitability of leaving happy childhood memories in the past, where they belong, in order to move toward the future. Tung-tung's loss of innocence is underscored by a moving scene in which his uncle Ch'ang-ming pours his heart out to Tung-tung as if the little boy were an adult peer. As Ch'ang-ming tries to explain his relationship with Pi-yun and his troubles with the family, Tung-tung does his best to be a good listener, even if he doesn't understand all the emotional frustrations his uncle is trying to express. When Ch'ang-ming and Pi-yun are married, Tung-tung is the only family member to attend the wedding ceremony. As the presiding official drones on about the importance of "good family order" to the strength of a nation, the little boy tries very hard to sit still in his adult-sized chair and give the occasion the dignity it deserves. In a letter to his parents,

Tung-tung expresses his empathy for his uncle's disappointment that no one else in the family came to the wedding, revealing a sensitivity and level of maturity well beyond his years. By the time Tung-tung's summer vacation in the country is over, he returns to the city with a new understanding of himself, human nature, and the world. Indeed, the initiation aspects of the film are foreshadowed by its very first sequence—an elementary school graduation ceremony that marks the end of childhood and the commencement of the journey toward adulthood.

The Urban Future: *The Boys from Feng Kuei*

The idea of the city, as Raymond Williams has noted, is often associated with the future; the image of the city exists in the cultural imagination as a place of progress and opportunity, both economic and educational. For many, then, the journey toward adulthood often involves a move from the country to the city.[59] Hou Hsiao-hsien's *The Boys from Feng Kuei* is precisely about such a search for change and opportunity. The adolescent boys who are the protagonists of this initiation story are first seen in the village where they were born and raised: Feng Kuei, a tiny fishing village on Peng-hu (彭湖), a small island off the southern coast of Taiwan. The opening scenes of the film emphasize the idyllic elements of the village's natural landscape: the vast expanses of blue sky, the rustic beauty of the colorful fishing boats floating in the water, the soothing rhythm of the crashing waves, and the leisurely pace of life in the village. At the same time, however, the sense of timelessness conveyed by these scenes underscores the backwardness of life in the remote fishing village. The boys, who spend their days wandering aimlessly around the village, get into senseless arguments and scuffles wherever they go. They feel that their lives are stagnating and yearn for something more. Says one: "I can't stay here in Feng Kuei any longer. I feel like I'm drying up!" It is this desire for change and growth that drives them to embark on their journey to the southern port city of Kaohsiung in search of jobs and the hope of a better future. Hou Hsiao-hsien underlines the universality of this migration to the cities by having the boys from Feng Kuei sneak into a movie theater to watch *Rocco and His Brothers*, Luchino Visconti's classic film about Italian peasants from the underdeveloped south who migrate to the industrial northern city of Milan in search of work and a new life.

Like Visconti's Parondi brothers, the boys from Feng Kuei each struggle in their own way to make it in the new, unfamiliar world of the city. Their first impressions of Kaohsiung as they arrive by boat evoke a commonly held image of the city as chaotic, noisy, and confusing. The very first shot

15. *The Boys from Feng Kuei*. The film's first shot of Kaohsiung, a crowded and multilayered mise-en-scène, conveys the sensory overload experienced by the boys from Feng Kuei as they approach the city for the first time.

of the city captures, in Raymond William's words, "its miscellanaeity, its crowded variety, its randomness of movement."[60] The sky is totally blotted out by a crowded and multilayered mise-en-scène that effectively conveys the sensory overload experienced by the boys as they approach the city for the first time. In the foreground is the gate of a railroad crossing; behind that is a jumble of multicolored taxis, bicyclists, and motorcyclists. A constant flow of pedestrians weaves in and out between the vehicles. In the background and on either side of the screen, tall buildings and the smokestacks of large ships in the port are also visible. The overwhelming confusion the boys experience is further emphasized by the sequence that finds them at a bus stop, struggling to decipher the information on a forest of signs. It takes them at least three tries before they find the bus they think will take them to Ah-jung's (阿容) sister's apartment, but when they get off the bus they still find themselves lost in the big city. As buses, motorcycles, and automobiles whiz by them on every side, the constant honking of horns threatening to drown out their conversation, the boys finally ask a passerby for directions. In a moment of quirky humor, Hou emphasizes the total disorientation of the urban experience by having the passerby point to a sign, which suggests that the road the boys are looking for is "right up there," straight up in the sky.

There are numerous scenes that underscore the contrast between the city's worldliness and corruption and the country's innocence and purity. The urban landscape is clearly constructed as a place defined by moral

16. *The Boys from Feng Kuei*. The view of Kaohsiung from the eleventh floor of a half-finished high-rise underscores the vastness of the city.

standards quite different from the values to which the boys are accustomed. When one of the boys, Ch'ing-ah (清仔), suggests that they take a taxi to the sister's apartment rather than struggle to find the right bus route, Ah-jung pointedly reminds him that taxi drivers in Kaohsiung are likely to take country bumpkins like them for a long and expensive ride! They are twice approached by a man on a motorcycle, who entices them with a promise of pornographic films ("They're European flicks . . . in big screen color!").[61] The first time they are too startled to accept his offer, but the second time they eagerly hand over their money—only to find themselves victims of a con. Angry at his own naïveté, Ch'ing-ah wants to find the man and beat him up. Again Ah-jung has to remind him of the realities of the city: "We're not going to find him. Kaohsiung is huge! Do you think you're still in Feng Kuei?"

The relative moral laxity of the big city is suggested throughout the film. Their neighbor and coworker Huang Chin-ho (黃錦和) steals from the factory where they all work. He shares his apartment with Hsiao-hsing (小杏), a woman the boys initially think is Huang's wife but then discover is his "live-in." Their response to the idea of a live-in is "hao shuang!" (好爽)—an expression that is translated in the film's subtitles as "fantastic!" but has more complex connotations, including frankness, spontaneity, and a bold disregard for conventional morality.[62] Even Ah-jung's sister, who arrived in Kaohsiung from Feng Kuei only a year or two before the boys, has an "as yet unregistered" husband. The boys have other experiences that contribute to a negative image of urbanization. Initially excited to see Kaohsiung's famous Love River (愛河), they are soon disgusted by its sickening, polluted stench. They also learn, from Ah-jung's sister and their own experiences, that jobs are not always easy to come by in the city. The work that they do find, dead-end jobs as unskilled workers in an electronics factory, also highlights a historical truth of urbanization and the development of global capitalism: that country people in the Third World provide cheap labor for metropolitan industries that are often controlled by foreign powers and markets.[63] The factory in which the boys work assembles audio equipment for Proton, a U.S. brand.

On the other hand, the film also depicts the city as a place of opportunity. It certainly promises educational advancement to the boys from the country. When they first meet Huang Chin-ho, he is on his way to his night school classes after a full day of work. Despite the taunts from his less ambitious friends, Ch'ing-ah studies Japanese on his own, hoping to better himself by acquiring special skills. Of the three boys who emmigrate to the city, Ch'ing-ah is the one who matures the most. While the others continue to behave as irresponsibly as when they were living in Feng Kuei, Ch'ing-ah seems truly to have changed. Like Tung-tung, he has grown by observing the behavior of others in Kaohsiung and through his own experience of the city. His passage into adulthood is marked by the death of his father. When he returns home for the funeral, he realizes that he has been irrevocably changed by his urban experience and can never go back to the rural life of his childhood. Hsiao-hsing comes to a similar realization. After she decides to break off her relationship with Huang Chin-ho, she leaves Kaohsiung but not to return to her home. Instead, she moves to an even bigger urban metropolis—the capital city of Taipei. The open-ended conclusion of the film conveys the ambivalence inherent in Hou's conception of the city. While the failure of Ah-jung's audiotape business suggests the difficulty—even the futility—of entrepreneurial endeavors in the crowded and competitive atmosphere of the city, the exuberance with which Ch'ing-ah and the boys hawk their wares in the final shots of the film demonstrates their determination to try their best to succeed.

The Undefined Present: *Dust in the Wind*

Geoffrey Nowell-Smith has said of *Rocco and His Brothers* that in that film, as in all of Visconti's works, there is "a constant tension . . . between an intellectual belief in the cause of progress and an emotional nostalgia for the past world that is being destroyed."[64] This type of ambivalence toward the modern city and all that it represents—urban living, a capitalist economy, "progress"—is precisely the kind of unresolved tension Raymond Williams refers to when he characterizes the modern era as "an undefined present" caught between the conflicting impulses associated with the country and the city. Both *Summer at Grandpa's* and *The Boys from Feng Kuei* are subtended by this ambivalent attitude toward both the rural and the urban worlds, but *Dust in the Wind* is the film that most effectively captures the tension of the present moment in Taiwan's development, using "the contrast of country and city to ratify an unresolved division and conflict of impulses."[65]

Like *The Boys from Feng Kuei*, *Dust in the Wind* is also a story about growing up and going away. Its young protagonists, a boy named Ah-Wan (阿遠) and a girl named Ah-Hun (阿雲), are friends and neighbors in a small fishing and mining village on the outskirts of Taipei. Like their counterparts in Feng Kuei, who migrate from the remote outer island to the main island of Taiwan, Ah-Wan and Ah-Hun travel from their rural homes in a peripheral village outside of Taipei to the alien center of the capital city. At first, they go to the city in pursuit of a formal education; later they are motivated by their hopes of getting jobs that will enable them to send money home to their families in the countryside. Ah-Wan ventures into the city first and finds a job at a printing company. By the time Ah-Hun follows him into the city, he has found himself a better job as a motorcycle courier and has arranged a position for Ah-Hun in a sewing factory.

Taipei clearly represents an entirely new kind of existence for the two, offering a different landscape, a different kind of work, and an altogether different way of life. The film evokes the differences between the country and the city at numerous levels but particularly in terms of their contrasting spatio-temporal configurations. In its visual construction of space, for example, the film conveys the contrasting psychological experiences of urban versus rural life. The scenes that take place in the village are dominated by a sense of stability and harmonious unity. Normally, each sequence is introduced with an extreme long shot of the village landscape, which clearly establishes the location of the village in relation to mountains, sea, and sky. In these shots, the smallness of the human figures in the landscape is reminiscent of classical Chinese landscape painting and also underscores the importance of nature for traditional rural culture. Other long shots of the village streets establish the physical positioning of the villagers' houses in relation to each other—a visual representation of the nature of their social relationship. A single shot that shows Ah-Wan's house right next to Ah-Hun's, for instance, metaphorically suggests their

17. In *Dust in the Wind*, close-up shots of cramped, confined spaces underscore the isolation and alienation Ah-Wan and Ah-Hun experience in the metropolis.

emotional intimacy. In fact, the two have been betrothed to one another since childhood. The dominance of shots like these establishes a pattern of familiarity, stability, and security—and hence creates an image of the country as a knowable community. Also of note in these village scenes is the importance of outdoor spaces in village life. Ah-Wan's gregarious grandfather, for example, likes to sit in the doorway or on the steps of his house to chat with passersby. The children of the village are frequently shown playing in the village square—the same square where the men of the village congregate to drink, gamble, or hold discussions.

In the city, in contrast, the tall buildings and crowded streets have blotted out the sky and the earth. In place of long shots of the natural land-scape, Hou uses tight close-up and medium shots of cramped, confined spaces such as narrow alleyways and covered train station platforms. The expansive outdoor spaces of the countryside are replaced with shots of interior spaces: Ah-Wan's dark and tiny bedroom, the back room of the movie theater where Ah Wan and his friends often meet, the dingy print-ing company where he works, and the prisonlike underground sewing factory where Ah-Hun spends her days, with a tiny barred window her only connection to the outside world and the sole source of light and air. Many of these scenes are accompanied by the noisy racket of machin-ery—the presses and sewing machines—which presents a stark contrast to the serene silence marking the scenes in the village. Moreover, the film never clarifies where these confined spaces are in relation to one another; they appear only as isolated fragments. The sense of space created by these

18. In *Dust in the Wind*, Ah-Wan's grandfather's rambling monologue about the annual sweet potato harvest mimics the cyclical nature of rural time.

images is fractured and disorienting—a reflection of the alienation and displacement that the characters, uprooted from the intimate and familiar environment of their village, experience in the urban metropolis.

The contrast between country and city is also underscored by the different conceptions of time that operate in each environment. Life in the countryside is characterized by a sense of timelessness, as traditional ways of life seem to have persisted over the centuries. The cyclical nature of rural time, based on seasonal changes and other familiar patterns of nature, is most strongly conveyed in the final scene of the film.[66] Standing in the middle of a field of sweet potatoes, the grandfather talks to Ah-Wan about this year's crop. Ah-Wan listens patiently while the old man goes on and on about the experience he has gained over many years of cultivating sweet potatoes: he tells Ah-Wan exactly the right number of vines to plant each year and insists that this year's unusual typhoon season will result in a smaller crop. As he rambles on, even his rhetorical style is cyclical. His monologue takes on a comforting, familiar rhythm as he punctuates his chatter with a single refrain: "Sweet potatoes are harder to grow than ginseng, you know!" Urban life, however, is measured in abstract time—divided into sequential units to be defined, counted, and consumed.[67] The city sequences in the film, for example, often begin with a shot of the big clock that hangs in the train station. In addition, the only time Ah-Wan ever has use for a watch is when he travels to the city. While he is attending school in Taipei, he carries his father's watch with him. When he decides to quit school, he returns the watch. Once Ah-Wan finds a job in the city, the first thing his father does is buy him his very own watch—even though it is a financial burden to the family—because a watch is something one needs to survive in the city.[68] In contrast to the leisurely pace of rural life, urban existence demands punctuality and efficiency. Not surprisingly, Ah-Wan is continually scolded by his employers for being too slow.

The greatest contrast between the country and the city lies in the different kinds of interpersonal relationships that characterize each kind of settlement. As the visual configuration of the village suggests, the community is a close-knit organic unit. Individual families in the village have lived there for generations and know and trust each other as if they were all part of a single family. Everyone in the village calls Ah-Wan's grandfather Grandpa, and when the old man sees his grandson off to the army they stop by nearly every house in the village to say good-bye. The intimacy of the village community is seen in small details: the shopkeeper calls Ah-Hun over to give her the rice her mother wanted; Ah-Wan helps the auntie from next door to write a letter to her children in the city. The city, on the other hand, is far too large and complex for these kinds of intimate, direct, personal relationships. Raymond Williams writes of the atomization of existence associated with the image of the city, particularly of the increasing separateness of individual human beings. In the city, he writes, "men and women do not so much relate as pass each other and sometimes collide."[69] In the large and anonymous city, interpersonal relationships are not based on familiarity and mutual trust. Ah-Hun learns this the hard way when she first arrives at the train station in Taipei, naively entrusting her bags and belongings to a stranger—from whom she then has to wrest them away. Even Ah-Hun's and Ah-Wan's relationship suffers. Their increasing separateness is underscored by the numerous scenes in which they are forced to talk through barriers and partitions—whether doors and gateways or the iron bars that separate the sewing factory from the street above. Eventually, their long-standing engagement is broken off, as Ah-Hun decides to marry another boy she meets in the city, a postman who, like her and all of their friends in Taipei, is an immigrant from a small village.

It is easy, of course, to contrast the country and the city and speak of them as separate modes of human existence. In reality, however, the transformation from a rural agrarian society to an urban industrial one is seldom so simple or neat. Third World nations whose economic development came in the latter half of the twentieth century, in particular, tend to have a more "compressed" experience of modernization characterized by a much more rapid and complete penetration of the city into the country. Therefore, while the persistence of the twin poles of country and city in the modern cultural imagination are significant, it is equally important to recognize the necessary interrelation of the two, to acknowledge the tension of the present as people feel torn by the pull of both a traditional rural past and a modern urban present.[70]

Though critics and scholars have largely focused on the pastoral and regional dimensions of both Hwang Chun-ming's fiction and Hou Hsiao-hsien's films, it would be wrong to see either of them simply as chroniclers of life in the Taiwanese countryside, the last voices of a bucolic rural existence that is rapidly disappearing. While Hwang's affection for his rural characters and their traditional ways of life is apparent, he also can laugh at their backwardness (Kam Kim-ah) and recognizes the inherent tragedy of clinging nostalgically to tradition (Uncle Ah-Sheng). Even more than Hwang's stories, Hou's films depart from hsiang-t'u literature's critical tradition of polarizing country and city by avoiding excessive sentimentality or idealization of the rural world. There is no doubt about the depth of Hou's love for village life and his nostalgia for rural traditions, but he is also very much interested in processes of change, understanding that the experiences of change and the difficulty of choosing between conflicting values are central to modern consciousness. *Dust in the Wind* is a film about change, about a nation in a continuing state of transition. The fates of its characters are fascinating precisely because they are living on the border between the old and the new. As the film clearly acknowledges, the idea of the country as a simpler, happier place where people live in complete harmony with nature and communicate directly and intimately is fantasy. The little village where Ah-Wan and Ah-Hun grew up has already been affected by the penetration of a capitalist economy into the countryside. Theirs is not a traditional agrarian village; in addition to farming and fishing, the inhabitants also work in coal mines—a curious cross between industrialism and the old agricultural way of life. As the sequences in the film that allude to mining accidents and the possibility of a strike illustrate, industrialization has already altered traditional labor relations. The agents of power and profit—the owners of the mine, who presumably live in Taipei—have become alienated from labor. Moreover, the children of this village have already been swept into a growing industrial economy, migrating from the country to the city to work in factories as soon as they reach adolescence. Nowhere is the incongruity between the idealized image of a simple agrarian existence and the complicated nature of the modern Taiwanese countryside more evident than in the scene in which the villagers gather to watch a movie in a makeshift outdoor cinema. What appears on the screen set up in the village square is a typical rural idyll: a happy-go-lucky peasant in a traditional straw hat herds his ducks across a quaint little bridge. As the conversations between members of the audience reveal, the realities of Taiwanese rural life are much more complex and much more brutal. A boy is scolded by his mother for not sending home enough money from his job in Taipei. When his mother asks him about the bruises on his body, he tells her that he fell off his motorcycle—an explanation that prompts his mother to scold him for his clumsiness and to exclaim in disgust: "You might as well be a coal miner like your father!" Later, the boy admits to his friends that his bruises are really the result of being beaten by his boss in the city.

A society on the border between the country and the city is a society in transition. One of the most important technological developments that facilitated this social transformation—and one of its most potent symbols—is the train. Luchino Visconti's *Rocco and His Brothers* begins with the arrival of the Parondi family at the train station in Milan. Significantly, *Dust in the Wind* also opens with a shot taken from the front of the train that carries the two young protagonists between their schools and jobs in Taipei and their homes in the village.[71] The youths are travelers doing their best to navigate their way between conflicting worlds: the country and the city, the past and the future, tradition and modernity. At the end of *Dust in the Wind*, what lies ahead of them remains unclear. Adolescence, after all, is a difficult period of transition during which one experiences both a sentimental nostalgia for childhood and a desire to achieve adulthood. One might therefore describe the current period of transition from country to city as the adolescence of Taiwanese society. For the present, then, it is important to focus on the dynamic interplay between the two poles of human settlement rather than solely on the country or the city, for, as Raymond Williams writes: "Between the simple backward look and the simple progressive thrust there is room for long argument but none for enlightenment."[72]

7

Exile, Displacement, and Shifting Identities:
Globalization and the Frontiers
of Cultural Hybridity

Multinational Capitalism, Global Consumer Culture, and Taiwan since the 1980s

Everywhere throughout the world, one finds the same bad movie, the same slot machines, the same plastic or aluminum atrocities, the same twisting of language by propaganda, etc. It seems as if mankind, by approaching *en masse* a basic consumer culture, were also stopped *en masse* at a subcultural level. Thus we come to the crucial problem confronting nations just rising from underdevelopment. In order to get on the road towards modernization, is it necessary to jettison the old cultural past which has been the *raison d'etre* of a nation? . . . Whence the paradox: on the one hand, it has to root itself in the soil of the past, forge a national spirit, and unfurl this spiritual and cultural revindication before the colonialists's personality. But in order to take part in modern civilization, it is necessary at the same time to take part in scientific, technical, and political rationality, something that very often requires the pure and simple abandonment of a whole cultural past. It is a fact: every culture cannot sustain and absorb the shock of modern civilization. There is the paradox: how to become modern and to return to sources; how to revive an old, dormant civilization and take part in universal civilization. — Paul Ricoeur

In this passage from a 1961 essay entitled "Universal Civilization and National Cultures," Paul Ricoeur seizes on the fundamental tensions between the rural and the urban, the past and the present, the traditional and the modern, and the indigenous and the foreign that underlie the process of modernization all around the globe but most dramatically in the developing nations of the Third World.[1] He also identifies the two primary forces whose intense competition and dynamic interaction lie at the heart of the varied cultural responses to modern civilization. On the one hand are localized, bounded nationalisms that seek to conserve and protect "old, dormant civilizations," and on the other is the desire to embrace the compelling forces of modernization and the new globalism—conflicting tendencies that have been with us since the age of empire. Global history in the modern era has been characterized primarily by a blossoming and complication of international and intercultural relationships that has radically altered sociocultural structures at all levels. Since the middle of the twentieth century, the mobility of people, goods, capital, and culture around the world has increased and intensified thanks to technological advancements in modes of transportation and media communications and to the development of a complicated multinational global economy. During the last two decades, in particular, these rapid and radical changes in geopolitical and geocultural interaction have fundamentally called into question our conventional assumptions about nationhood, cultural identity, and world order, as traditional formulations of the global system—such as the three worlds theory and the core-periphery model—are being replaced by visions of a world that is melding into a single, if increasingly complex, heterogeneous, and unstable, network.

Most scholars agree that this growing interconnectedness and interdependency can largely be attributed to three forces—the burgeoning of multinational business, the proliferation and global penetration of new media technologies, and an increase and shift in patterns of immigration—the profound effects of which are underscored by the dramatic changes since the 1980s that can be seen in nations such as Taiwan. The recent history of the island exemplifies in numerous ways the developmental strategies of the late capitalist world system.[2] Throughout the 1980s, for instance, the global dispersal of capital and internationalization of manufacturing were spurred by the removal of economic barriers between governments from Europe to Asia and the Americas as economic development strategies shifted emphasis from the nurturing of national industries to the negotiation of global trade relationships.[3] Taiwan has pursued just such a strategy since the end of the 1970s, shifting its focus from national development to the single-minded pursuit of multinational diversification and integration into the global order at all levels. It has focused its attention on expanding its markets and presence abroad, as well as on efforts to attract foreign capital to the island.[4] The "economic miracle" of the last few decades attests to the success of this strategy and has helped the island to become an integral part of the global network of finance, labor, and production. Today's Taiwan is a major manufacturer and exporter of consumer products—not only the inexpensive toys and clothing that once made the label "Made in Taiwan" a mark of inferior workmanship,[5] but also sophisticated consumer electronics and cutting-edge computer technology.[6] The island has become enormously wealthy, with impressive reserves of foreign capital and a standard of living that is among the highest in Asia.[7] During the 1980s, the Taiwanese government welcomed multinational businesses to the island, eliminating long-standing state monopolies on tobacco and alcohol, for example, and actively courting international franchises.[8] Today the island's supermarkets and department stores are stocked with the hottest fashions and newest consumer goods from Asia, Europe, and the Americas, and the streets of its cities are lined with international franchises like 7-Eleven, McDonald's, and IKEA. As personal income increases, the Taiwanese people have become avid and knowledgeable consumers (thanks to the internationalization of advertising) of brand name products from all over the world.[9]

Taiwan's integration into the world community in recent years has also been facilitated by its access to new media and communications technologies, as the government has committed itself to fully involving Taiwan in the global network of television, telephone, and computer technologies. It has steadily increased investments intended to upgrade the island's telecommunications systems.[10] During the 1980s, the home video revolution opened up a whole new world to the Taiwanese, as movies, cartoons, television programs, and even commercials from Hong Kong, Japan, the United States, and Europe began streaming in through both legal and illegal channels. Since then, the addition and astonishing proliferation of cable television (especially channels like CNN and MTV), direct satellite broadcasting, and the Internet[11] has offered up an even greater cultural smorgasbord.[12] In addition, imports of foreign magazines—covering not only news and business but also fashion and lifestyle issues—have been steadily on the rise, while the number of foreign books being translated is also increasing.[13] At the same time, Taiwan has used the new media technologies to extend its own global influence, exporting its news stories, movies, TV shows, and music to audiences all over the world.[14] The growing communities of the Taiwanese diaspora are now able to maintain links with the island and each other through local Chinese-language radio and TV broadcasts, by reading local editions of Chinese-language newspapers published by Taiwan's major papers, or by logging on to any number of Internet sites. Today's new technologies of electronic and digital capitalism allow nearly instantaneous transmission of news, ideas, fashion, and entertainment to and from almost anywhere in the world. Hence, the emotional and experiential bonds that are instrumental in building communities are increasingly being produced on a transnational scale.[15]

Exile, Displacement, and Identities   **213**

The new cosmopolitanism and global perspective that characterizes Taiwan today also owes much to the increasing mobility of its people. In the late 1970s, numerous restrictions governing travel and emigration were been lifted or loosened. In 1979, for example, tourist passports were issued to Taiwanese citizens for the first time and the island's airlines commenced international service.[16] These changes, coupled with Taiwan's economic successes and the continuing rise in personal income, meant that the 1980s saw an enormous boom in Taiwanese tourism, with groups and individuals traveling not only to such popular destinations as Japan, North America, and Europe but also to South America, Southeast Asia, Australia, and even the Middle East.[17] The liberalization of other government policies resulted in a dramatic increase in the number of Taiwanese conducting business or studying abroad. Moreover, the steady improvement in the quality of life in Taiwan and the island's growing cosmopolitanism have brought an end to the brain drain that had resulted from earlier generations of Taiwanese students traveling abroad. Rather than remaining abroad following the completion of their studies, an increasing number of talented and ambitious Taiwanese are bringing their experience and knowledge—as well as their living habits and popular tastes acquired while living abroad—back to Taiwan.

As a result of these dramatic economic, demographic, technological, and structural changes in international relationships, modern metropolises like Taipei have become sites where multiple cultures come together to continually confront, challenge, and ultimately change each other.[18] Today's geocultural exchange of people, capital, and culture, morever, is not a one-way street; that is, *globalization* no longer simply means the Americanization of the world.[19] The multidirectional flows of global cultural traffic have undercut traditional universalist conceptions of globalization and cosmopolitanism, which tend to presuppose the dominance and authority of the Western experience. Instead, cultural theorists are beginning to acknowledge that the "cosmopolitanisms" of the late capitalist era are both plural and particular.[20] Multinational business, transnational migration, and media technologies—the engines that drive the new globalization—have also empowered the smaller nations of what used to be called the Third World. As capital, people, and consumer and cultural products have begun to flow outward from the Third World, polycultural forces have dramatically transformed urban centers in the First World as well—a phenomenon that has been called "peripheralization at the core."[21] Thanks to the ascension of new global financial, industrial, and media players in Asia and elsewhere, *globalization* no longer means just McDonald's burgers in Beijing and Levi's jeans in New Delhi;

it also means Taiwanese *"boba"* shops in Los Angeles, Mexican cantinas in Prague, and Korean television in Topeka.[22] The same global media that have allowed the penetration of European and American culture into the remotest corners of Africa, Latin America, and Asia is also helping to bring the culture of the Third World to the First. The new immigrant communities in First World metropolises bring with them not only their food,[23] languages, and cultural practices but also—thanks to cable television, satellite broadcasting, video and computer technology—news, television dramas, movies, and popular music from their homelands. All of these immigrant cultures are rapidly and irrevocably infiltrating and reshaping the cultural mainstream of their adopted homes. In many cities of the world, the immediate juxtaposition of so many diverse cultures within increasingly porous national borders is already beginning to produce fascinating cultural hybridity, resulting in a complex heterogeneity that goes far beyond the imagination of older models of geocultural interaction.[24]

Exile and Displacement: The Multicultural Metropolis and Alternative Models of Identity Formation

One of the chief consequences of the dramatic changes that have radically altered modern global society has been what sociologist Fred Davis calls "massive identity dislocations": in a society subject to rapid change and clashes between multiple cultures, people find their fundamental beliefs, values, and modes of understanding constantly disrupted and shaken and find themselves losing their social, psychological, and moral bearings.[25] It is not surprising, therefore, that so many contemporary works of literature and art revolve around questions of identity—both individual and collective. One particularly creative exploration of identity can be seen in the work of Argentinian writer Alicia Dujovne Ortiz, whose best-known work, *Buenos Aires*, is an autobiographical meditation on herself, her city, and her nation.[26] In it, she confronts the rich multiplicity of cultures—native Indian, Russian, Spanish, Italian, and Irish, to name but a few—that make up modern Argentinian culture and raises what she considers to be "the oldest and most essential questions" she faces as a modern Argentinian: "What does it mean to say one is a *native* of Buenos Aires? To belong to Buenos Aires, to be *porteño*—to come from this port? . . . Who or what can we hang onto?"[27] In a provocative reading of Ortiz's work, Caren Kaplan identifies two different conceptions of cultural identity that might be seen as responses to the multiplicity of cultures endemic to the modern age in general but most pronouncedly to postcolonial societies.[28] The first, exile, which Kaplan identifies as a modernist mode of understanding, is based on the sense of separation and irrevocable loss that often results from dislocation—whether physical, cultural, social, or linguistic—and is characterized by anxiety and a passionate yearning to recover a sense of wholeness and rediscover some sort of unified, essential identity in a personal or historical past.[29] Underlying the notion of exile is the long tradition of European romantic nationalism so clearly articulated by Ricoeur: an absolutist, organic view of culture that, as Frederick Buell has noted, can be traced to the influential writings of eighteenth-century poet and philosopher Johann Gottfried von Herder.[30] It envisions culture as a coherent historical entity and the primordial basis for identity. Cultural conservationists of all political persuasions have embraced this view in order to decry the contamination of national cultures—whether by European colonialism, American cultural imperialism, or the cultural homogenization that is perceived to be the product of today's globalization.[31] The attitude of the exile, then, is shaped by fear, resistance to the unfamiliar, and mourning for a past that is lost.

Displacement, on the other hand, is conceived of as a recognition and acceptance of the new, of separation and multiplicity; it responds to the cultural mélange of modern civilization not with anxiety and estrangement but with a willingness to explore the spaces between cultures. It is a model of identity formation that Kaplan describes as postmodernist. While exile seeks to return to a fixed and knowable past, displacement looks to the past but refuses to be trapped by it, acknowledging the present and looking forward to the future. It offers, as Kaplan puts it, "a more processual, multi-cultural notion of identity." Identity is no longer simply a state of being but a more complex matter of continual becoming, "an ongoing process of displacement."[32] This second conception of identity has been advocated by many other writers and critics in different guises using terms such as *deterritorialization, travel,* and *nomadism.*[33] The critic Stuart Hall defines two ways of thinking about identity that are particularly close to Kaplan's: the first, based on the "vector of similarity and continuity," is an essentialized subject located in a fixed and idealized past and is "constructed through memory, fantasy, narrative, and myth."[34] In the Caribbean societies examined by Hall, this conception of identity manifests itself in a preoccupation with Africa as the lost homeland, the center of cultural meaning. The second, based on "the vector of difference and rupture," shifts its attention from Africa (the past) to the New World (terra incognita, the present and future), a "place of displacements" (78) defined by migration, difference, and diversity. Hence, this second way of thinking is defined "not by essence or purity, but by the recognition of a necessary heterogeneity, diversity, by a conception of 'identity' that lives with and through, not despite, difference; by *hybridity*" (80).

It is critical to emphasize here that *exile* and *displacement* are not strictly oppositional or mutually exclusive terms but exist along a continuum and often operate simultaneously—coexisting impulses in response to the challenges posed by the processes of modernization and globalization to the problem of cultural identity. There is a constant and unresolved tension between the need to clearly trace the boundaries of a definable, stable, and comprehensible self and the unavoidable pressure to somehow acknowledge the multicultural differences that are continually shaping and reshaping today's societies. This pairing of *exile* and *displacement* echoes the old quarrel between particularism and universalism that cultural analysts such as Paul Ricoeur have identified, but it differs in important ways. The problem with thinking about culture in Ricoeur's terms is that it allows only two options for identity formation: one either identifies with a localized, particular culture (nationalism) or "abandons . . . a whole cultural past" and assimilates into a single, homogenized, universal culture. The movement from exile to displacement, in contrast, is marked not by a choice between opposites but by a shift in the way one thinks about similarities and differences within and without. Exiles, for instance, form a sense of self by focusing on the similarities that bind the (national, racial, or gender) group with which they want to identify but even more strongly by focusing on the particular differences that separate the self from the external other. Hence, the exile fears the modern global interpenetration and rejects the homogenization—Riceour's universalism—that threatens to eventually erase differences *between* nation-states. While exile is linked to particularism, displacement does not exactly embrace its opposite, universalism. Universalism implies the suppression of local differences and specificities in favor of a monolithic global culture. Displacement, on the other hand, might be seen as a kind of cultural relativism that gives attention to both specific differences and global similarities, moving toward a looser, more flexible definition of *culture* that acknowledges not only differences between nations but also the myriad differences *within* societies and even within individuals. Instead of envisioning a single, uniform, global cosmopolitanism, it acknowledges the simultaneous existence of multiple cosmopolitanisms—partly rooted in local culture, partly in global networks—that are generated by specific histories of economic, political, and cultural interaction.[35]

"Exile" and the Poetics of Nostalgia

Alternative theories of identity such as Kaplan's notion of displacement are important interrogative attempts to escape the either-or binarisms of the national/global and particular/universal that underlie traditional paradigms for understanding cultures and the representation of identity. Her vocabulary of exile and displacement provides a particularly illuminating framework for an analysis of the different constructions of nation and Taiwanese identity that operate in both Hwang Chun-ming's fiction and Hou Hsiao-hsien's films. As noted earlier, the hsiang-t'u movement of which Hwang is a part grew out of a conservationist response to the cultural and political crises of the early 1970s, when the rapid influx of foreign capital and consumer culture into Taiwan was perceived as a threat to the island's native traditions. Hsiang-t'u advocates believed that Taiwan's embrace of Western-style capitalism had come at too high a price; they feared that wholesale Westernization would, in Ricoeur's words, result in "the simple abandonment of a whole cultural past." Hwang's hsiang-t'u stories are therefore structured around the very types of simple binary oppositions—between the particular and the universal, the native and the foreign, the old and the new, the past and the present, and the rural and the urban—that underlie the essentialist conception of culture and identity to which the exile clings. The works, though sometimes comic, are above all suffused with a sense of loss, of mourning for an idealized past. Hwang's stories represent an attempt to retrace the parameters of a way of life threatened by the encroachment of modern civilization in general and foreign cultures in particular. In "The Drowning of an Old Cat" and "The Gong," the Mandarin Chinese dialect is depicted as colorless and flat in comparison with the island's native tongue, and its growing dominance is perceived as responsible for the Taiwanese nation's loss of linguistic coherence. The idea that Taiwan's cultural purity had been contaminated by modernization and the invasion of foreign ideologies is underscored by the familiar feminization of native culture—so often employed by cultural nationalists—in stories such as "Sayonara, Tsai-chien," "Little Widows," and "A Flower in the Rainy Night." Hwang's characters often seem to be adrift in the tides of sociocultural change, and they long to regain a sense of belonging and attachment. The metaphorical home for which these exiles yearn lies somewhere in the Taiwanese countryside, as the rural village is repeatedly evoked as the origin and stronghold of authentic Taiwanese culture. In "The Story of Ch'ing-fan Kung" and "Two Sign Painters," the familiar order, serenity, and security of village life is idealized and contrasted with the chaos, cacophony, and estrangement of urban life.

Exile is a significant motif in many of Hou Hsiao-hsien's films as well. The family of mainlanders in *A Time to Live and a Time to Die* is representative of the displaced persons who characterize the modern age. Torn from their homes by warfare, they find themselves adrift, "loosened from their past, not yet anchored to their present."[36] Like so many exiles, their existence is defined primarily by a painful sense of forced separation, an unbearable rift between the self and its true home.[37] In their desperation to overcome the anxiety of estrangement from their native soil and to recover a sense of identification with their lost homeland, the older generation of the family—the parents and the grandmother—engages in the practice of *nostalgia*, a psychological and cultural response that often occurs in reaction to traumatic dislocations.[38] Nostalgic exiles cling desperately to the past and the homeland that has been lost. In their continual efforts to restore that past, they often cannot—or will not—find anchorage in the world they presently inhabit. Modern literature and film are filled with exiles who respond to their forced dislocation by locking themselves away in isolation and despair. The first two reels of Jonas Mekas's autobiographical film *Lost, Lost, Lost* (1975), for example, depict a group of Lithuanians living in exile who have clustered together in the Williamsburg section of Brooklyn. This defensively self-contained group of exiles creates its own little haven—a safe, symbolic community—that serves two important functions: it distinguishes them from the host country, in which they consider themselves to be transient visitors; and it reinforces their sense of connection to each other and the homeland from which they have all been separated.[39] The exiled mainlanders in *A Time to Live and a Time to Die*, victims of the civil war between Mao Zedong's Communists and Chiang Kai-shek's Nationalists, have been forced to flee their homes on the mainland to an island that is literally on China's periphery. Living in exile, they, too, alienate themselves from the life that surrounds them in a Taiwanese village. Their isolation is both physical and linguistic. In one family both parents confine themselves to living within the secure boundaries of their house; the father's isolation is forced, due to illness, but the mother's self-containment seems to be by choice. She seems to leave the house only when necessary—to buy food or see a doctor. Moreover, the older members of the family speak only their own Hakka dialect; they are either unable or unwilling (the parents seem to understand the children, who often insist on speaking Mandarin or Taiwanese) to speak the languages of the island. The grandmother often ventures into the village but only to walk and wander in a poignantly futile search for the road back to her native village, the figure of the wanderer so common in exilic literature and film. Like Ah-Hao's grandmother, the Lithuanian exiles in *Lost, Lost, Lost* also spend endless hours taking long walks—as if they are trying to walk off their pain, loneliness, and despair.[40]

Throughout Mekas's film, the song of Ulysses is repeated as a sort of rhythmic chant: "Oh sing, Ulysses / Sing your travels / Tell the story of a man / Who never wanted to leave his home / Who was happy / And lived among the people he knew / And spoke the language / Sing how then he was thrown out into the world." His invocation of Ulysses underscores the parallels between the fate of modern exiles and that of the traditional wandering hero of epic literature. The story of Ulysses the exile is also a story of return, for, as Salman Rushdie has said, "exile is a dream of glorious return."[41] The exile is consumed by a longing to return to a point of origin—to a motherland, childhood, a rural past, a familiar community, or a unified sense of self—that can provide a stable center of meaning. Hence, Ah-Hao's grandmother sets out every day in search of the road back to her ancestral home. She wants to take Ah-Hao with her, back to his roots, so he can learn who he really is. For most exiles, however, an actual return to the homeland or the past is impossible, and it is precisely this inability to realize the desired return that gives rise to nostalgia.[42] Interestingly, one of Hwang's most romanticized hsiang-t'u stories, "A Flower in the Rainy Night," provides a notable exception, for the prostitute Pai-mei achieves the glorious return of which all exiles dream. She returns to her childhood home (a rural past, a familiar community) and is able to regain a unified and stable sense of self through motherhood.

Pai-mei achieves a restored sense of self only because she has erased from her memory the years of prostitution that took her away from her home in the countryside. Nostalgia, then, can be seen as a denial of history—that is, a denial of the inexorable progression of historical time and the irreversible changes it has wrought.[43] The life of the exile is a life held in suspension. Stuart Hall has suggested that the exile constructs this idealized past "through memory, fantasy, narrative, and myth."[44] Mekas's Lithuanian exiles, obsessed with their native soil as the source of authentic identity, frequently gather to tell stories and sing songs about life in the old country: "How I watched you that day singing with your faces transfixed, transported back to Lithuania. Oh no, never, never you'll be able to uproot it from your minds, from your heart, from the very cells of your body." In Hwang Chun-ming's "Two Sign Painters," the laborer named Monkey compulsively sings songs from his rural village as a defense against the alienation and loneliness of life in the city. Hou Hsiao-hsien's exiled mainlanders, too, are transported back to their homes and their past lives on the mainland through their memories and fantasies. The parents live in their memories, the father writing in his diary, the mother compulsively narrating her recollected past to the children. For the grandmother, the fantasies are so real, the past so tangibly present, that she cannot distinguish between the mainland Chinese landscape in her imagination and the real Taiwanese countryside that surrounds her. Their memories and fantasies are a way of bridging the distance—both spatial and temporal—between their past and their present. For these exiles, letters are also an important nostalgic object that helps diminish the gap separating those living at home and those living in exile.[45] They provide a form of connection, however tenuous, to the beloved home-land and a happier life in the past. In *A Time to Live and a Time to Die*, a long sequence depicts the family receiving a letter bearing long-awaited news from relatives on the mainland. Both parents read it intently and in solemn silence, as a cutaway shot shows the children working on their stamp collection—also underscoring the centrality of letters in their lives. Significantly, the arrival of the letter triggers yet another flood of memories for both the mother and the father.

The anxiety and sense of dislocation that characterize the modern era affect not only displaced persons forced to migrate across national borders but even those whose dislocations are less clearly or dramatically defined. In the wake of urbanization and industrialization, for example, laborers uprooted from their rural communities to work in the city suffer a kind of internal exile.[46] As Hou Hsiao-hsien's *Dust in the Wind* suggests, the metaphorical home that is idealized in this case is often a childhood associated with the countryside.[47] When Ah-Wan and Ah-Hun first move to Taipei, they also experience exile in the city. Their sense of alienation and dislocation is conveyed in part by the spatial, temporal, and social disorientation they experience but also by their behavioral responses to these changes. For example, the film contains numerous scenes in which the pair gather with other young people who have come to the city to find work—building a self-contained little community with other exiles from "somewhere else." The young prostitutes in Hwang Chun-ming's "A Flower in the Rainy Night" form a similar kind of surrogate family, offering each other comfort and support and gathering together to share their dreams of one day returning to their childhood village homes. For young people like these, letters also take on a special significance as necessary connections to their homes and families—their cultural and emotional centers of meaning. Several scenes in *Dust in the Wind* foreground the writing and receiving of letters: early in the film, Ah-Wan helps a neighbor to write a letter to her son in the city. Not long after Ah-Hun arrives in Taipei, Ah-Wan finds her in tears because she hasn't received a letter from the village in a very long time. When Ah-Wan is sent to a peripheral island off the coast for his military service, he and the other soldiers look forward every day to the letters from home. In one of the letters Ah-Wan receives, he learns that in his absence Ah-Hun has married . . . a mail-carrier.

Toward Postmodernism: The "Global Teenager" and Hou Hsiao-hsien's *Daughter of the Nile*

I had come into town the previous afternoon watching video reruns of *Dance Fever* on the local bus. As I wandered around, looking for a place to stay, I noted down the names of the few stores: the Hey Shop, the Hello Shop, Easy Rider Travel Service, T.G.I. Friday restaurant. After checking into a modest guesthouse where Vivaldi was pumping out of an enormous ghetto blaster, I had gone out in search of a meal. I ran across a pizzeria, a sushi bar, a steak house, a Swiss restaurant, and a slew of Mexican cafes. Eventually, I wound up at T.J.'s, a hyper-chic fern bar, where long-legged young blondes in tropical T-shirts were sitting on wicker chairs and sipping tall cocktails. Reggae music floated through the place as a pretty waitress brought me my chips and salsa.[48]

The idea of exile can be useful for understanding the experiences of those who find themselves torn between two cultures and value systems —whether between a native homeland and an alien country or between traditional rural existence and modern urban society—and who turn to the more familiar and secure past for a sense of authentic identity. But it hardly seems adequate to cope with the kind of postmodern pastiche and cultural heterogeneity, for example, that Pico Iyer describes on his arrival in Bali. In today's postcolonial world of transnational capitalism and global consumer culture, life has become perhaps too complicated for interpretive models based on simple dualities and dialectical oppositions. Today's metropolises—in both the Third World and the First—have become complex, multilayered spaces that Fredric Jameson has described as "postmodern hyperspace." These are "sites in which transnationally organized circuits of capital, labor, and communications intersect with one another and with local ways of life"[49] or "a field of stylistic and discursive heterogeneity without a norm."[50]

In the last ten years, Taiwan's phenomenal economic growth has secured it a position in the multinational global economy, and its capital city, Taipei, has become a nodal point on the complex network of transnational capital, global communications, and mass consumer culture. Its inhabitants, too, have become active and avid participants in global circuits of economic and cultural exchange. Hou Hsiao-hsien's 1987 *Daughter of the Nile*—the only one of his films before the 1996 *Goodbye South, Goodbye* (南國再見, 南國) to attempt to deal with Taiwan's modern city life and youth culture—might be described as a vision of Taipei as postmodern hyperspace, a place where various forms of American, European, and Japanese mass culture confront, compete, and eventually comingle with indigenous traditional ideologies. Caught in the middle of this confusing cultural mélange are Hsiao-yang (曉陽), the teenage heroine of the film, and her friends and family. Perhaps more than any other segment of the world's population, young people—or "teenagers"—have been deeply affected by the globalization of popular culture.[51] Thanks to technological innovations such as television, videos, stereos, compact discs, and computers, and to the internationalization of marketing, teenagers around the world have more in common with each other than ever before.

Hsiao-yang works at a Taipei branch of Kentucky Fried Chicken.[52] The restaurant looks just like any other branch of the chain in the United States or elsewhere in the world: instantly recognizable from the red and white striped decor, the familiar face of Colonel Sanders, and the tidy uniforms. Like teenagers the world over,[53] she and her friends listen to American pop music,[54] which blasts from their car stereos, boom boxes, and Sony Walkmans.[55] They cruise around on motorcycles and in Japanese cars, hang out in restaurants and coffee houses with names like "Pink House," and dance the night away at a club called "Touch." Hsiao-yang's little sister, like so many elementary school girls, is crazy about the Hello Kitty and Little Twin Star products made in Japan and sold in specialty boutiques all over the world, including in Taiwan and the United States. Many have condemned, of course, the penetration of brand names and corporate icons into the consciousnesses of Third World peoples as yet another example of cultural imperialism. The effects of a global consumer language need not, however, necessarily be negative, especially given the realities of today's global migrations.[56]

It is important to point out here that despite the massive invasion of American pop culture into Third World cities like Taipei, these societies are not merely copycat cultures, not simply passive and uncritical recipients of ready-made images and consumer goods from the West. Rather, they are, as Caren Kaplan notes, "complex, sophisticated cultures which filter and mediate first world imports, recreating local meanings, producing hybrid cultural artifacts and subjects."[57] Frederick Buell similarly sees in today's global cultural carnival "not assimilation—the subjection of one culture to another—but of postmodern boundary violating and syncretistic cultural intersections." He emphasizes how "American material is not just absorbed but actively used by different national cultures. The material is used, on the one hand, as part of people's sometimes limited, but sometimes quite successful, attempts to negotiate and unseat American hegemony and, on the other, as a part of the formation of a new, syncretic, hybridized media-based global culture."[58] This cultural hybridity is visible in something as simple as the sign that hangs outside the Kentucky Fried Chicken store where Hsiao-yang works: the picture of Colonel Sanders is familiar to the West, but the Chinese characters—a transliteration of *Kentucky*—are not. The characters themselves (肯塔基) have no coherent meaning when strung together, but they do evoke a homophonous pun—(啃它雞, "chew the chicken")—whose meaning would be lost on a non-Chinese speaker. Inside the store, the decor, the uniforms, and the packaging are recognizably American, but the music on the radio is Japanese pop. These young people may watch American television shows and read Japanese comic books, but in school they learn classical Chinese philosophy.[59] Teenagers in the metropolises of the First World, where the demographics are also rapidly metamorphosing thanks to the massive influx of cultures from all over the world, are similarly discovering the reality of multicultural hybridity. In Los Angeles, for instance, where "Central and South America meet the Pacific Rim and West Indies," cultural assimilation is definitely not a one-way street, with everyone trying to fit into Anglo culture.[60] With so many disparate cultures living cheek by jowl, cultural exchange is not a one-way or even a two-way street; negotiating the free-form and multidirectional flow of languages and cultures in today's Los Angeles requires an unprecedented cultural dexterity and adaptibility that many of the city's residents—particularly its young people—are beginning to display.[61]

In an era of global mass communications and marketing that surrounds people with a confusing jumble of multiple cultures, the notion of an essential or authentic "identity" that one can recover by returning to a point of origin no longer seems valid. How, for example, would Hsiao-yang and her friends define an origin? A home? A community? They have no knowledge or experience of an agricultural Taiwan, only an urban present characterized by manic consumerism, commodity fetishism, and alienation. For Hsiao-yang, there is no longer a rural past to which she

19. *Daughter of the Nile*. Like the title character of the comic book she reads, Hsiao-yang is a "daughter of the Nile," a river whose mystery and significance lies precisely in the inaccessibility of its origin.

can nostalgically return. The closest she comes to communing with nature is in the tiny rooftop garden her grandfather tends. Nor is there any sense of childhood innocence; Hsiao-yang has been aware of her brother's life of petty thievery since she was very young, and her little sister is already stealing money to buy the toys and trinkets she so badly wants. In an era when people are increasingly mobile, not even the family is available as a stable center of meaning and identity. Many of the families in Hsiao-yang's world are fragmented. The mother of Ah-San, a friend of Hsiao-yang's brother, lives thousands of miles away in Japan.[62] Hsiao-yang's own mother is dead, and her father lives apart from the family in Taichung. Increasingly, people communicate not face to face but through a vast electronic communications network of telephones and beepers.[63] Hsiao-yang struggles gamely, with the help of her grandfather and her aunt, to try to make the familial center hold, but she cannot succeed. The only point of origin she can cling to as her center of meaning lies, ironically, in distant mythical Egypt: she is a "daughter of the Nile," a river whose mystery and significance lies precisely in the inaccessibility of its source.[64] Hsiao-yang's search for an origin of identity is destined to be futile.

Displacement and the Politics of Travel:
Border Crossings and Exploring the Space in Between

> The metropolis is an allegory; in particular it represents the allegory of the crisis of modernity that we have learnt to recognize in the voices of Baudelaire, Benjamin, and Kafka. To go beyond these bleak stories of exile and that grey, rainy country of the anguished soul, is to establish a sense of being at home in the city, and to make of tradition a space of transformation rather than the scene of a cheerless destiny. For this metropolis is not simply the final stage of a poignant narrative, of apocalypse and nostalgia, it is also the site of the ruins of previous orders in which diverse histories, languages, memories and traces continually entwine and recombine in the construction of new horizons.[65]

In our increasingly complex and confusing world of "crisscrossed economies, intersecting systems of meaning, fragmented identities" and multiple cultures in contention, the search for a single unified source of identity is sorely inadequate and is bound to lead to frustration and despair of the kind experienced by Hou Hsiao-hsien's exiles.[66] Those who mourn the dissolution of organic cultures will argue that the cultural mixing we see today dilutes culture and creates lost souls. Others, however, envision a brave new world of opportunity and creativity in postmodern cultural heterogeneity and perceive it to be ultimately enriching. The very contradictions and tensions between cultures that the exile finds so troubling can be exploited, as Caren Kaplan suggests, "towards a rewriting of the connections between the different parts of the self in order to make a world of possibilities."[67] Once one moves from a conception of identity as an essential subject to be retrieved or recovered from a fixed past to the more fluid, ever-evolving sense of self, a migratory or nomadic identity that Kaplan calls an "ongoing process of displacement," one needs no longer be paralyzed, like the exile, by the experience of marginalization and dislocation. A nomadic subject explores and celebrates separation and difference, probing cultural border zones and attempting to turn a negative position into a positive force.[68] The ability to move between marginal and central discourses, to travel between multiple cultures and value systems, is a crucial part of this strategy.

In Hou Hsiao-hsien's Taiwan, it is the younger generation that has begun to embrace this dynamic and evolutionary sense of self. The children in *A Time to Live and a Time to Die*, for example, can be seen as nomadic subjects who construct a sense of identity by learning to move between multiple cultures. As they mature and leave the familial sphere, they encounter the different cultural realities of Taiwanese village life, then of the island's educational system. Gradually, Ah-Hao and his siblings learn to move comfortably between the three cultural-linguistic worlds they inhabit. In *Dust in the Wind*, Ah-Wan and Ah-Hun are also travelers between worlds, moving between the fast-paced, anonymous life of the city and the more familiar rural ways of the country. The signifier of their nomadic identity is the train that carries them between their jobs in Taipei and their families in the village. It is the link that binds the urban metropolis to its rural satellites, the present to the past, and modernity to tradition. *Dust in the Wind*, *The Boys from Feng Kuei*, *Daughter of the Nile*, and the more recent *Goodbye South, Goodbye* all contain many other images of travel—boats, cars, taxicabs, and motorcycles—which carry the young protagonists through different landscapes, multiple cultures, and diverse experiences.[69] The young drifters and would-be gangsters of *Goodbye South, Goodbye* are particularly restless in their pursuit of economic opportunity. The film's protagonist, a tattooed ruffian named Ah-Kao (阿高), who is constantly talking on his cell phone or driving in his car, leads his gang of cohorts all around the island chasing various get-rich-quick schemes. Ah-Kao and his buddies want their share of Taiwan's economic miracle and are willing to go wherever opportunity takes them. Like so many Taiwanese investors, who see mainland China as a potential gold mine, Ah-Kao wants to go to Shanghai and open a restaurant. His girlfriend contemplates joining her sister in America, where she is making a comfortable living selling real estate to more recent arrivals from Taiwan. She is unfazed by any barriers of language or culture: English is easy enough to learn, she suggests, and life in the Taiwanese diasporic communities in the United States is not all that different from life in Taiwan. For the young people in Hou's films, identity becomes less and less a matter of ethnicity, geography, linguistic heritage, or cultural tradition and more and more a matter of choice. In a sense, these young people embody the tension between the coexisting impulses of exile and displacement: at times they suffer the loneliness and disorientation of the exile, yearning for a sense of belonging and hoping to rediscover a familiar and stable sense of self. At the same time, however, they realize that like it or not they are being reshaped by the multiplicity of cultures they encounter. They have also begun to recognize the fresh possibilities that these new and diverse experiences offer. In *Dust in the Wind*, for example, Ah-Hun's decision to back out of her traditionally arranged marriage with Ah-Wan in order to marry a postal worker she meets in Taipei reveals her understanding that her urban experience has changed her, that she is not the same person she was before she left the village. Similarly, in *The Boys from Feng Kuei*, Ching-ah, despite the difficulties he has suffered in the city, rejects his mother's suggestion that he remain in the village after his father's funeral. By opting to return to Kaohsiung, he acknowledges that he, too, has been changed by the culture of the city. There is no turning back; there can be no simple return to the past.

Hybridity, Multiplicity, Difference: "I Am a Crowd"

Underlying this nomadic sense of self is a gradual acceptance, rather than a crippling fear, of multiplicity and difference. The exile experiences isolation and despair because he or she clings to a conception of identity rooted in a lost homeland or irretrievable past and searches endlessly and futilely for utopian wholeness and plenitude. The nomadic subject, on the other hand, lets go of this obsession with origins and seeks alternatives to an imaginary unified self. As Alicia Dujovne Ortiz asks: "Why do we have such an absurd need for a solid, robust, and pink-cheeked identity, a peasant identity rooted for centuries in the same land? Why not embrace an empty self? What is so awful about emptiness once you get used to it?"[70] The beauty of emptiness is that it can be filled with not just one but a shifting multitude of cultural identities. Ortiz writes: "I have no roots. It's a fact. A tragic mixture of blood runs through my veins. Jews, Genovese, Castillians, Irish, Indians, maybe Blacks, find in me a bizarre and motley meeting place. I am a crowd."[71] Like Buenos Aires—and like so many other modern metropolises around the world—Ortiz's self is a site where multiple cultures and value systems intersect and meld. To accept this plurality of cultures is to embrace nomadism: "To be porteño is to accept wandering." To position oneself in the continuous flow of history—rather than seeking refuge in an idealized and fixed past—can be seen as a liberating embrace of life: "To know you are a carnival of characters, nations, sexes, epochs . . . aren't these all the elements of the human condition, in its total uncertainty?"[72]

Beneath the celebratory tone of these theories of multicultural hybridity, however, lies an ambivalence toward the destablization of conventional notions of identity that must be acknowledged. They represent, as James Clifford has observed, less a utopian vision of the future than a "utopic/dystopic tension."[73] The cultural inventiveness of these alternative models of identity formation have less to do with liberating transgressions than with tactical strategies for survival in an increasingly complex world; they are pragmatic responses that attempt to make the best of the given realities of postmodern, postcolonial situations. Alicia Dujovne

Ortiz's idea that we can abandon the "absurd need for a solid, robust, and pink-cheeked identity" and "embrace an empty self," Caren Kaplan's theory of "displacement," and Stuart Hall's conception of identity based on difference and rupture do indeed reveal mixed feelings. Indeed, Ortiz's own plaintive questioning—"Why not embrace an empty self? What is so awful about emptiness once you get used to it?"—suggests that the emotional tug of stable and comprehensible identities remains strong. Yet, given the blossoming multiculturalism and increasing global interconnectedness that are the inevitable results of today's economic, political, technological, and demographic developments, the notion of a traveling identity does offer a sense of hope and possibility, a pragmatic strategy for coping with the massive cultural challenges and dislocations we now face. For Ah-Hao, Ah-Wan, Ah-Hun, and the other young people in Hou Hsiao-hsien's Taiwan, it is the gradual acceptance of cultural multiplicity and nomadism that saves them from the alienation and loneliness of exile they initially experience in the modern metropolis and allows them to emerge with a richer, fuller sense of self. Reenvisioning the notion of identity to acknowledge, even celebrate, the new cultural hybridity allows us to move beyond apocalypse and nostalgia and embrace the multicultural global future with optimism and hope. As Ortiz declares: "I heal myself, then, in saying: to be a crowd: what a marvelous gift!"[74]

Conclusion
From Nation to Dissemi-Nation:
Postmodern Hybridization and Changing
Conditions for the Representation
of Identity

The portrait of Taiwan that ultimately emerges from Hou Hsiao-hsien's films departs significantly from earlier, more conventional formulations of the island's nationhood—both from the KMT government's historical attempts to integrate Taiwan into a larger Chinese nation and from the nostalgic rural vision of the island imagined by Hwang Chun-ming and his fellow hsiang-t'u writers of the 1970s. Indeed, it would be difficult, if not impossible, to trace in Hou's films the outlines of Taiwan as an organic, unified, and stable entity whose cultural parameters are readily definable. Instead, they paint a picture of the island as an increasingly complex and hybrid social space, an ever-changing formation that is continually being shaped and reshaped by the multiple languages, cultures, social classes, and value systems with which it comes into contact. Unlike his hsiang-t'u predecessors, Hou's constructions of a Taiwanese imagined community go beyond merely offering a nativist narrative of nation to counterbalance the Kuomintang's rhetoric of Chinese homogeneity and coherence. Rather, they question the very possibility of continuing to define a native or authentic Taiwanese cultural identity against a foreign other, whether that be the Japanese, mainland Chinese, or westerners. By simultaneously evoking and undermining the polar binarisms of classical nationalism, Hou challenges the essentialist rhetoric embraced by the earlier nativism of hsiang-t'u literature—a strategic realignment that moves Taiwan toward a more flexible and meaningful position in the arena of global culture by recognizing that today's world of multidimensional and multidirectional cultural flows demands acknowledgment of the myriad differences found within societies—and even within individuals—rather than just between them. His films foreground the forces of cultural hybridity and cosmopolitanism that began to alter Taiwanese society in the 1980s and 1990s and have accelerated in the new millenium.

Hou Hsiao-hsien's Taiwan is a constantly changing space criss-crossed by complex and intricate networks of historical, political, sociocultural, and linguistic differences. Moreover, his films remind us that the island's cultural hybridization is not a recent phenomenon. Taiwan has been enmeshed in global circuits of political interaction and intercultural exchange ever since the first colonizers set foot on its soil centuries ago. In *City of Sadness* and *The Puppetmaster*, for example, the island's long-standing official identification with the Chinese mainland and its cultural heritage is challenged by a multilayered examination of the island's complex colonial history and the violent internal conflicts that have shaped its past. At the same time, the exploration and sometimes sympathetic portrayal by these films of the island's lingering Japanese heritage also complicates the simple image of authentic indigenous Taiwanese culture envisioned by Hwang Chun-ming and his fellow nativist writers. The idea of an eternalized Taiwanese peasant identity is further destabilized by the subtle subversions, in *Summer at Grandpa's*, *The Boys from Feng Kuei*, and *Dust in the Wind*, of the urban-rural dichotomy on which the nativism of hsiang-t'u nationalism was based. In *Daughter of the Nile* and later films that depict the culturally heterogeneous, consumer-oriented milieu of modern Taipei, the utopian vision of Taiwan as an organically unified society—whose communal strength was celebrated in stories such as Hwang's "A Flower in the Rainy Night"—has all but disappeared.

It is, however, the complex linguistic diversity of Hou's films that most effectively constructs Taiwan as a hybrid space and perhaps best illustrates how far Taiwanese New Cinema has moved from the simple binarisms of hsiang-t'u nationalism. Hou's mixed use of Japanese, Mandarin, Taiwanese, English, and Shanghainese in *A Time to Live and a Time to Die* and *City of Sadness* not only captures the multilingual reality of Taiwanese life, but its differential deployment in specific social situations also marks the multiple legacies of colonialism and delineates shifting structures of power on the island. Moreover, the ability of individual characters to switch seamlessly between languages places them firmly on the frontiers of hybrid cultural identity.[1] The shift from the bipolar opposition of Taiwanese and Mandarin in the fiction of Hwang Chun-ming and other nativist writers during the 1970s to the naturalistic use of multiple languages in the films of Hou Hsiao-hsien and other Taiwanese New Cinema directors in the 1980s demonstrates to a large degree just how much Taiwanese society and its cultural representations have changed in recent decades. Taiwan in the 1970s and early 1980s, of course, was a totalitarian state in which society was perceived to be divided into two antagonistic groups: the ruling mainlander elite and the native Taiwanese populace. The decision by hsiang-t'u writers and the pioneers of New Cinema to use the Taiwanese dialect in their works was therefore politically charged, a deliberate oppositional act intended to challenge a state-imposed mono-linguism that discouraged the use of Taiwanese in the public sphere. Taiwan in the twenty-first century, however, is a democratic society in which political pluralism and free speech are not only tolerated but encouraged. In this postdictatorship era, the native tongue is well on its way to total rehabilitation; it is employed in more and more public media and is spoken freely even in official contexts. Today linguistic hybridity is the norm in Taiwanese filmmaking, not only in art films but in mainstream commercial cinema as well. Indeed, while Taiwanese spoken on-screen was once startling, it now goes almost unnoticed. It is not at all uncommon to find characters in films who switch among Taiwanese, Cantonese, Mandarin, Japanese, and English naturally and with ease, sometimes combining words and phrases from several languages in a single sentence.

Just as the dissipation of tension between Mandarin and Taiwanese has allowed for the emergence of a more complex picture of the island's linguistic heritage, the breakdown of other binarisms on which hsiang-t'u nationalism was based have radically altered the conditions for the representation of identity in Taiwan. Foremost among these is the dramatically changed relationship between China and Taiwan. Under the KMT dictatorship, China was revered as the sacred motherland. Taiwan was envisioned as a mere leaf, whose very existence depended on the support of the strong branches and solid trunk of the ancient tree (China) on which it grew.[2] In the wake of Taiwan's political democratization and the liberalization of governmental travel policies, however, China has been gradually demythologized. As increasing numbers of Taiwanese travel to the mainland and experience it for themselves, China has been stripped of the rosy glow of nostalgia that memory, fantasy, and official mythologies once created for it. For the younger generation of Taiwanese—including the first generation Taiwanese from mainlander families such as Hou hsiao-hsien and Chu T'ien-wen—China carries no special emotional or symbolic import. Many, especially those involved in international commerce, see it as just another developing nation in the growing economy of the Asia-Pacific region: a source of cheap labor, a land of many investment opportunities, and a huge and as yet unfulfilled market of potential consumers for Taiwanese products and expertise. Particularly in the last decade, so many Taiwanese have visited the mainland, invested in businesses there, moved their families to its coastal cities, and even brought home Chinese spouses that the old mainlander versus islander distinction has become increasingly irrelevant. Democratization has also undermined the conventional opposition between the official history promulgated by the government and the popular memory of the people. While the KMT's suppression of local history once provided a clear rallying point for Taiwanese nationalists, today much of that lost history has been recovered thanks to the island's new freedoms of speech and press, another example of how the political and cultural liberalizations of the 1990s have dramatically diminished the need to seek out and restore a coherent, authentic, native experience. The focus now is more on uncovering the remarkable diversity of the historical experiences of the island's people.

In addition, with their increasing affluence and mobility, today's Taiwanese have greatly strengthened their international presence, further hastening the disintegration of the East versus West dichotomy that fueled the rhetoric of the hsiang-t'u debates in the mid-1970s. While earlier generations of immigrants and students moved to a new country and often did not return home for years, today's ease of travel has made it possible for members of this generation to travel frequently between Taiwan and their adopted homes in the Americas, Europe, Australia, and elsewhere around the globe. Indeed many people choose to live transnationally, moving constantly between Taiwan and Chinese diasporic communities worldwide. These days it is not at all uncommon for Taiwanese families to be split. Often mothers and children—or sometimes just the children—live in America, Australia, or some other foreign country, taking advantage of local education and earning rights of residency. Fathers frequently remain in Taiwan to continue conducting business in the growing economies of the Asia-Pacific region. Family members maintain contact via phone, fax, the Internet, and, with the relatively low-cost of air travel these days, by commuting several times a year.[3] This phenomenon of living between nations and cultures has given rise to a whole new vocabulary, which reflects the sense of displacement and suspension experienced by these modern nomads. They are the new "trans-Pacific families,"[4] sometimes nicknamed "trapeze artists" (空中飛人).[5] Children brought to the United States by their parents then left to fend for themselves (albeit with a new house, new cars, and plenty of spending money), are sometimes referred to as "parachute kids,"[6] while the father who remains alone in Taiwan is called an "astronaut" (太空人), a term that can also be translated literally as "person without his wife." The wife, who is deposited in suburban American communities and left to manage the real estate and look after the children, is coyly referred to as an "inner beauty" (內在美), a shortened version of "my wife in the Beautiful Country [America] (內人在美國)."[7]

Most of these Chinese transnationals choose to accept their lives of fragmentation, impermanence, and displacement for tactical and pragmatic reasons. Despite the prosperity that the island's economic successes have built, many Taiwanese feel less confident about the island's political stability and status in the global political community and fully understand that acquiring rights of residency, or even citizenship, in another country is the safest bet for a secure future. Sometimes the motivating factors are economic rather than political: as Taiwanese professionals and businesspeople—like their counterparts in Hong Kong and other parts of the Chinese diaspora—become more involved in the circuits of global capitalism, they also realize that possession of an American, Canadian, or other passport greatly facilitates their global mobility and increases their economic opportunities. In addition, many of these trans-Pacific Taiwanese move their families across oceans to take advantage of what they perceive to be superior educational choices for their children. The active border crossing, comfortable mobility, and increasingly pragmatic view of citizenship embraced by modern-day Chinese from both Taiwan and Hong Kong pose interesting challenges to reigning notions of Chinese identity, which, as a number of critics have pointed out, have been particularly static and monolithic in Western cultural scholarship.[8] Western notions of Chineseness stubbornly cling to the idea that China's long history has somehow produced a stable cultural core that is seen as the chief determinant of Chinese identity, immune to historical change. Some may identify devotion to ancient cultural traditions as a particularly Chinese trait; others may idealize familial solidarity and the Confucian ideology of filial piety as the core of Chinese values. The complex realities of the contemporary Chinese diaspora, however, subvert such essentializing views. Modern history has proven that Chinese have been willing to abandon indigenous traditions when necessary and selectively embrace foreign cultural practices and make them their own. As the growing number of trans-Pacific migrants suggests, the Chinese family is now thoroughly mediated by a variety of political and economic considerations and has become both fragmented and bound by technologies of travel and communication. Significantly, the willingness of contemporary Chinese to explore and adapt themselves to the realities of the new transnational flows—to take, for example, a more flexible and instrumental approach to citizenship—offers interesting models for less traditional ways of thinking about identity in the new global order.

Transnationalism and the Transition into the
New Millenium: Taiwan in the 1990s and Beyond

We have seen how Taiwan's active participation in transnational capitalism, global migration, and rapidly expanding media and communications networks has transformed the island into a postmodern hyperspace,
a nexus on the intersecting networks of global exchange. Like individuals the world over, today's Taiwanese—particularly the young people—
are increasingly hybrid creatures who no longer fit into conventional cultural molds. They are likely to be continually shaped and reshaped not
only by traditional Chinese values and beliefs but also by a wide and unpredictable variety of cultural influences, both local and global. Many Taiwanese films of the 1990s are populated with characters who exemplify
this new cultural hybridity; two filmmakers whose recent work illustrates the increasing futility of trying to pin down a singular Taiwanese
identity particularly well are Ang Lee and Edward Yang.[9] Lee's domestic
comedy *Eat Drink Man Woman* (1994) features characters fairly typical of
Taiwan's middle-class urbanites: working professionals whose commit-
ments to their careers and individual futures have already begun to undermine traditional family unity. Each member of the Chu family, whose
loves and conflicts are the main focus of the film, confounds conventional cultural stereotypes of Chinese familial roles. Old Chu, the wid-
owed father, seems at first glance to be very much the traditional Chinese gentleman. He lives in a formal courtyard-style house (not many of
which remain in Taipei), listens to classical Chinese music, and is a master chef of classical Chinese cuisine who used to oversee the kitchens at
Taipei's Grand Hotel—a monumental landmark building whose massive
red lacquer pillars, ornate wood carvings, and elaborate gold ornamen-
tation are the very embodiment of imperial Chinese decor. This head of
household, however, is not enjoying the kind of retirement a traditional
Chinese father might expect. Instead of enjoying the pampering and filial
respect of his three daughters, the old widower finds himself cooking
their meals and doing their laundry as the young ladies pursue their own
careers. Chia-chen, the eldest, is a prim and proper schoolteacher, who,
after a failed romance (which later turns out to have been entirely fab-
ricated), has found solace in the embrace of a Western God. Chia-ch'ien,
the middle daughter, is an executive on the rise at an international airline
and is due to be transferred to the company's Amsterdam office. The most
Westernized and stylish of the three, she has a lover named Raymond,
who is a gallery owner, and has put a down payment on a new condo-

minium in a luxury development called Little Paris in the East. Chia-ning, the youngest, is a student who works part time at the local Wendy's and has a boyfriend who is obsessed with the works of Fyodor Dostoevsky. Although they all live under the same roof, each is very much self-focused and is quite unaware of developments in the lives of her sisters. The only time they talk, it seems, is over Sunday dinner—which is mandated by their father and is often characterized by uncomfortable silences. Even then, they don't really talk. Instead, they use the weekly forum to make announcements about plans they have already made or actions already taken.

The friends, colleagues, and neighbors of the Chu family live similarly fragmented lives. Chin-jung, their neighbor and Chia-chen's best friend, is a single working mother who has just survived a nasty divorce. Her sister is married to an (Anglo) American and lives in the United States. Her mother, Mrs. Liang, is a lively and talkative widow who splits her time between the United States and Taiwan and has her eye on Old Chu. Chia-ch'ien's handsome colleague at the airline, Li Kai, is one of those transnational "astronauts," who when not traveling on business to Amsterdam, Sydney, and other cities around the world splits his time between the office in Taipei and his family in suburban America. Chia-ning's boyfriend (and later her husband), Guo Lun, lives alone in Taipei while his parents, busy and successful real estate speculators, pursue deals in the United States and China. Consequently, not only has Guo Lun been left to fend for himself but his grandmother—rather than being taken in by her children in the traditional manner—has been sent to an old folks' home. As "un-Chinese" as these familial arrangements seem, what is most striking is that these departures from the traditional family order are presented in the film without a strong sense of loss or despair. Instead, they are put forth in a rather matter of fact manner, as simple realities of modern Taiwanese life.

The unpredictability of Taiwanese identity is further underscored as over the course of Lee's film all three of the Chu daughters turn out to be quite different from what they initially seem. The oldest, who seems to be the most reserved and conservative, pursues and marries a flamboyant, motorcycle-riding gym teacher. The youngest, seemingly the most obedient and complacent, surprises everyone with the sudden announcement that she is pregnant and getting married. Ironically, it is the middle daughter—by all appearances the most cosmopolitan and most impatient to leave the family nest—who ends up leading the most conventional life: she gives up her promotion and posting to Amsterdam in order to stay home and care for her father, even assuming some of his cooking duties, taking pleasure in creating the Chinese dishes she learned from him as a child. Indeed, nearly all of the characters in Lee's film defy easy categorization, illustrating not only the variety of cultural influences that shape today's Taiwanese but also the slipperiness of identity. Even Old Chu turns out to be less traditional than anyone could have guessed. At the end of the film, the elderly gentleman surprises everyone by remarrying—not the widow Mrs. Liang but her daughter, Chin-jung, Chia-chen's best friend! Not only does he become a father to Shan-shan, Chin-jung's little girl (who has always called him Grandpa) but he also decides to start a new family and a new life with his young wife. The conclusion of *Eat Drink Man Woman* is notably free of nostalgic yearning for past traditions or a return to the old order. Instead, it looks forward to a new and exciting—if uncertain—future. At the end of the film, Chu has sold the old family home and moved into a new house with Chin-jung, who is expecting their daughter. Chia-ch'ien is also planning to leave, to take up that executive position in Amsterdam after all. Their final meal together at the old house, then, is a particularly important one: a poignant farewell to tradition and the past but also a hopeful embrace of the future.

One of Lee's earlier films, *The Wedding Banquet* (喜宴, 1992), features a wonderfully humorous example of the cultural hybridity that marks modern Taiwanese. The film, set in New York City, features several characters who do not fit conventional images of the Chinese immigrant, illustrating the diversity of today's diaspora. Wei-wei is an illegal alien from mainland China who has been ducking the immigration authorities and working in restaurants to make ends meet. Her waitressing, though, is only a part-time job to pay the rent; primarily, she is a struggling artist who paints abstract oils. Her landlord, Wei-t'ong, is a Taiwanese businessman (with a U.S. passport) who invests in New York real estate. He is young, handsome . . . and gay. When his parents in Taiwan ask him to fill out an application for a matchmaking service, Wei-t'ong and Simon, his American companion, have fun describing his ideal mate: she must be a Taiwanese woman who is at least five feet nine inches tall, holds two Ph.D.s (one in physics), speaks five languages, and sings Western opera. They are confident, of course, that this is an impossible order to fill. Imagine Wei-t'ong's astonishment, then, when a prospective match is found in only a matter of weeks! The young woman has only one doctorate—in biology—but she is indeed fluent in five languages and, having sung professionally in San Francisco for two years, is an accomplished opera singer as well. She recognizes at once that Wei-t'ong is not interested in a match. Neither is she. Like Wei-t'ong, she has a "white boyfriend" and completed the application just to mollify her parents. To amuse Wei-t'ong, she sings a passage from

Madame Butterfly, that classic orientalist fantasy of the Asian woman—a stereotype that she clearly defies.

While films like Lee's foreground the cultural complexity of its contemporary citizens, Taiwan's leap into postmodern global society has not been without its difficulties. The collision of so many different cultures and value systems has not simply resulted in a society full of happy hybrids. Edward Yang's *A Confucian Confusion* (獨立時代, 1994) is a humorous yet bitingly satirical look at the social and moral fallout from the country's stunning economic growth, which, he believes, has irreversibly altered and complicated the old relationships between Taiwan and the West.[10] The Chinese title of Yang's film translates as "The Age of Independence" and alludes in part to the many exhilarating and confusing new freedoms that Taiwan is exploring—including, of course, the possibility of political independence. Taken together with the English title, it also points to one of the film's central themes—that Confucianism, which is based on strict social hierarchies and rigid standards of interpersonal behavior (倫理), has crashed head-on with Western value systems, which emphasize individual rights and responsibilities above all. The Taiwanese yuppies in Yang's film struggle to make sense of the fallout from this cultural collision. Taiwan's economic prosperity and its participation in transnational commerce and cultural exchange have brought Yang's young men and women material pleasures and new opportunities. Molly is an elegant, wealthy young woman who runs a public relations firm involved in a variety of "culture industry" concerns: publishing, records, and soap operas. Her fiancé, Akeem, is equally wealthy; he does business with mainland China and is basically underwriting Molly's company. Akeem's right-hand man, Larry, is a slippery hypocrite who understands best the idea that in the postmodern world image is everything. Full of false praise and practiced responses, he seems unable to say anything sincere. Molly's assistant and best friend is Ch'i-ch'i, an Audrey Hepburn type of charmer whom everyone adores but who is so sweet, unselfish, and accommodating that nobody (especially not cynical Larry) can quite believe she is for real. Her fiancé, Ming, is a gentlemanly and hardworking bureaucrat. Other characters in the film include Molly's sister, a popular television talk-show hostess; her ex-husband, once a popular author of romance novels but now a recluse who writes existential novels with titles like *A Confucian Confusion*; and Molly's friend Birdy, a celebrity director of "postmodern Chinese operas." Birdy believes in the globalization of culture (世界大同), which for him means creating the kind of popular cultural hybrid that will attract the broadest possible audience and sell the most tickets: "This is the age of democracy! What's more democratic than box office?" They are all stylish, cosmopolitan professionals, as comfortable watching NBA basketball and drinking coffee at T.G.I. Friday's as they are slurping noodles at the neighborhood stand.

As the film, progresses, however, it becomes clear that their assimilation of Eastern and Western cultures remains relatively superficial. Their cultural hybridity is a sort of pastiche of commodified cultural images and products, a transitional process through which they continue to struggle. Birdy, for example, is first seen conducting a press conference while restlessly rollerblading around his studio. He is dressed in a long Chinese scholar's gown and has decorated his studio in the gaudy reds and golds that typically signify "Chinese" in the West. Clearly, then, Birdy understands the commodification of Chinese culture and the techniques required to market it in the rest of the world. At the same time, however, he has difficulty grasping other Western concepts, such as the notion of intellectual property rights. Molly may run her own PR firm but only because Akeem has agreed to finance her ambitions in the hopes that she will become frustrated by failure and will finally settle into the role of a good Chinese wife. Their impending union seems more like a corporate merger than a marriage. Molly's sister has successfully marketed her "happy homemaker" image to her television audiences, but behind the camera her own marriage has fallen apart. Ch'i-ch'i, too, finds her relationship with Ming vaguely unsatisfying. Like the others, she cannot yet reconcile the individualism of the West and the Confucian traditions of the East and is torn between her own needs and ambitions and her sense of obligation and loyalty to others. Yang has argued that Confucianism is an excessively restrictive and authoritarian system and that far too much emphasis has been placed on its teachings as the cornerstone of Chinese culture.[11] Its ideals have outlived their usefulness in the modern age, Yang seems to suggest, and consumer capitalism and Western democratic ideals have finally given Confucianism the good shaking up it has always needed. Yet, as the turmoil and confusion of Molly and her friends attest, for better or worse the Confucian tradition provided for Taiwanese society a frame of reference whose collapse, in this "age of independence," has resulted in a moral and spiritual vacuum. With the unraveling of conventional social relationships, contemporary Taiwanese are still struggling to find a foothold on the unfamiliar and unstable ground of a postcolonial world. Like so many today, Taiwan remains a "society in process," still learning to negotiate the omnidirectional currents of multiple and often conflicting cultures.

Representations of Taiwanese society in films of the 1990s have clearly acknowledged the myriad external cultural influences that have irreversibly altered contemporary Taiwanese society. Equally important, however, are the multiplicity of conflicts and differences *within* Taiwanese society—including class, gender, ethnic, and sexual differences—that are increasingly gaining recognition in the island's film and literature. The growing attention given to Taiwan's internal diversity has been manifested in many ways, including, for example, the recent spate of films featuring realistic and sympathetically portrayed homosexual characters.[12] In addition, a growing number of women writers and filmmakers are making their voices heard. Films such as Ho P'ing's (何平) *Eighteen* (十八, 1993) and Ch'en Kuo-fu's (陳國富) *To Live One Day for You* (只要為你活一天, 1993) focus on the middle and lower-middle classes and are a reminder of the island's complex diversity beyond the world of Taipei's yuppies and transnational elites.[13] One of the most significant developments of the last few years is an emerging interest in the literature of the island's aboriginal peoples. The history of Taiwan's many aboriginal tribes has been, since the Japanese Occupation and perhaps before, one of oppression and forced assimilation. Their role in Taiwanese society has largely been limited to exotic spectacle—primarily in tourist areas such as Wu-lai (烏來) and Hua-lian (花蓮)—or objects of folkloric curiosity. Recent efforts in Taiwanese literary circles, however, are finally adding the aboriginal perspective to the island's postwar experience. In film, Huang Ming-ch'uan's (黃明川) independently produced *Man from Island West* (西部來的人, 1990) has made a significant contribution to these efforts. Huang's film tells the story of a young aboriginal man who has attempted assimilation and failed. His desire to escape Taipei and return to the familiar surroundings of his tribal home is matched only by the eagerness of the young men still in the aboriginal areas to leave. The ambivalence that the aborigines feel toward modernization and cultural change echoes the larger dilemma faced by Taiwanese society or for that matter any society caught up in the sweeping forces of globalization.

Thanks in large part to the innovations pioneered by the New Cinema of the 1980s, contemporary Taiwanese filmmaking is marked not only by growing thematic diversity but stylistic unpredictability as well. Despite the perennial box office dominance of martial arts costume dramas, action films, and slapstick comedies, and in the face of increased competition from Hollywood, there continues to be room for films of a more personal or experimental nature. Ang Lee's domestic comedies, Edward

Yang's social satires, Stan Lai's (賴聲川) modern parables *Peach Blossom Land* (暗戀桃花源, 1992) and *Red Lotus Society* (飛俠阿達, 1994), along with aesthetically challenging films like Ts'ai Ming-liang's *Vive L'Amour* (愛情萬歲, 1994), a spare study of urban alienation in the style of Antonioni, illustrate the diversity of an industry that has also seen growth in documentary and other nonfiction filmmaking.

In this age of multinational capitalism, mass migrations, and global media, the diversification and hybridization of cultural production is an inevitable trend. Like their counterparts in Hong Kong and other global cities in the world,[14] the cultural consciousness of today's Taiwanese artists—whether poets, novelists, painters, or filmmakers—has already been hybridized by exposure to an ever-widening variety of cultural influences.[15] Moreover, many of them have lived and worked abroad and increasingly divide their time among several countries. Even more than the comparatively Taiwan-centered filmmakers of the New Cinema movement, Taiwanese filmmakers in the 1990s are increasingly global in outlook and savvy in the ways of international marketing. They aim not only to promote their films on the prestigious international festival circuit but also to seek out foreign distribution deals and potential coproduction possibilities. Indeed, one of the most significant developments in 1990s Chinese filmmaking has been the rapidly growing number of films that are coproductions—transnational collaborations that combine financing, creative talent, and technical expertise from a variety of sources, including Taiwan, Hong Kong, the PRC, Japan, the United States, and Europe. In recent years, for example, many Chinese-language films have been complex collaborations among Hong Kong, Taiwan, and the PRC. While distributed variously as films from one of the three areas, they have typically involved shifting constellations incorporating financing from Taiwan, Hong Kong, and sometimes Japan, shooting locations and crews from the Chinese mainland, and creative talent from all three.[16] In addition, European production companies have become increasingly involved in films that are nominally from Taiwan, Hong Kong, or the People's Republic.

The transnationalization of Chinese film talent has been most emphatically underscored in the last few years by the highly publicized expansion efforts of several of Hong Kong's best-known action film directors and stars into the Hollywood mainstream.[17] While many working filmmakers who are categorized as Taiwanese are also involved in international coproductions, very few actors or directors have succeeded in crossing over to the American film industry with the success of their Hong Kong counterparts. The one exception—and he is a very noteworthy example—is Ang Lee.[18] Lee is very much representative of the new breed of globally oriented, transnational filmmakers, and his body of work dramatically illustrates the unpredictable hybridity of today's cultural production and the challenges such hybridity poses for the concepts of nation and cultural identity. Born in 1954 in Taiwan to a mainlander family, he moved to the United States in 1978 to study drama at the University of Illinois. From there, he went on to earn an M.F.A. in filmmaking at New York University, and he has lived and worked in New York ever since. His award-winning thesis film attracted the attention of Taiwan's Central Motion Picture Company, which produced his first three features *Pushing Hands*, *The Wedding Banquet*, and *Eat Drink Man Woman*.[19] Though nominally Taiwanese films, all three were thoroughly collaborative efforts, as Lee recruited talent from among both Taiwanese and American artists and technicians. The question of how to categorize Lee's films and his cultural identity as a filmmaker first became a problem when British actress Emma Thompson selected him to direct her adaptation of Jane Austen's *Sense and Sensibility*. Many in the industry were surprised by the choice and wondered how Lee's identity as a modern Taiwanese man could possibly fit a film about the social and romantic trials of two nineteenth-century Englishwomen. The film, of course, was a great success, winning multiple Oscar nominations and an award for Thompson's screenplay. Yet, despite the critical plaudits for the film and Lee's direction, he failed to garner an Oscar nomination. More importantly, every article, review, or interview about *Sense and Sensibility*—whether positive or negative—inevitably focused on the difference of identity between Lee and the film's subject matter. Even though most articles applauded the film and argued that he was the right choice to direct it, the very fact that everyone felt Lee needed to be defended highlights the fact that as a Taiwanese he was seen as a cultural outsider. His next film, *The Ice Storm* (1997), based on the 1994 novel by Rick Moody, also received high marks from critics. Nevertheless, in praising his direction critics once again emphasized the disjuncture between Lee and the world of suburban Connecticut in the 1970s. Reviewing the film in the *New York Times*, for example, Janet Maslin took pains to point out that Lee had "spent the era of Rick Moody's novel in Taiwan" and that his depiction of the spiritual and moral malaise of America in the 1970s is strikingly powerful precisely because he "understands it as only an outsider can."[20] Since Lee continues to be classified as a Taiwanese director, the thorny question of how his various films should be categorized becomes a constant issue. Is *Sense and Sensibility* a British film, Taiwanese-British, or British-Taiwanese? Can *The Ice Storm* truly be considered an American film if its director is Taiwanese?[21] Ang Lee's films, of course, are not the only ones for which this problem of classification arises. However, films such as his critical and commercial hit *Crouching Tiger, Hidden Dragon* (2000), which is classified as a U.S./Hong Kong/China/Taiwan production, effectively illustrate that with the increasing volume of international exchange, global migration, and transnational collaboration it is becoming ever more difficult to trace cultural products to a single point of origin. What we are witnessing, then, might be described as a gradual deterritorialization of culture.[22]

Even as cultural production becomes increasingly hybridized, however, the desire to localize persists. Taiwan may be rushing headlong toward integration into global circuits of commerce, communications, and culture, but the strongly territorial impulses of the "back to the earth" (回歸 鄉土) movement that gave rise to Taiwanese hsiang-t'u literature of the 1970s and inspired New Cinema of the 1980s have not disappeared. As cultural theorist Stuart Hall has noted, the most critical juncture in the development of any postcolonial society is the moment of "rediscovery," the search for roots. The act of what Hall calls "imaginary political re-identification and re-territorialization" is a strategy for political, economic, social, and cultural mobilization whose appeal can be quite stubborn.[23] Hence, even as Taiwan acknowledges its inclusion in the intricate networks of global exchange and looks forward to an increasingly complex and multicultural future, the emotional pull of the kind of essentialist nationalism that inspired hsiang-t'u literature persists. Its force can be felt in the indigenization trends sweeping Taiwanese politics today. It can be seen in continuing efforts to recover Taiwan's native past, such as the recent proliferation of books, journals, and university courses specializing in Taiwanese literature. Archival interest in preserving Taiwanese culture and history is expanding on other fronts as well. Archaeologists and architectural historians, for instance, continue to explore and campaign to preserve significant buildings and sites throughout the island.[24] In addition, a strikingly large number of documentaries examining local history and recording indigenous arts have been produced in recent years. It seems that Taiwan is becoming, as Stuart Hall observed to be typical of the postmodern era, at once more global *and* more local.[25] Although they no longer dominate, Taiwan-centered feature films reminiscent of early Taiwanese New Cinema also continue to be made. Wu Nien-chen's directorial debut, *To-san* (多桑, 1994),[26] a nostalgic look back at rural life during the years immediately following the Japanese Occupation, clearly draws on the yearning for the kind of village-based Taiwanese identity that shaped hsiang-t'u literature and on the traditions of social realism that marked New Cinema in its earliest days.[27] Thanks primarily to political and cultural liberalization, but also in part to the progress made by Hou's generation of directors toward constructing a Taiwanese nation, the new filmmakers seem less burdened by historical and cultural responsibilities—such as the need to redefine a coherent and authentic Taiwanese identity or carve out a space for a distinctively Taiwanese cinema—and less limited by the aesthetic expectations that challenged their predecessors.[28] Indeed, they seem to have found a sense of liberation and possibility in Taiwan's fast-paced, globally connected, and ever-changing new culture of the 1990s.

Postcolonial, Postmodern . . . Postnational?

> In a world which is increasingly compressed (and indeed identified as *the* world) and in which its most formidable units—namely, nationally-constituted societies—are increasingly subject to the internal, as well as external, constraints of multiculturality . . . the conditions of and for the identification of individual and collective selves and of individual and collective others are becoming ever more complex.[29]

The changing representations of the Taiwanese nation in Hou Hsiao-hsien's films and those of the younger generation of Taiwanese filmmakers help to illuminate many of the recent debates in the West surrounding postcolonialism and the rhetoric of nation. The increasingly global conditions under which contemporary culture is consumed and produced—whether in literature, the visual arts, or cinema—has led over the past two decades to a flurry of efforts by scholars and cultural intellectuals to reassess the category of nation as an appropriate unit of social and cultural analysis. This theoretical reconsideration of the national model of cultural discourse has included, for example, a resurgence of interest in the writings of Frantz Fanon. Fanon argued that the liberation of a society in the aftermath of colonialism depends to a large extent on an articulation of a national culture, but he also emphasized that merely searching for an indigenous counterdiscourse with which to rebut the forces of colonialism is insufficient. To identify a national identity with specific cultural characteristics rooted in quasi-natural attachments to a homeland only replicates the model imposed by imperialist discourse. Instead, he insisted, we must open our eyes, ears, and minds to all facets of the complex web of multiple discourses that make up cultural-historical experience: "We must not be content with delving into the past of a people in order to find coherent elements which will counteract colonialism's attempts to falsify and harm. . . . A national culture is not a folklore, nor an abstract populism that believes it can discover a people's true nature. A national culture is *the whole body of efforts* made by a people in the sphere of thought to describe, justify and praise the action through which that people has created itself and keeps itself in existence."[30]

The shift from the simple binarisms of Taiwanese hsiang-t'u literature to the linguistic differences and complex class, ethnic, gender, and intellectual hierarchies within a supposedly unified nation that can be found in Hou Hsiao-hsien's films seems to demonstrate what Fanon calls for: a movement away from monologic and coherent models of interpretation— even if they are anti-imperialist—toward more sophisticated models that acknowledge and embrace fragmentation, heterogeneity, and inconclusiveness. The postcolonial/postmodern rejection of essentialist or dualistic definitions of *identity* as something stable and coherent in favor of models that emphasize contingency and internal multiplicity marks a similar step in the evolutionary direction that Fanon proposes.

Similarly, the work of Homi K. Bhabha recasts Fanon's implicit critique of reified nationalist narratives by introducing the idea of "Dissemi-Nation": a "double-writing" that simultaneously evokes and erases the narrative structures—particularly the various binary divisions—through which essentialist national identities are traditionally constructed. Nation is revealed to be an unstable discursive space, "internally marked by cultural difference and heterogeneous histories of contending peoples, antagonistic authorities, and tense cultural locations," a hybrid space whose boundaries are constantly drawn and redrawn by these contending forces.[31] Any sense of unity or identity can only be transitory and illusory, sure to be fragmented by the eruption of difference from within. Bhabha shifts his emphasis away from the pedagogical past to the performative present, locating nation in what Fanon calls the "occult zone of instability" or "the fluctuating movement that the people are *just giving shape to.*"[32] Bhabha's reconceived idea of nation, based on ever-shifting articulations of cultural difference, brings to mind the efforts of Edward Yang's Taiwanese yuppies in *A Confucian Confusion* to negotiate the cultural smorgasbord that is modern Taipei. In Bhabha's words, it "addresses the jarring of meanings and values generated in-between the variety and diversity associated with cultural plenitude; it represents the process of cultural interpretation formed in the perplexity of living."[33] His disavowal of the fixity and coherence of nations raises the possibility of envisioning a world that is not only postcolonial and postmodern but also postnational. If, indeed, we live in a postmodern global system of mass migrations, multinational capitalism, and intersecting cultures, the idea of nations existing as separate and integral entities seems hopelessly outdated and inadequate.[34] As rapid globalization continues its erosion of the nation-state, national economies, and national cultural identities, we find ourselves, as Stuart Hall has observed, in a moment of extreme danger and complexity,[35] a moment of crisis that is being welcomed by some as an opportunity for change and renewed creativity but has caused many others to regress to the most defensive and dangerously exclusionary forms of nationalism.[36]

For Taiwan, the unresolved tension between these two coexisting modes of cultural understanding is a very real presence in its everyday existence. Its politicians, constantly under pressure from both the "one China" rhetoric of the PRC and the "formal independence" demands of Taiwanese nativists, pursue increasingly creative ways to assert the island's undeniable existence as an independent identity without actually declaring itself a nation. At the same time, its secure integration into the important networks of global exchange—financial, industrial, educational, and cultural—have rendered the question of nationhood somewhat moot. Controversies about Taiwan's official status continue to flare up on occasion—as it did recently when Los Angeles unveiled a public monument honoring its sister cities, including Taipei—but the debates are largely over semantics.[37] The Taiwanese people have in many ways already embraced the new globalism—living, working, and creating within an increasingly multicultural and transnational reality.

Postnationalism and the Chinese Diaspora:
Some Final Thoughts on Future Directions

Cultural nationalisms have for many decades dictated the way in which non-Western literatures and arts have been taught in the United States, and, even as the forces of globalization erode traditional cultural boundaries, the language of the nation-state remains deeply ingrained in American academic life. The study of Third World literatures and arts is still dominated by a kind of scholarly nativism whose theoretical attachment to notions of cultural purity and national coherence is fundamentally at odds not only with current developments in cultural discourse but with the realities of multicultural interaction on a global scale. Modernization and Westernization in countries whose otherness vis-à-vis the West was once so clearly demarcated have unsettled the assumptions of traditional methods of cultural analysis. Those informed by conventional approaches to the non-West, for instance, are understandably unnerved by the fact that the boundaries separating "us" and "them" are disintegrating and troubled by the emergence of the so-called inauthentic native—

the modern individual who is perceived to have betrayed his or her true cultural heritage (as if it were singular and coherent) because he or she no longer fits the cultural framework that the West has constructed.[38] One of the central points that Rey Chow makes in her provocative *Writing Diaspora*, for instance, is that modern Chinese history—that is, the fate of an ancient civilization turned modern—epitomizes and anticipates many of the problems that current cultural criticism in the West now faces.[39] She argues that Western scholars continue to be fascinated by Chinese literature and art that conform to existing notions about "authentic" Chinese culture but have stubbornly resisted cultural products that are more complexly hybridized by modernization and Westernization. The reception of recent Chinese films in the West certainly underscores her basic argument.[40] While exotic period films like those of the PRC's Zhang Yimou and Chen Kaige have received extravagant praise from Western critics and attracted respectably large audiences, many wonderful films by Hong Kong and Taiwanese filmmakers—and even films with contemporary themes by other PRC directors—have been ignored because they are too "modern," not "different" enough. As the boundaries separating cultures grow ever more porous, traditional scholarship that clings to the language of coherent national cultures will undoubtedly find it progressively more difficult to deal with the messiness of postmodern global culture and the hybridity of contemporary cultural production not only in the Third World but in the increasingly multicultural First World as well. In the United States, scholars of minority literatures and arts are realizing that the changes brought about by rapid globalization have made it necessary to rethink the essentialist categories that are the legacy of 1960s cultural nationalisms. The new paradigms of identity now emerging in ethnic studies offer interesting variations of cultural hybridity and syncretism. Not surprisingly, scholars of Asia and Asian America are very much at the forefront of these shifts in critical thinking.[41] After all, the sociocultural changes that have led to an increasingly hybrid and unstable sense of identity in Asian communities like Taiwan—changing immigration patterns, multinational capitalism, the ascendance of Third World nations as new economic powers, the ease of global travel and communications, and the emergence of a growing transnational elite—are the same factors that are rapidly undermining traditional definitions of ethnic identity in America. Over the last several years the study of Asian American literature and arts has been marked by gradual tactical and rhetorical shifts—from self-determination to diaspora, from internal colonization to the postcolonial, and from the building of an Asian American nation to denationalization.[42] Like the contemporary experiences of Taiwan, Hong

Kong, and other Asian communities, Asian American experiences are no longer limited to the simple duality between two cultural heritages, one Eastern and one Western, but involve a more radical ability to shuttle between multiple and competing cultural influences.[43] The multicultural and transnational consciousness of today's Asian diaspora has played a significant part in forcing a shift in critical discourse from essentialist or binary definitions of categories such as nation and identity to more radical approaches that emphasize not multicultural plurality (with its discrete alternative canons, the logical consequence of identity politics) but a multivoiced hybridity (hybrid cultural difference within one disseminated space). As the spirited debates over new methodologies for cultural analysis continue, the pragmatic problem remains of how to translate these new theoretical approaches to the teaching of non-Western literatures in the university—an institution borne of Enlightenment rationalism and driven by a fundamental impulse to categorize, define, and draw boundaries. The challenge for those of us in the academy will be to find constructive, rather than merely destructive, ways to break down traditional classifications and categories, to reassess existing disciplinary divisions, to move away from the isolated or dualistic study of national literatures, and to question modal and generic separations (verbal versus visual arts, documentary versus fiction, novel versus poem, and so on). As the cultures and arts of the postcolonial world continue to change and grow, the institutions of critical discourse must find new approaches to understanding newly emerging hybrid forms.

NOTES

Introduction

In the notes and bibliography, sources originally published in Chinese have been translated into English. The original Chinese characters follow the translation at the first mention of each source. Entries in the bibliography have been grouped into two categories: works published in Chinese and works published in English. The bibliography concludes with a list of the films of Hou Hsiao-hsien.

1   See, for instance, Seth Faison, "Taiwan's New Doctrine Unintelligible in Chinese," *New York Times*, July 21, 1999, A6.

2   Since its rise in the late eighteenth century and the early nineteenth, the idea of nation, which divides the world into a mosaic of distinct and differentiated entities, has been one of the most important and formative concepts in modern Western thought—a concept Benedict Anderson has called "the most universally legitimate value in the political life of our time" (Benedict Anderson, *Imagined Communities: Reflections on the Origins and Spread of Nationalism*, rev. ed. [London: Verso, 1991], 3).

3   Michael Hardt and Antonio Negri, *Empire* (Cambridge: Harvard University Press, 2001).

4   As one observer noted, many scholars and activists saw the master theory proposed by the book as an appealing blueprint for understanding the complexities of current global interaction and conflict—particularly after the events of September 11 spotlighted the intricate and widely distributed networks of global terrorism. See Dean Kuipers, "The Rise of the New Global 'Empire,'" *Los Angeles Times*, October 1, 2001.

5   Hardt and Negri, *Empire*, xii–xiii.

6   In addition to Benedict Anderson's frequently cited book, a few of the more important works in English include Peter Worsley's *The Third World* (Chicago: University of Chicago Press, 1964), Hans Kohn's *Nationalism: Its Meaning and History* (New York: Van Nostrand, 1965), Ernest Gellner's *Nations and Nationalism* (Oxford: Basil Blackwell, 1983), Partha Chatterjee's *Nationalist Thought and*

the Colonial World: A Derivative Discourse (London: Zed, 1986), Tom Nairn's *The Break-Up of Britain: Crisis and Neo-Nationalism* (London: New Left Books, 1977), Hugh Seton-Watson's *Nations and States: An Enquiry into the Origins of Nations and the Politics of Nationalism* (Boulder: Westview, 1977), and Eric Hobsbawm's *Nations and Nationalism since 1780: Programme, Myth, Reality* (Cambridge: Cambridge University Press, 1991).

7 Chon Noriega points to this paradox in his introduction to Chon Noriega, ed., *Visible Nations: Latin American Cinema and Video* (Minneapolis: University of Minnesota Press, 2000), noting that, following a period in which a pan-national approach to films from Latin American (best exemplified by the New Latin American Cinema movement of the 1970s and 1980s) dominated, the study of Latin American cinema has become insistently "national," resulting in the simultaneous existence of competing metanarratives (xi–xxv).

8 Ernest Renan, "What Is a Nation?" translated and annotated by Martin Thom, in Homi K. Bhabha, ed., *Nation and Narration* (London: Routledge, 1990), 8–22; Anderson, *Imagined Communities*.

9 See, for example, Chantal Mouffe, "Citizenship and Political Identity," *October* 61 (1992): 28–32.

10 China is a country for which the ideal of unity and the concepts of centralization, harmony, and stability have historically been dominant themes in social and political thought. The Central Kingdom's first emperor, Ch'in Shih Huang (秦始皇), is revered precisely because he was the first to succeed in unifying the fragmented rival fiefdoms of the Warring States period (475–221 B.C.) under a single centralized government. Since that time, the idea of the indivisibility of China has become deeply ingrained in the Chinese psyche. Despite the ethnic, religious, and ideological diversity within China's borders and even though the historical record shows that the country has experienced nearly as many years of division as unity in the millennia since Ch'in Shih Huang, the tradition of *ta-i-t'ung* (大一統)—"unity and cohesion"—remains the ideal in Chinese political thought. It was with an almost visceral sense of conviction that the Middle Kingdom, as Benedict Anderson observes, "imagined itself not as Chinese, but as central" (*Imagined Communities*, 12–13).

11 The emergence of concepts such as "three lands, two shores" (*san di liang an* [三地兩岸], encompassing Taiwan, Hong Kong, and the PRC) and "greater China" (which includes 30 million people in the Chinese global diaspora) attest to a newly transnationalized sense of Chineseness and acknowledges the reality of multiple Chinese cultural spaces. The ethnic and cultural hybridity of current artistic productions has also engendered a lively debate over the increasingly complex issue of Chinese cultural authenticity. See, for instance, David Henry Hwang, "In Today's World, Who Represents the 'Real' China?" *New York Times*, April 1, 2001.

12 Some of the details of Lee's biography are culled from Willem van Kemenade, *China, Hong Kong, Taiwan, Inc.: The Dynamics of a New Empire* (New York: Knopf, 1997), esp. 107–9; and Marcus W. Brauchli, "Rising in the East: Why Historic Election in Taiwan Is Rattling Both China and U.S.," *Wall Street Journal*, February 26, 1996, A1, 6.

13 Van Kemenade, *China, Hong Kong, Taiwan, Inc.*, 108.

14 Lee Teng-hui, *The Road to Democracy: Taiwan's Pursuit of Identity* (Tokyo: PHP Institute, 1999).

15 Van Kemenade, *China, Hong Kong, Taiwan, Inc.*, 113. "Dollar diplomacy" refers to Lee's efforts to use Taiwan's financial clout—as the world's fourteenth-largest trading power and the holder of its largest financial reserves—to establish unofficial relations with Third World nations. With mixed success, Taiwan has tried to win the goodwill and support of emerging nations through generous offers of developmental aid programs and investments in local industries. One might include in this category of diplomatic targets the People's Republic of China, where Taiwan is a major investor. While Taiwan has no formal diplomatic relations with any of its Western trading partners, it has managed to exchange Economic and Cultural Affairs Offices—which are staffed by former diplomats and function as embassies in all but name—with nearly all of them. Since Lee is not able to participate in official meetings with foreign government authorities, he relies on "vacation" or "golf" diplomacy, meeting them on golf courses or at other, politically neutral locales. Perhaps the most famous case of vacation diplomacy in recent years was President Lee's unofficial visit to the United States in May 1995. The visit was ostensibly a personal trip to attend a reunion at Cornell, which was conferring on him an honorary doctorate, but it was undoubtedly calculated to stir up a political tempest. While the visit did not result in any formal diplomatic gains for Taiwan, China's irate protests did generate a great deal of positive publicity and international sympathy for Taiwan.

16 Efforts to restore the island's Taiwanese identity can be seen, for instance, in the symbolic gesture of changing street names from those given by the KMT regime—often names of provinces, cities, and other sites on the mainland—to names that honor the island's native population. The most pointed example of this move to reclaim the island's geography for the Taiwanese can be found in Taipei, where the wide boulevard leading up to the presidential palace—once named Chieh-shou Street (介壽路), meaning "long live Chiang Kai-shek"—was, in 1995, rechristened Kai-De-Ge-Lan Boulevard (凱德葛蘭大道) in honor of the tribe of aborigines that lived in the area in the seventeenth century, before the arrival of the first Chinese immigrants. See van Kemenade, *China, Hong Kong, Taiwan, Inc.*, 107.

17 It was once a punishable offense to speak the native tongue in schools or official settings. See Alan Wachman, *Taiwan: National Identity and Democratization* (Armonk, N.Y.: M. E. Sharpe, 1994), 108.

18 Ibid., 109.

19 All indications are that Lee Teng-hui has remained actively involved in shaping Taiwan's path toward defining its global status. Indeed, late last year Lee openly declared that he was joining forces with President Chen to help increase Taiwan's presence on the global scene—a move that resulted in his expulsion from the KMT. See Erik Eckholm, "Nationalist Party Expels Taiwan's Ex-President," *New York Times*, September 22, 2001.

20 Chen seems to share Lee's belief that Taiwan's economic development is the central pillar supporting its continued democratization and indeed its very existence. He has continued to move toward strengthening Taiwan's position in the fast-growing global economy, including expanding ties with the mainland. See Tyler

Marshall, "Taiwan Sees New Ties with Mainland," *Los Angeles Times* (August 27, 2001); and Marshall, "Taiwan Hails Shift toward Mainland," *Los Angeles Times* (August 28, 2001).

21 See, for instance, Henry Chu, "In Taiwan, Gay Life Has Zest," *Los Angeles Times* (May 10, 2000) and Chu, "The Tale of Taiwan's Aborigines," *Los Angeles Times* (June 1, 2001).

22 Mark Landler, "One China? Perhaps Two? Little Things Mean a Lot," *New York Times* (March 7, 2002).

23 Many recent studies address the political and economic changes that have transformed the island over the last several decades and grapple more directly with that dimension. These include: Tien Hung-mao, *The Great Transition: Political and Social Change in the Republic of China* (Stanford: Hoover Institution Press, 1988); John F. Copper, *Taiwan: Nation-State or Province?* (Boulder: Westview, 1990); Simon Long, *Taiwan: China's Last Frontier* (London: Macmillan, 1991); Peter Moody, *Political Change on Taiwan: A Study of Ruling Party Adaptability* (New York: Praeger, 1992); Tun-jen Cheng and Stephan Haggard, eds., *Political Change in Taiwan* (Boulder: Lynne Reiner, 1992); Wachman, *Taiwan*; and Van Kemenade, *China, Hong Kong, Taiwan, Inc.*

24 As Benedict Anderson and other cultural theorists remind us, modern notions of nation are inextricably linked to the development and proliferation of media for public expression such as books, newspapers, and, in the electronic age, television and films. See Anderson, *Imagined Communities*, particularly chapter 2, "Cultural Roots," and chapter 3, "The Origins of National Consciousness." Many cultural theorists debating the future of the nation in our increasingly integrated global system have also focused on the complex relationship between the national and television, film, and other media of "electronic capitalism."

25 The correct Wade-Giles romanization is Huang Ch'un-ming, but I have retained the spelling that the writer himself prefers.

26 This is partly attributable, perhaps, to Huang's own experiences as a documentary filmmaker of some note.

27 *His Son's Big Doll* (兒子的大玩偶, 1983). The film's title segment was directed by Hou Hsiao-hsien.

28 See, for example, Huang Chien-yeh (黃建業), *The Quest of Humanist Cinema* (人文電影的追尋) (Taipei: Yuan-liu Publications, 1990), 27. The extent to which Hou Hsiao-hsien has come to stand for all of Taiwanese New Cinema in Taiwan is underscored by the cultural debates surrounding the cinematic trend that occurred during the balloting for the 1985 Golden Horse Awards (Taiwan's Oscars). Those supporting Taiwanese New Cinema were dubbed the "pro-Hou" (擁候) camp while those opposed were "anti-Hou" (反候). See Chiao Hsiung-p'ing (焦雄屏), ed., *Taiwanese New Cinema* (臺灣新電影) (Taipei: Jen-chien Books, 1988), 83. Hou has become such an iconic figure that one film scholar, wary of perpetuating a monolithic view of Taiwanese filmmaking, felt compelled to remind us that "Taiwanese cinema is more than Hou Hsiao-hsien." See Wen Ko-chih (文戈止), "The *Rashomon* Quality of *City of Sadness*" (悲情城市的羅生門本質), *Tsu-li Morning Post* (自立早報), October 10, 1989.

1 Structural domination is an imbalance of power between colonizer and colonized that allows the former to dominate the latter not only politically, economically, and socially but also culturally. See Robert Stam and Louise Spence, "Colonialism, Racism, and Representation," *Screen* 24, no. 2 (March–April 1983): 4. It is this emphasis on cultural structural domination as the key feature of the colonial experience that has allowed the critical discourse of postcolonialism to encompass the literatures and cinemas of not only the historical victims of European imperialism but also the cultural products of other groups that are oppressed, marginalized, stigmatized as underdeveloped, or otherwise dominated.

2 As Douglas Mendel notes, Taiwan was one of the very few former colonies that did not win self-determination after World War II. Instead, it merely changed from Japanese to Chinese control. He writes: "Whether or not one believes that the Formosan majority is under Chinese colonial domination today, the reaction of the native Formosans to their past Japanese and present Chinese overlords is relevant to any study of Asian colonialism" (*The Politics of Formosan Nationalism* [Berkeley: University of California Press, 1970], 3).

3 Although Taiwan's cultural inheritance is predominantly Chinese, it also bears the heritage of years of European and Japanese colonization. The influence of Dutch and Japanese architectural styles, for example, remains highly visible in many cities and towns. European blood runs in the veins of some of the island's inhabitants. The Taiwanese dialect is distinct from Mandarin, the language of Chinese officialdom, and the two dialects are mutually unintelligible when spoken. (They certainly have less in common than the languages of England and its American colonies had in 1776.) Over the centuries, the island's language has also absorbed words and phrases from its European and Japanese colonizers. Since 1949, five decades of Communist rule in the People's Republic and capitalist development in Taiwan facilitated by the United States and Japan have certainly further widened the sociocultural gap between the mainland and the island.

4 Andreas Huyssen, for example, has addressed the problems that the newly unified Germany has had to face in attempting to construct a coherent sense of nation after so many decades of separation and independent development. As he observes, "There now seem to be emerging, as a result of unification, two national identities, an FRG and a GDR identity, within what is supposed to be *one* nation-state. Unification at the level of state and currency . . . is indeed not accompanied by unification on the level of discourse, culture, experience, and everyday life" ("The Inevitability of Nation: German Intellectuals after Unification," *October* 61 [1992]: 69). The German situation offers a particularly illuminating point of comparison for "the two Chinas," which have similarly taken divergent paths on the level of state, currency, discourse, culture, and experience since World War II. Indeed, the Taiwanese have been paying close attention to developments in the new Germany, particularly to the woes of what used to be West Germany. Taiwanese who are opposed to reunification with China point to the incredible problems West Germany has encountered in trying to absorb the impoverished, undisciplined, and

demanding population of communist East Germany and fear that the burden the population of the PRC would impose on Taiwan would be exponentially greater. See Wachman, *Taiwan*, 115.

5 What Rey Chow calls the "myth of consanguinity"—the claim of Chinese ethnicity as the ultimate signified—has been exploited for political and social purposes by Chinese governments throughout history. See her *Writing Diaspora: Tactics of Intervention in Contemporary Cultural Studies* (Bloomington: Indiana University Press, 1993), 24–25. Benedict Anderson's example of the tsarist "Russification" of a heterogeneous population also provides an informative parallel. For another interesting comparison, see Marvin D'Lugo, "Catalan Cinema: Historical Experience and Cinematic Practice," *Quarterly Review of Film and Video* 13, nos. 1–3 (1991): 131–46.

6 For a brief description of Taiwan's early history, see chapter 1 of Long, *Taiwan*, 1–11.

7 See George Kerr, *Formosa: Licensed Revolution and the Home Rule Movement, 1895–1945* (Honolulu: University of Hawaii Press, 1974), 3.

8 Ibid., 6. In this sense, Taiwan is like Australia, whose earliest European settlers were British convicts and their warders. It has been argued that because of the penal origins of the settlements Australians viewed themselves as dispossessed and despised and consequently developed a culture based on denial of the dominant culture of England. See, for example, Neil Rattigan, *Images of Australia: 100 Films of the New Australian Cinema* (Dallas: Southern Methodist University Press, 1991), 10–17. Interestingly, nineteenth-century European governments felt that the lawless island posed a threat to international shipping and among the many proposals they considered to remedy the situation was a plan to make Taiwan a penal colony following the Australian pattern. See Kerr, *Formosa*, 9–10.

9 See Long, *Taiwan*, 13; and Kerr, *Formosa*, xiii.

10 See Kerr, *Formosa*, 7; and Long, *Taiwan*, 11.

11 Long, *Taiwan*, 19–20 and Kerr, *Formosa*, 10–11.

12 Kerr, *Taiwan*, xiv.

13 Edgar Snow, *Red Star over China*, cited in van Kemenade, *China, Hong Kong, Taiwan, Inc.*, 144.

14 Wachman, *Taiwan*, 93.

15 Alan Wachman cites one Taiwanese native who remembered how disillusioning those initial encounters with the mainland Chinese were. The ignorant, coarse Nationalist troops and the corrupt, decadent KMT officers caused many Taiwanese to acknowledge, with chagrin, that the Japanese culture into which they had been assimilated was in many ways superior to that of the Chinese. Says the Taiwanese eyewitness of his change of heart: "We all took up flags and went to welcome them [the KMT]. . . . President Chiang has come to take over Taiwan! That was really how we felt—entering the embrace of our fatherland. But although we genuinely accepted the mainland takeover, we immediately began to sense the conflict of culture. Moreover, that conflict of culture was extremely intense. It was discovered that the Japanese culture which we had originally loathed was, as compared to the culture of our fatherland, a strong culture, a superior culture. And the culture of the rulers is a worthless, inferior—an inferior kind of barbaric culture. . . .

That kind of conflict is extremely intense and transformed us from the heights of identification to the heights of hostility" (Wachman, *Taiwan*, 95).

16   See Long, *Taiwan*, 53.

17   Ibid., 55.

18   See ibid., 54.

19   The incident is only the bloodiest example of the kind of KMT brutality and high-handedness that led to the deep sense of injustice and victimization that has unified the Taiwanese. As one Western observer of the Taiwanese situation wrote: "The communal feeling that has developed since 1947 is, in many respects, a *negative* reaction. The result of discrimination and persecution, it has led to a deep-seated self-consciousness of Taiwanese as Taiwanese." See Mark Mancall's introduction to Mark Mancall, ed., *Formosa Today* (New York: Praeger, 1964), 24.

20   Cited in ibid., 6–7, emphasis mine. Note that the Chinese term translated as "compatriot" is 同胞, which literally means "of the same placenta."

21   Anderson, *Imagined Communities*, 11. See also Eric Hobsbawm, "Introduction: Inventing Traditions," in Eric Hobsbawm and Terence Ranger, eds. *The Invention of Tradition* (Cambridge: Cambridge University Press, 1983). Hobsbawm writes: "'Invented tradition' is taken to mean a set of practices, normally governed by overtly or tacitly accepted rules and of a ritual and symbolic nature, which seek to inculcate certain values and norms of behavior by repetition, which automatically implies continuity with the past. In fact, where possible, they normally attempt to establish continuity with a suitable historical past" (1).

22   Cited in Marshall Johnson, "Making Time: Historic Preservation and the Space of Nationality," *positions: east asia cultures critique* 2, no. 2 (fall 1994): 177–249. Johnson's article is a fascinating analysis of how the institutions of national historic preservation in Taiwan have been used to construct a Chinese nation under KMT rule and now, in the postdictatorship era, a Taiwanese nation.

23   See Anderson, *Imagined Communities*, chapter 10, in which the author discusses the role of museums and two other institutions of power—the census and the map—that he feels profoundly shape the way in which a colonial state imagines its dominion. Significantly, the residents of Taiwan—even those who were born on the island and have never been to the mainland—are categorized on their identification cards by the mainland provinces from which their ancestors originally came. See Mancall, *Formosa Today*, 26; and Johnson, "Making Time," 189, on *chi-kuan* (one's native place or hometown, 籍貫). In geography classes, Taiwanese students are expected to recognize the location not just of Taiwan but of all China's provinces, mountains, and rivers. See, for instance, the textbook illustration reproduced in Johnson, "Making Time," 240, depicting China as a tree and Taiwan as a leaf.

24   The KMT's vision of China is itself a modern construction—the product of China's own experience of colonization by foreign invaders. As Dru Gladney has observed, Sun Yat-sen's vision of China as an ethnic and cultural unit based on the Han nationality (漢民族) was created in response to, and mobilized as a tool of resistance against, the Manchu dynasty. See Dru Gladney, *Muslim Chinese: Ethnic Nationalism in the People's Republic* (Cambridge: Council on East Asian Studies, Harvard University, 1990), 82–85, cited in Wachman, *Taiwan*, 86–87.

25　See, for example, the prizewinning poster design for the celebration of the Republic of China's eightieth year (5,000 + 80), reproduced in Johnson, "Making Time,"
187.

26　Ibid., 206.

27　The bitterness expressed by one Taiwanese interviewee illustrates native impa-
tience with the KMT's incessant focus on the Chinese mainland and resentment
over being deprived of the local heritage: "My daughter now is in high school. She
has to memorize all the cities, all the agricultural products and industrial products
of every province [of China], the weather, the rivers, and the natural resources.
Everything. We had to memorize all this before, thirty years ago. I forget everything. Now, my daughter . . . has to memorize what I memorized and we know so
little about Taiwan. . . . We are forbidden to learn. We have no access. No resources"
(Wachman, *Taiwan*, 82).

28　These icons are common tools used to reinforce the feeling of unisonance. See
Anderson, *Imagined Communities*, 145.

29　A recent article in the *New York Times* (June 29, 2002) reported that Taiwan's
interior ministries had ordered that all portraits of Chiang Kai-shek and his son
Chiang Ching-kuo hanging in public places be removed. Only portraits of Sun Yat-
sen and Taiwan's current president are now allowed.

30　See, for example, Ch'iu Kuei-fen (邱貴芬), "'Discovering Taiwan': Constructing a
Theory of Taiwanese Post-Coloniality" (發現臺灣: 建構臺灣後殖民述), in Cheng
Ming-li (鄭明利), ed., *Contemporary Literary Criticism in Taiwan*, vol. 3: *The
Novel* (當代臺灣文學評論大系: 小說批評) (Taipei: Cheng-chung Books, 1993),
162.

31　Wachman, *Taiwan*, 108.

32　See, for example, ibid., 101.

33　Other groups in Taiwan include the Hakka (客家), who migrated over the course of
several centuries from Honan (河南) Province in central China southward through
numerous provinces to eventually settle in Kwangtung (廣東). Some of the Hakka
in Taiwan came with early settlers in the seventeenth century, while others came
from the mainland at the same time as the KMT. Taiwan also has many non-
Chinese aboriginal tribes that have inhabited the island since long before any
Chinese arrived. Of course, decades of intermarriage between mainlanders and
Taiwanese have also rendered this dichotomous system of labeling people increasingly imprecise. See ibid., 16–17.

34　For a more comprehensive discussion of early nativism in Taiwan, see Wang Jing,
"Taiwan *Hsiang-t'u* Literature: Perspectives on the Evolution of a Literary Movement," in Jeannette L. Faurot, ed., *Chinese Fiction from Taiwan: Critical Perspectives* (Bloomington: Indiana University Press, 1980), 43–70. See also Yeh Shih-t'ao
(葉石濤), "An Introduction to Taiwanese *Hsiang-t'u* Literature" (臺灣鄉土文學
導論), in Yu T'ien-ts'ung (尉天聰), ed., *A Collection of Essays on* Hsiang-tu *Literature* (鄉土文學討論集) (Taipei: Yuan-ching Publications, 1978), 69–92.

35　As with modern nationalist movements all over the world, a sense of Taiwanese identity was most strongly felt among the intelligentsia. Intellectuals helped
to articulate, and shape, feelings of national solidarity within society at large.
During this anti-Japanese period, Taiwanese patriots still identified most strongly

with the Chinese mainland, drawing part of their inspiration for the hsiang-t'u movement from the regionalist writing of mainland authors such as Shen Ts'ong-wen (沈從文). During the Sino-Japanese War, the Japanese military invasion of the mainland precipitated the emergence of a similarly anti-imperialist literature of nationalism, particularly in northeastern China, where fighting was heaviest. Writers such as Hsiao Hung (蕭紅), author of *Field of Life and Death* (生死場), de-picted with gritty realism Japan's destruction of the Chinese countryside and the brutalities committed by the invaders. See Hu Ch'iu-yuan (胡秋原), "The Restora-tion of a Chinese Position" (中國人立場之復歸), in Yu, *A Collection of Essays on* Hsiang-tu *Literature*, 15.

36 These are the writers most often cited as exemplary. See, for example, Wang T'o (王拓), "'Realism,' Not 'Ruralism,'" (是《現實主義》文學, 不是《鄉土文學》), in Yu, *A Collection of Essays on* Hsiang-tu *Literature*, 113. Chung Chao-cheng is also edi-tor of an anthology of native Taiwanese literature: *The Selected Works of Native Taiwanese Writers* (本省籍作家作品選集), 10 vols. (Taipei: Wen-t'an, 1965).

37 According to Wang Jing, the movement for adopting the Taiwanese dialect for cre-ative writing was advocated by Huang Shih-hui and Kuo Ch'iu-sheng, who also encouraged native writers to depict the reality of Taiwan and tap into the rich vo-cabulary of oral dialect. See Wang, "Taiwan *Hsiang-tu* Literature," 68, n. 6.

38 See Maurice Meisner, "The Development of Formosan Nationalism," in Mancall, *Formosa Today*, 147–62.

39 See, for instance, Huyssen, "The Inevitability of Nation," 65–73.

40 Meisner, "The Development of Formosan Nationalism," 151–53.

41 As one Taiwanese literary critic notes, "The early policies of the Kuomintang gov-ernment on Taiwan simply replicated the nightmare of colonization under the Japanese Occupation" (國民政府遷臺初期的種種策略無異複製了臺灣日據時代的被殖民夢魘). See Ch'iu, "Discovering Taiwan," 162.

42 The depth and breadth of the penetration of Japanese culture into Taiwanese so-ciety is particularly evident in Hou Hsiao-hsien's films—from the traditional Japa-nese-style houses (with their sliding *shoji* screens and *tatami* rooms) his charac-ters inhabit to the Japanese words and phrases interspersed throughout their dia-logue and the manner in which they sit, speak, and carry themselves. As Hou points out, Taiwanese knowledge and appreciation of Western classical music, lit-erature, and philosophy—all of which are featured in *City of Sadness*—also reflect the Japanese cultural influence. See Chiao Hsiung-p'ing (焦雄屏), "The Camera-swept Back Alleys of History: An Interview with Hou Hsiao-hsien" (鏡頭掃過歷史的暗巷), China Times (中國時報), September 4–5, 1989.

43 Modernization, it has often been argued, is simply another form of colonization. During the age of empire, European imperial powers justified their invasion and subjugation of non-Western peoples by claiming to civilize them—to offer them culture—as if they had none of their own. In the twenty-first century, the myth of progress persists in the guise of modernization—hence the emergence of *develop-ing nations* as an umbrella term used to describe the nations of the Third World. The underlying assumption, of course, is that development must necessarily lead to the achievement of the ultimate goal: the model of·industrial society as per-sonified by the Western powers. As Taiwan has industrialized, it has also suffered

Notes to Chapter 1   **257**

cultural colonization by the two economic superpowers to which it is most indebted: Japan and the United States. Both the Japanese and American consumer cultures have penetrated Taiwanese society to such an extent that native cultural awareness, some fear, is nearing the point of extinction.

44 The economic and cultural recolonization of Taiwan is one of the major concerns addressed by hsiang-t'u writers and theorists. See, for example, Ch'en Ying-chen's *Taiwan under American Rule* (美國統制下的台灣), vol. 13 of his *Collected Works* (Taipei: Jen-chien, 1988). See also two essays by Wang T'o in Yu, *A Collection of Essays on* Hsiang-tu *Literature*, "Embrace the Healthy Earth" (擁抱健康的大地), 384–62; and "'Colonialism' or 'Self-Determination'" (《殖民地意願》還是《自主意願》), 578–86. In both essays, Wang argues that neo-imperialism is a global phenomenon. Economic cooperation, technological cooperation, and the structures of the transnational corporation are merely disguises for the West's relentless recolonization of so-called underdeveloped and developing nations. In addition, see Hu Ch'iu-yuan, "On Nationalism and Economic Colonization" (談民族主義與殖民經濟), an interview with Hu collected in Yu, *A Collection of Essays on* Hsiang-tu *Literature*, 561–77.

45 The Taiwanese response was similar to the patriotic demonstration by Chinese students on May 4, 1919, protesting the Treaty of Versailles, which turned over German-held parts of the Northeast to Japan rather than returning them to China.

46 Participation in institutions of international exchange such as the United Nations and the Olympic Games are a constitutive part of nation building, hence Taiwan's expulsion from these arenas inevitably precipitated a crisis of nationhood. These particular political defeats are frequently cited as crucial turning points in Taiwanese history. See, for instance, Wang T'o's "'Realism,' Not 'Ruralism,'" 101; his "Embrace the Healthy Earth," 357–58; and Hu, "The Restoration of a Chinese Position," 17.

47 Ch'en Ying-chen (陳映眞), "A Tenth Anniversary Retrospective Look at the Hsiang-t'u Literary Debates" (《鄉土文學》論戰十周年的回顧), in *The Poverty of Ideology* (思想的貧困), vol. 6 of his *Collected Works* (Taipei: Jen-chien, 1988), 99.

48 See Lucy Chen, "Literary Formosa," in Mancall, *Formosa Today*, 131–41; Jules Nadeau, "Orphaned Authors in a More-or-Less Free China," in his *Twenty-Million Chinese Made in Taiwan*, translated by David Homel (Montreal: Montreal Press, 1990), 287–305. See also Ch'en, "A Tenth Anniversary Retrospective Look at the Hsiang-t'u Literary Debates," 98.

49 Chang Hsi-kuo (張系國), "Realism in Taiwan Fiction: Two Directions," in Jeannette L. Faurot, ed., *Chinese Fiction from Taiwan: Critical Perspectives* (Bloomington: Indiana University Press, 1980), 33.

50 The works of a few selected mainland writers—Hu Shih (胡適), Hsu Chih-mo (徐志摩), and Chu Tsu-ch'ing (朱自清) among them—were permitted.

51 As Chiu Kuei-fen notes, KMT censorship tightly controlled literature and all other forms of culture and media in Taiwan for decades. In the early years of KMT rule, all native publications were forced to shut down and the editorships of major newspapers and magazines were held by mainland writers, effectively creating a mainland-dominated literary canon. See Chiu, "Discovering Taiwan," 159–63. The writing of the mainland authors was criticized by the hsiang-t'u advocates as being

"ossified" (僵硬刻板) and "alienated from reality" (脫離現實). See, for instance Wang, "'Realism,' Not 'Ruralism,'" 109.

52 One critic refers to the work of the transients as "airport literature" (機場文學). See Su San, "Looking at Taiwan through Its Fiction," cited in Chang, "Realism in Taiwan Fiction," 31. Chang also uses the term *literature of the wanderer* (浪子文學) to describe works set on the mainland.

53 Chiang Meng-lin (蔣夢麟), "On the Chinese New Arts Movement" (談中國新文藝運動), originally published in 1961, cited in Ho Hsin (何欣), "The Modern Chinese Literary Heritage" (中國現代小說的傳統), in Yu, *A Collection of Essays on Hsiang-tu Literature*, 465–66.

54 Contemporary Poetry might also be translated as *Modern Poetry*, as suggested by Leo Ou-fan Lee in his essay "'Modernism' and 'Romanticism'" in Taiwan Literature," in Faurot, *Chinese Fiction from Taiwan*, 8. Many of these journals are still in publication. The dates in parentheses indicate their years of greatest influence. The literary supplements of Taiwan's major newspapers, such as the *China Times* (中國時報) and the *United Daily News* (聯合報), also provided an important forum for creative writing.

55 The journal was short-lived, beginning publication in 1936 and ceasing in 1937 when its printing plant in Shanghai was destroyed by Japanese cannon fire. During its brief existence, however, it brought together a number of Chinese writers who were interested in Western modernist poetry. In addition to Chi Hsien, editorial board members included Feng Chih (馮至), Pien Chih-lin (卞之琳), Liang Tsung-tai (梁宗岱), Sun Ta-yu (孫大雨), and Hsu Ch'ih (徐遲). See ibid., 8.

56 These are some of the guiding principles formulated by Chi Hsien. See ibid., 10.

57 A number of anthologies offer a sampling of their works in translation. See, for example, Wai-lim Yip, *Modern Chinese Poetry* (Iowa City: University of Iowa Press, 1970); Cyril Birch, ed., *Anthology of Chinese Literature*, 2 vols. (New York: Grove, 1972), 449–71, col. 2; and Ch'i Pang-yuan et al., eds., *An Anthology of Contemporary Chinese Literature, Taiwan, 1949–1974: Poetry Collection* (Taipei: National Institute for Compilation and Translation, 1975).

58 Quoted in Joseph S. M. Lau, "How Much Truth Can a Blade of Grass Carry? Ch'en Ying-chen and the Emergence of Native Taiwanese Writers," *Journal of Asian Studies* 32, no. 4 (August 1973): 624–25.

59 See Lee, "'Modernism' and 'Romanticism,'" 9.

60 Modern Literature, no. 1 (March 1960): 2, quoted in Lee, "'Modernism' and 'Romanticism,'" 14.

61 The long stream of consciousness monologue in "Wandering in the Garden, Waking from a Dream" (遊園驚夢) is a famous example of Pai's mastery of Western modernist technique.

62 Lucy Chen, "Literary Formosa," *Taipei People* (台北人) (Taipei: Ch'en-chung, 1971).

63 Ch'en Ying-chen, Wang T'o, and Yang Ch'ing-chu were all imprisoned by the Kuomintang government for their cultural and political activities. In the case of Ch'en Ying-chen, it is particularly important to separate Ch'en the politician/polemicist from Ch'en the fiction writer. His earliest stories dealt with the kinds of psychological issues treated by the modernists, and, as with Hwang Chun-ming's work, even his later hsiang-t'u stories often employed modernist techniques.

64 These are the authors most often cited as exemplifying hsiang-t'u literature. See, for instance, Ch'en Ying-chen, "Literature Comes from Social Self-Reflection" (文學來自社會反應社會), in Yu, *A Collection of Essays on* Hsiang-tu *Literature*, 64.

65 Most notable were the best-selling novels by Ch'iung Yao (瓊瑤), a sort of Taiwanese Barbara Cartland.

66 While Japanese era Taiwanese writing is cited as the most direct precursor, other sources of inspiration for the nativist hsiang-t'u movement include the Chinese literature of the May Fourth period as well as—ironically, given the fervent anti-Western rhetoric of the hsiang-t'u theorists—American Southern Renaissance literature and the Gaelic revival in Ireland. Hwang has expressed his admiration for both Hunanese writer Shen Ts'ong-wen (沈從文) and William Faulkner.

67 This was most notable in Wang Chen-ho, whose works are often so heavily laced with Taiwanese dialect that copious footnotes are needed to render it intelligible to nonnative readers. Defending the profusion of local dialect in his stories, Wang asks, "Why shouldn't a Taiwanese describe local life in his dialect when his readership is mainly Taiwanese?" See Nadeau, "Orphaned Authors in a More-or-Less Free China," 299.

68 Russian theorist Mikhail Bakhtin's theory of language, which will be given more detailed consideration in a later chapter, can be found throughout his writing, most notably: Mikhail Bakhtin and V. N. Volosinov, *Marxism and the Philosophy of Language*, translated by Ladislav Matejka and I. R. Titunik (Cambridge: Harvard University Press, 1986); Mikhail Bakhtin, *Rabelais and His World*, translated by Helene Iswolsky (Bloomington: Indiana University Press, 1984); and Bakhtin, *The Dialogic Imagination*, edited by Michael Holquist, translated by Caryl Emerson (Austin: University of Texas Press, 1982).

69 See, for instance, Wang, "'Realism,' Not 'Ruralism,'" 116. The village is often celebrated in rural Third World nations. Indian filmmaker Satyajit Ray, for example, similarly believes the village to be the one place where authentic national culture survives under colonial domination. See Teshome Gabriel, *Third Cinema in the Third World* (Ann Arbor: University of Michigan Press, 1983), 16.

70 The problem of how to utilize the past in the process of decolonization is infinitely complex. While indigenous traditions are considered to be a primary source of strength for anticolonial resistance, the constant danger of falling into an excessively nostalgic mode is also widely recognized. Frantz Fanon, for example, recognized that an emerging nationalistic art and literature must pass through a "remembrance phase," which is marked by a nostalgic return to childhood or a simpler past full of legends and folklore. At the same time, however, he emphasized that merely substituting the inherited culture of the oppressed for the culture of the oppressor is not a sufficient basis for the creation of a new culture: "A national culture is not a folklore." See Franz Fanon, *The Wretched of the Earth* (New York: Grove, 1968), 188. Instead, he argues that the elements of the past must be brought into a dialectical interpresence with the present reality of the people. See also Reed Way Dasenbrock's essay on the sociopolitical implications of nostalgia in contemporary African literature, "Creating a Past: Achebe, Naipaul, Soyinka, Farah," *Salmagundi* (fall 1985–winter 1986): 312–32.

71 The debates largely took the form of essays published in a variety of journals and literary supplements. Many of the crucial essays from this period are compiled in Yu, *A Collection of Essays on* Hsiang-tu *Literature*. Not surprisingly, Yu's selection of essays is heavily weighted in favor of the hsiang-t'u position.

72 Hundreds of books and articles have been devoted to this formative period of modern Chinese culture, which those readers interested in a better overview of the May Fourth Movement might want to consult. Two excellent introductions in English are Chow Tse-tsung, *The May Fourth Movement: Intellectual Revolution in Modern China* (Stanford: Stanford University Press, 1967); and Merle Goldman, ed., *Modern Chinese Literature in the May Fourth Era* (Cambridge: Harvard University Press, 1977). As Chow points out in his introduction, there has been some disagreement not only over the dating of the May Fourth era, but also over the precise relationship between the terms *May Fourth Movement* and *New Culture Movement*. The campaign for new literature and thought in China predated the May 4, 1919, student uprising by two years, but the sociopolitical demands of the latter were undeniably intimately connected to the revolution in thought advocated by the former. The 1919 demonstration itself is often thought of as a turning point for the May Fourth era. See Chow, *The May Fourth Movement*, 1–6.

73 Van Kemenade, *China, Hong Kong, Taiwan, Inc.*, 367.

74 Hu Shih, "On Constructive Revolution in Chinese Literature," cited in Chow, *The May Fourth Movement*, 277–78.

75 See chapter 13, "The New Thought and Later Controversies," in Chow, *The May Fourth Movement*, 314–37. See, in particular, the section entitled "The Controversy over Eastern and Western Civilizations," 327–32.

76 Ibid., 328.

77 The slogan was originally used in a positive sense by reformists such as Hu Shih, who suggested it as a substitute for the term *wholehearted modernization*. See ibid., 332, n. h. In later years—for instance, during the hsiang-t'u period—the term took on negative connotations.

78 Ch'en, "A Tenth Anniversary Retrospective Look at the *Hsiang-t'u* Literary Debates," 97–98. See also his "Literature Comes from Social Self-Reflection," 58.

79 Ch'en Ying-chen believes that the hsiang-t'u debates of the late 1970s were a logical continuation of the dialogue initiated by the modern poetry debates of 1972. Both, he argues, were essentially anti-imperialist, anti-Western movements. See Ch'en, "A Tenth Anniversary Retrospective Look at the *Hsiang-t'u* Literary Debates," 98–100.

80 See ibid., 99. Kwan's attack on Western modernism in modern Chinese poetry was published as an October 1972 review article in Yip, *Modern Chinese Poetry*. See Wang "Taiwan *Hsiang-t'u* Literature," 69, n. 17.

81 *Modern Literature*, no. 46 (March 1972): 5, cited in Lee, "'Modernism' and 'Romanticism,'" 12.

82 Wang, "'Realism,' Not 'Ruralism,'" 102. Wang goes on to cite numerous examples of tragedies and indignities suffered by Taiwanese laborers in American- and Japanese-owned factories (107). See also his "'Colonialism,' or 'Self-Determination,'" 578–86, translation mine.

83 Ch'en, "Literature Comes from Social Self-Reflection," 56. See also his *Taiwan under American Rule.*

84 In Wang Chen-ho, *An Oxcart for Dowry* (嫁妝一牛車) (Taipei: Yuan-ching, 1975).

85 Wang Chen-ho, *Rose, Rose, I Love You* (玫瑰玫瑰我愛你) (Taipei: Yuan-ching, 1984).

86 In Hwang Chun-ming, *Little Widows* (小寡婦) (Taipei: Yuan-ching, 1975), 57–92.

87 In Hwang Chun-ming, *Sayonara, Tsai-chien* (莎喲娜啦, 再見) (Taipei: Yuan-ching, 1974), 27–57.

88 Ibid., 127–90.

89 In Hwang, *Little Widows*, 93–213.

90 See, for instance, the publisher's note in Yu, *A Collection of Essays on* Hsiang-tu *Literature*, 3. Not surprisingly, these are the two stories most often derided by opponents of hsiang-t'u as the most polemical and simplistically ideological. See, for example, Yin Cheng-hsiung (銀正雄), "From Whence Come the Bells in the Graveyard?" (墳地裡哪來的鐘聲), in Yu, *A Collection of Essays on* Hsiang-tu *Literature*, 200.

91 Edward Said's *Orientalism*, (New York: Vintage, 1979), of course, is seminal for its analysis of the feminization of the Orient by the West. Another useful text is Francis Barker, Peter Hulme, Margaret Iversen, and Diana Loxley, eds., *Europe and Its Others*, vols. 1–2 (Colchester: University of Essex, 1985). For examples of some recent articles examining specific colonialist narratives, see Louis Montrose, "The Work of Gender in the Discourse of Discovery," *Representations* 33 (winter 1991): 1–41; and Ella Shohat, "Gender and the Culture of Empire: Toward a Feminist Ethnography of the Cinema," *Quarterly Review of Film and Video* 13, nos. 1–3 (1991): 45–84, a special issue on the "Discourse of the Other: Postcoloniality, Positionality, and Subjectivity," edited by Hamid Naficy and Teshome H. Gabriel.

92 Joan Wallach Scott, *Gender and the Politics of History*, cited in Montrose, "The Work of Gender in the Discourse of Discovery," 1.

93 Late-sixteenth-century English accounts of exploration and discovery in the New World, for example, make it clear that in the European imperialist imagination the conquest of "new" territories goes hand in hand with masculine sexual aggression against native women. See ibid., 18–19. In the twentieth century, the Japanese imperial army was notorious for enslaving the women of conquered territories. In Korea, for example, the Japanese colonizers forced untold numbers of women to prostitute themselves, serving as "comfort women" for the soldiers of the Occupation. Though Japan's brutal exploitation of Korean women has received more publicity, Taiwanese women suffered the same fate under Occupation forces.

94 Ella Shohat has noted the long history of the topos of the harem in orientalist fantasy ("Gender and the Culture of Empire," 72). The brothel might be seen as a variation on harem imagery—a place of leisure and sensual pleasure where a man can choose from any number of willingly submissive women. See also David Spurr, *The Rhetoric of Empire* (Durham: Duke University Press, 1993), particularly chapter 11, "Eroticization: The Harems of the West," 170–83.

95 The club, we are told, was originally a community teahouse. In order to take advantage of the moneymaking opportunities presented by the vacationing Ameri-

can soldiers, it was hastily remodeled as a Western-style bar—complete with an English-language name written in neon (Hwang, *Little Widows*, 93–94). The conversion of the community teahouse into a privately owned bar/brothel is symbolic of the replacement of traditional Chinese values and social institutions by Western capitalist structures and practices.

96 Ibid., 122, 156.

97 Ella Shohat has noted that the power of naming—to name is to control or possess—is central to both gender mythologies and narratives of colonialism ("Gender and the Culture of Empire," 46).

98 Hwang, *Little Widows*, 96.

99 Ibid., 115. The fact that they have to borrow traditional costumes from a television studio underscores the artificial, constructed nature of "Chineseness." As David Spurr notes, images of women representing exotic ethnic types have long been a part of colonialist discourse. French colonizers in Algeria between 1900 and 1930, for instance, often sent home postcards depicting native women dressed in "traditional" costumes and reenacting local customs or rituals. The captions accompanying the images—titles such as "Moorish Woman at Home"—further commodified the image of the colonized native for easy consumption by the West.

100 Spurr, *The Rhetoric of Empire*, 174.

101 Hwang, *Little Widows*, 107, translation mine.

102 Montrose, "The Work of Gender in the Discourse of Discovery," 8.

103 See, for example, Yu T'ien-ts'ung, "Nationalism and Our Society" (我們的社會和民族精神教育), in Yu, *A Collection of Essays on* Hsiang-tu *Literature*, 23.

104 Li Fung (李豐), "Save Medicine from Its Colonized Status" (把醫學從殖民地的地位挽救回來), cited in Ch'en, "Literature Comes from Social Self-Reflection," 58–59.

105 Ch'en, "Literature Comes from Social Self-Reflection," 59–60. A somewhat extremist reaction to the Westernization of Taiwanese cultural and academic discourse can be seen in Wu Ming-jen (吳明仁), "From the 'Adulation of the West' to the Awakening of a 'Nationalistic Consciousness'" (從崇洋媚外到民族意識的覺醒), in Yu, *A Collection of Essays on* Hsiang-tu *Literature*, 3–13. Wu advocates a complete resinicization of scientific and academic discourse and proposes radical measures to encourage native education and eliminate the privileges of foreign degree holders.

106 See, for example, Hu, "The Restoration of a Chinese Position," 9. In his essay "*Hsiang-t'u*, Nationalism, Autonomy" (鄉土, 民族, 自立自強), Chang Chung-tung (張忠棟), who offers a more measured criticism of hsiang-t'u, similarly argues for a more critically reflective approach to modernization, at once recognizing the inevitability of increased global interdependency and reaffirming the importance of maintaining military, economic, and cultural self-determination for Taiwan. See 495–500 of Yu, *A Collection of Essays on* Hsiang-tu *Literature*.

107 Ho Shin's "The Modern Chinese Literary Heritage" typifies this appeal to the legacies of modern Chinese anti-imperialism. Yu T'ien-ts'ung ed., pp. 451–70.

108 Yu T'ien-ts'ung, "Nationalism and Our Society," 25.

109 It must be pointed out that in addition to poetry and fiction modern painting in Taiwan was also criticized—in nearly identical language—for falling under the

spell of the West. Writing under the pseudonym Hsu Nan-ts'un (許南村), for example, Ch'en Ying-chen accuses modern Taiwanese art of having become commodified. He bolsters his arguments for a return to native artistic traditions by citing the words of a painter who believes that under Western capitalism Taiwanese paintings have become "no different from stocks, real estate, or any other plaything of the opportunistic investor" ("The Taiwanese Art World's First Spring in Thirty Years" [台灣畫界三十年來的初春]) in Yu, p. 132. Denouncing the formal experimentation of modernist "pure art," Ch'en reminds his audience that "art is inseparable from humanity, life, and labor" (135) and calls for a return to "the earth that has borne and nurtured us" (140).

110 See, for example, Ch'en Ying-chen, "Literature Comes from Social Self-Reflection," 62. Yu T'ien-ts'ung is similarly critical of those modernist writers "whose bodies are in Taiwan, but whose hearts remain in foreign lands" (身在台灣, 心存異邦). See Yu, "Literature in the Service of Life" (文學為人生服務), in Yu, ed., 158.

111 Yeh, "An Introductory History of Taiwanese *Hsiang-t'u* Literature," 72.

112 See Ch'en, "Literature Comes from Social Self-Reflection," 62.

113 This is a variation on 浪子文學. See Yeh, "An Introductory History of Taiwanese *Hsiang-t'u* Literature," 72. Yeh's criticism is aimed primarily at writers like Pai Hsien-yung.

114 Wang, "'Realism,' Not 'Ruralism,'" 111.

115 Yu T'ien-ts'ung, "The Path Wasn't Made by One Man Walking Alone" (路不是一個人走出來的), cited in Ho Shin (何欣), "How *Hsiang-t'u* Literature Is '*Hsiang-t'u*'" (鄉土文學怎樣《鄉土》)," in Yu, *A Collection of Essays on* Hsiang-tu *Literature*, 272, translation mine.

116 See Yu, "Nationalism and Our Society," 24.

117 《鄉土文學 . . . 與現代文學恰成對照, 也可說上對抗前者而起的。》 See Hu, "The Restoration of a Chinese Position," 18.

118 Chen Ying-chen, "A Compassionate Outlook on Life (關懷的人生觀)," in Yu, *A Collection of Essays on* Hsiang-tu *Literature*, 342–47.

119 Chao Kuang-han (趙光漢), "*Hsiang-t'u* Literature Is a National Literature" (鄉土文學就是國民文學), in Yu, *A Collection of Essays on* Hsiang-tu *Literature*, 281.

120 The original Chinese reads《文學的目的, 就是在使人快樂, 僅此而已。》. See Wang Wen-hsing (王文興), "The Merits and Faults of *Hsiang-t'u* Literature" (鄉土文學的功與過), in Yu, *A Collection of Essays on* Hsiang-tu *Literature*, 520.

121 Ibid., 524.

122 Ibid., 529.

123 See also Sun Po-tung (孫伯東), "Is Taiwan a Colonized Economy?" (台灣是殖民經濟嗎), in Yu, *A Collection of Essays on* Hsiang-tu *Literature*, 501–7; and P'eng Ko (彭歌), "Without Humanity, How Can There Be Literature?" (不談人性, 何有文學), in Yu, *A Collection of Essays on* Hsiang-tu *Literature*, 245–63, esp. 246–47.

124 Wang, "The Merits and Faults of *Hsiang-t'u* Literature," 533.

125 Ibid., 540–41.

126 See, for example, Wang, "Taiwan *Hsiang-tu* Literature," 43–45.

127 Among the defenders of modernist literature who employed this kind of political rhetoric are Wang Wen-hsing ("The Merits and Faults of *Hsiang-t'u* Literature," 525) and Yu Kuang-chung (余光中), whose brief essay "Crying Wolf" (狼來了), was

among the more inflammatory essays of the debates (in Yu, *A Collection of Essays on* Hsiang-tu *Literature*, 264–67).

128 Ironically, of course, the government's symposium and its subsequent attempts to censure the hsiang-t'u writers amounted to precisely the kind of politically determined orthodox policy for the arts that they wanted to condemn.

129 One government supporter thinks that the Chinese Communists are actively involved in stirring up tensions between Taiwanese natives and refugee mainlanders. See P'eng Ko, "Notes by San-san" (三三草), in Yu, *A Collection of Essays on* Hsiang-tu *Literature*, 235.

130 See Ch'en, "A Tenth Anniversary Retrospective Look at the *Hsiang-t'u* Literary Debates," 104. As Ch'en points out, the push for "literature in Taiwanese" dates back to the anti-Japanese resistance movement that preceded the Hsiang-t'u literary debates by decades. He compares it to the Chinese *pai-hua* movement of the 1910s, noting that one of its primary goals was to increase literacy and improve popular access to literature. He also denies any suggestion of separatism, arguing that the use of the Taiwanese dialect is merely intended to achieve a more accurate depiction of the island's complex linguistic reality.

131 In mid-December of 1979, an anti-KMT protest rally organized by *Formosa* (美麗島), a journal with ties to the pro-Taiwanese independence movement (台獨), was broken up by armed government troops. Scores of Taiwanese demonstrators were brutally beaten in the ensuing violence. Ch'en Ying-chen believes that this was a crucial turning point in the deterioration of the relationship between native Taiwanese and Chinese mainlanders. See ibid., 106–7.

132 鄉土文學必然是反對分裂的地方主義. See Yu T'ien-tsung, "*Hsiang-t'u* Literature and Nationalist Spirit" (鄉土文學與民族精神), in Yu, *A Collection of Essays on* Hsiang-tu *Literature*, 163.

133 Hsu Nan-ts'un (許南村), "The Blind Spot of *Hsiang-t'u* Literature" (鄉土文學的盲點), in Yu, *A Collection of Essays on* Hsiang-tu *Literature*, 93–99.

134 Chang, "*Hsiang-t'u*, Nationalism, Autonomy," 497.

135 Hsu Nan-ts'un (許南村), "A Preliminary Discussion of Ch'en Ying-chen" (試論陳映眞), in Yu, *A Collection of Essays on* Hsiang-tu *Literature*, 172–74.

136 Ch'en Ying-chen (陳映眞), "Establishing a Style for a National Literature" (建立民族文學的風格), in Yu, *A Collection of Essays on* Hsiang-tu *Literature*, 335, translation mine.

137 Yeh Shih-t'ao, "An Introduction to Taiwan *Hsiang-t'u* Literature," 71.

138 The seductiveness of binary thinking is reflected in much of the critical writing on Hwang's fiction. See, for example, Howard Goldblatt's introduction to his translations of Hwang's stories in Hwang Chun-ming, *The Drowning of an Old Cat and Other Stories*, translated by Howard Goldblatt (Bloomington: Indiana University Press, 1980). Also see Howard Goldblatt, "The Rural Stories of Hwang Chun-ming," in Faurot, *Chinese Fiction from Taiwan*, 110–33.

139 Wu Wan-ju (吳婉茹), "Seeing the World through Warm and Sympathetic Eyes: The Social Engagement of Writer Hwang Chun-ming" (用溫柔的眼睛觀看紅塵: 奮力淑世的小說家黃春明), *Central Daily News* (中央日報), July 15–16, 1995.

140 Wang T'o and Yang Ch'ing-ch'u decided to run for parliament in 1978. See Wang Jing, 47.

141 Interview with the author, August 20, 1983.

142 See Hwang Chun-ming, "One Writer's Humble Thoughts" (一個作者的卑鄙心靈), in Yu, *A Collection of Essays on* Hsiang-tu *Literature*, 634.

143 Hwang Chun-ming, "The Tomato Tree on the Roof" (屋頂上的番茄樹), in Hwang Chung-ming, *Awaiting the Name of a Flower* (等待一朵花的名字) (Taipei: Huang-kuan, 1989), 32–44.

144 Ibid., 32–33, 37.

145 Hwang, *Sayonara, Tsai-chien*, 1–30.

146 Ch'en Ying-chen, under the pseudonym Hsu Nan-tsun, engages in a similar self-critique of his early fiction in "A Preliminary Discussion of Ch'en Ying-chen." Like Hwang, he criticizes the work as excessively bleak and nihilistic—the sign of a "petit bourgeois urban intellectual writer." The fundamental problem with such a writer, he argues, is his failure to look beyond the self to society, his community, or his nation and his failure to connect his personal experience with the experiences of others. The writer who turns inward and flees the realities of life for a world of inner torment betrays not only himself but also "the very homeland that bore and nurtured him" (164–65).

147 Hwang, "The Tomato Tree on the Roof," 33.

148 See Lin Yaofu, "Language as Politics: The Metamorphosis of Nativism in Recent Taiwan Literature," *Modern Chinese Literature* 6, nos. 1–2 (spring–fall 1992): 7–22, esp. 16, a special issue on contemporary Chinese fiction from Taiwan guest edited by William S. Tay.

149 Sung-sheng Yvonne Chang, "Chu T'ien-wen and Taiwan's Recent Cultural and Literary Trends," *Modern Chinese Literature* 6, nos. 1–2 (spring–fall 1992): 61–83, esp. 63, a special issue on contemporary Chinese fiction from Taiwan guest edited by William S. Tay.

150 Ibid., 63; Lin, "Language as Politics." Lin notes that for a few years the journal was edited by Yang Ch'ing-ch'u (16).

151 Other partisan journals that feature Taiwanese literature and arts include *Literary Taiwan* (文藝台灣) and *New Taiwan Culture Monthly* (台灣新文化月刊), as well as the literary pages of the *Independence Evening News* (自立晚報).

152 See Lin, "Language as Politics," 16–17. As Lin points out, the fact that Taiwanese has no standard system of writing is a major problem for many of these writers. Nevertheless, the movement to encourage the use of Taiwanese seems to be gaining momentum (18–20).

153 Sung Tse-lai, *The Self-Pursuit of the Taiwanese* (台灣人的自我追尋), cited in Lin, "Language as Politics," 18.

154 Chang, "Chu T'ien-wen and Taiwan's Recent Cultural and Literary Trends," 63, n. 5.

155 Ibid., 61–83.

156 Another of the San-san writers, Ting Ya-min (丁亞民), is also considered to be one of the principal screenwriters in the New Cinema movement.

157 Chang, "Chu T'ien-wen and Taiwan's Recent Cultural and Literary Trends," 65.

158 Ibid., 66. In her article, Chang discusses specific examples from both Chu's fiction and her screenplays.

159 Ibid., 67.

1   Hsu Nan-ts'un (許南村), "The Taiwanese Art World's First Spring in Thirty Years" (台灣畫界三十年來的初春), in Yu, *A Collection of Essays on* Hsiang-t'u *Literature*, 130–47.

2   Ho, "How *Hsiang-t'u* Literature Is '*Hsiang-t'u*,'" in 271.

3   In his perceptive article on the role of national historic preservation in the construction of nationhood in Taiwan, Marshall Johnson argues that sites such as Lu Kang are important loci of struggle and competing historical narratives. See his "Making Time," 177–249.

4   See Wang, "Taiwan *Hsiang-t'u* Literature," 70, n. 22.

5   Marsha Kinder, *Blood Cinema: The Reconstruction of National Identity in Spain* (Berkeley: University of California Press, 1993), 7–8.

6   In her fascinating book on contemporary cinema in the PRC, for instance, Rey Chow examines the emergence of a twentieth-century modernity that is specifically grounded in visuality. See her *Primitive Passions: Visuality, Sexuality, Ethnography, and Contemporary Chinese Cinema* (New York: Columbia University Press, 1995). Beginning with a quote from the philosopher Martin Jay on "the ubiquity of vision as the master sense of the modern era" (12), Chow argues that the historical shift from the written word to the technologized visual image has radically altered human perception—not only the way we perceive ourselves and our communities (peoples and nations) but also the way we comprehend others. The power of the visual is such that it has even, she argues, transformed writing and the way writers think about literature. As her title suggests, Chow is very much interested in discourses of nationalism, particularly within the context of the complex historical relations between the West and the rest of the world.

7   *Interpellation*, a term now frequently used in cultural studies, refers to the way institutional discourses pull individuals into constructed social positions. See Louis Althusser, "Ideology and Ideological State Apparatuses (Notes towards an Investigation)," in *Lenin and Philosophy and Other Essays*, translated by Ben Brewster (New York: Monthly Review Press, 1971), 170–83. In film studies, the idea of interpellation has been particularly important for theories of spectatorship.

8   Most of my information on the early decades of the film industry in Taiwan is taken from John A. Lent, *The Asian Film Industry* (Austin: University of Texas Press, 1990), 61–91.

9   Ibid., 63.

10   Ibid., 64.

11   See ibid., 76–77, for some examples.

12   Taiwanese film critic Huang Chien-yeh (黃建業) believes that the 1970s marked a giant step backward for Taiwanese film. Unlike such films of the 1960s as *The Duck Breeders* (養鴨人家), *Good-Bye, Ah-lang* (再見阿郎), and *My Home Is in Taipei* (家在台北), which did not shrink from addressing various social issues in contemporary Taiwanese life, the films of the 1970s retreated into "genre-bound" (類型化) commercialism. See Huang Chien-yeh, "A Retrospective Look at the Taiwanese Cinema of 1983" (一九八三年台灣電影回顧), in Chiao, *Taiwanese New Cinema*, 49.

13 The popularity of escapist film dramas was overwhelming. According to the 1979 *Yearbook of Motion Pictures in the Republic of China*, martial arts movies and Ch'iung Yao romances alone accounted for 70 percent of film production in 1978.

14 Lent, *The Asian Film Industry*, 62.

15 See Huang, "A Retrospective Look at the Taiwanese Cinema of 1983," 48.

16 The GIO was extremely worried about its inability to control the flood of illegal (and therefore unregulated) videos, fearing that they would dilute "Chinese culture" and corrupt the morality of Taiwanese society. See Lent, *The Asian Film Industry*, 81.

17 This "movement," which began in 1978–79, generally refers to a group of young Hong Kong directors, including Ann Hui (許鞍華), director of *The Secret* (瘋劫, 1979) and *Boat People* (投奔怒海, 1982); Allen Fong (方育平), director of *Father and Son* (父子情, 1981) and *Ah Ying* (半邊人, 1983); Tsui Hark (徐克), director of *Butterfly Murders* (蝶變, 1979); and a number of others, most of whom studied at film schools in the United States before beginning their careers. Many of the films of the New Wave were noteworthy not only for their technical sophistication but also for their attempts to tackle a wide variety of contemporary social and political issues facing Hong Kong and its people. For an introduction to the Hong Kong New Wave, see Chiao Hsiung-p'ing (焦雄屏) ed., *Hong Kong Cinema Style* (香港電影風貌) (Taipei: Jen-chien Books, 1987). Articles in English include Tony Rayns, "Chinese Changes," *Sight and Sound* 54, no. 1 (winter 1984–85): 24–29; and a special "midsection" guest edited by David Chute, entitled "Made in Hong Kong," *Film Comment* 24, no. 3 (May–June 1988): 33–56. More recent studies include Ackbar Abbas, *Hong Kong: Culture and the Politics of Disappearance* (Minneapolis: University of Minnesota Press, 1997); articles by Li Cheuk-to, Esther Yau, and Leo Ou-fan Lee collected in Nick Browne, Paul G. Pickowicz, Vivian Sobchack, and Esther Yau eds., *New Chinese Cinemas: Forms, Identities, Politics* (New York: Cambridge University Press, 1996).

18 See, for example, Li Yung-wei (李詠薇) and P'eng Hsiao-fen (彭小芬), "Interviews with Seventeen Taiwanese 'New Cinema' Film Workers" (台灣 "新電影" 工作者訪問錄), *Film Appreciation* (電影欣賞), no. 26 (March 1987): 5–16.

19 Beginning in 1973, Hou worked as a scriptwriter, production assistant, and assistant director under several established directors. He made his directorial debut in 1980 with three commercial genre films—*Cute Girl* (就是溜溜的她, 1980), *Cheerful Wind* (風兒踢踏踩, 1982), and *Green Green Grass of Home* (在那河畔青草青, 1982)—which are generally not considered to be significant.

20 See Li and P'eng, "Interviews with Seventeen Taiwanese 'New Cinema' Film Workers," 13.

21 Also known as *The Sandwich Man*.

22 It is also worth noting that as the largest producer of motion pictures on the island, the CMPC has always been in good financial health and could afford to give the young directors of the New Cinema the chance to experiment with financially risky but artistically and thematically more innovative films. See Lent, *The Asian Film Industry*, 68. Nevertheless, the fact that a studio long recognized as the propaganda arm of the KMT would sponsor these films was an indication of the rapidly changing political attitudes of the times.

23 Interview with Wu, in *HHH: Portrait of Hou Hsiao-Hsien* (AMIP, 1997), directed by Oliver Assayas and produced as part of the French television series *Cinema of Our Time* (*Cinema de Notre Temps*).

24 Interview with Tseng Chuang-hsiang in Li and P'eng, "Interviews with Seventeen Taiwanese 'New Cinema' Film Workers," 12. The use of unknowns was also an economic decision, of course, since star salaries escalated out of control during the 1970s and have been blamed in part for the decline in film production at the end of that decade. (see Lent, *The Asian Film Industry*, 66).

25 On formula films, see interview with Liao Ch'ing-song in Li and P'eng, "Interviews with Seventeen Taiwanese 'New Cinema' Film Workers," 14.

26 *In Our Time*, for example, was the first Taiwanese film to use a 1:1.85 screen ratio (interview with Edward Yang in ibid., 13). Later films continued to improve the technical standards of Taiwanese filmmaking. Hou Hsiao-hsien, for instance, has discussed the improvements in sound editing that his films introduced. Before the arrival of New Cinema, he notes, not only were all films in Taiwan postsynchronized, but all of the dialogue was dubbed by a handful of actors—so every film sounded the same. His early films were among the first in which dialogue was dubbed by the actual actors appearing in the film, and his *City of Sadness* (1989) was the first to use direct sound. Hou notes that he used his own money to buy new sound and editing equipment and to train technicians not only for his own film but "for the future of Taiwanese filmmaking." See Hou's comments in, *HHH*.

27 See Chiao, *Taiwanese New Cinema*, 81–88.

28 See interviews in Li and P'eng, "Interviews with Seventeen Taiwanese 'New Cinema' Film Workers."

29 Ibid., 16, translation mine.

30 Looking back on the early 1980s, when Taiwanese New Cinema was just emerging, director Ch'en Kun-hou fondly recalls the first time he went to Edward Yang's house: *everyone* associated with the movement was there, and the whole gathering was buoyed by "an incredible sense of camaraderie and excitement." During the five- or six-year heyday of New Cinema, Ch'en remembers meeting with the others every one or two days to discuss films they had seen, exchange ideas, critique each other's work, or talk about their goals and ideals. It was, Ch'en says wistfully, a period whose creative intensity he greatly misses. Ch'en Kun-hou interviewed in *HHH*.

31 Hu Yin Meng (胡茵夢), a popular actress who was a star in the 1970s, when she was featured in many popular melodramas, but who has also worked with some of the new directors, believes that the more collaborative methods of the younger directors marked an important change in Taiwanese filmmaking. Before the New Cinema, she notes, actors had no professional training and were merely manipulated like props by the director. She much prefers the attitude of the new directors, who communicate their cinematic vision to the actors beforehand and solicit their input throughout the process. This newly respectful attitude toward actors and their craft, she says, has helped to improve the image of actors in Taiwan and has contributed to the overall professionalism of the industry. See interviews cited in Lent, *Asian Film Industry*, 69–70.

32 Hou, interviewed in *HHH*.

33 Interview with Wu Nien-chen in Li and P'eng, "Interviews with Seventeen Taiwanese 'New Cinema' Film Workers," 9.

34 Interview with K'o Yi-cheng in ibid., 10.

35 See Lent, *The Asian Film Industry*, 88.

36 Chan Hung-chih (詹宏志), "The Origins and Future Path of Taiwanese New Cinema" (台灣新電影的來路與去路), in Chiao, *Taiwanese New Cinema*, 31–32.

37 Interview with Wan Jen in Li and P'eng, "Interviews with Seventeen Taiwanese 'New Cinema' Film Workers," 15. The audience for Taiwanese New Cinema likely overlaps with the audience that supported hsiang-t'u literature.

38 Interview with Li Ya-min in ibid., 6, translation mine.

39 Interview with K'o Yi-cheng in ibid., 10.

40 Interview with Wan Jen in ibid., 14.

41 In postwar France, for example, *Cahiers du Cinema* founder André Bazin argued for a new French cinema that would turn away from escapism and become more attuned to the everyday realities of modern French life. In his words, French cinema "has been marked by a social exile that has diluted its sap. If the incontestable artistic value, the suppleness and exactitude of our cinema's style are to survive under the new circumstances, they must adapt to the new climate. We cannot stand up against the gust of grandeur, violence, hate, tenderness, and hope that will sweep over us with the American cinema unless we too set down the deepest roots in the soul of our time—in its angers and its sorrows as well as its dreams. French cinema will only save itself if it learns to be greater by rediscovering an authentic expression of French society" (André Bazin, "Reflections for a Vigil of Arms," cited in Alan Williams, *Republic of Images: A History of French Filmmaking* [Cambridge: Harvard University Press, 1992], 299).

42 New German Cinema was similarly in part an effort to resist cultural colonization by American films and popular culture by creating a distinctively German cinema more in touch with the specificities of modern Germany's cultural and political history. See Timothy Corrigan, *New German Film: The Displaced Image* (Austin: University of Texas Press, 1982), especially chapter 1, "A History, a Cinema: Hollywood, Audience Codes, and the New German Cinema," 3–24.

43 See Darrell William Davis, *Picturing Japaneseness: Monumental Style, National identity, Japanese Film* (New York: Columbia University Press, 1996), 17–18.

44 Pat Aufderheide, "Dynamic Duo" (Interview with Tsui Hark and Nansun Shi), in Chute, "Made in Hong Kong," 44.

45 See, for example, interview with Tseng Chuang-hsiang in Li and P'eng, "Interviews with Seventeen Taiwanese 'New Cinema' Film Workers," 12.

46 See Chiao, *Taiwanese New Cinema*; and Chang, "Chu T'ien-wen and Taiwan's Recent Cultural and Literary Trends," 68. The New Cinema Latin American movements similarly have looked to literary antecedents within their respective national traditions as a source of anti-imperialist inspiration. See Paul Willemen, "The Third Cinema Question: Notes and Reflections," in Jim Pines and Paul Willemen, eds., *Questions of Third Cinema* (London: British Film Institute, 1990), 22.

47 The transition to more socially conscious filmmaking was initiated by a number of cinematic adaptations of "serious" literature of both the modernist and hsiang-t'u movements. Directors such as Li Hsing (李行) and Pai Ching-jui (白景瑞) made

film versions of Pai Hsien-yung's (白先勇) stories, helping to pave the way for the cinematic adaptions of hsiang-t'u that followed.

48 Hou Hsiao-hsien, for instance, was born in 1947 in Kwangtung Province on the Chinese mainland. His family fled to Taiwan in 1949, and Hou grew up in the Taiwanese countryside.

49 Hou interviewed in Assayas, *HHH*.

50 Echoes of hsiang-t'u works continually surface in Taiwanese New Cinema. For example, traces of Ch'en Ying-chen's "The Mountain Path" (山路) and "The Country Teacher" (鄉村的教師) are clearly visible in Hou Hsiao-hsien's *City of Sadness*. The stories are collected in Ch'en Ying-chen, *The Mountain Path* (山路) (Taipei: Yuan-ching, 1984), 1–42, 101–16.

51 Wu Nien-chen, for instance, has explicitly expressed his continuing commitment to the hsiang-t'u vision. See Hsieh Jen-ch'ang (謝仁昌), "Interview with Wu Nien-chen," *Film Appreciation*, no. 71 (September–October 1994): 50–57.

52 Interview with Hou in *Hou Hsiao-hsien: The Making of a Director* (侯孝賢: 一個 導演的來歷), coordinated by Chan Hung-chih (詹宏志), Taiwan and Hong Kong 1993, color video, translation mine.

53 Hou in ibid.

54 John A. Lent notes that Taiwanese-dialect pictures—including films dealing with local history, famous Taiwanese traditional folktales, and local popular songs—flourished in the late 1950s. The heyday of these films was short-lived, however, as the government became actively involved in motion picture production and the Mandarin language quickly became the norm (*The Asian Film Industry*, 63).

55 The Chinese original is collected in Hwang, *Little Widows*, 17–39. An English translation can be found in Hwang Chun-ming, *The Drowning of an Old Cat and Other Stories*, translated by Howard Goldblatt (Bloomington: Indiana University Press, 1980), 158–84. Page numbers cited in the text refer to this translation.

56 The Chinese text appears in Hwang, *Sayonara, Tsai-chien*, 1–25. There are no available English translations of this story.

57 Interview with Huang Chien-yeh in Chan, *Hou Hsiao-hsien: The Making of a Director*.

58 Ibid.

59 There have been reports, for example, of "pilgrimages," organized by Hou's Japanese fans, to the Taiwanese villages featured in his films.

60 Hong Kong Film critic Luo Ming (羅明) has noted the unfair limitations of this characterization of Taiwanese New Cinema in his program notes to the exhibition Selected Works of Taiwanese New Cinema, held in Hong Kong in March 1984. Cited in Shao Yi-te (邵懿德), "On the 'New' in Taiwanese New Cinema of the 1980s" (關於八十年代台灣新電影環境 "新" 的聲音), *Film Appreciation*, no. 26 (March 1987): 28–29.

61 Even at its peak, Taiwanese New Cinema never represented more than 1 or 2 percent of total cinematic production in Taiwan. Few of the films have succeeded in making a significant impression at the domestic box office, despite winning critical success at home and overseas. Hou Hsiao-hsien's *City of Sadness* is one notable exception.

62 See Willemen, "The Third Cinema Question," 27.

63 Timothy Brennan points out the ambivalent position occupied by the Third World metropolitan intellectual by citing Bruce King's observation that "Nationalism is an urban movement which identifies with the rural areas as a source of authenticity, finding in the 'folk' the attitudes, beliefs, customs and language to create a sense of national unity among people who have other loyalties. Nationalism aims at . . . rejection of cosmopolitan upper classes, intellectuals, and others likely to be influenced by foreign ideas" (cited in Brennan, "The National Longing for Form," in Bhabha, *Nation and Narration*, 53).

64 In "The Tendencies of Taiwanese Film Criticism" (台灣電影批評的傾向), Ch'i Lung-jen (齊隆壬) discusses the importance of the journals *Theater* (劇場) and *Influence* (影響), which introduced foreign films and film theories—particularly the French New Wave and auteurism—to Taiwanese readers during the 1970s and 1980s. In Chiao, *Taiwanese New Cinema*, 40–46.

65 Chan, Hung-chih (詹宏志), "A Proclamation for Taiwanese Cinema, 1987" (七十年 台灣電影宣言), in Chiao, *Taiwanese New Cinema*, 111–18. Some critics have argued that because of its polemical nature this manifesto marks the end of Taiwanese New Cinema. See, for example, Mi Tsou (迷走) and Liang Hsin-hua (梁新華), eds., *The Death of Taiwanese New Cinema* (台灣新電影之死) (Taipei: T'ang-shan Publications, 1991), especially 1–8. See also Shao, "On the 'New' in 1980s Taiwanese New Cinema," 29–31.

66 Edward Yang declared, "I want to challenge contemporary Taiwanese cinema, to shatter the ossified traditions of established filmmaking." Quoted in "Taiwan Comes of Age" (台灣的成熟), originally published in *Asiaweek*, May 25, 1984, and reprinted in Chiao, *Taiwanese New Cinema*, 413–18.

67 See for example, T'ong Wa (童娃), "Language Laws and Colored Pens" (語法與彩 色筆), *Film Appreciation*, no. 20 (March 1986): 34: "The call for establishing a nationalist cinema originated in the desire to protect nonmainstream films and culture; the most urgent goal was to resist the spreading global hegemony of Hollywood film culture."

68 As Paul Willemen explains in "The Third Cinema Question," the notion of Third Cinema was born in Latin America during the late 1960s and was a part of a broader institutionalization of national cinemas—which called for the rejection of the formulaic styles and subjects of Hollywood in favor of more culturally authentic and culturally specific themes and forms of expression—during that decade. Counting among its original sources of inspiration the Cuban Revolution (1959) and Brazil's Cinema Novo (the most important impetus being Glauber Rocha's 1965 polemic "The Aesthetics of Hunger"), the theory of Third Cinema was launched by Argentinian filmmakers Fernando Solanas and Octavio Getino with their 1969 essay "Towards a Third Cinema." Another influential Latin American manifesto was Cuban Julio Garcia Espinosa's 1969 "For an Imperfect Cinema." Willemen notes that simultaneously filmmakers in various parts of North Africa were publishing similarly themed manifestos (4–6). In Bolivia, the Ukamau group led by Jorge Sanjines, Oscar Soria, and Antonio Eguino defined itself as a counterdiscourse by calling for a new cinema "that is away from the commercial mainstream strongly influenced by Hollywood and that looks dialectically at historical and contemporary situations." Quoted in Antonio Eguino, "Neorealism in Bolivia (an Interview)," in

Julianne Burton, ed., *Cinema and Social Change in Latin America* (Austin: University of Texas Press, 1986), 163–64. Originally called Third World Cinema, Third Cinema now includes politically conscious oppositional films produced by Third World segments of the population within the First World.

69   Willemen, "The Third Cinema Question," 5. Third World film movements are also important because their histories highlight the complex and volatile intersections of film culture and discourses of nationalism. Many Third World cinemas emerged in clearly imperialist contexts or under conditions of economic and cultural dependency. Moreover, because cinema is a technological means of cultural expression, it is a site where questions of industrial infrastructure, economic independence, and cultural self-determination coalesce, deeply implicating filmmaking in any project of decolonization.

70   In his influential 1983 study, for instance, Teshome Gabriel called Third Cinema "that cinema of the Third World which stands opposed to imperialism and class oppression in all their manifestations" (*Third Cinema in the Third World*, 2).

71   Willemen, "The Third Cinema Question," 4.

72   Ibid., 5. One is reminded here of Soviet theorist Mikhail Bakhtin's view of culture as an ever-changing open text: "Culture cannot be enclosed within itself as something ready made. The unity of culture is an open unity [in which] lie immense semantic possibilities that have remained undisclosed, unrecognised, and unutilised" (Bakhtin, *Speech Genres and Other Late Essays*, translated by Vern W. McGee, edited by Caryl Emerson and Michael Holquist [Austin: University of Texas Press, 1986], 5–6).

73   This is not to downplay, however, the important role played by New Cinema in the development of a Taiwanese consciousness separate and distinct from China. Indeed, Chu T'ien-wen has said that the very experience of traveling the international film festival circuit, where Taiwanese films compete with PRC films (which invariably attract more attention from Western audiences), has sharpened her own self-awareness as a Taiwanese artist. See Chang, "Chu T'ien-wen and Taiwan's Recent Cultural and Literary Trends," 67.

74   Wimal Dissanayake, "Nationhood, History, and Cinema: Reflections on the Asian Scene," in Wimal Dissanayake, ed., *Colonialism and Nationalism in Asian Cinema* (Bloomington: Indiana University Press, 1994), xvi.

75   Critics, of course, have tried to pigeonhole Hou's politics. *City of Sadness*, in particular, has been used for political purposes.

76   Salman Rushdie, "In Good Faith: A Pen against the Sword," *Newsweek*, February 12, 1990: 52.

3   Remembering and Forgetting, Part I

1   Ernest Renan, "What Is a Nation?" 19.

2   Johnson, "Making Time," 206.

3   Julia Watson and Sidonie Smith, "Introduction: De/Colonization and the Politics of Discourse in Women's Autobiographical Practices," in Julia Watson and Sidonie Smith, eds., *De/Colonizing the Subject: The Politics of Gender in Women's Autobiography* (Minneapolis: University of Minnesota Press, 1992), xix.

4 Teshome Gabriel, "Third Cinema as Guardian of Popular Memory: Towards a Third Aesthetics," in Pines and Willemen, *Questions of Third Cinema*, 53–64. Gabriel's ideas about history and popular memory—like those of many postcolonial theorists concerned with power, knowledge, and representation—clearly show the influence of Michel Foucault's theories of history. A similarly inclined but more sophisticated view is offered by Nancy Fraser, who challenges Jürgen Habermas's "institutional confinement of public life to a single, overarching sphere" by suggesting the coexistence of a multiplicity of "subaltern counterpublics . . . parallel discursive arenas where members of subordinated social groups invent and circulate counterdiscourses to formulate oppositional interpretations of their identities, interests, and needs." Nancy Fraser, "Rethinking the Public Sphere," in Craig Calhoun, ed., *Habermas and the Public Sphere* (Cambridge: MIT Press, 1992), 122–23. Instead of Fraser's description of these counterpublics as parallel, which implies that they are fixed, discrete, and autonomous, I prefer to think of them as overlapping, flexible, and interactively engaged.

5 Edward Said, "Foreword," in Ranajit Guha and Gayatri Chakravorty Spivak, eds., *Selected Subaltern Studies* (New York: Oxford University Press, 1988), vii.

6 Georg Gugelberger and Michael Kearney, "Voices for the Voiceless: Testimonial Literature in Latin America" *Latin American Perspectives* 70 (summer 1991): 5. For example, films like *The Other Francisco* (Cuba, 1975), *The Last Supper* (Cuba, 1976), and *Sugar Cane Alley* (Martinique, 1984) reevaluate and represent the Afro-Caribbean experience of slavery and the struggle for liberation from a black perspective, challenging and ultimately subverting official Western histories.

7 In the United States, for example, the demand for a more inclusive and multidimensional historical portrait of America has fueled a growing interest in personal narratives by groups whose experiences have been left out of canonized Anglo-European versions of the birth and growth of the nation: the working classes; women, gays and lesbians; and African American, Native American, Asian American, Chicano, and other ethnic groups. A quick look at the recent offerings of any university press catalog attests to the strength of this trend. Some examples that focus on autobiographies and other personal narratives of marginalized groups include William L. Andrews, *The First Century of Afro-American Autobiography, 1760–1865* (Urbana: University of Illinois Press, 1988); James Robert Payne, ed., *Multicultural Autobiography: American Lives* (Knoxville: University of Tennessee Press, 1992); Paul John Eakin, ed., *American Autobiography: Retrospect and Prospect* (Madison: University of Wisconsin Press, 1991); and Janice Morgan and Colette Hall, eds., *Gender and Genre in Literature: Redefining Autobiography in Twentieth-Century Women's Fiction* (New York: Garland, 1991).

8 For insights into German debates about history and national identity, I am indebted to Anton Kaes, *From Hitler to Heimat: The Return of History as Film* (Cambridge: Harvard University Press, 1989). Kaes's analysis of representations of German history in recent German films also provides provocative parallels to developments in Taiwanese New Cinema.

9 Alltagsgeschichte has been quite controversial in Germany. Its critics have primarily attacked what they perceive to be its apologetic tendencies of normalizing or even trivializing the Nazi past: the key question is whether, by separating the

activities of the Nazi regime and the elite social groups that supported its policies from the quotidian existence of the "little people," Alltagsgeschichte absolves the ignorant German masses of responsibility for Nazi atrocities. For an overview of the debate in English, see Martin Jay, "Songs of Experience: Reflections on the Debate over *Alltagsgeschichte*," *Salmagundi*, no. 81 (winter 1989): 29–41. Jay concludes that Alltagsgeschichte's understanding of past experience is far less naive than its critics allow and that in its critical mode the historiography of the everyday is a necessary complement to more structurally inclined, conventional historiography. As he notes, "the history of everday life" has also been the (less controversial) focus of recent theoretical and practical historiographical movements in other countries: Michel de Certeau's *The Practice of Everyday Life* (Berkeley: University of California Press, 2002), the Annales school in France, the History Workshop in England, and the work of historians Natalie Zemon Davis, Warren Susman, and Robert Darnton in America (33).

10   Kaes, *From Hitler to Heimat*, 83. On the distinction between Geschichte and Geschichten, see also Wolfgang Ernst, "DIstory: Cinema and Historical Discourse," *Journal of Contemporary History* 18, no. 3 (July 1983): esp. 403–4.

11   Richard Evans, "The New Nationalism and the Old History: Perspectives on the West German *Historikerstreit*," *Journal of Modern History* 59, no. 4 (December 1987): 761–97; Jay, "Songs of Experience," 31.

12   Kaes, *From Hitler to Heimat*, 172.

13   Hsu, "The Taiwanese Art World's First Spring in Thirty Years," 130–47.

14   Yu, "Nationalism and Our Society," 26, translation mine.

15   The linguistic issue is dealt with extensively in chapter 4.

16   A great deal has been written on the intersections of cinema and history. Recent books of interest include Marc Ferro, *Cinema and History*, translated by Naomi Greene (Detroit: Wayne State University Press, 1988); Robert Sklar and Charles Musser, eds., *Resisting Images: Essays on Cinema and History* (Philadelphia: Temple University Press, 1990); and Leger Grindon, *Shadows on the Past: Studies in the Historical Fiction Film* (Philadelphia: Temple University Press, 1994).

17   Susan Sontag, *On Photography* (New York: Farrar, Straus and Giroux, 1977).

18   As Kaes notes in *From Hitler to Heimat* (195–98), history films are increasingly replacing not only historical experience but also historical imagination.

19   D. W. Griffith's *Birth of A Nation* (1915) and Abel Gance's *Napoleon* (1927) are early examples, as are Sergei Eisenstein's *Strike* (1924), *The Battleship Potemkin* (1925), and *October* (1928).

20   Kaes imagines "the 'Third Reich' as film: Germany as the location, Hitler as producer, Goebbels and his officers as directors and stars, Albert Speer as set designer, and the rest of the population as extras" (*From Hitler to Heimat*, 4).

21   This is the main thesis of Kaes's *From Hitler to Heimat*. See also Thomas Elsaesser, *New German Cinema: A History* (New Brunswick, N.J.: Rutgers University Press, 1989).

22   Articles on German cinema often appear in the pages of *Film Appreciation*, the most important critical film journal closely associated with Taiwanese New Cinema. Several books on New German Cinema are also available in Chinese. A

common interest in questions of history and historiography is evidenced by the journal's publication of two special issues entitled "Film, History, and Popular Memory" (*Film Appreciation*, no. 44 [March 1990]; no. 45 [May 1990]), which bring together articles on both recent German films and Taiwanese New Cinema. German films are also frequently shown at Taiwan's National Film Library. The schedule for spring of 1990, for instance, included Leni Riefenstahl's *Triumph of the Will* (1936) and the German anthology film *Germany in Autumn* (*Deutschland im Herbst*, 1978).

23 Wu, Ch'i-yen (吳其諺), "The Taiwanese Experience on Film" (台灣經驗的影像塑造), in Mi and Liang, *The Death of Taiwanese New Cinema*, 50–52; Wei Ch'i-yen, "Historical Memory, Film Aesthetics and Politics" (歷史記憶, 電影藝術與政治), in Mi and Liang, *The Death of Taiwanese New Cinema*, 41–43.

24 Wu, "Historical Memory, Film Aesthetics and Politics," 180.

25 Underscoring the broader political and cultural concerns behind the current resurgence of interest in Taiwanese history, one critic has cited the African American struggle for representation as a point of comparison. See Ho Fang (何方), "Foucault, Film, and Popular Memory" (傅柯, 電影與人民記憶), in Mi and Liang, *The Death of Taiwanese New Cinema*, 194–96.

26 An important part of revisionist historiography and the shift in focus toward popular memory has been a growing interest in women's stories. See Jay, "Songs of Experience," 36; and Kaes, *From* Hitler *to* Heimat, 139–60.

27 See Wachman, *Taiwan*, 59–64.

28 The experiences of the ruling elite and refugee mainlander families on Taiwan are so different that one film critic considers the two groups to constitute separate nationalities. See Ho Fang, "Reshaping Memory" (記憶的重塑), in Mi and Liang, *The Death of Taiwanese New Cinema*, 184–89. Ho's use of the term *nationalities* tends toward hyperbole, but the point he is trying to make is clear.

29 *Banana Paradise* and *Long Live Youth* are discussed in a number of the essays collected by Mi and Liang, including *The Death of Taiwanese New Cinema*, Ho, "Foucault, Film, and Popular Memory," 190–207; Liang Hsin-hua (梁新華), "*Banana Paradise*: Evocation of a Divisive Era" ("香蕉天堂": 分裂時代的心情故事), 208–13; and Chang Ch'ing-yang (張擎陽), "History and Cinema" (歷史與電影), 214–19. While these films took only discreet and tentative steps toward reopening controversial eras in Taiwanese history, such as the white terror years, films made in the mid- and late 1990s tackle political taboos head on. Chapter 4 discusses some of these films in further detail.

30 Sung-sheng Yvonne Chang, "Chu T'ien-wen and Taiwan's Recent Cultural and Literary Trends," 66.

31 Chang Ch'ing-yang, "History and Cinema," 215.

32 Sung-sheng Yvonne Chang, "Chu T'ien-wen and Taiwan's Recent Cultural and Literary Trends," 66; Wachman, *Taiwan*, 62. Both refer to children of mainlander refugee families born on the island following the KMT's exile to Taiwan in 1945. The variance in terminology underlines the crisis of identity in which this group finds itself.

33 See chapter 3, "Conflicting Identities on Taiwan," in Wachman, *Taiwan*, 56–90, for a more detailed discussion of these issues.

34 See ibid., 62.

35 Sung-sheng Yvonne Chang, "Chu T'ien-wen and Taiwan's Recent Cultural and Literary Trends," 66, n. 9.

36 Doris Sommer, "'Not Just a Personal Story': Women's *Testimonios* and the Plural Self," in Bella Brodzki and Celeste Schenck, eds., *Life/Lines: Theorizing Women's Autobiography* (Ithaca: Cornell University Press, 1988), 11.

37 Anton Kaes has made a similar observation about Germany's postwar generation of writers and filmmakers. Upon approaching their midlife point in the late 1970s and early 1980s, young Germans looked back on their childhoods and asked: How did we become what we are today? See chapter 5, "Our Childhoods, Ourselves," in Kaes, *From Hitler to Heimat*, 139–60.

38 In the French-produced documentary *HHH: Portrait of Hou Hsiao-hsien*, directed by Oliver Assayas (AMIP, 1997), Wu Nien-chen asserts that Hou's film is not only the best of Taiwanese New Cinema but one of the greatest Taiwanese films ever made.

39 The Hakka people arrived in Taiwan beginning in the late 1700s, settling mostly in the foothills and lower mountainous regions of the island (primarily in the northeast and northwest) rather than the fertile lowlands settled by earlier immigrants from coastal Fukien. Their origins are obscure, but their ancestors are said to have migrated from northern China to the mountain hinterlands of Kwangtung Province, where their distinct dialect and way of life resulted in isolation and discrimination—a sense of separateness that carried over to their experience in Taiwan. See Kerr, *Formosa*, 8–9. The term *Hakka*, meaning "guest people," suggests their transient and marginalized existence.

40 Albert Memmi refers to this kind of person, who is nominally a colonizer but enjoys none of the privileges, as a colonial. See his *The Colonizer and the Colonized*, translated by Howard Greenfield (Boston: Beacon Press, 1967), 10.

41 See Chiao, *Taiwanese New Cinema*, 282. Chu also talks briefly about the experience of filming at her childhood home in *HHH*. Wu has since made another autobiographical film, *A Borrowed Life* (Toosan, 多桑, 1994.) *Toosan* means "father" in Japanese, and the film is partly about his difficult relationship with his father and partly about the difficulty his father's generation had in adjusting to the transition from Japanese to Nationalist Chinese rule.

42 Susanna Egan, "'Self'-Conscious History: American Autobiography after the Civil War," in Eakin, *American Autobiography*, 71. Egan argues that the post–Civil War era in America—marked by turbulent economic, technological, and sociological change—witnessed both a blossoming and a revolutionary transformation of American autobiographical writing. She sees the autobiographies of this period as attempts to grapple with the identity crisis precipitated by postwar change, noting that their most recognizable characteristic is "a distinct tendency toward what is American." The autobiographies, she asserts, "drew attention to an independent America struggling . . . for inheritance of the future . . . to the nature of America in relation to Europe, in relation to Europeans immigrating to the Promised Land, in relation to the places that constitute America—New England, the South, the West—and, most important, in relation to notions of what America could or should be" (72).

43 See, for example, many of the essays collected in James Olney, ed., *Autobiography: Essays Theoretical and Critical* (Princeton: Princeton University Press, 1980).

44 The writings on this subject are far too voluminous to enumerate. Two collections of essays that I found illuminating are James Olney, ed., *Studies in Autobiography* (New York: Oxford University Press, 1988); and Watson and Smith, *De/Colonizing the Subject.*

45 Phillipe Lejeune, *On Autobiography*, translated by Katherine Leary (Minneapolis: University of Minnesota Press, 1987), 198. Also compare German feminist films of the 1980s in which, as Anton Kaes notes, "the gesture of remembering and the coming to terms with a national past is . . . reflected and inscribed in personal biography" (*From* Hitler *to* Heimat, 158).

46 Lejeune, *On Autobiography*, 164. Note again the emphasis on times of dramatic change or trauma as periods that particularly invite autobiographical narration. In a similar vein, see Avrom Fleishman's analysis of storytelling situations in films in his *Narrated Films: Storytelling Situations in Cinema History* (Baltimore: Johns Hopkins University Press, 1992). He notes that experimentation with autobiographical and other forms of first-person narration in films proliferates in immediate postwar periods. In addition, many of the autobiographical storytelling situations dramatized in the films he analyzes are motivated by trauma (e.g. *Rashomon* and *Hiroshima, Mon Amour*).

47 Molly Hite, "Foreword," in Morgan and Hall, *Gender and Genre in Literature*, xv.

48 bell hooks, *Talking Back: Thinking Feminist, Thinking Black*, cited in Caren Kaplan, "Resisting Autobiography: Out-Law Genres and Transnational Feminist Subjects," in Watson and Smith, *De/Colonizing the Subject*, 130–31.

49 As Barbara Harlow puts it in "From the Women's Prison: Third World Women's Narratives of Prison": "In the same way that institutions of power . . . are subverted by the demand on the part of dispossessed groups for an access to history, power, and resources, so too are the narrative paradigms and their textual authority being transformed by the historical and literary articulations of those demands" (cited in ibid., 120).

50 This reconception of autobiography seems particular useful for film, which is, more than a written text, experienced as a "present unfolding."

51 James Olney, "Autobiography and the Cultural Moment: A Thematic, Historical, and Bibliographic Introduction," in Olney, *Autobiography*, 3–27.

52 See Janice Morgan, "Subject to Subject/Voice to Voice: Twentieth-Century Autobiographical Fiction by Women Writers," in Morgan and Hall, *Gender and Genre in Literature*, 5.

53 Fleishman, *Narrated Films*, 1–19, esp. 17.

54 The distinctions that Fleishman draws between "external" and "internal" voice-over are important because the two terms reflect two very different sets of claims to attention and authority. While "external" narrators stand outside the action and claim an objective perspective on historical "truth," an internal narrator marks the film as memory, subjective representations of a past inevitably shaped by present attitudes and motivations. See ibid., 78–79.

55 Gabriel, "Third Cinema as Guardian of Popular Memory," 58.

56 Diaries and journals differ from autobiography in its strictest sense because they

are "written to the moment" rather than from a retrospective stance, presenting not a coherent life story but discontinuous fragments of an existence. See Felicity A. Nussbaum, "Toward Conceptualizing Diary," in Olney, *Studies in Autobiography*, 128–40.

57 Salman Rushdie, "Imaginary Homelands," in *Imaginary Homelands* (London:
Granta, 1991), 9–21. Rushdie writes that those in his position—"exiles, emigrants,
or expatriates"—who are haunted by a sense of loss and struggle to reclaim their
lost homes by creating fictions, inhabit "not actual cities or villages, but invisible
ones, imaginary homelands" (10).

58 Avrom Fleishman points to Alain Resnais's film *Hiroshima, Mon Amour* as the
most illuminating illustration of this impulse (*Narrated Films*, 112–27).

59 See Caren Kaplan, "The Poetics of Displacement in Alicia Ortiz's *Buenos Aires*,"
Discourse, no. 8 (fall–winter 1986–87): 84–100. Kaplan discusses the many "ghosts"
or "structuring absences" that haunt the consciousnesses of the *porteños* in Ortiz's
Buenos Aires.

60 Said, *Orientalism*, 55. "Imaginative geography" refers to a sense of space and time
that is shaped by emotion rather than logic.

61 In an interview, Hou has acknowledged that at the time of the film's release he
feared he would be criticized for undercutting the myth of the "return to the mainland." He was. See *HHH*.

62 Sung-sheng Yvonne Chang has observed that Hou's rejection of KMT authority is
memorably depicted in *A Time to Live and a Time to Die*, when Ah-Hao angrily
throws rocks at an old KMT soldier who has commanded him to listen respectfully
to the radio broadcast of the vice president's funeral ceremony ("Chu T'ien-wen
and Taiwan's Recent Cultural and Literary Trends," 66).

4   Remembering and Forgetting, Part II

1   Walter Benjamin, "Theses on the Philosophy of History," in *Illuminations*, edited
by Hannah Arendt, translated by Harry Zohn (New York: Schocken, 1969), 255.
Further references to this essay are cited parenthetically in the text.

2   Benjamin's philosophy of history is decidedly modernist, particularly its emphasis on gaps, ruptures, the dialectical relationship between past and present, and its
tendency to disrupt linear narrative progression. Hayden White addressed similar
issues of modernism and history in the Tenth Patricia Doyle Wise Lecture, entitled
"The Fact of Modernism: The Fading of the Historical Event," delivered April 8,
1992, at the University of California, Los Angeles.

3   He has also referred to this elsewhere as his "Trilogy of Sadness" (悲情三部曲).
See Hsieh Jen-ch'ang (謝仁昌), "A Report on My Life" (我生命過程的一個報告),
an interview with Hou Hsiao-hsien published in *Film Appreciation*, no. 64 (July–
August 1993): 45–62. As a point of comparison, Rainer Werner Fassbinder, one of
the key figures of New German Cinema, also made a trilogy of films examining
German history and identity. His FRG Trilogy consists of *The Marriage of Maria
Braun* (1979), *Lola* (1981), and *Veronika Voss* (1982).

4   Hou Hsiao-hsien and Wu Nien-chen (a coscriptwriter for *City of Sadness*) briefly
discussed their views on the current political and cultural liberalization in Tai-

wan, its impact on their work, and the changing relationship between Taiwan and China in an interview with Tobari Higashi-o (戶張東夫) entitled "New Creative Directions in the Post-martial-law Era," *The People Biweekly* (百姓), no. 210, February 26, 1990, 46–47; no. 211, March 1, 1990, 36–37. Despite liberalization, *City of Sadness* did not entirely escape controversy. Government censors initially cut a scene depicting KMT soldiers tracking down and shooting Taiwanese patriots in their mountain hideaways from the domestic version of the film. After the film's success on the European festival circuit and Hou's well-publicized protests over the cuts, the scene was restored. See Chang Ching-pei (張靚蓓), "Two Versions of *City*? Domestic Print Lacks a Scene" (兩種"悲情": 國內版少一段), *China Times*, September 13, 1989.

5 See, for example, "*City of Sadness* and the February 28 Incident: A Symposium" (悲情城市二二八), *Contemporary* (當代), no. 43 (November 1, 1989): 111–30. Film scholar and critic Ch'i Lung-jen (齊隆壬) makes the comment on 116.

6 This is the characterization of the current era of social critic and former dissident Bo Yang (白楊). For a brief account of the changes that have swept Taiwan since the end of martial law, see Nicholas D. Kristof, "A Dictatorship That Grew Up," *New York Times Magazine*, February 16, 1992, 16–22, 53–57. For more comprehensive accounts in English, see Wachman, *Taiwan*; and van Kemenade, *China, Hong Kong, Taiwan, Inc.*

7 The largest and most active of these is the Democratic Progressive Party, of which the current president, Chen Shui-bian, is a member.

8 In an interview with Taiwanese film scholar Chiao Hsiung-p'ing, Hou said that he was in the midst of editing *City of Sadness* when the massacre in Tiananmen occurred. He immediately sensed the connection between Tiananmen and the massacres alluded to in his film, wondering "Why do such tragedies keep befalling the Chinese people?" He hoped that his film would evoke the same pain and anger in its audiences. See Chiao, "The Camera-Swept Back Alleys of History." Audiences did indeed seize on the parallels between events in the film and events in Beijing. Lin Huai-ming, for example, explicitly compares Provincial Governor Chen Yi's radio announcement of martial law in Taiwan in 1947 to Li P'eng's radio broadcasts following the Tiananmen incident. See Lin Huai-ming (林懷民), "Warm Affections, Deep Sighs: On Watching *City of Sadness* in New York" (溫潤的關照, 深沉的探思: 紐約看 "悲情城市"), *China Times*, October 18, 1989. European film festival audiences made the comparison so often that the Taiwanese government news agency became quite unsettled—enough to pressure the film's distributors to carefully reword their overseas press materials. See "Overseas Press Materials for *City of Sadness* Stir Controversy" ("悲" 海外宣材引起震憾), *Ming Sheng News* (明生報), August 30, 1989. Some have even argued that the film owes part of its success—winning the Golden Lion in Venice, for instance—to the coincidence of its release at the time of the Tiananmen massacre. See Wu Ch'i-yen (吳齊諺), "Notes on the Release of *City of Sadness*" ("悲情城市" 現象記), in Mi and Liang, *The Death of Taiwanese New Cinema*, 84.

9 See Chiao, "The Camera-Swept Back Alleys of History," translation mine.

10 Michael S. Roth, "Foucault's 'History of the Present,'" cited in Anton Kaes, "History, Fiction, Memory: Fassbinder's *The Marriage of Maria Braun* (1979)," in Eric

Rentschler, ed., *German Film and Literature* (New York: Methuen, 1986), 276–88. This essay was later reprinted as chapter 4, "The Presence of the Past: Rainer Werner Fassbinder's *The Marriage of Maria Braun*," in Kaes's *From Hitler to Heimat*, 73–103.

11 Gabriel, "Third Cinema as Guardian of Popular Memory."

12 See, for example, Chiao, "The Camera-Swept Back Alleys of History."

13 Memmi, *The Colonizer and the Colonized*, 91, 103–5.

14 Sergio Giral's *El Otro Francisco* and Tomas Gutierrez Alea's *The Last Supper* are the most notable. Significantly, both films rely heavily on traditional African storytelling, popular music, and other forms of oral culture to construct a powerful counterdiscourse to subvert official history.

15 Humberto Solas, "Every Point of Arrival Is a Point of Departure (Interviewed by Marta Alvear)," in Julianne Burton, ed., *Cinema and Social Change in Latin America* (Austin: University of Texas Press, 1986), 146, 150.

16 Ping-hui Liao, "Rewriting Taiwanese National History: The February 28 Incident as Spectacle," *Public Culture* 5, no. 2 (1993): 287.

17 Ying-hsiung Chou, "Imaginary Homeland: Postwar Taiwan in Contemporary Political Fiction," *Modern Chinese Literature* 6, nos. 1–2 (spring–fall 1992): 23–37.

18 Chou considers hsiang-t'u literature to have been a precursor to the political fiction of the 1980s (ibid., 36).

19 Tse-han Lai, Ramon H. Meyers, and Wou Wei, *A Tragic Beginning: The Taiwan Uprising of February 28, 1947* (Stanford: Stanford University Press, 1991), 1 (also cited in Liao, "Rewriting Taiwanese National History," 287).

20 Liao Ping-hui has observed that the historiographical strategies employed in these works are similar to those used by the subaltern studies group in India ("Rewriting Taiwanese National History," 287).

21 Wu, Ch'i-yen, "The Taiwanese Experience on Film," 182.

22 The numerous contributions of Hayden White have been most influential, particularly his groundbreaking *Metahistory: The Historical Imagination in Nineteenth Century Europe* (Baltimore: Johns Hopkins University Press, 1973) and his subsequent *Tropics of Discourse: Essays in Cultural Criticism* (1978) and *The Content of the Form: Narrative Discourse and Historical Representation* (Baltimore: Johns Hopkins University Press, 1986).

23 Jean-François Lyotard, *Instructions païennes* (Paris: Galilee, 1977), 39. See also Kaes 1985, 281.

24 Bakhtin, *The Dialogic Imagination*. The collection contains four essays: "Epic and Novel" (hereafter cited in the text as "Epic"), 5–40; "From the Prehistory of Novelistic Discourse," 41–83; "Forms of Time and Chronotope in the Novel," 84–258; and "Discourse in the Novel," 259–422.

25 Mikhail Bakhtin, *Problems of Dostoevsky's Poetics*, edited and translated by Caryl Emerson (Minneapolis: University of Minnesota Press, 1984).

26 Michael Holquist, "Introduction." In Bakhtin, *The Dialogic Imagination*, xx.

27 Bakhtin elaborates on the relationship between the idea of national tradition and the complete, conclusive, and immutable world of the epic in "Epic and Novel" (*The Dialogic Imagination*, 16–17).

28 Holquist, "Introduction," xxxi.

29 The marketing strategy for the film clearly played up its historical aspects, promising, in particular, revelations about the politically taboo topic of the February 28 Incident. Publicity posters for the film, for example, included a domestic version that read: "A story which you could not hear, and could not discuss . . . before today." A foreign version read: "Taiwan, 1945. The Japanese colonizers have gone. Nationalist troops from China have just arrived. A page of history is about to be turned." See Mi and Liang, *The Death of Taiwanese New Cinema*, 120. Liao Ping-hui also notes that Hou Hsiao-hsien specifically entered the film in the political film category at the Venice Film Festival ("Rewriting Taiwanese National History," 291).

30 Wu Ch'i-yen, "Thru the Narrow Cracks of History" (透過歷史的那道狹窄隙縫), in Mi and Liang, *The Death of Taiwanese New Cinema*, 123–28.

31 Hou explains, for example, that his admiration for Yasujiro Ozu (a director to whom he is often compared but whose films he claims to have seen relatively late in his career as a filmmaker) arises from Ozu's interest in and mastery of family drama. See interview collected in *Imagekeeper Monthly* (影響) 1 (November 20, 1989): esp. 15–16.

32 See Hayden White, "The Value of Narrativity in the Representation of Reality." *Critical Inquiry* 7, no. 1 (autumn 1980): 5–27.

33 The names are rough transliterations of the Taiwanese—not Mandarin—pronunciations used in the film.

34 It is tempting to read a great deal into this character, seeing the deaf-mute as a metaphor for Taiwan's voiceless, marginalized existence, for example. See Ping-hui Liao, "A Deaf, Dumb Photographer" (即聾又啞的攝影師), in Mi and Liang, *The Death of Taiwanese New Cinema*, 129–34. Hou, however, has coyly explained that the creation of this character was partially inspired by an encounter with a deaf-mute artist (Ch'en T'ing-shih [陳庭詩]) and partially a pragmatic solution to the inability of the actor—who is from Hong Kong—to speak Taiwanese.

35 Hiroe and Hiromi are the Japanese pronunciations of K'uan-jung and K'uan-mei, respectively. During the Occupation, most Taiwanese names were given Japanese pronunciations. This was especially true for people like Hiroe, who teaches in a Japanese-run school, and Hiromi, who was trained by Japanese doctors.

36 In his fascinating article on historic preservation and the construction of the nation, Marshall Johnson points to Chiu-fen (九份), the real-life mining town where *City of Sadness* was filmed, as an exemplary illustration of the complex ideological struggles tied up in current projects of preservation in Taiwan. What Johnson finds most significant in the Chiu-fen campaign is that, unlike other recent campaigns to preserve local sites and buildings around the island, the project neither "substantiates the Taiwanese Nation and denaturalizes the Chinese Nation, or vice versa." Rather, the plan is to demonstrate how historically specific domination, autonomy, and commodification are integral to the struggle over historic preservation. See Johnson, "Making Time," 233–35.

37 For a more detailed analysis of the different narratorial effects and claims to authority associated with conventional cinematic language, see Fleishman, *Narrated Films*, particularly the introduction and chapters 1 and 4.

38 The term *bricoleur* is frequently associated with Walter Benjamin, but it origi-

nated, as Anton Kaes points out, in Claude Lévi-Strauss's *The Savage Mind* (Chicago: University of Chicago Press, 1966). See Kaes 1985, 242, n. 36.

39 Note that the film's publicity poster for the international market read in part: "The saga of a family . . . The saga of a nation." See Mi and Liang, *The Death of Taiwanese New Cinema*, 120.

40 It is a common strategy in postcolonial writing to link the births, deaths, and other significant life events of characters directly to major events in national history. See, for example, Aruna Srivastava's essay on Salman Rushdie, "'The Empire Writes Back': Language and History in *Shame* and *Midnight's Children*," in Adam and Tiffin, *Past the Last Post*, 65–78.

41 As Anton Kaes notes in "History, Fiction, Memory," his essay on *The Marriage of Maria Braun*, Fassbinder also uses radio broadcasts to weave public, political history into the personal narratives of Maria and her friends.

42 Intertitles in films (primarily in the presound era) have traditionally functioned as an omniscient narrative voice—a voice of authority. See Fleishman, *Narrated Films*, 31–32. This was particularly true in the case of historical films. In Hou's film, however, the voice of history represented by the opening and closing intertitles becomes only one of many voices represented by intertitles—many of them conveying highly personal narratives—and its authority is therefore undercut.

43 See, for example, Max Horkheimer and Theodor Adorno, "The Culture Industry: Enlightenment as Mass Deception," in *Dialectic of Enlightenment*, translated by John Cumming (New York: Continuum, 1988), 120–67.

44 The December 1988 issue of the *American Historical Review* (93, no. 5) features a forum dealing precisely with the problems and possibilities of portraying history on film. Included are essays by Robert A. Rosenstone ("History in Images/History in Words," 1173–85), David Herlihy ("Am I a Camera? Other Reflections on Film and History," 1186–92), Hayden White ("Historiography and Historiophoty," 1193–99), John E. O'Connor ("History in Images/Images in History," 1200–09), and Robert Brent Toplin ("The Filmmaker as Historian," 1210–27). On the advantages and disadvantages of cinema's reality effect, see in particular those by Rosenstone (1177) and Herlihy (1187).

45 One Taiwanese critic has compared the treatment of the past in *City of Sadness* to that in *Rashomon*, Akira Kurosawa's famous meditation on the relativity of truth. See Wen "The *Rashomon* Quality of *City of Sadness*."

46 The critical reaction to *City of Sadness*, which was heated and noisy, focused almost immediately on the issue of politics and Hou's treatment of the February 28 massacre. Hou was attacked for his historical inaccuracies, for not fully depicting KMT brutalities, for being too sympathetic to the Japanese, for not properly restoring the dignity of the Taiwanese people, and for trivializing a traumatic event in Taiwanese history by packaging it as a commercial film. Many of these criticisms can be found in essays collected in Mi and Liang, *The Death of Taiwanese New Cinema*, esp. 79–168. The controversy over the film was not unlike the debate recently surrounding Oliver Stone's JFK (1991). Interestingly, Stone also invoked *Rashomon* in his defense, arguing that his film does not pretend to offer a single, comprehensive conspiracy theory but instead barrages the viewer with snippets of verbal and visual information—fragments of multiple theories that the viewer

must sort out. See Oliver Stone, "The Flicker of an Eye Means Nothing in Print," *Los Angeles Times*, March 26, 1992, B7.

47 Chu T'ien-wen (朱天文), "Thirteen Questions on *City of Sadness*" ("悲情城市十三問), *Tzu-li Morning Post*, July 11–13, 1989, translation mine.

48 Philip Rosen has made a similar argument about the conception of history in Ousmane Sembene's *Ceddo*. See his "Making a Nation in Sembene's *Ceddo*," *Quarterly Review of Film and Video*, 13, nos. 1–3 (1991): 147–72.

49 White, "The Value of Narrativity in the Representation of Reality," 14.

50 Even a volume like Feng Tsuo-min's (馮作民) *One Hundred Lessons of Taiwan History* (台灣歷史百講) (Taipei: Youth Culture Press, 1965), though unusual in its detailed examination of local history, stresses the kinship between the experiences of the island and the mainland, emphasizing the proper place of Taiwanese history *within* the larger context of Chinese history (see especially the publisher's preface, 3). There is absolutely no attempt to assess the island's experiences under KMT rule. Instead, the historical narrative ends on October 25, 1945, when the Japanese formally relinquished control of the island to the new KMT governor-general, returning Taiwan to "the motherland's embrace." Not surprisingly, the book ends on a victorious note. On that day, Feng writes, the jubilant Taiwanese masses, "of their own accord," hung a pair of celebratory banners to welcome the KMT troops (249–50).

> Joyously, we leave behind the days of bitter rain and bleak horizons
> (喜離苦雨泣風景).
> Enthusiastically, we look forward to blue skies and brilliant sunshine
> (快睹晴天白日旗).

Note that "blue skies and brilliant sunshine" refers to the Nationalist Chinese flag.

51 See George Kerr, *Formosa Betrayed* (Boston: Houghton Mifflin, 1965), 72. Kerr, who was the U.S. vice-consul in Taipei during those years of transition, is clearly sympathetic to the Taiwanese people. His book may be somewhat colored by his sympathies and American interests, but his account of the events of the 1940s, based on personal experiences, correspondence, and eyewitness accounts, appears to be reliable.

52 See, for example, Memmi, *The Colonizer and the Colonized*, 79–85.

53 In the film, Taiwanese often refer to mainlanders using the derisive term *Ah-sua-eh* (阿山的). Roughly translated as "the one from the mountains," it distinguishes those from the provinces on the mainland from native islanders (who presumably are more closely associated with the sea).

54 The most notable of these is the scene in which the eldest son, Bun-heung, pleads with the Shanghai bosses to use their influence to get him released from a KMT prison.

55 For Wu Nien-chen, mainland China is not a motherland at all, but "another country, another place . . . like Singapore, or like Hong Kong" (Hsieh Jen-ch'ang, "Interview with Wu Nien-chen"). Any interest he has in China, he says, is simple curiousity, the kind of interest any foreigner might have; it has nothing to do with genuine affection or nostalgia. Hou Hsiao-hsien, whose parents came to Taiwan from the mainland as refugees in 1949, feels more of an emotional attachment. Nevertheless, he makes clear that he considers Taiwan to be his home and that

his primary concern and love are for Taiwan and its people. See interviews with Chiao Hsiung-p'ing ("Caught in the Tides of Sweeping Change") and with Tobari Higashi-o ("New Creative Directions in the Post-Martial Law Era").

56 Benjamin, "Theses on the Philosophy of History," 256. In the eyes of some, Taiwan continues to be colonized, forced into an inferior and dependent status by the KMT government and American political, military, and economic interests. See Ch'en, *Taiwan under American Rule*. As Ch'en makes clear, the island's status as a colony is an extremely complicated issue (45–60).

57 Kerr notes that Ch'en's appointment was particularly disappointing to the United States, which considered Taiwan a "clean slate . . . a unique opportunity [for the Nationalist Party] to show that the 'Three Peoples Principles' and the 'New Life Movement' were something more than empty slogans used *ad nauseum* to mask incompetence, corruption, and the brutality of totalitarian Party rule." From the U.S. point of view, Chiang had squandered a chance to prove "what the Christian missionaries and their friends in the United States for a century had dreamed of achieving for China proper": to demonstrate that "any province of China, given orderly and relatively honest government, could be brought forward successfully into the 20th century" (48–49). Kerr's point is well taken despite the imperialistic attitudes his remarks reveal.

58 Kerr describes both Ch'en Yi's notoreity and Chinese and American criticism of his appointment as Taiwan's governor-general (ibid., 47–57).

59 Ibid., 97.

60 In a section called "The KMT Military Scavengers," Kerr describes the widespread looting of property by KMT officials, as well as by "thousands of carpetbaggers" who heard of Taiwan's relative wealth and streamed in from Shanghai to seize all they could. See ibid., 97–103.

61 Ibid., 124–42.

62 The Lim family has been described as a microcosm of Taiwanese society, with many different socioeconomic groups represented: Ah-luk-sai belongs to the older generation, which lived through the entire Japanese Occupation and can therefore measure the new regime against the old; Bun-heung represents the criminal element of society; Bun-hsim stands in for the educated professional class; Bun-leung is a former military man; and Bun-ch'ing represents the artist/intellectual. There are also the women and children, who, with the exception of Hiromi, who serves as a sort of guiding consciousness throughout the film, mostly remain in the background.

63 A brief account of the events of February and March 1947 appears in *Imagekeeper Monthly* (影響) 1 (November 20, 1989): 40. There are two collections of essays and documents dealing specifically with the incident and its aftermath. The volume edited by Wai Min (韋名), *The February 28 Incident in Taiwan* (台灣的二二八事件) (Hong Kong: Seventies Magazine Publications, 1975), reflects leftist views—not only the PRC response but also the views of overseas Chinese who support Taiwanese independence. The second collection is Li Ao (李敖), ed., *Research on the February 28 Incident* (二二八事件研究), 3 vols. (Taipei: Li Ao Publications, 1989). Volume 1 consists mostly of documents and articles from 1947. Volume 2 brings together testimonials, recollections, and essays by individuals caught up in

the turmoil, including perspectives from mainlanders and aboriginal peoples. Volume 3 examines the life and career of Ch'en Yi. For an early eyewitness account in English of the February Incident and the violence that erupted in the weeks to follow, see Kerr, 254–310. A comprehensive analysis of the uprising has recently been published in English: Lai, Meyers, and Wei, *A Tragic Beginning*.

64 Kerr, who was nearby when the shooting began, describes what he saw on rushing to the scene.

> As our jeep came into the intersection dominated by the Generalissimo's [Chiang Kai-shek's] gilded statue, we found ourselves running between a line of heavily armed Nationalist soldiers, before the Governor's gate, and a silent crowd of Formosans, facing them across the plaza.
>
> On the macadam roadway between lay the bodies of unarmed civilians who had been shot down as the demonstrators approached the entrance to Government grounds.
>
> The anticipated crisis had come at last. (256)

65 In his account of the crisis, Kerr repeatedly emphasizes that the majority of the Taiwanese protesters wanted reform not revolution. It was the KMT government that, seeking justification for its brutality in crushing the uprising, painted the activists as traitorous rebels (ibid.).

66 Ibid., 299–301.

67 Huang Mei-ying (黃美英), "The Reproduction of 'February 28'" (再造的 "二二八"), in Mi and Liang, *The Death of Taiwanese New Cinema*, 153–57.

68 Ibid., 154.

69 Albert Memmi has commented on the importance of radio and the press to colonizing forces. By monopolizing these media, they are able to ensure that their version of history will prevail and that they can successfully deny historical subjectivity to the colonized (*The Colonizer and the Colonized*, 92).

70 For a full translation of Chiang Kai-shek's official speech defending Ch'en Yi's management of the affair (made in Nanking on March 10 and distributed in leaflet form in Taiwan's major cities on March 12), see Kerr, 307–9.

71 Bakhtin defines discourse as "language in its concrete living totality" (*Problems of Dostoevsky's Poetics*, 181).

72 "After all," writes Bakhtin, "the boundaries between fiction and nonfiction, between literature and non-literature are not laid up in heaven" ("Epic," 33).

73 The scene alludes to the practice of the Taiwanese during the period following the February Incident of stopping people in the street and asking "Are you sweet potato or pig?" Anyone suspected of being a pig (a mainlander) was immediately beaten. See Kerr, 257, 279. Critics of the film who felt Hou did not go far enough in restoring Taiwanese dignity or condemning the KMT authorities often cite this scene, with its unflattering portrayal of Taiwanese, as an example. See Huang Mei-ying, "The Reproduction of 'February 28,'" 156. To expect from Hou's film simply a Taiwanese version of historical truth, however, is to miss the point of the far more radical historiographical project Hou has undertaken.

74 In Chinese: 生離祖國死歸祖國. *Motherland* refers to Taiwan, not China, and *separation* refers to psychic rather than physical separation from a homeland—a sense of profound dislocation resulting from years of colonization. This is one of several

scenes in the film that allude to a short story by Chen Ying-chen entitled "The Mountain Path." It is collected in Ch'en, *The Mountain Path*, 1–42.

75 The disintegration of the patriarchal family structure is a recurring theme in Hou's films. In all of them, the fathers are either absent (*Daughter of the Nile*), ill (*Dust in the Wind, A Time to Live and a Time to Die*), or otherwise debilitated (*The Boys from Feng Kuei*). The strongest figures in his films are often women.

76 See David Holley, "Army Killed Thousands in '47 Massacre, Taiwan Admits," *Los Angeles Times*, February 24, 1992.

77 Tsai, Ling-ling (紫玲玲), "The Critical Fog Surrounding *City of Sadness*" (環繞著 "悲" 的論述霧), *Tzu-li Evening News*, October 10, 1989.

78 Chiao, Hsiung-p'ing (焦雄屏), "Caught in the Tides of Sweeping Change" (縱浪大 化中), Interview with Hou Hsiao-hsien, *China Times*, in seven parts, June 7–13, 1993.

79 Hsieh, "A Report on My Life," 55.

80 Here we might recall the German idea of Geschichten, another anecdotal approach to history.

81 Ping-hui Liao, "Rewriting Taiwanese National History: The February 28 Incident as Spectacle," *Public Culture* 5, no. 2 (1993): 281–96, p. 287.

82 See Ping-hui Liao, "A Rejection of History?" (歷史的楊棄), in Mi and Liang, *The Death of Taiwanese New Cinema*, 158–61.

83 See Hsieh, "A Report on My Life," 58, and Chiao, "Caught in the Tides of Sweeping Change," June 7.

84 Zhang Yimou's film also shares with *The Puppetmaster* an interest in popular theater, as the protagonist, Xu Fuguei, is a shadow puppeteer. In style, however, Zhang's film is radically different from Hou's. *To Live* is a straightforward melo-drama, Zhang's most conventional film.

85 Li Er-mo (李爾莫), "Regression or Innovation? A Discussion with Zhang Yimou of *To Live*" (是回歸還是創新? 與張藝謀談 "活著"), *Film Appreciation*, no. 69 (June 1994): 105–14.

86 For a useful overview of the Japanese Occupation period, see Kerr, *Formosa*. Kerr's focus is on the independence movement under the Occupation. See also Lai, Mey-ers, and Wei, *A Tragic Beginning*, 13–49.

87 See Kerr, 196. Hou also mentions the suppression of puppetry in the interview with Chiao, *China Times*, June 13, 1993.

88 Contrast Hou's matter of fact treatment of this episode in Li's life with a parallel sequence in Chen Kaige's (陳凱歌) *Farewell My Concubine* (霸王別姬, 1993), in which Chen Die-yi's decision to sing for the Japanese is derided as an act of treason.

89 Cited in Kaes, 171.

90 Hou has described his oblique and elliptical style as essentially Taoist in nature. See Hsieh's interview with Hou, p. 52. It might also be worth recalling here James Olney's comments about autobiography in his introduction to the 1980 anthology *Autobiography: Essays Theoretical and Critical*. "Autobiography," he notes, "pro-duces more questions than answers, more doubts by far (even of its existence) than certainties" (5).

91 Again, Bakhtin's ideas about the deliberate discontinuity and flexibility of the novel are informative here. He contrasts, for instance, the "finalized unity" of the

hero in the epic world with the radical restructuring of the individual in the world of the novel, which calls attention to the "hero's inadequacy to his fate or his situation"—that is, his inability to ever fully comprehend himself or his experiences. In the very fluidity and multilayeredness of its form, argues Bakhtin, the novel emphasizes the surplus of human experience and the inexhaustibility of the self, which is always incomplete. See "Epic," 34–37.

92 See, for example, Vincent Canby's review of the film in the *New York Times*, October 11, 1993, B5.

93 The processes of memory are always unpredictable and unreliable. Hou notes, for example, that during the making of the film Li T'en-luk's stories about his past changed with every retelling. See Hsieh's interview with Hou ("A Report on My Life," 46).

94 Compare Michael Holquist's observations on the Bakhtinian novel, which "dramatizes the gaps that always exist between what is told and the telling of it, constantly experimenting with social, discursive, and narrative asymmetries" ("Introduction," xxviii).

95 Kaes, 19–21.

96 See Chiao's interview with Hou ("Caught in the Tides of Sweeping Change," June 9, 1993).

97 Hou's emphasis on the theatrical and illusionary harkens back, in a sense, to the often forgotten nonmimetic origins of the medium in the fantasy and trick films of George Meliès. It is the other cinematic tradition—the realistic narrative tradition initiated by the Lumière films—that has dominated mainstream filmmaking.

98 Ernest Bloch, cited in Kaes, 121.

99 Peter Handke, cited in ibid., 139.

100 This is not unlike Hou's deliberate blurring of *play*, *dream*, and *life*. For thoughts on the relationship between history and fairy tales, see ibid., 123–27.

101 A third film released that year, Hsu Hsiao-ming's (徐小明) *Heartbreak Island* (去年冬天, literally, "Last Winter"), is based on another violent political incident in the island's past: the 1979 Formosa Incident in the southern city of Kaohsiung, in which participants in a demonstration organized by the underground dissident journal *Formosa* were beaten by police and the suspected leaders of the protest jailed until 1987. It is similar in theme, centering on a woman jailed in the aftermath of the incident, who upon her release many years later finds herself feeling lost and disappointed in a world that has changed in her absence. It is a world, she laments, in which "the martyrs have all died." See Hsiung-ping Chiao, "White Terror and the Formosa Incident: Introspection on Recent Political Films from Taiwan," translated by Sam Ho, *Cinemaya* 32 (1996): 22–24.

102 Liao, "Rewriting Taiwanese National History," 287; Chou, "Imaginary Homeland," 23–27.

103 Lan Po-chou (藍博洲), *Song of the Swinging Chariot* (幌馬車之歌) (Taipei: Times Cultural Publications 時報文化出版社, 1991).

104 The first violation is the theft of the diary and the second is the intrusion of the faxes—sent by an unknown individual from an unknown location—into the private space of her apartment. Interestingly, a fax machine also becomes an instrument of electronic harassment in *Supercitizen K'o*: after K'o's son-in-law decides

to run for public office, his enemies send threatening faxes, including pictures of guns, to his home.

105 I doubt that these images represent the completed film in which Liang Ching is to star because her voice-over at the conclusion of *Good Men, Good Women* suggests that the principal photography on her film is just beginning. Of course, the name of the film in which she is to appear is also called *Good Men, Good Women*, further confusing the multiple layers of reality in Hou's film.

106 At the end of the film, Liang Ching reports in voice-over that Chiang died the day before principal photography on the film about her life was to begin. The real patriot dies, only to be almost immediately resurrected on-screen by the actress, who feels, after lengthy preparations, that she has "become Chiang."

107 See Liao, "Rewriting Taiwanese National History," 290. In Wan Jen's film, there is a scene in which K'o visits with the KMT soldier who arrested him. The old soldier, who now owns a noodle stand, talks with K'o about those years of hysteria when his job was to arrest anyone and everyone, regardless of the severity of their crime, who dared do or say anything deemed subversive by the government.

5   Language and Nationhood

1 Bakhtin's complex and highly distinctive conception of language underlies almost everything he writes, but a particularly useful articulation of his main ideas can be found in the essay "Discourse in the Novel." See also Bakhtin and Volosinov, *Marxism and the Philosophy of Language*. As Bakhtin asserts elsewhere: "Languages are philosophies, penetrated by a system of values inseparable from living practices and class struggle." See Bakhtin, *Rabelais and His World*, 471.

2 Mikhail Bakhtin, "Discourse in the Novel," in Bakhtin, *The Dialogic Imagination*, 270–75.

3 A national language is one that succeeds in accessing and wielding power, a language that "gives expression to forces working toward concrete verbal and ideological unification and centralization, which develop in vital connection with the processes of socio-political and cultural centralization" (ibid., 270–71). As Benedict Anderson, who is similarly interested in the concrete functions of language in sociocultural struggles, has noted, the emergence of national languages in nineteenth-century Europe dramatically illustrates the ideological and political importance of this kind of linguistic centralization. See Anderson, *Imagined Communities*, particularly chapter 5, "Old Languages, New Models," 67–82.

4 Anderson, *Imagined Communities*, 134.

5 Ibid., esp. 37–46.

6 In his analysis of the sociocultural meaning of print language in eighteenth-century America, for example, Michael Warner argues that the invention and widespread dissemination of print media radically transformed relations between individuals, and between people and power, making possible the emergence of the idea of an American republic. Moreover, he identifies literacy as a crucial mark of authority, important for defining the parameters of the national community and in particular for maintaining the racial divide. Literacy and access to the linguistic technologies of the written and printed word, he argues, constituted and distin-

guished a specifically *white* community. They were more than neutral media that whites simply managed to monopolize; they were an integral component of social and racial identity. White colonists thought of themselves as inhabiting a social sphere defined by "a pure language of writing" that matched their social superiority, while blacks were defined by their merely oral "dialect," the intelligibility (to whites) of which was perceived to be an expression of their lack of mastery of language and hence as a natural sign of their condition of servitude. At the same time, blacks came to perceive the printed word as a sign of power and to understand literacy in the white man's language as the key to legitimacy and authority. The relationship between white colonists and the indigenous Indian population was similarly constructed. Warner goes on to note that gender barriers were likewise marked and reinforced by the different relationships men and women had with writing and printing. See Michael Warner, *The Letters of the Republic: Publication and the Public Sphere in Eighteenth-Century America* (Cambridge: Harvard University Press, 1990), esp. 11–19.

7 In *The Colonizer and the Colonized*, for instance, Albert Memmi provides an insightful analysis of the role that language plays in building empires and reinforcing the power that imperialist nations wield over their colonies.

8 Benedict Anderson calls the unifying languages of empire imperial languages and considers them to be directly related to the administrative languages or languages of state that were central to the European nationalisms of the nineteenth century. This is one of the reasons why he adopts Hugh Seton-Watson's sardonic term *official nationalisms* to describe the imperialist projects of the major European nations. See chapter 6, "Official Nationalism and Imperialism," in Anderson, *Imagined Communities*, 83–111. The reference to Seton-Watson is to his 1977 *Nations and States*.

9 In Bakhtinian terms, the dominant language of the colonizer functions as a centripetal force that aims to centralize and unify the verbal-ideological world of the empire: "the victory of one reigning language (dialect) over the others, the supplanting of languages, their enslavement, the process of illuminating them with the True Word, the incorporation of barbarians and lower social strata into a unitary language of culture and truth" (Bakhtin, "Discourse in the Novel," 271). The subordinated language(s) of the colonized, then, can be seen as the centrifugal forces of heteroglossia, suppressed but ever present beneath the seemingly unified surface of nation or empire, representing a source of potential subversion.

10 John Beverly, *Against Literature* (Minneapolis: University of Minnesota Press, 1993), 41.

11 Ibid., 3.

12 These range from the former Soviet Republics (where the use of Russian is being replaced as an official language) to Ireland (where writers of the Irish Renaissance promoted the use of Gaelic over English), the Philippines (where a cherished program of the Aquino government was the adoption of Tagalog as the medium of national discourse), and India (where filmmaker Satyajit Ray insists on making all his films in his native Bengali). In the case of Indian cinema, the issue of language centers more on regional identities.

13 It is not only the writer whose language choice acquires this kind of cultural mean-

ing, of course. The battle between languages is continual and affects everyone. For instance, many films from decolonizing nations in Africa and Latin America have foregrounded this linguistic battle as central themes. Ousmane Sembene's *Xala*, for example, pits the revolution-minded daughter's insistence on using the Wolof tribal dialect against her father's preference for French, the colonizer's tongue. Antonio Eguino's *Chuquiago* similarly depicts the tension between the indigenous Indian dialect spoken by the older generation of Bolivian natives and the Spanish preferred by their children.

14 Ngugi wa Thiong'o, *Decolonizing the Mind: The Politics of Language in African Literature* (London: James Currey 1986), 28. Ngugi's choice of Gikuyu was a rejection of not only English but of Swahili, which he saw (admittedly, an extremist position) as an artificially created intertribal language.

15 Some have noted that Ngugi's rather idealistic depiction of his indigenous language as the embodiment of a pure or authentic national consciousness is a late, politically motivated conversion that is at odds with the more materialist views of culture and ideology he espoused earlier in his career. See, for example, Simon Gikandi, "Ngugi's Conversion: Writing and the Politics of Language," *Research in African Literatures* 23, no. 1 (spring 1992): 131–44.

16 Ibid., 139.

17 See Thomas H. Jackson, "Orality, Orature, and Ngugi wa Thiong'o," *Research in African Literatures* 22, no. 1 (spring 1991): 5. For an overview and bibliography of the theoretical debate over the language issue in contemporary African writing, see David Westley, "Language and African Literature: A Bibliographic Essay," *Research in African Literatures* 23, no. 1 (spring 1992): 159–71.

18 See Bill Ashcroft, Gareth Griffiths, and Helen Tiffin, *The Empire Writes Back: Theory and Practice in Post-colonial Literatures* (London: Routledge, 1989), 38–77. Others have described these poles somewhat differently. Simon Gikandi opposes universalist conceptions of language in favor of particularist views ("Ngugi's Conversion"), while Peter Wollen refers to the two strategic tendencies as archaism and assimilation (*Raiding the Icebox: Reflections on Twentieth-Century Culture* [Bloomington: Indiana University Press, 1993], esp. 200).

19 As Ngugi asserted in a 1979 lecture, a backward glance at the precolonial past is often seen as necessary for true national liberation: "Only by a return to the roots of our being in the languages and cultures and heroic histories of the Kenyan people can we rise up to the challenge of helping in the creation of a Kenyan patriotic national culture that will be the envy and pride of Kenyans" ("Return to the Roots: National Languages as the Basis of a Kenyan National Literature and Culture," cited in Gikandi, "Ngugi's Conversion," 132).

20 For brief comments on the hybridization of languages and the potential for cultural decolonization in African literature, see Katherine Williams, "Decolonizing the Word: Language, Culture and the Self in the Works of Ngugi wa Thiong'o and Gabriel Okara," *Research in African Literatures* 22, no. 4 (winter 1991): 53–61; and James McGuire, "Forked Tongues, Marginal Bodies: Writing as Translation in Khatibi," *Research in African Literatures* 23, no. 1 (spring 1992): 107–16.

21 Ulf Hannerz, *Transnational Connections: Culture, People, Places* (London: Routledge, 1996), 71.

22 In addition to the African example, Taiwanese nativist writers also frequently cite the Gaelic revival in Ireland and the Southern Renaissance in the United States (particularly Faulkner) as comparative points of reference. See, for instance, Ho Shin, "How *Hsiang-t'u* Literature Is '*Hsiang-t'u*,'" 271–80.

23 See Anderson, *Imagined Communities*, 94–99.

24 Anderson, *Imagined Communities*, 40–41.

25 Walter J. Ong, *Orality and Literacy: The Technologizing of the Word* (London: Methuen, 1982). Ong's contributions to the cultural study of writing and print occupy an interesting position. His assessment of the intellectual, literary, and social effects of literacy, a systematic analysis of the transition from the psychodynamics of an oral tradition to the mind-set of a literate society, has often been criticized as overly deterministic and reductive and excessively sentimentalized (see, e.g., Warner, *The Letters of the Republic*, 5). This criticism is to a large extent justifiable, particularly in view of Ong's notion that orality and literacy are two fundamentally antithetical states of consciousness, separated by a radical restructuring of human consciousness that begins with the invention of writing and is solidified by the technological development of printing. On the other hand, many of Ong's observations about the social and cultural meaning of literary languages, those essentially controlled by writing rather than oral speech such as learned Latin and Classical Chinese (25, 33, 35, 114), and grapholects, vernaculars whose ties to the technologies and institutions of writing and print give them special status and authority such as the national languages that developed in nineteenth-century Europe (106–7), are remarkably similar to Benedict Anderson's.

26 Patrick Hanan, *The Chinese Vernacular Story* (Cambridge: Harvard University Press, 1981), 3.

27 In Bakhtinian terms, Mandarin functions on the island as a "unitary language," an expression of the centripetal forces constantly working toward verbal and ideological unification, and contrasts with a subordinated dialect like Taiwanese, a centrifugal force that struggles to reassert social and linguistic multiplicity. Mendel points out that while the use of Mandarin is legally required in most spheres of public life the Taiwanese dialect has been tolerated, though it is definitely marginalized. See Mendel, *The Politics of Formosan Nationalism*, 46–47. From my own experiences in Taiwanese elementary schools during the early 1970s, I know that students caught speaking Taiwanese at school were often subject to corporal punishment and public humiliation. The institutionalized legitimacy of Mandarin is so deeply ingrained in the Taiwanese mind that until only very recently young people from Taiwanese-speaking homes would always speak Mandarin to their classmates in public settings, even outside of the school environment. The Nationalists hoped, of course, to mold the postwar generation of Taiwanese children into "pure" Chinese citizens who spoke Mandarin, knew the writings of Sun Yat-sen and would ultimately follow Chiang Kai-shek in his dream of regaining the mainland (42–63).

28 Beverly, *Against Literature*, 58–59.

29 The rhetorical opposition of city and country is examined in more detail in chapter 6.

30 See, for example, Albert B. Lord's study of oral composition, *The Singer of Tales*

(New York: Atheneum, 1976). Lord believes that there are profound and irreconcilable differences between "the oral way of thought and the written way" (125).

31 Walter Benjamin, "The Storyteller: Reflections on the Work of Nikolai Leskov," in Benjamin, *Illuminations*, 83–109. Benjamin is clearly influenced by Georg Lukács's distinctions between the (oral) epic and the (written) novel. See Georg Lukács, "The Epic and the Novel," in *The Theory of the Novel*, translated by A. Bostock (Cambridge: MIT Press, 1971), 56–93. Lukács sees the Homeric epic as the product of an "integrated civilization," an age characterized by "the blessed existent totality of life" (58). The novel, in contrast, is the naturally appropriate form for the modern bourgeois world of "transcendental homelessness" (61), in which "the extensive totality of life is no longer directly given, in which the immanence of the meaning of life has become a problem" (56).

32 Gabriel, *Third Cinema in the Third World*. See also the two essays by Gabriel collected in Pines and Paul Willemen, *Questions of Third Cinema*: "Towards a Critical Theory of Third World Films" (30–52); and "Third Cinema as Guardian of Popular Memory" (53–64). In the former essay, Gabriel even includes a two-column table that explicitly contrasts the characteristics of "folk (or oral) art forms" with those of "print (or literate) art forms" (42–43). Another table (46–47) contrasts "Western dominant [filmic] conventions" with the "Non-Western use of conventions." While this table includes an advisory warning that "these are tendencies, not absolutes," the table comparing folk and print art forms, interestingly, does not.

33 Hsiang-t'u literature, for example, can be seen as a kind of cultural populism that was a direct reaction against the privileging of the literary culture of the metropolis—exemplified by the difficult and formalistic writing of the university-based Modernist writers. The stories of Hwang Chun-ming and other nativist writers manifest in part a desire to counter the hegemony of literary culture with indigenous oral forms expressed in the native tongue. For an interesting comparison in the Latin American context, see John Beverly's essay on the meaning of the "Spanish literary baroque" in *Against Literature*, 47–65.

34 Chen Ying-chen offers a brief discussion of the role of language during the Japanese Occupation in *The Poverty of Ideology* (思想的貧困), vol. 6 of his *Collected Works* (Taipei: Jen-chien, 1988), 104–5.

35 Personal interview with Hwang, August 20, 1983.

36 See the essays collected in Hwang, *Awaiting the Name of a Flower*.

37 Ibid., 50–51. Discussing the formative stages of his creative writing career, Wang Chen-ho similarly emphasizes his delight in discovering the richly expressive power of the Taiwanese dialect. When he first began to write, he recalls, "I discovered the vividness and vitality of the folk language. I was fascinated and inspired by the evocative richness of its imagination and its subtle possibilities of manipulation. From then on, whenever I found older people speaking in Taiwanese, I would perk up my ears—like a cat—to listen." See Wang Chen-ho, "The Eternal Quest: On My Fiction-Writing Experiences (永恆的尋求: 談我的小說寫作經驗)," (素葉文學), nos. 20–21 (November 1983): 14.

38 "I Love You" (我愛你), in Hwang, *Awaiting the Name of a Flower*, 90–91. Compare Edward Said on indigenous culture and decolonization: "Local slave narratives,

spiritual autobiographies, prison memoirs form a counterpoint to the Western powers' monumental histories, official discourses, and pan-optic quasi-scientific viewpoint" (*Culture and Imperialism* [New York: Knopf, 1993], 215).

39 Personal interview with Hwang, August 20, 1983.

40 This is one of the chief dilemmas that a postcolonial writer faces. Ezekial Mphahle, for instance, has pointed out the untenable choice an African writer faces: either accept a limited audience speaking a particular African language or strive to reach a larger but politically and linguistically compromised audience that speaks the language of the colonizers. See Williams, "Decolonizing the Word," 58. As Yeh Shih-t'ao (葉石濤) has noted, hsiang-t'u writers also lacked a firmly established indigenous literature (i.e., a written tradition) on which to draw. See Yeh, "An Introduction to Taiwanese *Hsiang-t'u* Literature," 69–92.

41 Compare, for example, John Beverly's comments on the case of Richard Rodriquez, whose autobiographical *Hunger of Memory: The Education of Richard Rodriquez* he cites as an illustration of how the assimilation of ethnic writers into the dominant culture of the United States—and particularly their acceptance into literary culture and the university milieu—requires their abandonment of the Spanish language (*Against Literature*, 15–16).

42 This appropriative mixing of languages is a common strategy in cross-cultural writing. Writing on the historical development of Chinese vernacular literature, Patrick Hanan in *The Chinese Vernacular Story* similarly notes that early vernacular stories were written using a mixture of Classical (literary) and spoken Chinese. Only much later did writers begin to use "pure" vernacular. An interesting and informative case for comparison can be found in James Snead's analysis of "cultural eclecticism" and "linguistic miscegenation" in postcolonial African literatures. See his "European Pedigrees/African Contagions: Nationality, Narrative, and Communality in Tutuola, Achebe, and Reed," in Bhabha, *Nation and Narration*, 231–49.

43 Because Taiwanese lacks an established written tradition, many of these words and phrases are transliterated using homophonic Mandarin Chinese characters or phonetic spelling. See, for example, a brief piece Hwang wrote on Taiwanese folk songs, "A Lovable Country Balladeer (一個可愛的農村歌手)," in Hwang, *Awaiting the Name of a Flower*, 131–33.

44 Ashcroft, Griffiths, and Tiffin, *The Empire Writes Back*, 65.

45 James Snead has pointed out identical strategies in African literature ("European Pedigrees/African Contagions," 241).

46 See, for example, his essays on and transcriptions of Taiwanese folk songs in Hwang, *Awaiting the Name of a Flower*. As he notes, it is often impossible to fully explain the lyrics of these songs to a nonnative islander. The best one can offer is "crude translations into Mandarin" (142–43).

47 Compare Michael Warner's observations on the "cognitive dissonance" experienced by women writers in colonial America: "Despite the universalizing claims made by writing in its role as communication, these exceptional women felt themselves to be particularized in the given being of their bodies with relation to their pens. Holding pens, they entered a contradictory relation to the implicitly male community that was constituted in writing" (*The Letters of the Republic*, 15).

48 The Chinese original of this story is collected in Hwang Chun-ming, *The Gong*

(鑼)(Taipei: Yuan-ching, 1974), 27–31. An English translation by Howard Goldblatt can be found in the summer 1981 issue of the Taipei Chinese Center, International PEN's publication, *The Chinese Pen*, 94–98.

49 As Goldblatt notes, Ah-Ban is a uniquely Taiwanese nickname for the youngest child in a family. It expresses the implicit hope for a son. Ibid.

50 Hwang has pointed out that the Chinese Nationalists' assumption of control included changing the names of villages and towns all over the island, even in the remote countryside. See, for example, his "From 'Confucius Says . . .' to 'According to the Newspapers'" (從'子曰'到'報紙說'), in Hwang, *Awaiting the Name of a Flower*, esp. 60–61. Not surprisingly, an earthier Taiwanese name is usually replaced by a more "elegant," abstract Mandarin name. The example Hwang cites is the replacement of Bang-ah-k'ang (蚊子坑, "Mosquito Ditch") with Fu-ku-ts'un (福谷村, "Lucky Valley Village"). Similarly, Gwei-liao-ah means something like "tribal hut."

51 The Chinese original is collected in Hwang, *Sayonara, Tsai-chien*, 27–57. An English translation by Howard Goldblatt is available in Hwang, *The Drowning of an Old Cat and Other Stories*, 158–84. Further references to this translation appear parenthetically in the text.

52 The Chinese original is collected in Hwang, *Little Widows*, 17–39. An excellent English translation can be found in Hwang, *The Drowning of an Old Cat and Other Stories*, 12–36. Further references to this translation appear parenthetically in the text.

53 The fear of death, interestingly, is seen by Walter Benjamin as a modern phenomenon associated with the decline of oral storytelling and a diminished ability to communicate life experiences. In the oral world of "story," death is a natural, meaningful part of the organic continuum of human experience and not at all something to be feared. See Benjamin, "The Storyteller," 93–95.

54 The central importance of the well to the village community is encapsulated in the phrase "li-hsiang pei-ching" (離鄉背井). It refers to the act of leaving one's home to explore the world, but literally mean's "leaving the country and turning one's back on the well." See Hwang, "I Remember . . ." (使我想起來), in Hwang, *Awaiting the Name of a Flower*, 143.

55 Hwang has noted elsewhere that the temple is always the cultural center of the village community. In the Taiwanese countryside, he observes, young people have deserted their villages in search of new careers, sometimes moving into the city and settling there to begin their families. Left behind in the villages are "old people, old houses, old dogs, and old cats." It is around the old trees in the courtyard of the village temple that these remnants of an older way of life congregate "to talk about the past, and to sing old songs." See Hwang, "From 'Confucius Says . . .' to 'According to the Newspaper,'" esp. 58.

56 Ong observes that "Writing is a solipsistic operation" (*Orality and Literary*, 101). He believes that the literate mind is more introspective, more concerned with the problems of individual self-identity, than with the community at large. Compare Benjamin's comment on communal storytelling and novel writing: "The novelist has isolated himself. The birthplace of the novel is the solitary individual" ("The Storyteller," 87).

57 Writing about the novels of Chinua Achebe, Thomas Jackson describes a similar opposition between the more "authentic" and earthy speech that issues from the lips of African elders in *Things Fall Apart* and the clichéd and sterile language of the educated young bureaucrats in *Arrow of God* ("Orality, Orature, and Ngugi wa Thiong'o," 6–7).

58 In his analysis of the Latin American narrative form called *testimonio*, John Beverly argues that the deliberate orality of the narrative is an important tool for sociocultural decolonization because its restoration of a once-silenced "voice" implies a challenge to the loss of authority in the context of processes of cultural modernization that privilege literacy and literature as a norm of expression. It permits the entry into literature of persons who would normally—in those societies (most societies) where literature is a form of class privilege—be excluded from direct literary expression (*Against Literature*, 76).

59 This stylistic hybridization has been identified as an appropriationist strategy of linguistic decolonization. See Ashcroft, Gareth, and Tiffin, *The Empire Writes Back*, 68–72.

60 See Hanan, *The Chinese Vernacular Story*, 20.

61 John Beverly considers these "interlocutive and conversational markers" to be critical to the testimonio's ability to affect change by "deautomatizing the reaction of the reader" (*Against Literature*, 77).

62 I have slightly altered Goldblatt's translation of the passage in order to emphasize the use of the words *that, those,* and *these.*

63 See "A Balladeer from Home" (來自故鄉的歌手), *Yu-shih wen-yi* (幼獅文藝), no. 297 (September 1978).

64 See for example, Yen Yuan-shu (諺元叔), "Social Realism in Recent Chinese Fiction in Taiwan," in *Thirty Years of Turmoil in Asian Literature* (Taipei: Taipei Chinese Center, International PEN, 1976), 218.

65 Goldblatt, "The Rural Stories of Hwang Chun-ming," 129.

66 Lord, *The Singer of Tales.*

67 The importance of storytelling for the formation of a cultural heritage applies to every level of sociocultural organization, beginning with the family. As Karen Baldwin has observed: "In many instances, family folk traditions are the first linguistic, plastic, and dramatic arts we know, and they become for formally developed artists, the most meaningful, coherent references to ethnicity and region." See Karen Baldwin, "'One Thing about Your Grandad—He Never Lied, He Just Told Stories': The Importance of Family Narratives to Ethnic and Regional Studies," *MELUS*, 10, no. 2 (summer 1983): 71.

68 These are the two "archaic types" of oral storyteller identified by Walter Benjamin in "The Storyteller," 84–85. Compare Ngugi wa Thiong'o's belief in the centrality of storytelling in agrarian life: "The story-within-a-story was part and parcel of the conversational norms of the peasantry" (*Decolonizing the Mind*, 76).

69 Gabriel, "Third Cinema as Guardian of Popular Memory," 53.

70 The Chinese original appears in Hwang, *Sayonara, Tsai-chien*, 1–25. Page references in the text refer to this edition. There are no available English translations of this story, so the translations included in the text are my own. In translating the title, I have tried to preserve the ambiguity of the Chinese, which could mean

either "the story *about* Ch'ing Fan Kung" or "the story *told by* Ch'ing Fan Kung." A story with similar characters and themes is "The Dusk of Uncle Kam-Keng" (甘庚伯的黃昏), which is collected in Hwang, *The Gong*, 5–26.

71 Ah-Ming is an intimate nickname that could refer to Hwang Chun-ming himself. Ch'ing Fan Kung does appear to be modeled on Hwang Chun-ming's own grandfather, since a few of the plot elements in the story also figure in the autobiographical reminiscences Hwang has published elsewhere. See Hwang's "The Tomato Tree on the Roof," in *Awaiting the Name of a Flower*, 32–44.

72 Take, for example, Walter Ong's view of temporal apprehension in oral societies: "The psyche of a culture innocent of writing knows by a kind of empathetic identification of knower and known, in which the object of knowledge and the total being of the knower enter into a kind of fusion. . . . To personalities shaped by literacy, oral folk often appear curiously unprogrammed, not set off against their physical environment . . . unresponsive to abstract demands such as a 'job' that entails commitment to routines organized with abstract clock time (as against human, or lived, *felt* duration)" (*Interfaces of the Word: Studies in the Evolution of Consciousness and Culture* [Ithaca: Cornell University Press, 1977], 18). See also Gabriel, "Towards a Critical Theory of Third World Films," 43.

73 This kind of reverence for nature is thematized in numerous Third World films, including, to take only a few examples, Euzhan Palcy's *Sugar Cane Alley* (Martinique), Glauber-Rocha's *Barravento* (Brazil), and Akira Kurosawa's *Dersa Uzala* (Japan). In Kurosawa's film, for instance, Dersa Uzala is similarly fearful of "offending the gods" when he shoots a tiger in the forest.

74 Benjamin, "The Storyteller," 86.

75 Ibid., 89. Hwang makes a strikingly similar distinction when he contrasts the concrete authority of Confucian proverbs and the abstract authority of modern forms of information dissemination such as newspapers and how-to books. See his "From 'Confucius Says . . .' to 'According to the Newspaper,'" 52–77.

76 Benjamin, "The Storyteller," 87.

77 Note that this legend is similar to the "Ballad of Narayama" told in Japan. Other versions are told throughout Asia. Here it is unclear whether the story Ch'ing Fan Kung tells is a legacy of the Japanese Occupation or part of indigenous folk literature.

78 Hwang has repeatedly emphasized his belief in the organic links among language, oral culture, and the agrarian way of life. In addition to legends and folktales, Hwang also points to nicknames, riddles, and popular songs as sources of sociocultural truths and traditional wisdom. See, for example, "The Past Can Only Be Savored in Memory" (往事只能回味), in *Awaiting the Name of a Flower*, 24–31.

79 The villagers had no warning of the coming floods because, Ch'ing Fan Kung later learned, the reed-singing birds, harbingers of the floods, had been shot by Japanese hunters (9, 19), a reference to the Japanese Occupation. Hence, Ch'ing Fan Kung insists that Ah-Ming never shoot at birds.

80 See, for example, Hwang, "One Writer's Humble Thoughts," 637. See also his first and second prefaces to *The Gong*, ii, iii.

81 The Chinese original can be found in *The Gong*, 1–90. It was translated by Howard Goldblatt as "The Gong" and collected in Hwang, *The Drowning of an Old Cat and*

Other Stories, 61–145. Further references to this translation appear parenthetically in the text.

82 I offer a translation that differs slightly from Howard Goldblatt's in an attempt to better capture the oral rhythms of the Chinese. In Chinese, the orality is accomplished partly through the use of internal repetition (好久好久, "a long, long time") and by ending sentences with particles such as *pa* (吧) and *le* (了).

83 Chinua Achebe similarly employs metaphors, proverbs, and other storytelling devices from the Ibo oral tradition in his writing. See Snead, "European Pedigrees/ African Contagions," 241.

84 The concepts of carnival and the carnivalesque are most fully developed in Bakhtin's 1965 *Rabelais and His World*. He also discusses these ideas in his 1963 *Problems of Dostoevsky's Poetics*.

85 The concept of carnival that Bakhtin outlines in his study of Rabelais is unabashedly exuberant and utopian. For him, the Rabelaisian carnivalesque is nothing short of revolution, a radical populism that rejects everything official or authoritative: "No dogma, no authoritarianism, no narrow-minded seriousness can co-exist with Rabelasian images; these images are opposed to all that is finished and polished, to all pomposity, to every ready-made solution in the sphere of thought and world outlook" (*Rabelais and His World*, 3).

86 See Peter Stallybrass and Allon White, *The Politics and Poetics of Transgression* (Ithaca: Cornell University Press, 1986). The book begins with an attempt to map "the high/low oppositions in each of our four symbolic domains—psychic forms, the human body, geographical space and the social order" that are fundamental to "ordering and sense-making European culture" (3). The study then examines how these interlinked hierarchies are challenged and inverted by the counterhegemonic force of Bakhtinian carnival, taken as "one instance of a generalized economy of transgression and of the recoding of high/low relations across the whole social structure" (19).

87 Bakhtin, *Rabelais and His World*, 5.

88 See, for example, the dozen or more essays on Taiwanese folk music collected at the end of *Awaiting the Name of a Flower*. "A Lovable Country Balladeer" (131– 33) highlights the difficulty of trying to write Taiwanese songs in Mandarin Chinese and offers an interesting illustration of the subversive potential of folk music. In the period immediately following the Kuomintang's assumption of power over Taiwan, all the native islanders had to learn the new national anthem. In one village, an old balladeer manages to parody the KMT anthem by putting its unfamiliar (and very literary) Mandarin lyrics to the melody of a familiar Taiwanese folk ballad. In "I Remember . . ." (使我想起來) (142–46), Hwang underlines the importance of folk songs to the development of a sense of regional identity. "The Age of Folk Songs" (產生民謠的時代) (152–55) laments the passing of the era in which folk songs were meaningful expressions of an authentic way of life. "Folk Songs That Count" (算術民謠) (162–64) examines the songs of Taiwanese street merchants and, again underscoring linguistic difference, provides Mandarin glosses on their meanings. In "A Taboo Folk Song" (一支令人忌諱的民謠) (165–67), Hwang contrasts the intimate, heartfelt emotions of traditional funeral songs with the commercialized impersonal frivolity of modern creations. Finally, in "Notes on Tai-

wanese Folk Songs" (台灣民謠扎記) (171–77), Hwang observes that many of the rich double entendres of Taiwanese folk songs would be completely lost on non-native speakers.

89 Hwang, "Little Three-Character Classics, Old Three-Character Classics," in *Awaiting the Name of a Flower*, 78–88. The first half of the title refers to the Confucian *Trimetrical Classic*, which once was used as the first primer in school, while the latter refers to the curses and profanities of traditional folk culture. As in his other essays on language, Hwang contrasts the artificial rigidity and abstraction of the Confucian "three-character classics" with the earthy dynamism and concrete expressiveness of popular language. His idea that coarse language can be the purest expression of national culture is embodied in the term *kuo-ma* (國罵), "national profanities."

90 Bakhtin, *Rabelais and His World*, 319.

91 Ibid., 19.

92 Kam Kim-ah, in this respect, is reminiscent of Lu Hsun's famous "Ah Q."

93 The protagonist of Hwang's "His Son's Big Doll" is also a poor laborer, whose job as a walking advertisement (a "sandwich man") is supplanted by a loudspeaker on a pedicab. The Chinese version can be found in Hwang, *The Gong*, 33–62, and an English translation by Howard Goldblatt in Hwang, *The Drowning of an Old Cat and Other Stories*, 37–60.

94 McGuire, "Forked Tongues, Marginal Bodies," 107–16. McGuire's objective in this provocative essay is, as he puts it, "to use Walter Benjamin's model of translation [as outlined in "The Task of the Translator"], where it intersects with [bilingual Moroccan writer Abdelkebir] Khabiti's project, in proposing a reconceptualization of bilingual writing as an act of translation."

95 The Chinese original of this story is collected in Hwang, *Sayonara, Ts'ai-Chien*, 127–90. An English translation by Howard Goldblatt can be found in Hwang, *The Drowning of an Old Cat and Other Stories*, 217–70. All references to this translation appear parenthetically in the text. As Goldblatt notes, the title consists of the Japanese and Chinese words for "good-bye." The four sections of the story are titled after popular Japanese films—an indirect critique of Japanese cultural imperialism on the island but also an opportunity for subversion. The self-styled "seven samurai" of Hwang's story, for example, are a pointed parody of Kurosawa's well-known warriors.

96 In a long passage (219–20) explaining his "deep-seated struggle" to sort out his internal contradictions, Mr. Hwang stresses that "as a Chinese who has an understanding of modern Chinese history" he has learned to "abhor the Japanese," his willingness to learn Japanese, an indispensible tool for economic advancement, notwithstanding. He remembers how his grandfather had his leg smashed by the Japanese and how a respected teacher told him about Japan's evil and murderous war of aggression against the Chinese people. He recalls, with horror and hatred, photographs of the infamous Rape of Nanking that showed "decapitated Chinese, pregnant women whose bellies had been slit open by bayonets, and, most unforgettably, lines of Chinese, including mothers clutching their children, walking hand in hand into huge pits to be buried alive."

97 The young man's theory is further borne out by the fact that the Japanese sexual

warriors have notched conquests throughout the Third World—"South America, Southeast Asia, Korea, Taiwan" (231)—but none in North America or Western Europe.

98 McGuire, "Forked Tongues, Marginal Bodies," 112. McGuire appears to be quoting from Paul de Man, "Conclusions: Walter Benjamin's 'The Task of the Translator,'" *Yale French Studies* 69 (1985): 25–46.

99 This, of course, does not take into account the relatively small number of independent Taiwanese-language films made between 1955 and 1979. Taiwanese-language film production was an altogether separate—and extremely marginalized—industry about which little was known until recently, when the Cinema Resources Center in Taipei began researching the field as part of a continuing effort to examine the "colorful and multifaceted heritage of Taiwanese folk culture." See Ching Ying-jui (井迎瑞), "No Longer Adrift on the Long River of History" (在歷史的長河裏我們不在漂泊), preface to a special issue of *Film Appreciation*, no. 53 (September 1991), on Taiwanese-language films. It is important to note that the industry collapsed in the early 1980s—precisely when the Taiwanese dialect began to gain wider acceptance through the emergence of New Cinema.

100 This resembled the way black Americans were caricatured in Hollywood films for many years.

101 Anderson, *Imagined Communities*, 134.

102 The most prominent writers were Sung Tse-lai (宋澤萊) and Lin Tsung-yuan (林宗源).

103 Interview in Chiao, "The Camera-Swept Back Alleys of History."

104 "I Love Mary" (我愛瑪麗) and "Little Widows" are two that come to mind.

105 Hou Hsiao-hsien's belief that the growing global hegemony of the English language and American culture represents an alarming threat to indigenous languages and cultures is a concern that is echoed in the works of many Third World filmmakers. In Ousmane Sembene's *Xala* (Senegal, 1974) for example, the father's colonized mentality is suggested not only by his preference for the French language over his native Wolof dialect, but also by his taste for Evian water and Coca-Cola. Kidlat Tahimik's *Perfumed Nightmare* (Philippines, 1977) also attests to the power the English language and American culture holds over Third World minds: the imagination of his jeepney driver is shaped entirely by the English-language broadcasts of the Voice of America. He dreams—in English—not of Philippine things but of Disneyland, Cape Canaveral, and Werner von Braun.

106 Again this points up the frequent dependence on binary models of resistance such as Teshome Gabriel's dichotomy between folk (or oral) and print (or literary) culture as a paradigm for understanding the differences between Western and non-Western cultural forms.

107 These modern modes are represented by scientific discourse and the formal school system, with its emphasis on memorization of abstract facts, testing, and so on.

108 Chow, *Primitive Passions*. See especially chapter 1, "Visuality, Modernity, and Primitive Passions," 1–52. See also Hannerz, *Transnational Connections*, 21.

109 Chow, *Primitive Passions*, 10.

110 Any number of works which, as Chow puts it, "derive their ethical impetus from Edward Said's *Orientalism*" (ibid., 12).

111 The critical literature on the complexities of the "dominant" Western gaze is voluminous and far beyond the scope of this study. Rey Chow's book, however, offers an insightful engagement with many of its major concerns, including its implications not only for literature and film studies but for gender studies, ethnography, anthropology, and so on.

112 Chow sees in modern China, for example, a "contempt for visuality" (13) that includes a "reaffirmation of culture as literary culture" (14) as an expression of resistance against the hegemony of the "technologized visuality" of the West (*Primitive Passions*). This association of the image with victimization and envisioning the "return" to the traditional written word as a form of cultural empowerment provide a provocative parallel to the more common dichotomy, which sees writing as the instrument of conquest and idealizes oral culture as an authentic form of cultural resistance. Compare also Hou Hsiao-hsien's deliberate suppression of the visual and foregrounding of the written word in his 1989 *City of Sadness* (see chapter 4).

113 See Davis, *Picturing Japaneseness*, 21.

114 Noel Burch, *To the Distant Observer: Form and Meaning in the Japanese Cinema* (Berkeley: University of California Press, 1979).

115 David Bordwell, Janet Staiger, and Kristin Thompson, *The Classical Hollywood Cinema: Film Style and Mode of Production to 1960* (New York: Columbia University Press, 1985).

116 Davis, *Picturing Japaneseness*, 22. Later in his discussion, Davis makes direct reference to Benedict Anderson's analysis of language, power, and the rise of national consciousness.

117 Paul Willemen has noted the relevance here of Mikhail Bakhtin's notion of a chronotope: a time-space articulation that is determined by specific social and historical factors. See Willemen, "The Third Cinema Question," 15–16.

118 Gabriel, "Towards a Critical Theory of Third World Films," 44.

119 Fernando Solanas, cited in Willemen, "The Third Cinema Question," 9.

120 Julio Garcia Espinosa, cited in ibid., 7.

121 See, for example, Chan, "The Origins and Future Path of Taiwanese New Cinema," 25–39.

122 See Chiao Hsiung-p'ing, *Taiwanese New Cinema*, 413.

123 Paul Willemen points out, for example, that Fernando Birri, Tomas Gutierrez Alea, and Julio Garcia Espinosa all studied at the Centro Sperimentale in Rome ("The Third Cinema Question," 5).

124 For an overview of Italian neorealism, see the first five chapters of Peter Bodanella's *Italian Cinema: From Neo-realism to the Present* (New York: Frederick Ungar, 1990).

125 Ibid., 36.

126 Ibid., 24. Taiwanese New Cinema was similarly stimulated by contact with foreign cinematic movements.

127 See especially Gabriel, "Towards a Critical Theory of Third World Films," 44–47.

128 Taiwanese New Cinema departs from the Third Cinema paradigm in that its ties to established studios, financial and otherwise, were relatively tight. Hou and several others worked within the commercial industry for a number of years before

making the films that were to become New Cinema. Also, while the earliest films of Taiwanese New Cinema were exemplary works of low-budget independent filmmaking, Hou's *City of Sadness* was a major production that cost a record-breaking NT$30 million to complete. The average Taiwanese commercial film costs New Taiwan $6 to 7 million.

129 See the interview with Hou in *Imagekeeper Monthly* 1 (November 20, 1989): 12, 15; and Chu, "Thirteen Questions on *City of Sadness.*" This was also the case with Italian neorealism.

130 Luchino Visconti, "Anthropomorphic Cinema," in David Overby, ed., *Springtime in Italy: A Reader in Neorealism* (Hamden, Conn.: Archon, 1979), 83–85.

131 Death, for example, is often conveyed through a letter, as in *City of Sadness* and *The Boys from Feng Kuei.*

132 Peter Bodanella notes that the important contributions to neorealism made by Visconti's *Ossessione* (1942) include the downplaying of dialogue and the expressive use of silence (*Italian Cinema*, 28). Teshome Gabriel similarly observes that silence is an important aesthetic element of Third World films ("Towards a Critical Theory of Third World Films," 45).

133 See the essay by Huang Chien-yeh (黃建業) in Chiao, Taiwanese New Cinema, 131–35.

134 See the interview with Hou in *Imagekeeper Monthly*, 16.

135 This dispersion of narrative authority is something that clearly sets Hou's films apart from the conventions of Hollywood filmmaking. The goal of classical continuity editing has always been to establish a unified, authoritative narrative voice and a logical sequence of dramatic development that leave little room for multiple interpretation. Hou's films, in contrast, offer a polyphony of fragmentary narrative voices and offer little in the way of an externally imposed order or logic. This lack of narrative guidance is perhaps one of the reasons that Western audiences have found Hou's films so inaccessible.

136 See the interview with Hou in *Imagekeeper Monthly*, 16, and the discussion with Liao Ch'ing-sung (廖慶松), who helped edit *City of Sadness*, in the *China Times*, September 15, 1989.

137 One of Hou Hsiao-hsien's most extensive discussions of his stylistic choices appears in an interview with Hsieh Jen-ch'ang, "A Report on My Life," 45–62.

138 Ibid., 48–50.

139 This is the title of Lin's book on Chinese cinema and traditional aesthetics. See Lin Nien-t'ong, *Wandering in the Lens* 鏡游 (Hong Kong: Su-yeh Publications [素葉出版社], 1984). Note that I have chosen not to translate the term as "wandering lens," which would imply a moving camera. In Lin's conception of this visual aesthetic, it is not the camera that wanders but the viewer's imagination.

140 See ibid., 62.

141 See Hsieh, "A Report on My Life," 49, 52, as well as the interview with Hou in *Imagekeeper Monthly*, 14.

142 See Burch, *To the Distant Observer*, 154–85. Burch coined the term for Japanese director Yasujiro Ozu's hallmark shots, which momentarily suspend the film's diegetic flow in order to create a mood or deepen an emotion. Although comparisons between Hou and Ozu are frequently made (particularly by film critics in the West),

Hou has repeatedly insisted that he never saw an Ozu film until very late in his filmmaking career.

143   See Hsieh, "A Report on My Life," 52.

144   Ibid., 49.

145   Gabriel, "Third Cinema as Guardian of Popular Memory," 62.

146   Gabriel, "Towards a Critical Theory of Third World Films," 49.

147   Tomás Gutierrez Alea, translated by Julia Lesage and published as "The Viewer's Dialectic," *Jump Cut* 29 (February 1984): 18–21, cited by Gabriel in "Towards a Critical Theory of Third World Films," 50. Hou Hsiao-hsien, for his part, has said that in his filmmaking he seeks forms that will allow cinema to take up the social, moral, and educational roles once filled by folk theater and opera. See Hsieh, "A Report on My Life," 60–61.

6   The Country and the City

1   Williams, *The Country and the City* (New York: Oxford University Press, 1973), 2. Of the pattern of transition from rural to urban society, William says: "Since much of the dominant subsequent development, indeed the very idea of 'development' in the world generally, has been in these decisive directions, the English experience remains exceptionally important, not only symptomatic but in some ways diagnostic" (2).

2   Just as the European countryside had become economically dependent on and exploited by the industrialized cities, so, too, did colonies in Asia, Africa, and Latin America fall into a pattern of dependency vis-à-vis the Western powers. The organized system of colonization coupled with the development of an industrialized economy in Western Europe and North America therefore can be seen as chiefly responsible for the division of the world into the "advanced," "metropolitan" societies of the industrialized First World and the "underdeveloped" agricultural societies of the Third World. See ibid., 279–88. "What happened in England has since been happening ever more widely, in new dependent relationships between the industrialized nations and all the other 'undeveloped' but economically important lands. Thus one of the last models of 'city and country' is the system we now know as imperialism" (279). The logic of progress—the model of capitalist development—is that eventually all of the country will become the city. The reality of colonial exploitation, however, is that the economies of the dominated societies are developed only enough to fit the needs of the metropolitan countries (284). See also André Gubder Frank, "The Development of Underdevelopment," in Richard I. Rhodes, ed., *Imperialism and Underdevelopment: A Reader* (New York: Monthly Review Press, 1970), esp. 5. While Williams associates the beginnings of the urban-rural colonial dynamic with the rise of British imperialism in the mid–nineteenth century, Edward Said, commenting on *The Country and the City*, argues that the "new rural [mostly colonial] societies" entered the imaginative metropolitan economy of English literature much earlier than Williams acknowledges. See Edward Said, "Jane Austen and Empire," in Terry Eagleton, ed., *Raymond Williams: Critical Perspectives* (Boston: Northeastern University Press, 1989), 152.

3 Williams, *The Country and the City*, 286.

4 Ibid., 287.

5 While agrarian laborers accounted for 56 percent of the population in 1953, the figure had dropped to 19 percent by 1983, with most of them being absorbed by the growing industrial and service economies. Statistics cited by Wu Cheng-huan (吳正桓) in "Taiwanese Cinema Culture and Two Ways of Looking at Films," *Contemporary* 10, 97–98.

6 With Latin America in mind, Williams notes that "the last image of the city, in the ex-colonial and neo-colonial world, is the political capital or the trading port surrounded by the shanty-towns, the barriadas" (287).

7 In the Taiwanese case, one could argue that the "foreignness" of city life is particularly acute, given the long historical traditions of Chinese peasant society and the centrality of nature in Chinese philosophy and arts.

8 Williams draws on his own experience of coming from the country to the city for his education: "It is ironic to remember that it was only after I came [to the city] that I heard, from townsmen, academics, an influential version of what country life, country literature, really meant: a prepared and persuasive cultural history." The dilemma in which he finds himself is acute: "I find I keep asking the same question, because of the history: where do I stand in relation to these writers: in another country or in this valuing city? That problem is sharp and ironic in its cultural persistence" (*The Country and the City*, 6). The parallels to the difficult position of Third World peoples—who find themselves defined by their otherness to the West—are provocative.

9 See ibid., in particular the chapter entitled "Golden Ages" (35–45), as well as "Pastoral and Counter-pastoral" (13–34) and "Knowable Communities" (165–81).

10 There is a great deal of literature on the idea of Heimat, primarily in German. One useful resource in English is Celia Applegate, *A Nation of Provincials: The German Idea of Heimat* (Berkeley: University of California Press, 1990). See, in particular, chapter 1, "Heimat and German Identity," and chapter 8, "Heimat and the Recovery of Identity." Applegate includes a comprehensive bibliography. For a brief but insightful summary of the term's evolution in German history, see Kaes, *From Hitler to Heimat*, 164–67; and Michael E. Geisler, "'Heimat' and the German Left: The Anamnesis of Trauma," *New German Critique*, no. 36 (fall 1985): 25–66. My overview of the history of Heimat is based largely on these three sources.

11 To avoid confusion, Heimat refers to the concept and *Heimat* refers to Reitz's film.

12 Franz A. Birgel, "You Can Go Home Again: An Interview with Edgar Reitz," cited in Kaes, *From Hitler to Heimat*, 163. "Heimat" is similarly defined as "the familiar grown distant" in Andreas Kiryakakis, *The Ideal of "Heimat" in the Works of Hermann Hesse* (New York: Peter Lang, 1988), 30. Edgar Reitz has additionally offered a parallel definition for the Hunsruck (the region in which his film is set) dialect word *Geheischnis*, which he would have preferred for his film's title: "It means shelter and trust, a relationship to a very special, select group of people who occupy an important place in one's life, more than friendship, less than love, something indispensible" (cited in Geisler, "'Heimat' and the German Left," 42).

13 Applegate, *A Nation of Provincials*, 7.

14 Ibid., 13.

15 Celia Applegate cites several of the Heimat movements most frequently recognized by the historical literature and argues that the extremism of their antiurban and antimodern views may have served a polemical purpose but were not at all in keeping with the original spirit of Heimat (ibid., 104). She believes that the original intention underlying Heimat was to protect the diversity of local cultures against the homogenizing forces of centralization: "The city as such . . . could be and was both the seat of Heimat activites and a Heimat itself for its own inhabitants. . . . Indeed, the original impulse, the informing and defining concept behind Heimat, was not antimodernism at all but belief in the importance of regional identity" (ibid., 106).

16 See Kaes, *From* Hitler *to* Heimat, 165.

17 For the war-torn nation threatened on all sides by foreign enemies, Heimat conjured up timeless images of unspoiled old Germany and represented the promise of a return to peace and order. See Applegate's examination of the Heimat movement in the Pfalz region of Germany, which suffered French occupation during World War I, in *A Nation of Provincials*, 108–19.

18 It became, as Benedict Anderson has noted, part of a vocabulary of kinship and home that effectively "naturalized" the idea of nation, endowing the term with the kind of emotional appeal that could elicit a passionate and unquestioning patriotism comparable only to the unconditional love of family (*Imagined Communities*, 143). Note that Anderson's chapter is entitled "Patriotism and Racism."

19 Applegate's account of this period is fascinating (*A Nation of Provincials*, 197–227). In many ways, the symbols and concerns of the Heimat movement were ripe for appropriation by the Nazi regime. Its emphasis on family and love of the German countryside, for example, were readily incorporated into Hitler's radically chauvanist "blood (*Blut*) and soil (*Boden*)" movement. Its celebration of local culture and folk rituals was easily transformed into the Fascist penchant for orchestrating elaborate and grandiose displays of power. Most damaging, its antiforeign and antiurban tendencies fed directly into Nazi anti-Semitism, as cosmopolitan, city-dwelling Jews became obvious targets of National Socialists' hatred.

20 Applegate, for instance, repeatedly emphasizes that, unlike the homogenizing and exclusionary nationalistic ideology of the Nazis, the original conception of Heimat did not seek to construct a uniform German identity. Instead, it recognized the strength of Germany's identity in the very diversity of its regional cultures. See, in particular, ibid., 85–86.

21 Kaes, *From* Hitler *to* Heimat, 164.

22 For interesting perspectives on the country-city dynamic in post-1985 fiction in the People's Republic of China, see the first five essays (by Joseph S. M. Lau, Michael S. Duke, Jeffrey C. Kinkley, David Der-wei Wang, and Heinrich Fruehauf) in Ellen Widmer and David Der-wei Wang, eds., *From May Fourth to June Fourth: Fiction and Film in Twentieth-Century China* (Cambridge: Harvard University Press, 1993, 19–166. See also the introduction by David Der-wei Wang (1–18) and the afterword by Leo Ou-fan Lee (361–84).

23 There were plenty of writers and other artists who reveled in the urban phenomena of Shanghai, seeing the city's mix of traditional and Western cultures as a fascinating cultural laboratory in which a distinctive modern Chinese culture would even-

tually develop. See, for instance, Heinrich Fruehauf, "Urban Exoticism in Modern and Contemporary Chinese Culture," in Widmer and Wang, *From May Fourth to June Fourth*, 133–64.

24 For a brief overview of cinema in post-Mao China, see Esther Yau, "China after the Revolution," in Geoffrey Nowell-Smith, ed., *The Oxford History of World Cinema* (New York: Oxford University Press, 1996), 693–704.

25 Germany's defeat in World War II left the nation in ruins—cities and villages destroyed, millions of families displaced and sundered, and the country literally divided up by the victors. Not surprisingly, during the immediate postwar years the rebuilding of the (West) German nation again crystallized around the concept of Heimat. Recovered from the rubble of the Nazi Reich, the rural idyll of Heimat now served a conservative rehabilitative function, providing the emotional foundation for the reconstruction of a new German identity. Heimat was an integral part of the mourning process in postwar Germany, filling the vacuum left by the destruction of war with nostalgic memories and fantasies. The centrality of Heimat to Germany's postwar recovery is addressed in Eric L. Santner, *Stranded Objects: Mourning, Memory, and Film in Postwar Germany* (Ithaca: Cornell University Press, 1990), esp. 57–102. Popular novels, films, and sentimental songs offered a refuge from postwar realities, depicting Germany as an idealized rural homeland boasting beautiful landscapes and populated by simple, noble peasants who celebrated regional history, language, and folk culture. The idyllic images offered by the hundreds of Heimatfilme made during the 1950s, in particular, responded to the collective needs of the German masses left physically and spiritually homeless (*heimatlos*) by the devastation of war. Unfortunately, the homeland depicted in these immensely popular films was no less mythical and romanticized than the Nazi vision of the German nation. In fact, the most prolific directors of 1950s Heimatfilme received their training in Hitler's studios, and many of the most successful films were straight remakes of Nazi era films. One of every five films made in West Germany between 1947 and 1960 was a Heimatfilm. See Applegate, *A Nation of Provincials*, 4, n. 4; and J. Hoberman, "Once in a Reich Time," *Village Voice*, April 16, 1985, excerpted in Miriam Hansen, ed., "Dossier on *Heimat*," *New German Critique*, no. 36 (fall 1985): 10. See also Kaes, *From* Hitler *to* Heimat, 14–16, which likewise emphasizes the essentially conservative nature of the Heimatfilm. Kaes observes that the Heimatfilm is to Germany what the western is to America: it "shows imaginary spaces, pure movie lives, and a strong moral undercurrent" (15). He also reminds us of the Heimatfilm's strong ties to the Nazi regime's "blood and soil" tradition, noting that "Under Hitler, the Heimatfilm was an arch-German film genre, with all its negative connotations" (15).

26 The regionalist spirit of Heimat experienced another revival in the mid-1970s, but this time it acquired new layers of meaning, as it found itself caught up in new political alliances and Germans sought to strip Heimat of its associations with national chauvinism and the xenophobia of Hitler's blood and soil ideology. The reasons underlying the renaissance of Heimat during the 1970s are complex, but the most frequently cited factors include the disillusionment that followed the political failures of the previous decade (Vietnam, Cuba, and China), the strengthening influence of international (i.e., American) popular culture, and a

growing awareness of the physical threats to Germany's environment from industrial pollution and nuclear technology. See Kaes, *From Hitler to Heimat*, 166; and Geisler, "'Heimat' and the German Left," 39–42. Geisler specifically links the new regional consciousness with the rise of the environmental agenda of the Green Party. As a result of these anxieties, Germany entered a period of soul-searching. "Fears about the quality of life and the future caused the outer-directed political activism of the sixties to turn inward, to Germany itself"—as Germans began to examine the roots of their identity—"looking backward at origins implied the hope for an orientation in the present" (Kaes, *From Hitler to Heimat*, 166–67). The term Heimat, long associated with right-wing ideologies, was suddenly being embraced by the German Left. According to Michael Geisler, the Left sought to rehabilitate the much-maligned notion of Heimat by distancing it from its mythifying and hegemonic tendencies under the Third Reich and attempting to resurrect its original regionalist spirit by focusing not on a utopian vision of a coherent German nation but on the diverse concrete particularities of local German life. Geisler argues that the Left was able to appropriate the concept for its own purposes by separating Heimat (associated with the private, the maternal, and the local) from Deutschland (associated with the public/political, militarism, and centralization).

27 These humiliations included the international community's courtship of the PRC, which resulted in Taiwan's forced severance of diplomatic ties with major nations, its expulsion from the United Nations, and its exclusion from the Olympic Games.

28 Many of the specific themes and concerns common to both the Heimat and hsiang-t'u movements have been discussed in detail in preceding chapters. These include, for example, the reexamination of local history and the revival of interest in regional dialects, oral culture, and folklore. The Heimat historians sought, in particular, to restore popular, mass perspectives, collecting private histories as a counterbalance to history as written by the new centers of economic and political authority in Germany. Celia Applegate discusses the importance of historical study—community oral histories, regional museums, and so on—to the Heimat movement in *A Nation of Provincials*, 87–100. Hsiang-t'u writers and their followers similarly approached history from below, giving voice to the Taiwanese common folk, whose everyday experiences had long been left out of historical discourse. The study of dialect and regional folk culture was a crucial part of Heimat efforts; in contrast to standard German, an administrative language that some perceived as manufactured and tainted by the influence of foreign words, local dialects were celebrated as living, authentic languages, "the genuine expression of a people's character" (77–87). The restoration and realistic use of the Taiwanese dialect was, of course, one of the central polemical tenets of both hsiang-t'u literature and Taiwanese New Cinema. The colorful expressiveness of the native dialect enriched the works of writers such as Wang Chen-ho and Hwang Chun-ming, and its contrast with Mandarin, the language of officialdom, is thematized in several of Hwang's works, including "Ah Ban and the Cop" and "The Drowning of an Old Cat." References to Goldblatt's translation of the latter in *The Drowning of an Old Cat and Other Stories*, appear parenthetically in the text.

29 Both are collected in Hwang *Awaiting the Name of a Flower*, 24–44. In his preface

to the second edition of *The Gong*, entitled "A Letter to Kam Kim-ah" (給憨欽仔的
一封信), Hwang also expresses a deep nostalgia for the close-knit community he
remembers from his childhood in the I-lan countryside: "My little hometown was
just that sort of place, where everyone feels close to everyone else, simply from
seeing and greeting one another in familiar places each day."

30 Because of its associations with warmth, security, and family, Heimat has always
contained a strong maternal element. See, for instance, Kiryakakis, *The Ideal of
Heimat in the Works of Hermann Hesse*, 120–29, as well as Anton Kaes's discussions of Helma Sander-Brahms's *Germany, Pale Mother* (*From Hitler to Heimat*,
139–60) and Edgar Reitz's *Heimat* (163–92, esp. 168–71). Michael Geisler also suggests that in the German discourse of nationhood, many perceive a clear distinction between Germany as motherland (Heimat) as opposed to fatherland (Deutschland). See his "'Heimat' and the German Left," esp. 34–35.

31 The story is collected in Hwang, *Sayonara, Tsai-chien*, 59–126. Parenthetical page
citations in the text refer to this edition. The Chinese title translates literally as
"Days of Watching the Sea." The English translation, "A Flower in a Rainy Night,"
takes its title from a Taiwanese folk song (雨夜花) sung by the heroine, which expresses the loneliness and homesickness of the prostitutes in the story, who, like
fragile flowers battered by a storm, are blown by the wind far from their roots, from
the warmth and security of their families. See Hwang Chung-ming, "A Flower in
the Rainy Night," translated by Earl Wieman, in Joseph S. M. Lau ed., *Chinese
Stories from Taiwan, 1960–70* (New York: Columbia University Press, 1976), 195–
241.

32 The most detailed description of Bakhtin's conceptualization of space-time articulations that are sociohistorically determined can be found in his "Forms of Time
and Chronotope on the Novel," in Bakhtin, *The Dialogic Imagination*, 84–258. The
idea of chronotope has been widely embraced in cultural and literary studies. Theorists of Third World film, for example, have used Bakhtin's term to articulate the
different ways in which Euro-American and non-Western cinemas organize time
and space. See Willemen, "The Third Cinema Question," 15–16.

33 Those who have taken a philosophical interest in socio-temporal-spatial structures—particularly as manifested in the arts—include Michel Foucault and John
Berger. For an interesting account of the "spatialization" of modern critical social
theory, see Edward W. Soja, *Postmodern Geographies: The Reassertion of Space in
Critical Social Theory* (London: Verso, 1989). Soja devotes considerable attention
to the urban/regional problematic.

34 Bakhtin, "Forms of Time and Chronotope on the Novel," 225, cited by Eric L. Santner in his discussion of Edgar Reitz's film *Heimat* (*Stranded Objects*, 60). John
Berger also contrasts the cyclical view of time in traditional peasant cultures ("cultures of survival") versus the abstract, linear, temporal orientation of modern capitalist societies ("cultures of progress"). See John Berger, "Historical Afterword," in
Pig Earth (London: Writers and Readers Publishing Cooperative, 1979), 195–213.

35 This story is collected in Hwang, *Sayonara, Tsai-chien*, 1–25. Page references appear parenthetically in the text.

36 Edgar Reitz, interview with Eric L. Santner (July 1987), in Santner, *Stranded Objects*, 67.

37   This essay is collected in Hwang, *Awaiting the Name of a Flower*, 52–77.

38   Hwang's comments bring to mind some of the arguments made by Walter Benjamin in his important essay "The Work of Art in the Age of Mechanical Reproduction," in Benjamin, *Illuminations*, 217–51.

39   The story is collected in Hwang, *The Gong*, 63–105. Parenthetical page references in the text refer to this edition.

40   This story is collected in Hwang, *Sayonara, Tsai-chien*, 27–57.

41   Notably, the female breast has here lost its associations with maternal nurturing and been reduced to mere spectacle.

42   Michael Geisler discerns a comparable view of mass media's role in modern man's alienation in Edgar Reitz's *Heimat*: "There is [a] dialectical relationship between the development of mass communication (radio, telephone, television figure prominently in the series) and the destruction of "Heimat" ("Heimat and the German Left," 25).

43   "Man tragt wieder Erde," by Martin Raschke, appeared in the *Literarische Welt* of 1931. It is cited in Kaes, *From Hitler to Heimat*, 164.

44   Yin, "From Whence Come the Bells in the Graveyard?" 193–203.

45   See, for example, Wang T'o (王拓), "'Realism,' Not 'Ruralism,'" 117.

46   Michael Geisler uses the latter term ("'Heimat' and the German Left," 37) and Anton Kaes opts for the former. Some examples of the critical Heimatfilm cited by Kaes include Peter Fleischmann's *Hunting Scenes from Lower Bavaria* (1968), Volker Schlondorff's *The Sudden Wealth of the Poor People of Kombach* (1971), and Reinhard Hauff's *Mathias Kneissl* (1971) (16, 255, n. 10). Geisler cites Peter Schamoni's *Closed Season on Foxes* (1965) as an early precursor to the anti-Heimat-film (37).

47   See ibid., 38; Kaes, *From Hitler to Heimat*, 167. An interesting comparison can be made, I think, with the revisionist view of rural China undertaken during the 1980s by writers in the PRC's "search for roots" (*xungen*) movement. Writers such as Mo Yan—many of whom lived through Mao's Cultural Revolution and experienced his program of "learning from the peasants"—have produced what has been described as "anti-hsiang-t'u" literature, stories that depict the Chinese countryside not as a bucolic paradise, but as a nightmarish world of poverty, ignorance, pettiness, cruelty, and misery. See Michael S. Duke, "Past, Present and Future in Mo Yan's Fiction of the 1980s," in Widmer and Wang, *From May Fourth to June Fourth*, 43–70.

48   For a selection of commentaries on the film, see the dossier collected by Miriam Hansen, in "Dossier on *Heimat*."

49   See quotation from Reitz cited in Anton Kaes, *From Heimat to Hitler*, 167.

50   *Film Appreciation* no. 45 (May 1990). The material on Reitz's film consists primarily of translations of the commentaries and discussions collected in the fall 1985 issue of *New German Critique*.

51   Note that the Chinese term means "family compound," an enclosed, safe space.

52   *Film Appreciation*, no. 45 (May 1990): 27.

53   Kidlat Tahimik's *Perfumed Nightmare* (Philippines, 1976), Antonio Eguino's *Chuquiago* (Bolivia, 1977), and the three films in Satyajit Ray's Apu Trilogy are but a few examples of films that underscore the contrast between the Westernized cul-

ture of the city—inundated with foreign consumer goods and cultural products—and the indigenous traditions of the villages.

54 See, for instance, Fredric Jameson, "Remapping Taipei," in Nick Browne, Paul Pickowicz, Vivian Sobchak, and Esther Yau, eds., *New Chinese Cinemas: Forms, Identities, Politics* (Cambridge: Cambridge University Press, 1994), 117–50. Hou is the rural director and Edward Yang the urban one.

55 Williams, *The Country and the City*, 12.

56 On the importance of summer in the English pastoral tradition, see ibid., 18.

57 Ibid., 9.

58 See ibid., 4, on the dispersal of his own family.

59 Williams himself moved from the countryside to the city in the course of pursuing an education (ibid., 1–8). Third World films as diverse as Satyajit Ray's classic Apu Trilogy, *Sugar Cane Alley* (Martinique, 1984) and *Perfumed Nightmare* (Philippines, 1977) depict young people on the move from villages to metropolitan centers in search of education and/or economic opportunity.

60 Ibid., 154.

61 This is another illustration of the common association of moral decadence with the West.

62 For example, *shuang-fa* (爽法) means to "break regulations" or "disregard the law," while someone described as *shang-kuai* (爽快) is outspoken, straightforward, and refreshingly open-minded.

63 Williams, *The Country and the City*, 51.

64 Geoffrey Nowell-Smith, *Visconti*, 2d ed. (New York: Viking, 1973), 177. Quoted in Bondanella, *Italian Cinema*, 198.

65 Williams, *The Country and the City*, 297.

66 This scene is reminiscent of the exchanges between grandfather and grandson in Hwang Chun-ming's "The Story of Ch'ing Fan Kung."

67 See Iain Chambers, *Popular Culture: The Metropolitan Experience* (London: Routledge, 1990), 21.

68 The watch is a Timex.

69 Williams, *The Country and the City*, 155.

70 In *The Country and the City*, Raymond Williams singles out Thomas Hardy and D. H. Lawrence as examples of writers who were especially conscious of the sense of crisis precipitated by the British migration from country to city. They were aware, he writes, "of a difficult borderland and of frontiers that had to be crossed" (ibid., 264). Their works emphasized that it is the transition itself that is valuable and decisive and the complex interaction of country and city and the consequent conflict of values that are most informative and revealing (264–78, 197–214).

71 A train is also prominently featured and carries similar symbolic weight in Satyajit Ray's *World of Apu*, the first film in his Apu Trilogy.

72 Williams, *The Country and the City*, 37.

7 Exile, Displacement, and Shifting Identities

1 Paul Ricoeur, "Universal Civilization and National Cultures," in *History and Truth*, translated by Charles A. Kelbley (Evanston: Northwestern University Press,

1965), 276–77. The two conflicting impulses have also, of course, been analyzed under different names—for instance, in Nokai Sakai's "Modernity and Its Critique: The Problem of Universalism and Particularism," in Masao Miyoshi and H. D. Harootunian, eds., *Postmodernism and Japan* (Durham: Duke University Press, 1989), 93–122.

2 See Ernest Mandel, *Late Capitalism* (London: Verso, 1978). The most important and influential analyses of Mandel's late capitalism for literary and cultural studies have been undertaken by Fredric Jameson, whose seminal texts include "Postmodernism; or, the Cultural Logic of Late Capitalism," *New Left Review* 146 (1984): 53–92; "Third-World Literature in the Era of Multi-national Capitalism," *Social Text* 15 (1986): 65–88; "Cognitive Mapping," in C. Nelson and L. Grossberg, eds., *Marxism and the Interpretation of Culture* (Urbana: University of Illinois Press, 1988), 347–56; and *Postmodernism; or, the Cultural Logic of Late Capitalism* (Durham: Duke University Press, 1991), the latter being a substantial reworking and expansion of the 1984 essay. Many, of course, will insist that Taiwan's pursuit of the capitalist ideal is itself an example of its cultural colonization by the West. Such an unyieldingly negative portrayal of Taiwan's integration into the capitalist world order, however, replicates precisely what it sets out to oppose. By depicting Taiwan as culturally helpless, those who criticize its "Westernization" assume the imperialist viewpoint that Third World nations are weak and defenseless, perpetuating the rhetoric of victimology that has for too long contributed to the oppression of the Third World. Taiwan's economic successes, dramatically improved standards of living, and growing global presence demonstrate that foreign philosophies and technologies can be appropriated and employed in the service of a native agenda and that participation in the modern global community need not lead to the betrayal of indigenous values and beliefs.

3 See, for example, the analysis of this trend and its implications for the United States in Robert Reich, *The Work of Nations: Preparing Ourselves for Twenty-First-Century Capitalism* (New York: Knopf, 1991).

4 Beginning in the late 1970s, for example, the government and private industry negotiated several major agreements for joint investment projects in Taiwan with multinationals General Electric, General Motors, and Toyota. The early 1980s also saw the establishment of Taipei branches of major European and American monetary institutions, as well as the opening of Taiwanese bank offices abroad. Since then, every effort has been made to make Taipei a center of international finance. Many of the highlights and statistics concerning Taiwan's recent achievements in global finance, trade, telecommunications, and travel are culled from the chronologies offered in the annual reference books published by the Taiwanese government. I have consulted *The Republic of China Handbook* (Taipei: Government Information Office) for the years 1989 and 1994.

5 Recent advertising campaigns undertaken by the government to promote Taiwanese products—from high-end sporting goods to personal computers—acknowledge the island's earlier reputation with the tagline "Very Well Made in Taiwan."

6 This completely reverses earlier formulations of the international division of labor that envisioned peripheral Third World nations producing primary commodities and providing raw materials for the First World industrial core while receiving

more technologically sophisticated manufactured goods in return. See Frederick Buell, *National Culture and the New Global System* (Baltimore: Johns Hopkins University Press, 1994), 115–16.

7   Taiwan grew from being the twenty-fifth-largest trading country in the world in 1978 (as determined by the International Monetary Fund) to fourteenth-largest in 1987. The nation's trade surplus has become so large that regulations have been passed to keep foreign exchange reserves from growing too rapidly.

8   Many restrictions that had hampered foreign trade were lifted to encourage and strengthen Taiwan's trade relationships not only with Europe and America but also with its neighbors on the Pacific Rim. Postwar import bans on Japanese consumer products, for example, were lifted in 1982, and trade relationships with Hong Kong, Australia, New Zealand, the People's Republic of China, and the former Soviet Union have dramatically improved.

9   The greater spending ability of the Taiwanese people and their growing demand for an improved quality of life are also evidenced by the proliferation since the late 1980s of consumer-oriented magazines specializing in fashion, automobiles, sports, travel, and interior design. See the chapter "Mass Media" in *The Republic of China Handbook*, 1994.

10 See the chronologies in the various handbooks, as well as the "Mass Media" chapter in ibid.

11 As the global reach of the Internet continues to grow at astonishing speed, familiar fears about the hegemony of the English language and American culture have once again been raised. Since the Internet originated in the United States, English has become the lingua franca of the computer world, prompting many to worry that computer users in non-English-speaking countries will be at a disadvantage, unable to fully avail themselves of the resources of the information age. Others, however, believe that the Internet, like other global media, will become increasingly multicultural, pointing to the impressive number of software programs available with fonts for everything from Chinese characters and Russian Cyrillic to Sanskrit. Also in development are automatic translation programs for online service subscribers. It is important to point out here that translation is itself a problematic process. Related to conquest and conversion, it is deeply enmeshed in issues of power and hierarchy. See, for example, Vicente Rafael, *Contracting Colonialism: Translation and Christian Conversion in Tagalog Society under Early Spanish Rule* (Manila: Ateneo de Manila University Press, 1988).

12 Tun Ch'eng (敦誠), "Eye in the Sky: Direct Satellite Broadcasting and the Logic of Capital Distribution" (天眼: 從直播衛星電視看資本運作邏輯), *Contemporary* 50 (July 1990): 4–16.

13 Most of these are popular fiction, business books, and children's stories, but a fair number of educational and computer titles are also being made available to Taiwanese readers to supplement local books and periodicals.

14 In a conscious attempt to globalize, Taiwanese news services have sought to both increase their coverage of international news and transmit news of Taiwan abroad. The island's Central News Agency (中央通訊社), established in 1983, transmits news by satellite to subscribers worldwide and has twenty-eight international bureaus working in major cities around the world.

15 Bruce Robbins, extending Benedict Anderson's arguments on nationhood, suggests that the technologies and institutions of electronic and digital capitalism have taken the place of print capitalism in building and sustaining new imagined communities that are cosmopolitan and transnational. See his "Introduction Part I: Actually Existing Cosmopolitanism," in Pheng Cheah and Bruce Robbins, eds., *Cosmopolitics: Thinking and Feeling beyond the Nation* (Minneapolis: University of Minnesota Press, 1998), esp. 4–7.

16 China Airlines launched an effort to establish itself as a world-girdling commercial air service, inaugurating service from Taipei to the U.S. West Coast in 1978 and to New York and Amsterdam in 1983. See the chronology in *The Republic of China Handbook, 1994*. In recent years, Taiwan has added another major international airline, EVA Air.

17 Thanks to the global dispersion of Taiwanese overseas investments, there are also sizable communities of migrant Taiwanese professionals working in parts of the Middle East and Africa. I recently met, for example, a young woman, who before moving to Los Angeles to attend high school had spent most of her elementary and junior high school years in Saudi Arabia, where her parents (a chemist and a physician) worked in a large medical facility. She described a community of hundreds of Taiwanese professionals, who along with their families have created a whole town in the desert.

18 Stuart Hall, who has written extensively on Caribbean culture, speaks similarly of a "New World Presence" as "the juncture-point where the other cultural tributaries met . . . where strangers from every other part of the globe met. . . . It is the space where creolisations and assimilations and syncretisms were negotiated." See Stuart Hall, "Cultural Identity and Cinematic Representation," *Framework*, no. 36 (1989): esp. 81.

19 In today's world, culture flows in multiple and often unpredictable directions. As Hall has argued, the overarching framework of the new globalization may still be American, but it no longer tries to obliterate local differences; instead, it seeks to operate within them. The world is growing simultaneously more global *and* more localized. See Stuart Hall, "Old and New Identities, Old and New Ethnicities," in Anthony D. King, ed., *Culture, Globalization and the World-System: Contemporary Conditions for the Representation of Identity* (Binghamton: Department of Art and Art History, State University of New York at Binghamton, 1991), esp. 27–28. Ulf Hannerz similarly characterizes the new world culture as an organization of diversity rather than the replication of uniformity. See Ulf Hannerz, "Scenarios for Peripheral Cultures," in King, *Culture, Globalization and the World-System*, 107–28.

20 See Robbins, *Cosmopolitics*, 1–2.

21 As Frederick Buell notes (*National Culture and the New Global System*, 136–37, 214), this term has been used by both Anthony D. King and Saskia Sasson-Koob. King writes of the dual processes of "the peripheralization of the core and the co-realization of the periphery" that characterize the current era in his *Global Cities: Post-imperialism and the Internationalization of London* (New York: Routledge, 1990), 46. Sasson-Koob describes similar phenomena in "Recomposition and Peripheralization at the Core," *Contemporary Marxism* 5 (summer 1982): 88–100.

22 *Boba* are fruit, tea, and herbal beverages that combine bits of flavored gelatin with liquid—drinks long popular in Asia but now found in shops all over Los Angeles (and not only in Asian neighborhoods). A bottled version, called Jumpin' Gems, targets an even broader market. See the *Los Angeles Times*, August 3, 1995, H2.

23 The foods of immigrant communities are often quick to enter the mainstream. In Los Angeles, pad thai, dim sum, and naan are becoming as familiar as pizza, tacos, and bagels. In recent years, major metropolises such as Los Angeles, New York, and London have also seen a profusion of restaurants serving "fusion" cuisines: Chino-Latino, Franco-Japanese, and other imaginative hybrids. One positive review of a restaurant in Los Angeles, for instance, described the place as run by "a Japanese-influenced Iranian chef taking on an Italian-tinged California grill menu that happens to include tacos" (*Los Angeles Times*, September 14, 1995, H15).

24 Some of the most striking examples of cultural hybridization can be found in contemporary music, in which experimental mixes of multiple musical traditions are increasingly the norm. The work of musicians in London, New York, Los Angeles, and other centers of "Western" popular music, for example, is increasingly being influenced by Third World rhythms, forms, and instrumentation. See Stuart Hall, "The Local and the Global," in King, *Culture, Globalization and the World-System*, 38–39; and Janet Abu Lughod, "Going beyond Global Babble," in the same volume, 133.

25 Fred Davis, *Yearning for Yesterday*, cited in Christopher Lasch, "The Politics of Nostalgia: Losing History in the Mists of Ideology," *Harper's*, 269, no. 163 (November 1984): 69.

26 Like so many developing countries, modern Argentina is the product of European colonization, waves of global migration, and rapid industrialization. Traditionally a rural agrarian country, it now has an urban industrial center, the capital city of Buenos Aires, which attracts not only workers from the Argentinian countryside but also foreign cultures and capital from abroad—a typical Third World metropolis.

27 Alicia Dujovne Ortiz, "To Be *Porteño*," in *Buenos Aires*, translated by Caren Kaplan, *Discourse*, no. 8 (fall–winter 1986–87): 76.

28 Kaplan, "The Poetics of Displacement in Alicia Ortiz's *Buenos Aires*," 84–100.

29 Edward Said, for example, sees exile as one of the most potent motifs of modern culture: "We have become accustomed to thinking of the modern period itself as spiritually orphaned and alienated, the age of anxiety and estrangement" ("Reflections on Exile," 357).

30 The conception of national cultures as separate, bounded wholes owes much to Herder's assertion that each national group had its own clearly defined *Volksgeist* or *Nationalgeist*, its own language and therefore customs, mores, and worldview. See Buell, *National Culture and the New Global System*, 28.

31 Iain Chambers, for example, notes that intellectuals and social commentaters in postwar England who criticized the threat of American popular culture to "Englishness" espoused "an organic view of culture," which, "with its implicit appeal to a pre-industrial, rural world" was "increasingly at odds with the cosmopolitan modernism of twentieth-century popular tastes" (*Popular Culture*, 35–36).

32 Kaplan, "The Poetics of Displacement in Alicia Ortiz's *Buenos Aires*," 84.

33 Kaplan herself borrows the terms *deterritorialization* and *reterritorialization* from philosophers Gilles Deleuze and Félix Guattari to describe this process of identity formation as a constant traveling from culture to culture between the center and the margins. See Caren Kaplan, "Deterritorializations: The Rewriting of Home and Exile in Western Feminist Discourse," in Abdul Janmohamed and David Lloyd, eds., *The Nature and Context of Minority Discourse* (New York: Oxford University Press), 357–68. In anthropology, James Clifford has similarly advocated a theoretical shift from the traditional localizing of culture (culture as dwelling) to an acknowledgment of the intercultural exchanges, mediations, and tensions that produce modern subjectivities (culture as travel). See his "Traveling Cultures," in L. Grossberg, C. Nelson, and P. Treichler, eds., *Cultural Studies* (New York: Routledge, 1992), 96–116. Stephen Muecke, also elaborating on Deleuze and Guattari, focuses on their formulation of ex-centric nomad societies as models of "becoming and heterogeneity" that are opposed to "the stable, the eternal, the identical and the constant." See his "The Discourse of Nomadology: Phylums in Flux," *Art and Text* 14 (1984): 27. See also Teshome Gabriel, "Thoughts on Nomadic Aesthetics and the Black Independent Cinema: Traces of a Journey," in Cham Mybe and Claire Watkins, eds., *Blackframes: Critical Perspectives on Black Independent Cinema* (Cambridge, Mass.: Celebration of Black Cinema, 1988), 62–77.

34 Hall, "Cultural Identity and Cinematic Representation," 72. Page references are cited parenthetically in the text. See also Hall's "Old and New Identities, Old and New Ethnicities," in which he elaborates on the political and strategic benefits of shifting identifications.

35 These are what James Clifford calls discrepant cosmopolitanisms ("Traveling Cultures," 108).

36 Kaplan, "The Poetics of Displacement in Alicia Ortiz's *Buenos Aires*," 88.

37 As Leo Lee has observed, "the word *exile* in Chinese is often associated with negative or passive meanings—banishment as a form of punishment by government (*fangzhu, liufang*); seldom, if ever, does it connote the meaning of self-exile, or exile by voluntary choice as an act of protest by an individual." See Leo Ou-fan Lee, "On the Margins of the Chinese Discourse: Some Personal Thoughts on the Cultural Meaning of the Periphery," *Daedalus* 120, no. 2 (spring 1991): 212.

38 Lasch, "The Politics of Nostalgia," 69.

39 On the importance of a symbolic *communitas* for the exile, see Hamid Naficy, "The Poetics and Practice of Iranian Nostalgia in Exile," *Diaspora*, no. 3 (1992): 18–27. Naficy notes the importance of rituals for cementing this sense of communal solidarity and identity (19–20). Reels one and two of *Lost, Lost, Lost* are filled with marriages, baptisms, dances, and other tradition rituals that help the Lithuanian community to construct a sense of its heritage. Edward Said also described exile as a jealous state: "What you achieve in exile is precisely what you have no wish to share, and it is the drawing of lines around you and your compatriots that the least attractive aspects of being an exile emerge: an exaggerated sense of group solidarity as well as a passionate hostility towards outsiders" ("The Mind of Winter: Reflections on a Life in Exile," *Harper's*, September 1984, 51).

40 Scott MacDonald, "Lost, Lost, Lost over *Lost, Lost, Lost*," *Cinema Journal* 25, no. 2 (winter 1986): 25.

41 Salman Rushdie, *The Satanic Verses* (New York: Viking, 1988), 205. Of course, the very foundation of the KMT government's Republic of China on Taiwan was precisely such "a dream of glorious return."

42 "The exile must roam and pant to return, but never actually achieve it" (Naficy, "The Poetics and Practice of Iranian Nostalgia in Exile," 7).

43 See Lasch, "The Politics of Nostalgia," 65–70.

44 Hall, "Cultural Identity and Cinematic Representation," 72. See also Teshome Gabriel, "Theses on Memory and Identity: The Search for the Origin of the Nile," *Emergences*, no. 1 (1989): 131–37.

45 Letters are among a number of "nostalgic objects" or "fetish souvenirs" that Hamid Naficy identifies as central to exilic culture ("The Poetics and Practice of Iranian Nostalgia in Exile," 8–10).

46 See Williams, *The Country and the City*, 225.

47 On the significance of a "return to nature" in the poetics of exile, see Naficy, "The Poetics and Practice of Iranian Nostalgia in Exile," 11–18.

48 Pico Iyer, *Video Night in Kathmandu*, on his arrival in Bali, cited in Buell, *National Culture and the New Global System*, 4.

49 Jameson, "Postmodernism; or, the Cultural Logic of Late-Capitalism," 65. Iain Chambers similarly describes today's metropolises as "points of intersection, stations, junctions, in an extensive network whose economic and cultural rhythms, together with their flexible sense of centre, are no longer even necessarily derived from Europe or North America." See Iain Chambers, *Border Dialogues: Journeys in Postmodernity* (London: Routledge, 1990), 53.

50 Roger Rouse, "Mexican Migration and the Social Space of Postmodernism," *Diaspora* 1, no. 1 (1991): 9. The focus of Rouse's study is Los Angeles, but he makes it clear that the transformation of the city is symptomatic of a global phenomenon.

51 Iain Chambers observes that the teenager is often regarded as a post-1945 American invention associated with particular attitudes and a distinctive lifestyle: music (mostly American), hairstyles, fashion, coffee bars, clubs, dancing, and cruising in cars or on motorbikes. See Chambers, *Popular Culture*, 152–53.

52 American fast food chains—the quintessential icon of American mass culture—have proliferated all around Taipei. The popularity of McDonald's, Wendy's, Kentucky Fried Chicken, Pizza Hut, and Shakey's among Taiwanese young people has not only radically altered the country's dietary habits (a recent CBS Radio Network news item reported that so many pizzas, hot dogs, and hamburgers are consumed in Taiwan that the government is launching an official campaign to promote the increased consumption of rice) but also threatens to undermine an important tradition: the family meal. We have noted how frequently families are shown sharing a meal in Hou's films—most prominently in *City of Sadness* but also in *Daughter of the Nile*. The cultural weight assigned to the family meal—and traditional Chinese foods—takes center stage in a film by Taiwanese director Ang Lee (李安), *Eat Drink Man Woman* (飲食男女, 1994), in which the Chinese master chef's youngest daughter expresses her teenage rebelliousness in part by working at Wendy's. Throughout the film, the family's growing troubles are paralleled by the increasing discord around the dining table and by the sudden unreliability of the chef's once perfect taste buds. At the end of the film, restoration of family harmony in-

cludes not only the chef's miraculous recovery of his sense of taste but also the coming home of his Westernized middle daughter, who rediscovers her love for traditional Chinese cooking and takes over as family chef. Similarly, in Chinese-Canadian filmmaker Mina Shum's *Double Happiness* (1995), whenever the young heroine, Jade, angers her parents by doing something outrageously Western (such as staying out all night or dating a non-Chinese man) she tries to make amends and restore her position as a good Chinese daughter by buying her father his favorite red bean sweet buns. The film opens, incidentally, with a wonderful family meal, with the camera cleverly positioned in the middle of the lazy susan.

53 In 1989, Will Baker, a professor of English at the University of California at Davis, and a teenaged photographer interviewed teenagers in twelve countries on five continents and wrote a report called "The Global Teenager," *Whole Earth Review*, no. 65 (winter 1989): 2–37. Their findings, though statistically insignificant, are extremely interesting, suggesting that as billions of young people around the world begin to listen to the same music, watch the same movies, wear the same clothes, and eat the same foods there is a global teenager emerging. Like Chambers, Baker believes that this youth culture is predominantly American in origin.

54 Included are songs from many different periods of American pop music history. "Hey Big Spender," The Carpenters' "Top of the World," and The Bangles' "Walk Like an Egyptian" are among those most prominently featured. This sort of juxtaposition of songs, detached from their disparate cultural and historical origins and recirculated in a new context, is typical of postmodern pastiche.

55 It has been suggested that consumer brand names and famous labels have become a sort of universal language that has penetrated deeply into the consciousnesses of Third World peoples as a part of cultural imperialism. See Susan Strusser, "The Politics of Packaged Products," cited in Wai-lim Yip (葉維廉), "Colonialism, Culture Industry, and Consumer Desire" (殖民主義, 文化工業與消費欲望), *Contemporary*, no. 52 (August 1990): 58. One of the most provocative results of Will Baker's "The Global Teenager" was the so-called Icon Probe. Teenagers were asked to identify twenty icons ranging from religious symbols to corporate logos. Not surprisingly, the corporate logos (Levi's, Coca-Cola, Sony) were among the most recognized; only the Christian cross symbol rated higher.

56 I am reminded, for instance, of a young cousin who was very anxious about moving with his mother from Taiwan to faraway Australia. After arriving in Melbourne, he was greatly comforted by the familiar sights he spotted in the otherwise alien landscape: McDonald's and Pizza Hut! Mitchell Stephens relates a similar story about a graduate student from Kenya, who, upon arriving in the United States to study at Amherst, was relieved to discover he could get Kentucky Fried Chicken there. ("Pop Goes the World").

57 Kaplan, "Deterritorializations," 358. Kaplan is describing the world system of culture proposed by Ulf Hannerz in "The World System of Culture: The International Flow of Meaning and Its Local Management," 1985, manuscript.

58 Frederick Buell, *National Culture and the New Global System*, 5. Buell also cites a number of interesting media studies showing that American popular culture has been consumed globally in a very different way than anti-American cultural conservatives suggest. These include Ien Ang, *Watching Dallas: Soap Opera*

and the Melodramatic Imagination (London: Methuen, 1985); Mary Yoko Brannen, "'Bwana Mickey': Constructing Cultural Consumption at Tokyo Disneyland," in Joseph J. Tobin, ed., Re-made in Japan: Everyday Life and Changing Consumer Taste in a Changing Society (New Haven: Yale University Press, 1992), 216–34; and John Tomlinson, Cultural Imperialism (Baltimore: Johns Hopkins University Press, 1991).

59 Daughter of the Nile, the title of Hou's film, is taken from the Japanese comic book that Hsiao-yang is seen reading and whose first and last pages frame the film itself (pretitle sequence excepted).

60 See Lynell George, "Gray Boys, Funky Aztecs, and Honorary Homegirls," Los Angeles Times Magazine, January 17, 1993, 14–17, 37–39.

61 This is not to suggest, of course, that the increasing porosity of cultural borders in Los Angeles has alleviated problems of racial tension.

62 Roger Rouse, describing the changing sociospatial arrangements of the postmodern age, observes that most people today find that "their most important kin and friends are as likely to be living hundreds or thousands of miles away as immediately around them" ("Mexican Migration and the Social Space of Postmodernism," 6).

63 Hou's more recent films that depict modern Taiwanese life—Good Men, Good Women and Goodbye South, Goodbye—similarly depict people communicating primarily via telephone and fax. The young men and women in both of these films are seldom without their cell phones, and in Good Men, Good Women the main character finds herself pursued and harassed by anonymous phone calls and suspicious faxes.

64 The title Daughter of the Nile perfectly underscores the film's theme of the modern individual's futile quest for stable identity. As Teshome Gabriel has observed: "The Nile is much more than the river of rivers: it is a metaphor for an expedition of memory for all of us in seeking the source of our identities" ("Theses on Memory and Identity," 137).

65 Chambers, Border Dialogues, 112.

66 Rouse, "Mexican Migration and the Social Space of Postmodernism," 1.

67 Kaplan, "Deterritorializations," 368.

68 Rouse, "Mexican Migration and the Social Space of Postmodernism," 8–10. This idea of a border zone, which allows for a play of differences, runs throughout much of postcolonial, feminist, and other forms of minority discourse. Jonas Mekas's Lost, Lost, Lost, for example, ends with a scene in which the exiled Mekas achieves a moment of acceptance—a scene that takes place on a beach, "a physical margin between land and sea." See MacDonald, "Lost, Lost, Lost over Lost, Lost, Lost," 32. Homi Bhabha speaks of the creation of a "Third Space," a liminal zone, "that productive space of the construction of culture as difference." See Homi Bhabha, "The Third Space," in Jonathan Rutherford, ed., Identity, Community, Culture, Difference (London: Lawrence and Wishart, 1990), 207–21.

69 Today perhaps the best metaphor for modern nomadic existence is the airplane rather than the train. Iain Chambers, in Border Dialogues, offers the image of modern airports as the cities of the future, "transit points connecting the movement of millions between one megasuburb and another. . . . With its shopping malls,

restaurants, banks, post offices, bars, video games, television chairs, and security guards, it is a miniaturized city. As a simulated metropolis it is inhabited by a community of nomads: a collective metaphor of cosmopolitan existence where the pleasure of travel is not only to arrive, but also not to be in any particular place ... to be simultaneously everywhere. This is a condition experienced not only by the contemporary traveler, but also by many a contemporary western intellectual: the *flaneur* becomes a *planeur*" (57–58).

70 Ortiz, "To Be *Porteño*," 81.

71 Ibid., 81–82.

72 Ibid., 82.

73 James Clifford, "Mixed Feelings," in Cheah and Robbins, *Cosmopolitics*, 362–70.

74 Ortiz, "To Be *Porteño*," 82. Compare Salman Rushdie's defense of his novel *The Satanic Verses*: "Those who oppose the novel most vociferously today are of the opinion that intermingling with a different culture will inevitably weaken and ruin their own. I am of the opposite opinion. *The Satanic Verses* celebrates hybridity, impurity, intermingling, the transformation that comes of new and unexpected combinations of human beings, ideas, politics, movies, songs. It rejoices in mongrelization and fears the absolutism of the Pure. Melange, hotch-potch, a bit of this and a bit of that is *how newness enters the world*. It is the great possibility that mass migration gives the world, and I have tried to embrace it. *The Satanic Verses* is for change-by-fusion, change-by-conjoining. It is a love-song to our mongrel selves" ("In Good Faith," 52).

Conclusion

1 Many recent studies of minority literatures in the United States have also emphasized the strategic importance of language usage in the construction of new identities, particularly in multicultural contexts. Recent work on Chicana literature, for example, has stressed the importance of linguistic hybridity and the ability to "switch codes" to the formulation of ethnic and sexual identities on the borders between cultures. See Margaret R. Higonnet, "Comparative Literature on the Feminist Edge," in Charles Bernheimer, ed., *Comparative Literature in the Age of Multiculturalism* (Baltimore: Johns Hopkins University Press, 1995), 162.

2 In KMT geography textbooks, Taiwan was frequently depicted as a leaf on the tree of China. See the illustration reproduced in Johnson, "Making Time," 240.

3 Several members of my own extended family live this way, as do many of their friends. I am aware that this particular type of transnationalism is limited primarily to middle- and upper-class families and therefore should be used as a model of cultural dynamism only with great caution. Anthropologist Aihwa Ong, for instance, refers to these Chinese transnationals as an "elite diaspora community" and observes that the freedom of movement and pragmatic "flexible citizenship" they enjoy do not apply to "migrant workers, boat people, persecuted intellectuals and artists, and other kinds of less well-heeled refugees." See Aihwa Ong, "Flexible Citizenship among Chinese Cosmopolitans," in Cheah and Robbins, *Cosmopolitics*, 134–62. On the other hand, as James Clifford points out, migrant workers, refugees, and other types of "non-bourgeois travelers" have also been affected by

today's global flows and have developed their own forms of cosmopolitanisms, which deserve more attention than they have received. See Clifford, "Traveling Cultures," 106–8.

4 Sociological studies of recent Asian immigration have used this term. See Liu Hai-ming, "The Trans-Pacific Family: A Case Study of Sam Chang's Family History," *Amerasia Journal* 18, no. 2 (1991): 1–34.

5 Sau-ling C. Wong, "Denationalization Reconsidered: Asian American Cultural Criticism at a Theoretical Crossroads," *Amerasia Journal* 21, nos. 1–2 (1995): 7.

6 See Nina Chen, "Virtual Asian American Orphans: The 'Parachute Kid' Phenome-non," *Asian Week*, January 27, 1995, 1, 4. See also, Ong, "Flexible Citizenship among Chinese Cosmopolitans," 150.

7 Ong, "Flexible Citizenship among Chinese Cosmopolitans," 150.

8 Aihwa Ong focuses on this point (ibid., 134–35), and Rey Chow makes Western sinology's insistent orientalization of China one of the central focuses of her pro-vocative *Writing Diaspora*.

9 The proper romanization is Li An, but Ang Lee is the name he is known by in the West.

10 Yang believes that global balances of power have shifted dramatically with the eco-nomic ascendency of Asian nations in recent decades. He argues that we are on the threshold of the Chinese century and that "there are adjustments to be made for the West and the East because the old relativity between the two has been ir-reversibly altered ever since the continuous economic miracles and double-digit annual growths in the Confucian-inspired Asian nations" (cited by Andrea Alsberg in program notes for the 1995 Los Angeles Asian Pacific Film and Video Festival). See also Huang Chien-yeh's (黃建業) interview with Yang in *Film Appreciation*, no. 71 (September–October 1994): 15–26. Yang believes that the dramas played out in his film are common to any number of rapidly developing Asian nations.

11 See Huang, interview with Yang, esp. 24 and 26. Yang points out that there is much more to Chinese tradition than Confucianism and argues that Chinese culture was much more lively and tolerant before its rise. He wonders why people remain so wrapped up in Confucian ideas.

12 Some titles from the late 1990s include Tsai Ming-liang's (蔡明亮) *The River* (河流, 1997), and Lin Cheng-sheng's *Murmur of Youth* (美麗在歌唱, 1997).

13 As one Taiwanese film scholar notes, the diverse portraits of the island presented in films like these underscore the fact that "'Taiwan' is not a unified and coherent concept. Beyond the Taiwan that is Taipei, there is a Taiwan that is beyond Taipei" ("台灣" 並不是統一完整的概念, 一個台北的台灣之外, 還有台北之外的台灣。). See Wu Ch'i-yen, "Taiwan Enters an Era of Auteurist Cinema" (台灣邁入作者電影的時期), *Film Appreciation*, no. 68 (March–April 1994): 13–15.

14 Action film director John Woo (吳宇森) is a prime example of the cultural hy-bridity that is a fundamental characteristic of cosmopolitan cultures such as Hong Kong's. Even though Woo was trained entirely within the Hong Kong film industry, his films are remarkably hybrid, demonstrating the influences of multiple genres —not only the traditional Chinese genres of martial chivalry films and sword-play epics but also Hollywood genres such as the western, the gangster film, film noir, and even classic melodrama. For a discussion of Woo's transnationalism, see

Anne T. Cieko, "Transnational Action: John Woo, Hong Kong, Hollywood," in Lu, *Transnational Chinese Cinemas*, 224–37.

15 To take film culture as just one example of Taiwan's cultural wealth, serious film buffs (whose numbers remain small but are growing) can see any number of movies and videos from the United States, Europe, Latin America, Africa, the Caribbean, Southeast Asia, or practically anywhere in the world at screenings and festivals put together by cultural organizations such as the National Film Research Institute (國家電影資料館). Taiwanese filmmakers, of course, regularly cite foreign directors as being among their influences. Even the island's mainstream audiences, however, are exposed to a surprisingly wide variety of films. A videocassette of Ang Lee's *Eat Drink Man Woman*, for instance, included trailers for *I Love Trouble* (Hollywood mainstream) and *A Bronx Tale* (American independent), as well as for a traditional Chinese historical epic called *The Great Emperor's Concubine* (西楚霸王). For a similar perspective on the processes of hybridization from within, see also Rey Chow's praise for a recent book by Nancy Armstrong and Leonard Tennenhouse, *The Imaginary Puritan* (Berkeley: University of California Press, 1992), whose historical analysis of changing habits of reading and writing demonstrate how the supposedly pure intellectual heritage of English literature has always been "contaminated" from within by cultural influences from its colonies. See Rey Chow, "In the Name of Comparative Literature," in Bernheimer, *Comparative Literature in the Age of Multiculturalism*, 112–13.

16 See Chen Ju-hsiu (陳儒修), "A Report on Taiwanese Film Culture in the Nineties" (九零年代台灣電影文化生態調查報告), *Film Appreciation*, no. 75 (May–June 1995): 98–112.

17 The first, and certainly the most publicized, "defection" to Hollywood was that of the director John Woo (吳宇森), who, along with his producer Terence Chang, relocated in Los Angeles and became the first Asian to direct a major studio picture—Universal's $20 million production, *Hard Target* (1993). That film, starring Jean-Claude van Damme, received only a lukewarm response, but Woo has since made several more movies for major Hollywood studios, two of which, starring red-hot John Travolta, *Broken Arrow* (1995) and *Face/Off* (1997), were enormously successful. Significantly, his name is no longer always prefaced with the label "Hong Kong director." Two other Hong Kong action directors, Ringo Lam and Tsui Hark, followed John Woo's example and tried their luck in Hollywood but with less success. Chow Yun-fat (周潤發), long one of the most popular actors in Asia, has parlayed his reputation as "the coolest actor in the world" (the title of a profile written by R. J. Smith for the *Los Angeles Times Magazine*, March 12, 1995, 10–15) into multiple commitments in Hollywood. Other Hong Kong figures familiar to action film fans, such as Jet Li, Michelle Yeoh, and of course Jackie Chan, have also successfully crossed over into American films.

18 For a more detailed discussion of Lee's films, see Wei Ming Dariotis and Eileen Fung, "Breaking the Soy Sauce Jar: Diaspora and Displacement in the Films of Ang Lee," in Lu, *Transnational Chinese Cinemas*, 187–220.

19 Nancy Blaine, "East by Northeast: Wedding Banquet Director Ang Lee Discusses Sex, Food, Marriage, and the Politics of Filmmaking," *LA Village View*, August 13–19, 1993, 9. Lee loves New York and considers it his home. He says: "I live in New

York. It's a miniature world all its own. It's neither China nor America; it's New York. And when people ask me, 'Do you consider yourself an American director or a Chinese director?' I say, 'I'm a New York filmmaker.'"

20 Janet Maslin, "Suburbanites Pure as Driven Slush," *New York Times*, September 26, 1997, B1, 14. An article in the paper's Sunday edition similarly characterized Lee as an "outsider," lumping him together with several foreign directors (Agnieszka Holland, Jocelyn Moorhouse, John Woo, Wolfgang Peterson, and Wim Wenders) who have made films with "American" stories, even though Lee is the only one who lives in the United States and has done so for two decades. See Frank Bruni, "Arriving from Afar to Get Inside America," *New York Times*, September 21, 1997, Arts and Leisure section, 1, 18.

21 In the International Movie Database, the "country" under which *Ice Storm* is categorized is the United States, as are Lee's later films *Ride with the Devil* (about the American Civil War, released in 1999) and *The Hulk* (2003). *Sense and Sensibility* is credited as a joint U.S./U.K. production.

22 See Hannerz, "Scenarios for Peripheral Cultures," 107–28.

23 Hall, "Old and New Identities," 52–53.

24 See Johnson, "Making Time," 177–249.

25 Stuart Hall, "The Local and the Global," 19–39.

26 The title of Wu's film, which is the story of his father and other Taiwanese men of his generation, is a phonetic rendering of the Japanese term for *father*.

27 Wu, a novelist and screenwriter known primarily as one of Hou Hsiao-hsien's chief collaborators, acknowledges his debt to nativist writers such as Hwang Chun-ming and Ch'en Ying-chen. He also readily admits that he is something of a throwback to an earlier era in Taiwanese history and that he feels he is out of touch with contemporary Taiwanese culture and the current crop of young filmmakers. See Hsieh, "Interview of Wu Nien-chen," 50–57.

28 See articles by Chu T'ien-wen (朱天文) and Huang Chien-yeh (黃建業) in the *China Times*, September 15, 1994, 39.

29 Robertson, "Social Theory, Cultural Relativity and the Problem of Globality," 71–72.

30 Fanon, *The Wretched of the Earth*, cited in Hall, "Cultural Identity and Cinematic Representation," 81, emphasis mine.

31 Homi K. Bhabha, "DissemiNation: Time, Narrative, and the Margins of the Modern Nation," in Bhaba, *Nation and Narration*, 299.

32 Ibid., 303–4.

33 Ibid., 312.

34 See, for example, Arjun Appadurai, "Disjuncture and Difference in the Global Cultural Economy," *Public Culture* 2, no. 2 (spring 1990): 1–24. Appadurai describes a single world system structured around the complex and disjunctive relationships among five dimensions of global flow—human movement (ethnoscape), technological exchange (technoscape), monetary transfer (finanscape), image flow (mediascape), and the circulation of ideological keywords (ideoscape). It is an interactive system of constant deterritorializations and displacements that allows, as Appadurai puts it, "greater attention to global fragmentation." It corrects, then, one of the

chief flaws of nationalist or any other totalizing narrative: the supression of the multiplicity of significant difference.

35 Rey Chow, writing about the contradictory political sentiments in Hong Kong following the Tiananmen massacre, makes an interesting observation about the Chinese term for *crisis* (*weiji*, 危機). Made up of the characters for *danger* (危) and *opportunity* (機), it neatly juxtaposes the two conflicting responses to the crisis precipitated by globalization and the breakdown of traditional national categories. See Rey Chow, *Writing Diaspora*, 25.

36 Hall, "The Local and the Global," 25–26. The resurgence of nationalism that has led to violence in places like Germany and the former Yugoslavia illustrates the kind of defensive retrenchment that Hall describes.

37 The monument originally included a plaque honoring "Taipei, Taiwan." When the PRC government objected, the sign was changed to "Taipei municipality, Taiwan Province, China," which then led to protests from the local Taiwanese community. See Massie Ritch, "Sign Directs Sister Cities to Diplomatic Soap Opera," *Los Angeles Times*, November 16, 2002. The issue was finally resolved with a sign that reads simply "Taipei." The country affiliations of the other sister cities were also eliminated. Postnational, indeed!

38 On the inauthentic native, see Chow, *Writing Diaspora*, 27–30.

39 Ibid., 18.

40 The problems of the West's persistent orientalism in its reception of Chinese cinema and of self-orientalization by a number of Chinese filmmakers (most notably Zhang Yimou) have been hotly debated in numerous articles and essays in recent years but are regrettably too large in scope for the current discussion.

41 Latin American studies has also contributed significantly to current reconceptualizations of ethnic identity. Numerous Chicano writers, activists, and scholars, for example, have proposed syncretic categories that emphasize "border experiences." For an introductory list of some of these theorists, see Clifford, "Traveling Cultures," 109. Latin America and Asia are on the leading edge of political acknowledgment of the new transnationalisms as well. Mexico and Korea, for instance, officially recognized the reality of Mexican Americans and Korean Americans who live transnationally with their recent announcements that they would begin granting privileges of dual citizenship. See K. Connie Kang, "Dual U.S.-Korean Nationality Nears," *Los Angeles Times*, June 14, 1998, A1, 36.

42 Russell Leong, "Lived Theory (Notes on the Run)," an editor's preface to a special edition of *Amerasia Journal* guest edited by Michael Omi and Dana Takagi, "Thinking Theory in Asian American Studies," *Amerasia Journal* 21, nos. 1–2 (1995): xii. See also the chapter "The Construction of Asian-American Literature" in Buell, *National Culture and the New Global System*, 177–216.

43 Malaysian-born artist Cheng-sim Lim exemplifies the complexity of the contemporary Asian American experience when she describes the neighborhood in which she lives. She writes: "I live in Los Angeles and my neighbors are Mexican, Cuban, Chinese, Italian, Kampuchean, Vietnamese and Lebanese. During the last year, a golden-domed Ukrainian church has sprouted in full view of my living-room window that faces east while the south window looks onto downtown and its sky-

line of high-rise corporate egos. The Dodgers play ball on the hill at the end of the road. WASPs have found their way to the local Buddhist vegetarian restaurant. I heard Spanish rap at the laundromat the other day." See Cheng-sim Lim, "Rojak," in Russell Leong, ed., *Moving the Image: Independent Asian Pacific Media Arts* (Los Angeles: Asian American Studies Center and Visual Communications, UCLA, 1991), 197–98.

BIBLIOGRAPHY

Chinese Sources

Chao Kuang-han (趙光漢). "*Hsiang-t'u* Literature *Is* a National Literature" (鄉土文學就是國民文學). In Yu T'ien-ts'ung, *A Collection of Essays on* Hsiang-tu *Literature*, 281–91.

Chan Hung-chih (詹宏志). "The Origins and Future Path of Taiwanese New Cinema" (臺灣新電影的來路與去路). In Chiao Hsiung-p'ing, *Taiwanese New Cinema*, 25–39.

——. "A Proclamation for Taiwanese Cinema, 1987" (七十年臺灣電影宣言). In Chiao Hsiung-p'ing, *Taiwanese New Cinema*, 111–18.

Chang Ch'ien-p'ei (張靚蓓). "Two Versions of *City*? Domestic Print Lacks a Scene" (兩種"悲情": 國內版少一段). *China Times* (中國時報), September 13, 1989.

Chang Ch'ing-yang (張擎陽). "History and Cinema" (歷史與電影). In Mi and Liang, *The Death of Taiwanese New Cinema*, 214–19.

Chang Chung-tung (張忠棟). "*Hsiang-t'u*, Nationalism, Autonomy" (鄉土, 民族, 自立自強). In Yu T'ien-ts'ung, *A Collection of Essays on* Hsiang-tu *Literature*, 495–500.

Chen Ju-hsiu (陳儒修). "A Report on Taiwanese Film Culture in the Nineties" (九零年代台灣電影文化生態調查報告). *Film Appreciation* (電影欣賞), no. 75 (May–June 1995): 98–112.

Ch'en Ying-chen (陳映眞). "A Compassionate Outlook on Life" (關懷的人生觀). In Yu T'ien-ts'ung, 342–47.

——. "Establishing a Style for a National Literature" (建立民族文學的風格). In Yu T'ien-ts'ung, *A Collection of Essays on* Hsiang-tu *Literature*, 334–41.

——. "Literature Comes from Social Self-Reflection" (文學來自社會反應社會). In Yu T'ien-ts'ung, *A Collection of Essays on* Hsiang-tu *Literature*, 53–68.

——. *The Mountain Path* (山路). Taipei: Yuan-ching, 1984.

——. "Nationalism and Our Society" (我們的社會和民族精神教育). In Yu T'ien-ts'ung, *A Collection of Essays on* Hsiang-tu *Literature*, 23.

——. *Taiwan under American Rule* (美國統制下的台灣). Vol. 13 of his *Collected Works*, Taipei: Jen-chien, 1988.

——. "A Tenth Anniversary Retrospective Look at the *Hsiang-t'u* Literary Debates" (《鄉土文學》論戰十周年的回顧). In *The Poverty of Ideology* (思想的貧困), vol. 6 of his *Collected Works*, 99. Taipei: Jen-chien, 1988.

Ch'i Lung-jen (齊隆壬). "The Tendencies of Taiwanese Film Criticism" (臺灣電影批評的傾向). In Chiao Hsiung-p'ing, *Taiwanese New Cinema*, 40–46.

Chiao Hsiung-p'ing (焦雄屏). "The Camera-Swept Back Alleys of History: An Interview with Hou Hsiao-hsien" (鏡頭掃過歷史的暗巷). *China Times* (中國時報), September 4–5, 1989.

——. "Caught in the Tides of Sweeping Change" (縱浪大化中). Interview with Hou Hsiao-hsien, *China Times* (中國時報), June 7–13, 1993, in seven parts.

——. ed. *Hong Kong Cinema Style* (香港電影風貌). Taipei: Jen-chien Books, 1987.

——. *Taiwanese New Cinema* (臺灣新電影). Taipei: Jen-chien Books, 1988.

Ching Ying-jui (井迎瑞). "No Longer Adrift on the Long River of History" (在歷史的長河裏我們不在漂泊). *Film Appreciation* (電影欣賞), no. 53 (September 1991), 2–4.

Ch'iu, Kuei-fen (邱貴芬). "'Discovering Taiwan': Constructing a Theory of Taiwanese Post-Coloniality" (發現臺灣: 建構臺灣後殖民述). In Cheng Ming-li (鄭明利), ed., *Contemporary Literary Criticism in Taiwan*. Vol. 3, *The Novel* (當代臺灣文學評論大系: 小說批評). Taipei: Cheng-chung Books, 1993, 157–81.

Chu T'ien-wen (朱天文). "Thirteen Questions on *City of Sadness*" ("悲情城市" 十三問). *Tzu-li Morning Post* (自立早報), July 11–13, 1989.

Chung Chao-cheng (鐘肇政), ed. *The Selected Works of Native Taiwanese Writers* (本省籍作家作品選集). 10 vols. Taipei: Wen-t'an, 1965.

"*City of Sadness* and the Febuary 28 Incident: A Symposium" (悲情城市二二八). *Contemporary* (當代), no. 43 (November 1, 1989): 111–30.

Feng, Tsuo-min (馮作民). *One Hundred Lessons of Taiwanese History* (臺灣歷史百講). Taipei: Youth Culture Press, 1965.

Film Appreciation (電影欣賞), no. 45 (May 1990). Special issue on "Film, History and Popular Memory," which includes translations of articles discussing Edgar Reitz's film *Heimat* from the fall 1985 issue of *New German Critique*.

Ho Fang (何方). "Foucault, Film, and Popular Memory" (傅柯, 電影與人民記憶). In Mi and Liang, *The Death of Taiwanese New Cinema*, 194–96.

——. "Reshaping Memory" (記憶的重塑). In Mi and Liang, *The Death of Taiwanese New Cinema*, 184–89.

Ho Hsin (何欣), "How *Hsiang-t'u* Literature Is '*Hsiang-t'u*'" (鄉土文學怎樣 "鄉土"). In Yu T'ien-ts'ung, *A Collection of Essays on* Hsiang-tu *Literature*, 271–80.

——. "The Modern Chinese Literary Heritage" (中國現代小說的傳統). In Yu T'ien-ts'ung, *A Collection of Essays on* Hsiang-tu *Literature*, 465–66.

Hou Hsiao-hsien: The Making of a Director (侯孝賢: 一個導演的來歷). Coordinated by Chan Hung-chih (詹宏志). Taiwan: 1993. Color video.

Hsieh Jen-ch'ang (謝仁昌). "Interview with Wu Nien-chen" (吳念眞). *Film Appreciation* (電影欣賞), no. 71 (September–October 1994): 50–57.

——. "A Report on My Life" (我生命過程的一個報告). *Film Appreciation* (電影欣賞), no. 64 (July–August 1993): 45–62. Interview with Hou Hsiao-hsien.

Hsu Nan-ts'un (許南村) [Ch'en Ying-chen]. "The Blind Spot of *Hsiang-t'u* Literature" (鄉土文學的盲點). In Yu T'ien-ts'ung, *A Collection of Essays on* Hsiang-tu *Literature*, 93–99.

——. "A Preliminary Discussion of Ch'en Ying-chen" (試論陳映眞). In Yu T'ien-ts'ung, *A Collection of Essays on* Hsiang-tu *Literature*, 172–74.

——. "The Taiwanese Art World's First Spring in Thirty Years" (台灣畫界三十年來的初春). In Yu T'ien-ts'ung, *A Collection of Essays on* Hsiang-tu *Literature*, 130–47.

Hu Ch'iu-yuan (胡秋原). "On Nationalism and Economic Colonization" (談民族主義與殖民經濟). Interview collected in Yu T'ien-ts'ung, *A Collection of Essays on* Hsiang-tu *Literature*, 561–77.

——. "The Restoration of a Chinese Position" (中國人立場之復歸). In Yu T'ien-ts'ung, *A Collection of Essays on* Hsiang-tu *Literature*, 1–44.

Huang Chien-yeh (黃建業). Interview with Edward Yang. *Film Appreciation* (電影欣賞), no. 71 (September–October 1994): 15–26.

——. *The Quest of Humanist Cinema* (人文電影的追尋). Taipei: Yuan-liu Publications, 1990.

——. "A Retrospective Look at Taiwanese Cinema of 1983" (一九八三年台灣電影回顧). In Chiao Hsiung-p'ing, *Taiwanese New Cinema*, 48–60.

Huang Mei-ying (黃美英). "The Reproduction of 'February 28'" (再造的 "二二八"). In Mi and Liang, *The Death of Taiwanese New Cinema*, 153–57.

Hwang Chun-ming (黃春明). *Awaiting the Name of a Flower* (等待一朵花的名字). Taipei: Huang-kuan, 1989.

——. *Little Widows* (小寡婦). Taipei: Yuan-ching, 1975.

——. *Sayonara, Tsai-chien* (莎喲娜啦, 再見). Taipei: Yuan-ching, 1974.

——. *The Gong* (鑼). Taipei: Yuan-ching, 1974.

——. "One Writer's Humble Thoughts" (一個作者的卑鄙心靈). In Yu T'ien-ts'ung, *A Collection of Essays on* Hsiang-tu *Literature*, 629–47.

——. "From 'Confucius Says . . .' to 'According to the Newspaper . . .'" (從 "子曰" 到 "報紙說"). In Huang, *Awaiting the Name of a Flower*, 52–77.

——. "The Tomato Tree On the Roof" (屋頂上的番茄樹). In *Awaiting the Name of a Flower*, 32–44.

——. "A Lovable Country Balladeer" (一個可愛的農村歌手). In *Awaiting the Name of a Flower*, 131–33.

——. "I Remember . . ." (使我想起來). In *Awaiting the Name of a Flower*, 142–46.

——. "The Age of Folk Songs" (產生民謠的時代). In *Awaiting the Name of a Flower*, 152–55.

——. "Folk Songs That Count" (算術民謠). In *Awaiting the Name of a Flower*, 162–64.

——. "A Taboo Folk Song" (一支令人忌諱的民謠). In *Awaiting the Name of a Flower*, 165–67.

——. "Notes on Taiwanese Folk Songs" (台灣民謠札記). In *Awaiting the Name of a Flower*, 171–77.

——. "Little Three-Character Classics, Old Three-Character Classics." In *Awaiting the Name of a Flower*, 78–88.

Imagekeeper Monthly (影響) 1 (November 20, 1989). Inaugural issue, featuring interviews with Hou Hsiao-hsien (候孝賢), and Chu T'ien-wen (朱天文), as well as numerous articles on Hou's *City of Sadness* (悲情城市).

Lan Po-chou (藍博洲) *Song of the Swinging Chariot* (幌馬車之歌). Taipei: Times Cultural Publications, 1991.

Li Ao (李敖), ed., *Research on the February 28 Incident* (二二八事件研究). 3 vols. Taipei: Li Ao Publications, 1989.

Li Er-mo (李爾莫). "Regression or Innovation? A Discussion with Zhang Yimou of *To Live*" (是回歸還是創新? 與張藝謀談 "活著"). *Film Appreciation* (電影欣賞), no. 69 (June 1994): 105–14.

Li You-hsin (李幼新), ed. *Six Major Directors from Hong Kong and Taiwan* (港台六大導演). Taipei: Tzu-li News Publications, 1986.

Li Yung-wei (李詠薇) and P'eng Hsiao-fen (彭小芬). "Interviews with Seventeen Taiwanese 'New Cinema' Film Workers" (臺灣 "新電影"工作者訪問錄). *Film Appreciation* (電影欣賞), no. 26 (March 1987): 5–16.

Liang Hsin-hua (梁新華). "*Banana Paradise*: Evocation of a Divisive Era" (香蕉天堂: 分裂時代的心情故事). In Mi and Liang, *The Death of Taiwanese New Cinema*, 208–13.

Liao, Ping-hui (廖炳惠). "A Deaf, Dumb Photographer" (即聾又啞的攝影師). In Mi and Liang, *The Death of Taiwanese New Cinema*, 129–34.

——. "A Rejection of History?" (歷史的楊棄). In Mi and Liang, *The Death of Taiwanese New Cinema*, 158–61.

Lin, Huai-ming (林懷民). "Warm Affections, Deep Sighs: On Watching *City of Sadness* in New York" (溫潤的關照, 深沉的探思: 紐約看 "悲情城市"). *China Times* (中國時報), October 18, 1989.

Lin, Nien-t'ong (林年同). *Wandering in the Lens* (鏡游). Hong Kong: Su-yeh Publications, 1984.

Mi Tsou (迷走) and Liang Hsin-hua (梁新華), eds. *The Death of Taiwanese New Cinema* (臺灣新電影之死). Taipei: T'ang-shan Publications, 1991.

"Overseas Press Materials for *City of Sadness* Stir Controversy" (悲海外宣材引起震憾). In *Ming Sheng News* (明生報), August 30, 1989.

P'eng Ko (彭歌). "Without Humanity, How Can There Be Literature?" (不談人性, 何有文學). In Yu T'ien-ts'ung, *A Collection of Essays on* Hsiang-tu *Literature*, 245–63.

——. "Notes By San-san" (三三草). In Yu T'ien-ts'ung, *A Collection of Essays on* Hsiang-tu *Literature*, 227–44.

The Republic of China Handbook. Taipei: Government Information Office, 1989, 1994.

Shao, Yi-teh (邵懿德). "On the 'New' in Taiwanese New Cinema of the 1980s" (關於八十年代臺灣新電影環境 "新" 的聲音). In *Film Appreciation* (電影欣賞), no. 26 (March 1987): 27–31.

Sun Po-tung (孫伯東). "Is Taiwan a Colonized Economy?" (台灣是殖民經濟嗎). In Yu, *A Collection of Essays on* Hsiang-tu *Literature*, 501–7.

Tobari Higashi-o (戶張東夫). "New Creative Directions in the Post-martial-law Era." *The People Biweekly* (百姓), no. 210, February 26, 1990, 46–47; no. 211, March 1, 1990, 36–37.

T'ong Wa (童娃). "Language Laws and Colored Pens" (語法與彩色筆). *Film Appreciation* (電影欣賞), no. 20 (March 1986): 29–36.

Tsai, Ling-ling (紫玲玲). "The Critical Fog Surrounding *City of Sadness*" (環繞著 "悲" 的論述霧). *Tzu-li Evening News* (自立晚報), October 10, 1989.

Tun Ch'eng (敦誠). "Eye in the Sky: Direct Satellite Broadcasting and the Logic of Capital Distribution" (天眼: 從直播衛星電視看資本運作邏輯). *Contemporary* (當代), no. 50 (July 1990): 4–16.

Wai, Min (韋名), ed. *The February 28 Incident in Taiwan* (臺灣的二二八事件). Hong Kong: Seventies Magazine Publications, 1975.

Wang Chen-ho (王禎和). "The Eternal Quest: On My Fiction-Writing Experiences" (永恆的尋求: 談我的小說寫作經驗). (素葉文學), nos. 20–21 (November 1983): 14.

———. *An Oxcart for Dowry* (嫁妝一牛車). Taipei: Yuan-ching, 1975.

———. *Rose, Rose, I Love You* (玫瑰玫瑰我愛你). Taipei: Yuan-ching, 1984.

Wang T'o (王拓). "'Colonialism' or 'Self-Determination'" (《殖民地意願》還是《自主意願》). In Yu, *A Collection of Essays on* Hsiang-tu *Literature*, 578–86.

———. "Embrace the Healthy Earth" (擁抱健康的大地). In Yu, *A Collection of Essays on* Hsiang-tu *Literature*, 384–62.

———. "'Realism,' Not 'Ruralism,'" (是《現實主義》文學, 不是《鄉土文學》). In Yu T'ien-ts'ung, *A Collection of Essays on* Hsiang-tu *Literature*, 100–119.

Wang Wen-hsing (王文興). "The Merits and Faults of *Hsiang-t'u* Literature" (鄉土文學的功與過). In Yu T'ien-ts'ung, *A Collection of Essays on* Hsiang-tu *Literature*, 515–46.

Wen Ko-chih (文戈止). "The *Rashomon* Quality of *City of Sadness*" (悲情城市" 的 "羅生門本質). *Tsu-li Morning Post* (自立早報), October 10, 1989.

Wu Cheng-huan (吳正桓). "Taiwanese Cinema Culture and Two Ways of Looking at Films." *Contemporary* 10: 97–98.

Wu, Ch'i-yen (吳其諺). "Historical Memory, Film Aesthetics and Politics" (歷史記憶, 電影藝術與政治). In Mi and Liang, *The Death of Taiwanese New Cinema*, 229–34.

———. "Notes on the Release of *City of Sadness*" ("悲情城市" 現象記). In Mi and Liang, *The Death of Taiwanese New Cinema*, 84.

———. "Taiwan Enters an Era of Auterist Cinema" (台灣邁入作者電影的時期), *Film Appreciation* (電影欣賞), no. 68 (March–April 1994): 13–15.

———. "The Taiwanese Experience on Film" (臺灣經驗的影像塑造). In Mi and Liang, *The Death of Taiwanese New Cinema*, 179–83.

———. "Thru the Narrow Cracks of History" (透過歷史的那道狹窄隙縫). In Mi and Liang, *The Death of Taiwanese New Cinema*, 123–28.

Wu Ming-jen (吳明仁). "From the 'Adulation of the West' to the Awakening of a 'Nationalistic Consciousness'" (從崇洋媚外到民族意識的覺醒). In Yu T'ien-ts'ung, *A Collection of Essays on* Hsiang-tu *Literature*, 3–13.

Wu Wan-ju (吳婉茹). "Seeing the World through Warm and Sympathetic Eyes: The Social Engagement of Writer Hwang Chun-ming" (用溫柔的眼睛看紅塵: 奮力淑世的小說家黃春明). *Central Daily News* (中央日報), July 15–16, 1995.

Yearbook of Motion Pictures in the Republic of China, 1979.

Yeh Shih-t'ao (葉石濤). "An Introduction to Taiwanese *Hsiang-t'u* Literature" (臺灣鄉土文學討論). In Yu T'ien-ts'ung, *A Collection of Essays on* Hsiang-tu *Literature*, 69–92.

Yen Yuan-shu (顏元叔). "Social Realism in Recent Chinese Fiction in Taiwan." In *Thirty Years of Turmoil in Asian Literature* Taipei: Taipei Chinese Center, International PEN, 1976, 218. Proceedings of the Fourth Asian Writer's Conference.

Yin Cheng-hsiung (銀正雄). "From Whence Come the Bells in the Graveyard?" (墳地裡哪來的鐘聲). In Yu T'ien-ts'ung, *A Collection of Essays on* Hsiang-tu *Literature*, 93–203.

Yip, Wai-lim (葉維廉). "Colonialism, Culture Industry, and Consumer Desire" (殖民主義, 文化工業與消費欲望). *Contemporary* (當代), no. 52 (August 1990): 40–60.

Yu Kuang-chung (余光中). "Crying Wolf" (狼來了). In Yu T'ien-ts'ung, *A Collection of Essays on* Hsiang-tu *Literature*, 264–67.

Yu T'ien-ts'ung (尉天聰). "Literature in the Service of Life" (文學爲人生服務). In Yu T'ien-ts'ung, *A Collection of Essays on* Hsiang-tu *Literature*, 158–60.

——. "Nationalism and Our Society" (我們的社會和民族精神教育). In Yu T'ien-ts'ung, *A Collection of Essays on* Hsiang-tu *Literature*, 22–27.

Yu T'ien-ts'ung (尉天聰), ed. *A Collection of Essays on* Hsiang-tu *Literature* (鄉土文學討論集). Taipei: Yuan-ching Publications, 1978.

Western-Language Sources

Abbas, Ackbar. *Hong Kong: Culture and the Politics of Disappearance.* Minneapolis: University of Minnesota Press, 1997.

Abu Lughod, Janet. "Going beyond Global Babble." In King, ed., *Culture, Globalization and the World-System*, 131–38.

Adam, Ian, and Helen Tiffin, eds. *Past the Last Post: Theorizing Post-colonialism and Post-modernism.* Calgary: University of Calgary Press, 1990.

Ahmad, Aijaz. "Jameson's Rhetoric of Otherness and the 'National Allegory,'" *Social Text*, no. 17 (fall 1987): 3–25.

Alea, Tomás Gutiérrez. "The Viewer's Dialectic." Translated by Julia Lesage. *Jump Cut* 29 (February 1984): 18–21.

Allen, Robert C., and Douglas Gomery. *Film History: Theory and Practice.* New York: Knopf, 1985.

Althusser, Louis. "Ideology and Ideological State Apparatuses (Notes towards an Investigation)." In *Lenin and Philosophy and Other Essays.* Translated by Ben Brewster. New York: Monthly Review Press, 1971, 170–83.

American Historical Review 93, no. 5 (December 1988): 1127–73.

Anderson, Benedict. *Imagined Communities: Reflections on the Origin and Spread of Nationalism.* London: Verso, 1991.

Andrews, William L. *The First Century of Afro-American Autobiography, 1760–1865.* Urbana: University of Illinois Press, 1988.

Ang, Ien. *Watching Dallas: Soap Opera and the Melodramatic Imagination.* London: Methuen, 1985.

Appadurai, Arjun. "Disjuncture and Difference in the Global Cultural Economy." *Public Culture* 2, no. 2 (spring 1990): 1–24.

Applegate, Celia. *A Nation of Provincials: The German Idea of Heimat.* Berkeley: University of California Press, 1990.

Armes, Roy. *Third World Film Making and the West.* Berkeley: University of California Press, 1987.

Armstrong, Nancy, and Leonard Tennenhouse. *The Imaginary Puritan.* Berkeley: University of California Press, 1992.

Ashcroft, Bill, Gareth Griffiths, and Helen Tiffin. *The Empire Writes Back: Theory and Practice in Post-colonial Literatures.* London: Routledge, 1989.

Aufderheide, Pat. "Dynamic Duo" In Chute, "Made in Hong Kong," 44. Interview with Tsui Hark and Nansun Shi.

———. "Oriental Insurgents." *Film Comment* 23, no. 6 (November–December 1987): 73–76.

Baker, Will. "The Global Teenager." *Whole Earth Review*, no. 65 (winter 1989): 2–37.

Bakhtin, Mikhail. *The Dialogic Imagination*. Edited by Michael Holquist, translated by Caryl Emerson. Austin: University of Texas Press, 1982.

———. "Discourse in the Novel." In Bakhtin, *The Dialogic Imagination*, 259–422.

———. "Epic and Novel." In Bakhtin, *The Dialogic Imagination*, 5–40.

———. "Forms of Time and Chronotope in the Novel." In Bakhtin, *The Dialogic Imagination*, 84–258.

———. *Problems of Dostoevsky's Poetics*. Edited and translated by Caryl Emerson. Minneapolis: University of Minnesota Press, 1984.

———. *Rabelais and His World*. Translated by Helene Iswolsky. Bloomington: Indiana University Press, 1984.

———. *Speech Genres and Other Late Essays*. Translated by Vern W. McGee, edited by Caryl Emerson and Michael Holquist. Austin: University of Texas Press, 1986.

Bakhtin, Mikhail, and V. N. Volosinov. *Marxism and the Philosophy of Language*. Translated by Ladislav Matejka and I. R. Titunik. Cambridge: Harvard University Press, 1986.

Baldwin, Karen. "'One Thing about Your Grandad — He Never Lied, He Just Told Stories': The Importance of Family Narratives to Ethnic and Regional Studies." *MELUS* 10, no. 2 (summer 1983): 69–77.

Barker, Francis, Peter Hulme, Margaret Iversen, and Diana Loxley, eds. *Europe and Its Others*. Vols. 1–2. Colchester: University of Essex, 1985.

Benjamin, Walter. *Illuminations*. Translated by Harry Zohn, edited and with an introduction by Hannah Arendt. New York: Schocken, 1969.

———. "The Storyteller: Reflections on the Works of Nikolai Leskov." In Benjamin, *Illuminations*, 83–109.

———. "Theses on the Philosophy of History." In Benjamin, *Illuminations*, 253–67.

———. "The Work of Art in the Age of Mechanical Reproduction." In Benjamin, *Illuminations*, 217–51.

Bennington, Geoffrey. "Postal Politics and the Institution of the Nation." In Bhabha, *Nation and Narration*, 121–37.

Berger, John. "Historical Afterword." In *Pig Earth*. London: Writers and Readers Publishing Cooperative, 1979, 195–213.

Bernheimer, Charles, ed. *Comparative Literature in the Age of Multiculturalism*, Baltimore: Johns Hopkins University Press, 1995.

Beverly, John. *Against Literature*. Minneapolis: University of Minnesota Press, 1993.

Bhabha, Homi K. "DissemiNation: Time, Narrative, and the Margins of the Modern Nation." In Bhabha, *Nation and Narration*, 291–322.

———. "Of Mimicry and Man: The Ambivalence of Colonial Discourse." *October* 28 (spring 1984): 125–33.

———. "The Other Question: Stereotype and Colonial Discourse." *Screen* 5, no. 6 (November–December 1983): 18–36.

——. "Representation and the Colonial Text: Some Forms of Mimeticism." In Frank Gloversmith, ed., *The Theory of Reading*. Brighton: Harvester, 1984, 99–122.

——. "The Third Space." In Jonathan Rutherford, ed., *Identity, Community, Culture, Difference*. London: Lawrence and Wishart, 1990, 207–21.

Bhabha, Homi K., ed. *Nation and Narration*. London: Routledge, 1990.

Birch, Cyril, ed. *Anthology of Chinese Literature*. 2 vols. New York: Grove, 1972.

Blaine, Nancy. "East by Northeast: *Wedding Banquet* Director Ang Lee Discusses Sex, Food, Marriage, and the Politics of Filmmaking." *LA Village View*, August 13–19, 1993.

Blythe, Martin. "Third Cinema at Home in the First World." *The Independent*, November 1990, 24–27.

Bondanella, Peter. *Italian Cinema: From Neo-realism to the Present*. New York: Frederick Ungar, 1990.

Bordwell, David, Janet Staiger, and Kristin Thompson. *The Classical Hollywood Cinema: Film Style and Mode of Production to 1960*. New York: Columbia University Press, 1985.

Brannen, Mary Yoko. "'Bwana Mickey': Constructing Cultural Consumption at Tokyo Disneyland." In Joseph J. Tobin, ed., *Re-made in Japan: Everyday Life and Changing Consumer Taste in a Changing Society*. New Haven: Yale University Press, 1992, 216–34.

Brauchli, Marcus W. "Rising in the East: Why Historic Election in Taiwan Is Rattling Both China and U.S." *Wall Street Journal*, February 26, 1996.

Brennan, Timothy. "The National Longing for Form." In Bhabha, *Nation and Narration*, 44–70.

Browne, Nick, Paul G. Pickowicz, Vivian Sobshack, and Esther Yau, eds. *New Chinese Cinemas: Forms, Identities, Politics*. New York: Cambridge University Press, 1996.

Bruni, Frank. "Arriving from Afar to Get Inside America." *New York Times*, September 21, 1997.

Buell, Frederick, *National Culture and the New Global System*. Baltimore: Johns Hopkins University Press, 1994.

Burch, Noel. *To the Distant Observer: Form and Meaning in the Japanese Cinema*. Berkeley: University of California Press, 1979.

Burton, Julianne. *Cinema and Social Change in Latin America*. Austin: University of Texas Press, 1986.

——. "Marginal Cinemas and Mainstream Critical Theory." *Screen* 26, nos. 3–4 (May–August 1985).

Canby, Vincent. Review of *Farewell My Concubine*. *New York Times*, October 11, 1993, B5.

Chambers, Iain. *Border Dialogues: Journeys in Postmodernity*. London: Routledge, 1990.

——. *Popular Culture: The Metropolitan Experience*. London: Routledge, 1990.

Chanan, Michael, ed. *Twenty-Five Years of the New Latin American Cinema*. London: British Film Institute, 1983.

Chang Hsi-kuo. "Realism in Taiwan Fiction: Two Directions." In Jeannette L. Faurot, ed., *Chinese Fiction from Taiwan: Critical Perspectives*. Bloomington: Indiana University Press, 1980, 31–42.

Chang, Sung-cheng Yvonne. "Chu T'ien-wen and Taiwan's Recent Cultural and Literary Trends." *Modern Chinese Literature* 6, nos. 1–2 (spring–fall 1992): 61–83.

Chatterjee, Partha. *Nationalist Thought and the Colonial World: A Derivative Discourse.* London: Zed, 1986.

Cheah, Pheng, and Bruce Robbins, eds. *Cosmopolitics: Thinking and Feeling beyond the Nation.* Minneapolis: University of Minnesota Press, 1998.

Chen, Lucy. "Literary Formosa." In Mancall, *Formosa Today,* 131–41.

Chen, Nina. "Virtual Asian American Orphans: The 'Parachute Kid' Phenomenon." *Asian Week,* January 27, 1995.

Cheng, Tun-jen, and Stephan Haggard, eds. *Political Change in Taiwan.* Boulder: Lynne Reinner, 1992.

Ch'i Pang-yuan et al., eds. *An Anthology of Contemporary Chinese Literature, Taiwan, 1949–1974: Poetry Collection.* Taipei: National Institute for Compilation and Translation, 1975.

Chiao, Hsiung-p'ing. "The Distinct Taiwanese and Hong Kong Cinemas." In Chris Berry, ed., *Perspectives on Chinese Cinema.* London: British Film Institute, 1991, 155–65.

——. "White Terror and the Formosa Incident: Introspection on Recent Political Films from Taiwan." Translated by Sam Ho. *Cinemaya* 32 (1996): 22–24.

Chin, Daryl. "Multiculturalism and Its Masks: The Art of Identity Politics." *Performing Arts Journal,* no. 40 (vol. 14 no. 1) (January 1992): 1–15.

Chou, Ying-hsiung. "Imaginary Homeland: Postwar Taiwan in Contemporary Political Fiction." *Modern Chinese Literature* 6, nos. 1–2 (spring–fall 1992): 23–37.

Chow, Rey, "In the Name of Comparative Literature." In Bernheimer, *Comparative Literature in the Age of Multiculturalism,* 107–16.

——. *Primitive Passions: Visuality, Sexuality, Ethnography, and Contemporary Chinese Cinema.* New York: Columbia University Press, 1995.

——. *Writing Diaspora: Tactics of Intervention in Contemporary Cultural Studies.* Bloomington: Indiana University Press, 1993.

Chow Tse-tsung. *The May Fourth Movement: Intellectual Revolution in Modern China.* Stanford: Stanford University Press, 1967.

Chu Henry. "The Tale of Taiwan's Aborigines." *Los Angeles Times,* June 1, 2001.

——. "In Taiwan, Gay Life Has Zest." *Los Angeles Times,* May 10, 2000.

Chute, David, ed. "Made in Hong Kong." *Film Comment* 24, no. 3 (May–June 1988): 33–56.

Cieko, Anne T. "Transnational Action: John Woo, Hong Kong, Hollywood." In Lu, *Transnational Chinese Cinemas,* 224–37.

Clifford, James. "Mixed Feelings." In Cheah and Robbins, *Cosmopolitics,* 362–70.

——. "Traveling Cultures." In L. Grossberg, C. Nelson, and P. Treichler, eds., *Cultural Studies.* New York: Routledge, 1992, 96–116.

Combs, Richard. "Venice: Standing on the Tower of Babel." *Sight and Sound* 59, no. 1 (winter 1989–90): 4–5.

"Coming of Age in Taiwan." *World Press Review* 31, no. 7 (July 1984): 60.

Cooper, John F. *Taiwan: Nation-State or Province?* Boulder: Westview, 1990.

Cooper, Scott. "Third Cinema Reconsidered: Evolving Forms of Politicized Aesthetics." *The Spectator* 8, no. 2 (spring 1988): 66–73.

Bibliography **333**

Corrigan, Timothy. *New German Film: The Displaced Image.* Austin: University of Texas Press, 1982.

Dariotis, Wei Ming, and Eileen Fung. "Breaking the Soy Sauce Jar: Diaspora and Displacement in the Films of Ang Lee." In Lu, *Transnational Chinese Cinemas,* 187–220.

Dasenbrock, Reed Way. "Creating a Past: Achebe, Naipaul, Soyinka, Farah." *Salmagundi* (fall 1985–winter 1986): 312–32.

Davis, Darrell William. *Picturing Japaneseness: Monumental Style, National Identity, Japanese Film.* New York: Columbia University Press, 1996.

de Certeau, Michel. *The Practice of Everyday Life.* Berkeley: University of California Press, 2002.

de Man, Paul. "Conclusions: Walter Benjamin's 'The Task of the Translator.'" *Yale French Studies* 69 (1985): 25–46.

Dissanayake, Wimal, ed. *Colonialism and Nationalism in Asian Cinema.* Bloomington: University of Indiana Press, 1994.

Dissanayake, Wimal. "Nationhood, History, and Cinema: Reflections on the Asian Scene." In Dissanayake, *Colonialism and Nationalism in Asian Cinema,* ix–xxix.

D'Lugo, Marvin. "Catalan Cinema: Historical Experience and Cinematic Practice." *Quarterly Review of Film and Video* 13, nos. 1–3 (1991): 131–46.

Downing, John D. H., ed. *Film and Politics in the Third World.* New York: Automedia, 1986.

Duke, Michael S. "Past, Present and Future in Mo Yan's Fiction of the 1980s." In Widmer and Wang, *From May Fourth to June Fourth,* 43–70.

During, Simon. "Literature, Nationalism's Other? The Case for Revision." In Bhabha, *Nation and Narration,* 138–53.

Eakin, Paul John, ed. *American Autobiography: Retrospect and Prospect.* Madison: University of Wisconsin Press, 1991.

Eckholm, Eric. "Nationalist Party Expels Taiwan's Ex-President." *New York Times,* September 22, 2001.

Egan, Susanna. "'Self'-Conscious History: American Autobiography after the Civil War." In Eakin, *American Autobiography,* 70–94.

Eguino, Antonio. "Neorealism in Bolivia (an Interview)." In Burton, *Cinema and Social Change in Latin America,* 161–69.

Elsaesser, Thomas. *New German Cinema: A History.* New Brunswick, N.J.: Rutgers University Press, 1989.

Ernst, Wolfgang. "DIstory: Cinema and Historical Discourse." *Journal of Contemporary History* 18, no. 3 (July 1983): 396–409.

Evans, Richard. "The New Nationalism and the Old History: Perspectives on the West German *Historikerstreit.*" *Journal of Modern History* 59, no. 4 (December 1987): 761–97.

Faison, Seth. "Taiwan's New Doctrine Unintelligible in Chinese." *New York Times,* July 21, 1999.

Fanon, Frantz. *Black Skin, White Masks.* New York: Grove Press, 1967.

——. *The Wretched of the Earth.* New York: Grove, 1968.

Faurot, Jeannette L., ed. *Chinese Fiction from Taiwan: Critical Perspectives.* Bloomington: Indiana University Press, 1980.

Ferguson, Russell, with Martha Gever, Trinh T. Minh-ha, and Cornel West, eds., *Out There: Marginalization and Contemporary Cultures*. Cambridge: MIT Press, 1990.

Ferro, Marc. *Cinema and History*. Translated by Naomi Greene. Detroit: Wayne State University Press, 1988.

Fleishman, Avrom. *Narrated Films: Storytelling Situations in Cinema History*. Baltimore: Johns Hopkins University Press, 1992.

Frank, André Gubder. "The Development of Underdevelopment." In Richard L. Rhodes, ed., *Imperialism and Underdevelopment: A Reader*. New York: Monthly Review Press, 1970.

Fraser, Nancy. "Rethinking the Public Sphere." In Craig Calhoun, ed., *Habermas and the Public Sphere*. Cambridge: MIT Press, 1992.

Fruehauf, Heinrich. "Urban Exoticism in Modern and Contemporary Chinese Culture." In Widmer and Wang, *From May Fourth to June Fourth*, 133–64.

Gabriel, Teshome. "Towards a Critical Theory of Third World Films." In Pines and Willemen, *Questions of Third Cinema*, 30–52.

——. "Colonialism and 'Law and Order' Criticism." *Screen* 27, nos. 3–4 (May–August 1986).

——. "Theses on Memory and Identity: The Search for the Origin of the Nile." *Emergences*, no. 1 (1989): 131–37.

——. "Third Cinema as Guardian of Popular Memory: Towards a Third Aesthetics." In Pines and Willemen, *Questions of Third Cinema*, 53–64.

——. *Third Cinema in the Third World: An Aesthetics of Liberation*. Ann Arbor: University of Michigan Press, 1983.

——. "Thoughts on Nomadic Aesthetics and the Black Independent Cinema: Traces of a Journey." In Cham Mybe and Claire Watkins, eds., *Blackframes: Critical Perspectives on Black Independent Cinema*. Cambridge, Mass.: Celebration of Black Cinema, 1988, 62–77.

Gabriel, Teshome, and Hamid Naficy, eds. *Quarterly Review of Film and Video* 13, nos. 1–3 (1991). Special issue, "Discourse of the Other: Postcoloniality, Positionality, and Subjectivity."

Gates, Henry Louis. "'Authenticity,' or the Lesson of Little Tree." *New York Times Book Review*, November 24, 1991, 1, 26–30.

——. *Loose Cannons: Notes on the Culture Wars*. New York: Oxford University Press, 1992.

Gates, Henry Louis Jr., ed., *Race, Writing and Difference*. Chicago: University of Chicago Press, 1986.

Geisler, Michael E. "'Heimat' and the German Left: The Anamnesis of Trauma." *New German Critique*, no. 36 (fall 1985): 25–66.

Gellner, Ernest. *Nations and Nationalism*. Oxford: Basil Blackwell, 1983.

George, Lynell. "Gray Boys, Funky Aztecs, and Honorary Homegirls." *Los Angeles Times Magazine*, January 17, 1993, 14–17, 37–39.

Gikandi, Simon. "Ngugi's Conversion: Writing and the Politics of Language." *Research in African Literatures* 23, no. 1 (spring 1992): 131–44.

Gladney, Dru. *Muslim Chinese: Ethnic Nationalism in the People's Republic*. Cambridge: Council on East Asian Studies, Harvard University, 1990.

Goldblatt, Howard. Introduction to Hwang Chun-ming, *The Drowning of an Old Cat and Other Stories.* Translated by Howard Goldblatt. Bloomington: Indiana University Press, 1980, xi–xiv.

——. "The Rural Stories of Hwang Chun-ming." In Jeannette L. Faurot, ed., *Chinese Fiction from Taiwan: Critical Perspectives.* Bloomington: Indiana University Press, 1980, 110–33.

Goldman, Merle, ed. *Modern Chinese Literature in the May Fourth Era.* Cambridge: Harvard University Press, 1977.

Gramsci, Antonio. *An Antonio Gramsci Reader.* Edited by David Forgacs. New York: Shocken, 1988.

Grindon, Leger. *Shadows on the Past: Studies in the Historical Fiction Film.* Philadelphia: Temple University Press, 1994.

Gugelberger, Georg, and Michael Kearney. "Voices for the Voiceless: Testimonial Literature in Latin America." *Latin American Perspectives* 70 (summer 1991): 3–14.

Guha, Ranajit, and Gayatri Chakravorty Spivak, eds. *Selected Subaltern Studies.* New York: Oxford University Press, 1988.

Hall, Stuart. "Cultural Identity and Cinematic Representation." *Framework*, no. 38 (1989): 68–81.

——. "Gramsci's Relevance for the Study of Race and Ethnicity." *Journal of Communication Inquiry* 10, no. 2 (summer 1986): 5–27.

——. "The Local and the Global: Globalization and Ethnicity." In King, *Culture, Globalization and the World-System*, 19–40.

——. "Old and New Identities, Old and New Ethnicities." In Anthony D. King, ed., *Culture, Globalization and the World-System: Contemporary Conditions for the Representation of Identity.* Binghamton: Department of Art and Art History, State University of New York at Binghamton, 1991, 41–68.

Hanan, Patrick. *The Chinese Vernacular Story.* Cambridge: Harvard University Press, 1981.

Hannerz, Ulf. *Transnational Connections: Culture, People, Places.* London: Routledge, 1996.

——. "Scenarios for Peripheral Cultures." In King, *Culture, Globalization and the World-System*, 107–28.

Hansen, Miriam, ed. "Dossier on *Heimat.*" *New German Critique*, no. 36 (fall 1985): 3–24.

Hardt, Michael, and Antonio Negri. *Empire.* Cambridge: Harvard University Press, 2001.

Herlihy, David. "Am I a Camera? Other Reflections on Film and History." *American Historical Review* 93, no. 5 (1988): 1186–92.

HHH: Portrait of Hou Hsiao-hsien. Directed by Oliver Assayas. AMIP, 1997.

Higonnet, Margaret R. "Comparative Literature on the Feminist Edge." In Bernheimer, *Comparative Literature in the Age of Multiculturalism*, 155–64.

Hite, Molly. "Foreword." In Morgan and Hall, *Gender and Genre in Literature*, xiii–xvi.

Hoberman, J. "Once in a Reich Time." *Village Voice*, April 16, 1985.

Hobsbawm, Eric. "Introduction: Inventing Traditions." In Eric Hobsbawm and Terence Ranger, eds., *The Invention of Tradition.* Cambridge: Cambridge University Press, 1983.

——. *Nations and Nationalism since 1780: Programme, Myth, Reality.* Cambridge: Cambridge University Press, 1991.

Hobsbawn, Eric J., and Terence Ranger, eds. *The Invention of Tradition*. Cambridge: Cambridge University Press, 1983.

Holley, David. "Army Killed Thousands in '47 Massacre, Taiwan Admits." *Los Angeles Times*, February 24, 1992.

Holquist, Michael. "Introduction." In Bakhtin, *The Dialogic Imagination*, xv–xxxiv.

Horkheimer, Max, and Theodor Adorno. "The Culture Industry: Enlightenment as Mass Deception." In *Dialectic of Enlightenment*. Translated by John Cumming. New York: Continuum, 1988, 120–67.

Huyssen, Andreas. "The Inevitability of Nation: German Intellectuals after Unification," *October* 61 (1992): 65–73.

Hwang Chun-ming. *The Drowning of an Old Cat and Other Stories*. Translated by Howard Goldblatt. Bloomington: Indiana University Press, 1980.

——. "A Flower in the Rainy Night." Translated by Earl Wieman. In Joseph S. M. Lau, ed., *Chinese Stories from Taiwan, 1960–70*. New York: Columbia University Press, 1976, 195–241.

Hwang, David Henry. "In Today's World, Who Represents the 'Real' China?" *New York Times*, April 1, 2001.

Jackson, Thomas H. "Orality, Orature, and Ngugi wa Thiong'o." *Research in African Literatures* 22, no. 1 (spring 1991): 5–15.

Jameson, Fredric. "Cognitive Mapping." In C. Nelson and L. Grossberg, eds., *Marxism and the Interpretation of Culture*. Urbana: University of Illinois Press, 1988, 347–56.

——. *The Political Unconscious: Narrative as Symbolic Act*. Ithaca: Cornell University Press, 1981.

——. "Postmodernism: or, the Cultural Logic of Late-Capitalism." *New Left Review* 146 (1984): 53–92.

——. *Postmodernism: or, the Cultural Logic of Late Capitalism*. Durham: Duke University Press, 1991.

——. "Remapping Taipei." In Nick Browne, Paul Pickowicz, Vivian Sobchak, and Esther Yau, eds., *New Chinese Cinemas: Forms, Identities, Politics*. Cambridge: Cambridge University Press, 1994, 117–50.

——. "Third-World Literature in the Era of Multinational Capitalism." *Social Text*, no. 15 (1986): 65–88.

Janmohamed, Abdul R. *Manichean Aesthetics: The Politics of Literature in Colonial Africa*. Amherst: University of Massachusetts Press, 1983.

Janmohamed, Abdul R., and David Lloyd, eds. *The Nature and Context of Minority Discourse*. New York: Oxford University Press, 1997.

Jay, Martin. "Songs of Experience: Reflections on the Debate over *Alltagsgeschichte*." *Salmagundi*, no. 81 (winter 1989): 29–41.

Johnson, Marshall. "Making Time: Historic Preservation and the Space of Nationality." *positions: east asia cultures critique* 2, no. 2 (fall 1994): 177–249.

Kaes, Anton. "History, Fiction, Memory: Fassbinder's *The Marriage of Maria Braun*." In Eric Rentschler, ed., *German Film and Literature*. New York: Methuen, 1986, 276–88.

——. *From Hitler to Heimat: The Return of History as Film*. Cambridge: Harvard University Press, 1989.

Kang, K. Connie. "Dual U.S.-Korean Nationality Nears." *Los Angeles Times*, June 14, 1998.

Kaplan, Caren. "Deterritorializations: The Rewriting of Home and Exile in Western Feminist Discourse." In Janmohamed and Lloyd, *The Nature and Context of Minority Discourse*, 357–68.

——. "The Poetics of Displacement in Alicia Ortiz's *Buenos Aires*." *Discourse*, no. 8 (fall–winter 1986–87), 84–100.

Kerr, George. *Formosa: Licensed Revolution and the Home Rule Movement, 1895–1945.* Honolulu: University of Hawaii Press, 1974.

——. *Formosa Betrayed.* Boston: Houghton Mifflin, 1965.

Kinder, Marsha. *Blood Cinema: The Reconstruction of National Identity in Spain.* Berkeley: University of California Press, 1993.

King, Anthony D. "Introduction: Spaces of Culture, Spaces of Knowledge." In King, *Culture, Globalization and the World-System*, 1–18.

——. *Global Cities: Post-imperialism and the Internationalization of London.* New York: Routledge, 1990.

——. ed. *Culture, Globalization and the World-System: Contemporary Conditions for the Representation of Identity.* Binghamton: Department of Art and Art History, State University of New York at Binghamton, 1991.

Kiryakakis, Andreas. *The Ideal of "Heimat" in the Works of Hermann Hesse.* New York: Peter Lang, 1988.

Kohn, Hans. *Nationalism: Its Meaning and History.* New York: Van Nostrand, 1965.

Kristof, Nicholas D. "A Dictatorship That Grew Up." *New York Times Magazine*, February 16, 1992, 16–22, 53–57.

Kuipers, Dean. "The Rise of the New Global 'Empire.'" *Los Angeles Times*, October 1, 2001.

Lai, Tse-han, Ramon H. Meyers, and Wei Wou. *A Tragic Beginning: The Taiwan Uprising of February 28, 1947.* Stanford: Stanford University Press, 1991.

Landler, Mark. "One China? Perhaps Two? Little Things Mean a Lot." *New York Times*, March 7, 2002.

Lasch, Christopher. "The Politics of Nostalgia: Losing History in the Mists of Ideology." *Harper's* 269, no. 163 (November 1984): 65–70.

Lau, Joseph S. M. "How Much Truth Can a Blade of Grass Carry? Ch'en Ying-chen and the Emergence of Native Taiwanese Writers." *Journal of Asian Studies* 32, no. 4 (August 1973): 624–25.

Lee, Leo Ou-fan. "On the Margins of the Chinese Discourse: Some Personal Thoughts on the Cultural Meaning of the Periphery." *Daedalus* vol. 120, no. 2 (spring 1991): 207–26.

——. "Modernism and Romanticism in Taiwan Literature." In Jeannette L. Faurot, ed., *Chinese Fiction from Taiwan: Critical Perspectives.* Bloomington: Indiana University Press, 1980, 6–30.

Lee Teng-hui. *The Road to Democracy: Taiwan's Pursuit of Identity.* Tokyo: PHP Institute, 1999.

Lejeune, Phillipe. *On Autobiography.* Translated by Katherine Leary. Minneapolis: University of Minnesota Press, 1987.

Lent, John A. *The Asian Film Industry.* Austin: University of Texas Press, 1990.

Leong, Russell, ed. *Moving the Image: Independent Asian Pacific Media Arts.* Los Angeles: Asian American Studies Center and Visual Communications, UCLA, 1991.

Leong, Russell. "Lived Theory (Notes on the Run)." *Amerasia Journal* 21, nos. 1–2 (1995): v–x.

Lévi-Strauss, Claude. *The Savage Mind.* Chicago: University of Chicago Press, 1966.

Liao, Ping-hui. "Rewriting Taiwanese National History: The February 28 Incident as Spectacle." *Public Culture* vol. 5, no. 2 (1993): 281–96.

Lim, Cheng-sim. "Rojak." In Leong, *Moving the Image,* 197–99.

Lin Yaofu. "Language as Politics: The Metamorphosis of Nativism in Recent Taiwan Literature." *Modern Chinese Literature* 6, nos. 1–2 (spring–fall 1992): 7–22.

Liu Hai-ming. "The Trans-Pacific Family: A Case Study of Sam Chang's Family History." *Amerasia Journal* 18, no. 2 (1991): 1–34.

Long, Simon. *Taiwan: China's Last Frontier.* London: Macmillan, 1991.

Lord, Albert B. *The Singer of Tales.* New York: Atheneum, 1976.

Lowe, Lisa. "Heterogeneity, Hybridity, Multiplicity: Marking Asian-American Differences." *Diaspora,* no. 1 (1991): 24–44.

Lu, Sheldon Hsiao-peng, ed. *Transnational Chinese Cinemas: Identity, Nationhood, Gender.* Honolulu: University of Hawaii Press, 1997.

Lukács, Georg. "The Epic and the Novel." In *The Theory of the Novel.* Translated by A. Bostock. Cambridge: MIT Press, 1971.

Lyotard, Jean-François. *Instructions paiennes.* Paris: Galilee, 1977.

MacDonald, Scott. "Lost, Lost, Lost over *Lost, Lost, Lost.*" *Cinema Journal* 25, no. 2 (winter 1986).

Mancall, Mark, ed. *Formosa Today.* New York: Praeger, 1964.

Mandel, Ernest. *Late Capitalism.* London: Verso, 1978.

Marshall, Tyler. "Taiwan Hails Shift toward Mainland." *Los Angeles Times,* August 28, 2001.

——. "Taiwan Sees New Ties with Mainland." *Los Angeles Times,* August 27, 2001.

Maslin, Janet. "Suburbanites Pure as Driven Slush." *New York Times,* September 26, 1997.

McGuire, James. "Forked Tongues, Marginal Bodies: Writing as Translation in Khatibi." *Research in African Literatures* 23, no. 1 (spring 1992): 107–16.

Meisner, Maurice. "The Development of Formosan Nationalism." In Mancall, *Formosa Today,* 147–62.

Memmi, Albert. *The Colonizer and the Colonized.* Translated by Howard Greenfield. Boston: Beacon Press, 1967.

Mendel, Douglas H. *The Politics of Formosan Nationalism.* Berkeley: University of California Press, 1970.

Meucke, Stephen. "The Discourse of Nomadology: Phylums in Flux." *Art and Text* 14 (1984).

Miyoshi, Masao. *Off-Center: Power and Culture Relations between Japan and the U.S.* Cambridge: Harvard University Press, 1991.

Montrose, Louis. "The Work of Gender in the Discourse of Discovery." *Representations* 33 (winter 1991): 1–41.

Moody, Peter. *Political Change on Taiwan: A Study of Ruling Party Adaptability.* New York: Praeger, 1992.

Morgan, Janice. "Subject to Subject/Voice to Voice: Twentieth-Century Autobiographical Fiction by Women Writers." In Morgan and Hall, *Gender and Genre in Literature*, 3–19.

Morgan, Janice, and Colette T. Hall, eds. *Gender and Genre in Literature: Redefining Autobiography in Twentieth-Century Women's Fiction*. New York: Garland, 1991.

Mouffe, Chantal. "Citizenship and Political Identity." *October* 61 (1992): 28–32.

Nadeau, Jules. "Orphaned Authors in a More-or-Less Free China." In *Twenty-Million Chinese Made in Taiwan*. Translated by David Homel. Montreal: Montreal Press, 1990.

Naficy, Hamid. "The Poetics and Practice of Iranian Nostalgia in Exile." *Diaspora*, no. 3 (1992): 1–32.

Nairn, Tom. *The Break-up of Britain: Crisis and Neo-Nationalism*. London: New Left Books, 1977.

Ngugi wa Thiong'o. *Decolonizing the Mind: The Politics of Language in African Literature*. London: James Currey, 1986.

Noriega, Chon, ed. *Visible Nations: Latin American Cinema and Video*. Minneapolis: University of Minnesota Press, 2000.

Nowell-Smith, Geoffrey. *Visconti*. 2d ed. New York: Viking, 1973.

Nussbaum, Felicity A. "Toward Conceptualizing Diary." In Olney, *Studies in Autobiography*, 128–40.

O'Connor, John E. "History in Images/Images in History." *American Historical Review* 93, no. 5 (1988): 1200–1209.

Olney, James, "Autobiography and the Cultural Moment: A Thematic, Historical, and Bibliographic Introduction." In Olney, *Autobiography: Essays Theoretical and Critical*. Edited by James Olney. Princeton: Princeton University Press, 1980, 3–27.

Olney, James, ed. *Studies in Autobiography*. New York: Oxford University Press, 1988.

Omi, Michael, and Dana Takagi. "Thinking Theory in Asian American Studies." *Amerasia Journal* 21, nos. 1–2 (1995). Special issue.

Ong, Aihwa. "Flexible Citizenship among Chinese Cosmopolitans." In Cheah and Robbins, *Cosmopolitics*, 134–62.

Ong, Walter J. *Interfaces of the Word: Studies in the Evolution of Consciousness and Culture*. Ithaca: Cornell University Press, 1977.

——. *Orality and Literacy: The Technologizing of the Word*. London: Methuen, 1982.

Ortiz, Alicia Dujovne. "To Be *Porteño*." In *Buenos Aires*. Translated by Caren Kaplan. *Discourse*, no. 8 (fall–winter 1986–87): 73–83.

Pasolini, Pier Paolo. "New Linguistic Questions." In *Heretical Empiricism*. Edited and translated by Ben Lawton and Louise K. Barnett. Bloomington: Indiana University Press, 1988, 3–22.

Payne, James Robert, ed. *Multicultural Autobiography: American Lives*. Knoxville: University of Tennessee Press, 1992.

Pines, Jim, and Paul Willemen, eds. *Questions of Third Cinema*. London: British Film Institute, 1990.

Pollack, Andrew. "A Cyberspace Front in a Multicultural War." *New York Times*, August 7, 1995, C1, 6.

Rafael, Vicente. *Contracting Colonialism: Translation and Christian Conversion in*

Tagalog Society under Early Spanish Rule. Manila: Ateneo de Manila University Press, 1988.

Rattigan, Neil. *Images of Australia: 100 Films of the New Australian Cinema*. Dallas: Southern Methodist University Press, 1991.

Rayns, Tony. "Chinese Changes." *Sight and Sound* 54, no. 1 (winter 1984–85), 24–29.

Reich, Robert. *The Work of Nations: Preparing Ourselves for Twenty-First-Century Capitalism*. New York: Knopf, 1991.

Renan, Ernest. "What Is a Nation?" Translated and annotated by Martin Thom. In Bhabha, *Nation and Narration*, 8–22.

Rhodes, Richard I., ed. *Imperialism and Underdevelopment: A Reader*. New York: Monthly Review Press, 1970.

Ricoeur, Paul. "Universal Civilization and National Cultures." In *History and Truth*. Translated by Charles A. Kelbley. Evanston: Northwestern University Press, 1965.

Ritch, Massie. "Sign Directs Sister Cities to Diplomatic Soap Opera." *Los Angeles Times*, November 16, 2002.

Robertson, Roland. "Social Theory, Cultural Relativity and the Globality." In Anthony D. King, ed., *Culture, Globalization and the World-System: Contemporary Conditions for the Representation of Identity*. Binghamton: Department of Art and Art History, State University of New York at Binghamton, 1991, 69–90.

Robbins, Bruce. "Introduction Part 1: Actually Existing Cosmopolitanism." In Cheah and Robbins, *Cosmopolitics*, 1–19.

Rosaldo, Renato. *Culture and Truth: The Remaking of Social Analysis*. Boston: Beacon Press, 1989.

——. "Ideology, Place, and People without Culture." *Cultural Anthropology* 3, no. 1 (1988): 77–87.

Rosen, Phillip, "Making a Nation in Sembene's *Ceddo*." *Quarterly Review of Film and Video* 13, nos. 1–3 (1991): 147–72.

Rosenstone, Robert A. "History in Images/History in Words." *American Historical Review* 93, no. 5 (1988): 1173–85.

Rouse, Roger. "Mexican Migration and the Social Space of Postmodernism." *Diaspora* 1, no. 1 (1991): 8–23.

Rushdie, Salman. "In Good Faith: A Pen against the Sword." *Newsweek*, February 12, 1990, 52–57.

——. "Imaginary Homelands." In *Imaginary Homelands*. London: Granta, 1991, 9–21.

——. *The Satanic Verses*. New York: Viking, 1988.

Said, Edward. *Culture and Imperialism*. New York: Knopf, 1993.

——. "Foreword." In Guha and Chakravorty, *Selected Subaltern Studies*.

——. "The Mind of Winter: Reflections on a Life in Exile." *Harper's*, September 1984.

——. "Jane Austen and Empire." In Terry Eagleton, ed., *Raymond Williams: Critical Perspectives*. Boston, MA: Northeastern University Press, 1989.

——. *Orientalism*. New York: Vintage, 1979.

——. "Reflections on Exile." In Fergusson et al., *Out There*, 357–66.

——. "Representing the Colonized: Anthropology's Interlocutors." *Critical Inquiry* 15, no. 2 (winter 1989): 205–25.

——. *The World, the Text and the Critic*. London: Faber, 1984.

Sakai, Nokai. "Modernity and Its Critique: The Problem of Universalism and Particularism." In Masao Miyoshi and H. D. Harootunian, eds., *Postmodernism and Japan*. Durham: Duke University Press, 1989, 93–122.

Santner, Eric L. *Stranded Objects: Mourning, Memory, and Film in Postwar Germany*. Ithaca: Cornell University Press, 1990.

Sasson-Koob, Saskia. "Recomposition and Peripheralization at the Core." *Contemporary Marxism* 5 (summer 1982): 88–100.

Seton-Watson, Hugh. *Nations and States: An Enquiry into the Origins of Nations and the Politics of Nationalism*. Boulder: Westview, 1977.

Shohat, Ella. "Gender and the Culture of Empire: Toward a Feminist Ethnography of the Cinema." *Quarterly Review of Film and Video* 13, nos. 1–3 (1991): 45–84.

Sklar, Robert, and Charles Musser, eds. *Resisting Images: Essays on Cinema and History*. Philadelphia: Temple University Press, 1990.

Snead, James. "European Pedigrees/African Contagions: Nationality, Narrative, and Communality in Tutuola, Achebe, and Reed." In Bhabha, *Nation and Narration*, 231–49.

Snyder, Louis L. *Global Mini-nationalisms: Autonomy or Independence?* Westport: Greenwood, 1982.

Soja, Edward W. *Postmodern Geographies: The Reassertion of Space in Critical Social Theory*. London: Verso, 1989.

Solas, Humberto. "Every Point of Arrival Is a Point of Departure (Interviewed by Marta Alvear)." In Burton, *Cinema and Social Change in Latin America*, 143–59.

Sommer, Doris. "'Not Just a Personal Story': Women's *Testimonios* and the Plural Self." In Bella Brodzki and Celeste Schenck, eds., *Life/Lines: Theorizing Women's Autobiography*. Ithaca: Cornell University Press, 1989.

Sontag, Susan. *On Photography*. New York: Farrar, Straus and Giroux, 1977.

Spivak, Gayatri Chakravorty. "Can the Subaltern Speak?" In Cary Nelson and Lawrence Grossberg, eds., *Marxism and the Interpretation of Culture*. Urbana: University of Illinois Press, 1988, 271–313.

Spurr, David. *The Rhetoric of Empire*. Durham: Duke University Press, 1993.

Srivastava, Aruna. "'The Empire Writes Back': Language and History in *Shame* and *Midnight's Children*." In Adam and Tiffin, *Past the Last Post*, 65–78.

Stallybrass, Peter, and Allon White. *The Politics and Poetics of Transgression*. Ithaca: Cornell University Press, 1986.

Stam, Robert, and Louise Spence. "Colonialism, Racism, and Representation." *Screen* 24, no. 2 (March–April 1983): 4.

Stanbrook, Alan. "The Worlds of Hou Hsiao-hsien." *Sight and Sound* 59, no. 2 (spring 1990): 120–24.

Stephens, Mitchell. "Pop Goes the World." *Los Angeles Times Magazine*, January 17, 1993.

Stone, Oliver. "The Flicker of an Eye Means Nothing in Print." *Los Angeles Times*, March 26, 1992, B7.

Tien Hung-Mao. *The Great Transition: Political and Social Change in the Republic of China*. Stanford: Hoover Institution Press, 1988.

Tomlinson, John. *Cultural Imperialism*. Baltimore: Johns Hopkins University Press, 1991.

Toplin, Robert Brent. "The Filmmaker as Historian." *American Historical Review* 93, no. 5 (1988): 1210–27.

Visconti, Luchino. "Anthropomorphic Cinema." In David Overby, ed., *Springtime in Italy: A Reader in Neorealism*. Hamden, Conn.: Archon, 1979, 83–85.

Van Kemenade, Willem. *China, Hong Kong, Taiwan, Inc.: The Dynamics of a New Empire*. New York: Knopf, 1997.

Wachman, Alan. *Taiwan: National Identity and Democratization*. Armonk, N.Y.: M. E. Sharpe, 1994.

Wang Jing. "Taiwan Hsiang-t'u Literature: Perspectives in the Evolution of a Literary Movement." In Jeannette L. Faurot, ed., *Chinese Fiction from Taiwan: Critical Perspectives*. Bloomington: Indiana University Press, 1980, 43–70.

Warner, Michael. *The Letters of the Republic: Publication and the Public Sphere in Eighteenth-Century America*. Cambridge: Harvard University Press, 1990.

Watson, Julia, and Sidonie Smith, "Introduction: De/Colonization and the Politics of Discourse in Women's Autobiographical Practices." In Julia Watson and Sidonie Smith, eds., *De/Colonizing the Subject: The Politics of Gender in Women's Autobiography*. Minneapolis: University of Minnesota Press, 1992, xiii–xxxi.

Westley, David. "Language and African Literature: A Bibliographic Essay." *Research in African Literatures* 23, no. 1 (spring 1992): 159–71.

Widmer, Ellen, and David Der-wei Wang, eds. *From May Fourth to June Fourth: Fiction and Film in Twentieth-Century China*. Cambridge: Harvard University Press, 1993.

White, Hayden. *The Content of the Form: Narrative Discourse and Historical Representation*. Baltimore: Johns Hopkins University Press, 1986.

——. "Historiography and Historiophoty." *American Historical Review* 93, no. 5 (1988): 1193–99.

——. *Metahistory: The Historical Imagination in Nineteenth Century Europe*. Baltimore: Johns Hopkins University Press, 1973.

——. "The Value of Narrativity in the Representation of Reality." *Critical Inquiry* 7, no. 1 (autumn 1980): 5–27.

Willemen, Paul. "The Third Cinema Question: Notes and Reflections." In Pines and Willeman, *Questions of New Cinema*, 1–29.

Williams, Alan. *Republic of Images: A History of French Filmmaking*. Cambridge: Harvard University Press, 1992.

Williams, Katherine. "Decolonizing the Word: Language, Culture and the Self in the Works of Ngugi wa Thiong'o and Gabriel Okara." *Research in African Literatures* 22, no. 4 (winter 1991): 53–61.

Williams, Raymond. *The Country and the City*. New York: Oxford University Press, 1973.

——. *Culture and Society, 1780–1950*. New York: Columbia University Press, 1959.

——. *Keywords: A Vocabulary of Culture and Society*. New York: Oxford University Press, 1976.

Wollen, Peter. *Raiding the Icebox: Reflections on Twentieth-Century Culture*. Bloomington: Indiana University Press, 1993.

Wong, Sau-ling C. "Denationalization Reconsidered: Asian American Cultural Criticism at a Theoretical Crossroads." *Amerasia Journal* 21, nos. 1–2 (1995): 1–28.

Worsley, Peter. *The Third World*. Chicago: University of Chicago Press, 1964.

Yau, Esther. "China after the Revolution." In Geoffrey Nowell-Smith, ed., *The Oxford History of World Cinema*. New York: Oxford University Press, 1996, 693–704.

Yip, Wai-lim. *Modern Chinese Poetry*. Iowa City: University of Iowa Press, 1970.

Zahar, Renate. *Frantz Fanon: Colonialism and Alienation*. Translated by Willfried F. Feuser. New York: Monthly Review Press, 1974.

Films by Hou Hsiao-hsien

Cute Girl (就是溜溜的她), 1980.

Cheerful Wind (風兒踢踢踩), 1982.

Green Green Grass of Home (在那河畔青草青), 1982.

"His Son's Big Doll" (兒子的大玩偶), episode of *His Son's Big Doll* (兒子的大玩偶), 1983.

The Boys from Feng Kuei (楓櫃來的人), also known as *All the Youthful Days*, 1983.

Summer at Grandpa's (冬冬的假期), 1984.

A Time to Live and a Time to Die (童年往事), 1985.

Dust in the Wind (戀戀風塵), 1987.

Daughter of the Nile (尼羅河女兒), 1987.

City of Sadness (悲情城市), 1989.

The Puppetmaster (戲夢人生), 1993.

Good Men, Good Women (好男好女), 1995.

Goodbye South, Goodbye (再見南國, 再見), 1996.

Flowers of Shanghai (海上花), 1998.

Millennium Mambo (千禧曼波), 2000.

INDEX

Biography, *The Puppetmaster* as, 112. *See also* Autobiography, in film

The Boys from Feng Kuei (Hou Hsiao-hsien), 62–63, 67, 73; city and country-side in, 196; and the future, 201–204; images of travel in, 227–228; peasant identity in, 231

Brennan, Timothy, 272 n.63

A Brighter Summer Day (Yang), 74

Buell, Frederick, 216, 224, 317 n.58

Business, multinational: impact of, in Taiwan, 212–213. *See also* Economic boom

Capitalism, in Taiwan, 211–215

"Carnivalesque," Bakhtin on, 155–166, 298 n.85

Censorship, 51, 56, 258 n.51, 279 n.4

Chambers, Iain, 314 n.31, 316 n.51, 318 n.69

Chang, Sung-sheng Yvonne, 46–47, 75, 279 n.62

Chang Chung-tung, 263 n.106

Chang Hua-k'un, 54, 56

Chang Ta-ch'un, 90

Chang Yi, 54

Cheng Ch'eng-kung (Koxinga the Pirate), 13

Ch'en Jo-hsi, 36

Chen Kaige, 247

Ch'en K'un-hou, 54, 56, 269 n.30

Ch'en Kuo-fu, 240

Chen Shui-bian, 7–8

Ch'en Ta, 49

Ch'en Yi, 15; in *City of Sadness*, 107; and March Massacres, 106; during years of transition, 103–104

Ch'en Ying-chen, 9, 259 n.63, 261 n.79, 263 n.109, 266 n.146; and hsiang-t'u, 27, 32–33; on imperialism, 33; and literary debates, 28; on modernism, 37; on nationalism, 40–41; on 1970s, 31; on Western language, 35–36

Chiang Ching-kuo, 5

Chiang Kai-shek, 5; and March Massacres, 106; promotion of nationhood,

17; rule of, 15–17; and Shanghai, 187; during years of transition, 102–103

Chiang Meng-lin, 22

Childhood and adolescence: in Hou Hsiao-hsien's films, 76, 199–200, 226–227; in Hwang Chun-ming's stories, 189–190

China, as unified nation, 1, 4, 250 n.10, 254 n.5, 255 n.24

China, mainland. *See* Mainland China; Mainland Chinese

Chinese, Classical, 135–136

Chinese aesthetics, 176–178

Chinese Communist Party, and peasants, 187

Chinese diaspora, 234, 246–248

Chinese language, describing "nation" in, 1–2. *See also* Mandarin, speaking; Taiwanese, speaking

Chinese literature, political overtones of, 187

"Ch'ing Fan Kung's Story" (Hwang Chun-ming), 63, 146–151

Ch'ing government, Taiwanese rebellion against, 14

Ch'in Shih Huang, 250 n.10

Ching-yu technique, 177

Chiu Kuei-fen, 258 n.51

Ch'iung Yao, 53

Chow, Rey, 170, 247, 254 n.5, 267 n.6, 301 n.112, 323 n.35

"Chronotope" (Bakhtin), 190–191, 308 n.32

Chuang Tzu, and Hou Hsiao-hsien's films, 177

Chu Ming, 49

Chung Chao-cheng, 18

Chung Li-ho, 18

Chu T'ien-hsin, 44, 61

Chu T'ien-wen, 120; films of, 76; on representation of history, 99–100; and San-san Bookstore, 44; and Taiwanese consciousness, 46–47; and Taiwanese New Cinema, 54, 57

Cinema: and history, 72–75; and the national, 50–54; use in mythmak-

Historical knowledge, film as source of, 107

Historical narrative, in film, 108–109

Historical relationship, between Taiwan and mainland China, 14–15

Historiography, critical, 70, 85–86, 274 n.9, 279 n.2

History: and cinema, 72–75; and memory, 69–84, 117–118; narrative in, 91–100; and politics, 114; public versus private, 97–98; recuperation of, 87–91; representations of, 73, 99–100; and the self, 118–121; theater of, 111–117; writing and rewriting, 70–71, 91–100

Hollywood, as institution, 171

Holquist, Michael, 93

Hong Kong New Wave, 54, 59–60, 268 n.17

Hong T'ong, 49

Ho P'ing, 240

Hou Hsiao-hsien, 9, 252 n.28, 257 n.42, 268 n.19, 269 n.26, 271 n.48, 279 n.4, 280 n.8, 283 n.46; on *City of Sadness*, 111; on dignity of Taiwan, 61; and "His Son's Big Doll," 55; on Japanese occupation, 111–112; and language, 166–168; and Taiwanese New Cinema, 54; Taiwan Trilogy of, 85–130; and Vittorio De Sica, 176

Hou Hsiao-hsien, films of: characteristics of, 75–76; children in, 226–227; Chinese aesthetics in, 177–178; city and countryside in, 196–197, 209; exile in, 219; historical awareness in, 86–87; and Hwang Chun-ming's literature, 9–10; lack of drama in, 174–175; land in, 62–63, 178; linguistic diversity in, 231–232; and mainland Chinese, 231; narration in, 175–176; nation in, 66–67; representation of Taiwan in, 230–231, 244–246; Taiwanese identity in, 67–68; and Taoism, 177–178; themes in, 10; village life in, 63; visual language in, 176–180

Hsiang-t'u debates. *See* Debates, hsiang-t'u

Hsiang-t'u literature, 9; childhood in, 189–190; countryside and city life in, 192; emergence of, 10–11, 25–28; and Heimat, 188 (*see also* Heimat); and Japanese occupation, 18–19; language in, 164–166; and May Fourth writers, 185–186; and modernism, 37; and nationalism, 18–19; ordinary people in, 71–72; peasantry in, 194; versus political fiction, 90; and the rural idyll, 185–189; and Taiwanese consciousness, 39–40; and Taiwanese New Cinema, 61–62, 195–197; as term, emergence of, 187–188; theorists of, 40–41; writers of, 27–28, 138. *See also* Debates, hsiang-t'u

Hsiang Yang, 44–45

"Hsiao-ch'i's Hat" (Hwang Chun-ming), 33–34

"Hsiao-ch'i's Hat" (Tseng Chuang-hsiang), 55

"Hsiao Lin in Taipei" (Wang Chen-ho), 33

Hsiao Yeh, 54, 56–57

Hsia Tsi-an, 23

Hsu Hsiao-ming, 288 n.101

Hu Yin Meng, 269 n.31

Huang Chien-yeh, 267 n.12

Huang Ming-ch'uan, 240

Huillet, Danielle, 120

Huyssen, Andreas, 253 n.4

Hwang Chun-ming, 9, 298 n.88, 299 nn.89, 96; background of, 42; and childhood, 189–190; and hsiang-t'u debates, 41–44; as hsiang-t'u writer, 27; on literature, 43

Hwang Chun-ming, fiction of: characters in, 151; countryside in, 62–63, 209; and Hou Hsiao-hsien's films, 9–10; language in, 138–140, 162–164, 231–232; oppositions in, 218–222; ordinary people in, 71–72; popularity of, 32; praise of, 33–34; and rural idyll, 188–189; and Taiwanese New Cinema directors, 54–55, 61; themes in, 10; time and space in, 191; tradition and modernity in, 150. *See also titles of specific works*

Hybridity, cultural: and difference, 228–229; and globalization, 211–229; and

Hybridity (*continued*)
identity, 230–248; in Ang Lee's films, 237–238; in Taiwanese films, 235; theories of, 2, 216–217, 222, 228–229

The Ice Storm (Lee), 242

Identity: of Chinese, 234; Fanon on, 244–245; formation of, 215–218; and hybridization, 230–248; and language, 132–133 (*see also* Language); and nomadism, 228–229; Ortiz on, 215–216; of Taiwan and Mainland China, 12–13; of Taiwan, 4, 8–9, 12–13, 230–234; of Taiwanese, 8–9, 17, 67–68, 236–237

Illusion, and reality, in Chinese literature, 118–119

Images, visual: and narration, 119–120; power of, 72; in *The Puppetmaster*, 118; suppression of, in *City of Sadness*, 99–100

Immigration, 212, 214, 233–234, 313 n.17

Imperial China, language used during, 135–136

Imperialism: and gender, 34–35, 262 nn.91, 93, 94; and nationhood, 2–3; and the novel, 93

Indigenization, of post-martial law Taiwan, 5–8

In Our Time (anthology film), 54–56, 73

Intellectuals, disillusioned, during years of transition, 104–105

International presence, of Taiwanese, 233, 313 n.17

Italian neorealism, 173–176

Jackson, Thomas H., 296 n.57

Jameson, Fredric, 222, 311 n.2

Japan: influence of, on Taiwanese society, 20, 33–35, 162–163, 223, 257 n.42

Japanese Occupation, 12, 14; and hsiangt'u literature, 18–19; impact on Taiwanese life, 114–116, 282 n.35, 299 n.96; language used during, 135, 167–168; in *City of Sadness*, 115; in *The Puppetmaster*, 111–117; transition from, 100–105

Johnson, Marshall, 267 n.3, 282 n.36

Kaes, Anton, 185, 196, 275 nn.18, 20, 277 n.37

Kaplan, Caren, 215–216, 226, 229, 315 n.33

Kerr, George, 284 n.51, 285 n.57, 286 n.64; on Chiang Kai-Shek, 102–103; on March Massacres, 106

KMT (Kuomintang): and February 28 Incident, 105–107; literature under, 21–24; and myth of nation, 16–17, rule of, 12, 14–18; and Shanghai, 187; during years of transition, 101–103

Ko Ching, 101–102

K'o Yi-cheng, 54, 58

Kuan Chieh-ming, 32

Kuomintang. *See* KMT (Kuomintang)

Lai, Stan, 241

Land, in fiction and film, 62–63, 178. *See also* Countryside

Language: in African literature, 133–135; Bakhtin on, 131–132; and colonialism, 132–135, 290 nn.8, 9; of mainlanders and Taiwanese natives, 102; and nationhood, 130–180, 290 nn.8, 9; and power, 132–144; in Taiwanese film and fiction, 81–83, 154–156, 164–169, 231–232; visual, 169–173, 176–180; writers' choice of, 133–134, 162–164, 290 n.13. *See also* Mandarin, speaking

Lao She, 22, 185–186

Lee, Ang, 235–237, 322 n.20

Lee, Leo Ou-fan, 315 n.37

Lee Teng-hui, 251 n.19; and February 28 Incident, 90–91, 110; as native-born Taiwanese, 5–6; on Taiwan, 6–7; on Taiwan's relationship to China, 1

Lejeune, Phillipe, 77

Lent, John A., 271 n.54

Liang Ching, 289 n.105–106

Liao Ch'ing-sung, 54, 121

Liao Ping-hui, 281 n.20

Lien Chan, 6

Lim, Cheng-sim, 323 n.43

Linguistic diversity. *See* Language

Lin Huai-min, 49–50

Lin Nien-t'ong, 177–178

June Yip is an independent scholar. She has a Ph.D. in
Comparative Literature from Princeton University and an
M.A. in Cinema Studies from the University of California,
Los Angeles, where she has taught Chinese film.

Library of Congress Cataloging-in-Publication Data
Yip, June Chun, 1962–
Envisioning Taiwan : fiction, cinema, and the nation in the
cultural imaginary / June Yip.
p. cm. — (Asia-Pacific)
Includes bibliographical references and index.
ISBN 0-8223-3357-0 (alk. paper)
ISBN 0-8223-3367-8 (pbk. : alk. paper)
1. Popular culture—Taiwan. I. Title. II. Series.
HM621.Y56 2004 306'.095124'9—dc22 2004005069